# ROSARIO + VAMPIRE
## Season II

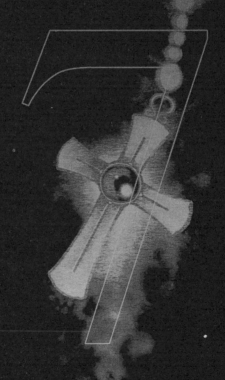

7

AKIHISA IKEDA

## Horror Story Thus Far

Tsukune Aono accidentally enrolls in Yokai Academy, a high school for monsters! After befriending the school's cutest girl, Moka Akashiya, he decides to stay...even though Yokai has a zero-tolerance policy toward humans. (A *fatal* policy.) Tsukune has to hide his true identity while fending off attacks by monster gangs. He survives with the help of his News Club friends—Moka, Kurumu, Yukari and Mizore.

But then a student riot nearly destroys the school and classes are cancelled for half a year for "remodeling." It's already spring by the time the gang (now sophomores) return...and meet Moka's rowdy little sister, Koko, who has enrolled as a freshman.

Talking to a former Yokai student named San who is trying to make it in the real world has all our friends contemplating their futures...until they realize that Outer-Moka and Inner-Moka's frequent switcheroo is causing the Rosario seal to disintegrate!

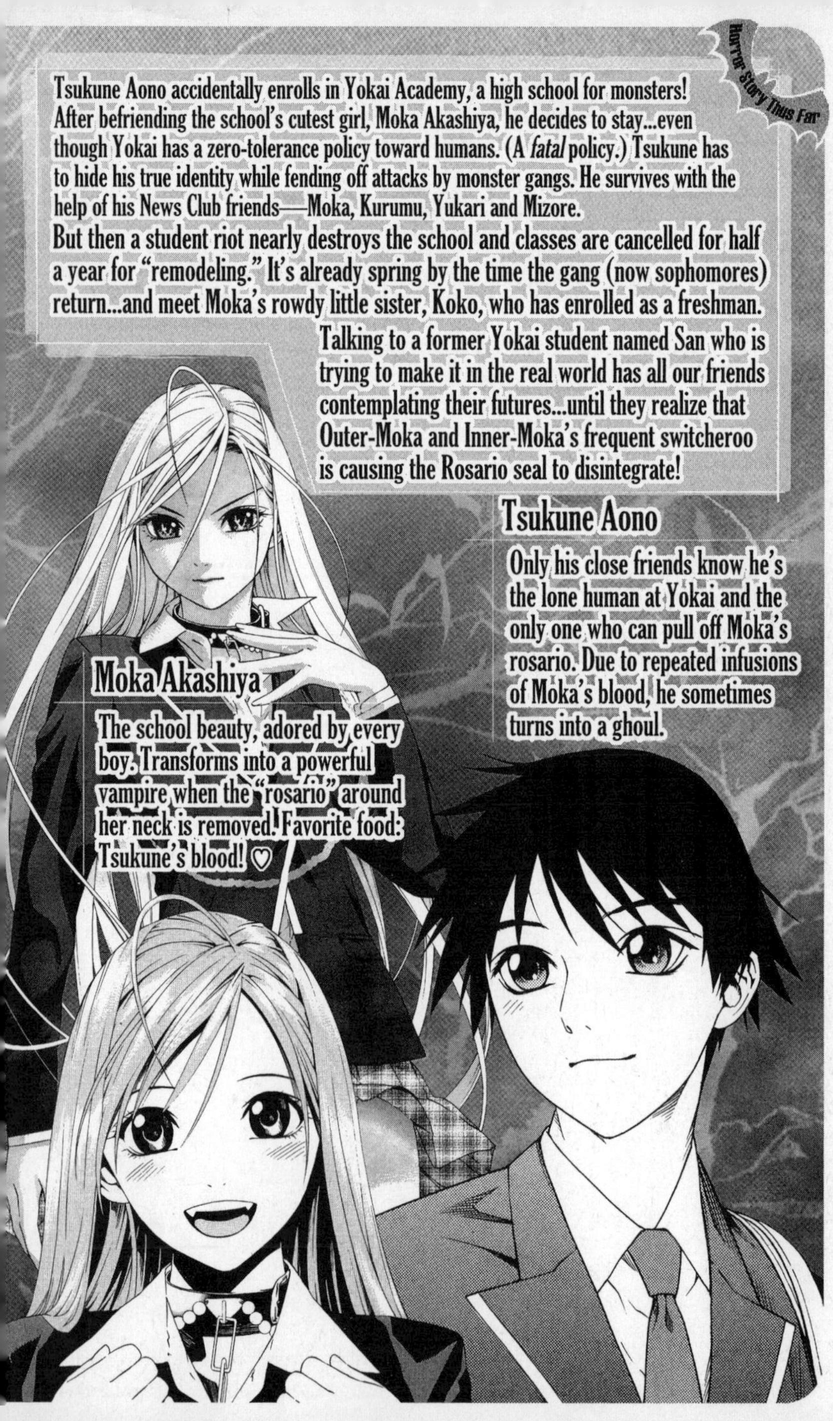

### Tsukune Aono

Only his close friends know he's the lone human at Yokai and the only one who can pull off Moka's rosario. Due to repeated infusions of Moka's blood, he sometimes turns into a ghoul.

### Moka Akashiya

The school beauty, adored by every boy. Transforms into a powerful vampire when the "rosario" around her neck is removed. Favorite food: Tsukune's blood! ♡

## Kurumu Kurono

A succubus. Also adored by all the boys—for two obvious reasons. Fights with Moka over Tsukune.

## Yukari Sendo

A mischievous witch. Much younger than the others. A genius who skipped several grades.

## Mizore Shirayuki

A snow fairy who manipulates ice. She fell in love with Tsukune after reading his newspaper articles.

## Ruby Tojo

A witch who only learned to trust humans after meeting Tsukune. Now employed as Yokai's headmaster's assistant.

## Koko Shuzen

Moka's stubborn little sister. Koko worships Moka's inner vampiric self but hates her sweet exterior. Koko's pet bat transforms into a weapon.

## Huang Fangfang

A freshman and the only son of a family that controls many of China's most dangerous monsters. Also a Yasha, a Chinese demon who excels at transformation and sorcery. In awe of Tsukune's power.

## Huang Lingling

Fangfang's elder sister, who is also late. Because she's dead! Reanimated as a Jiang Shi, a hopping zombie. A junior transfer student at Yokai.

ROSARIO+VAMPIRE
Season II

7

Contents

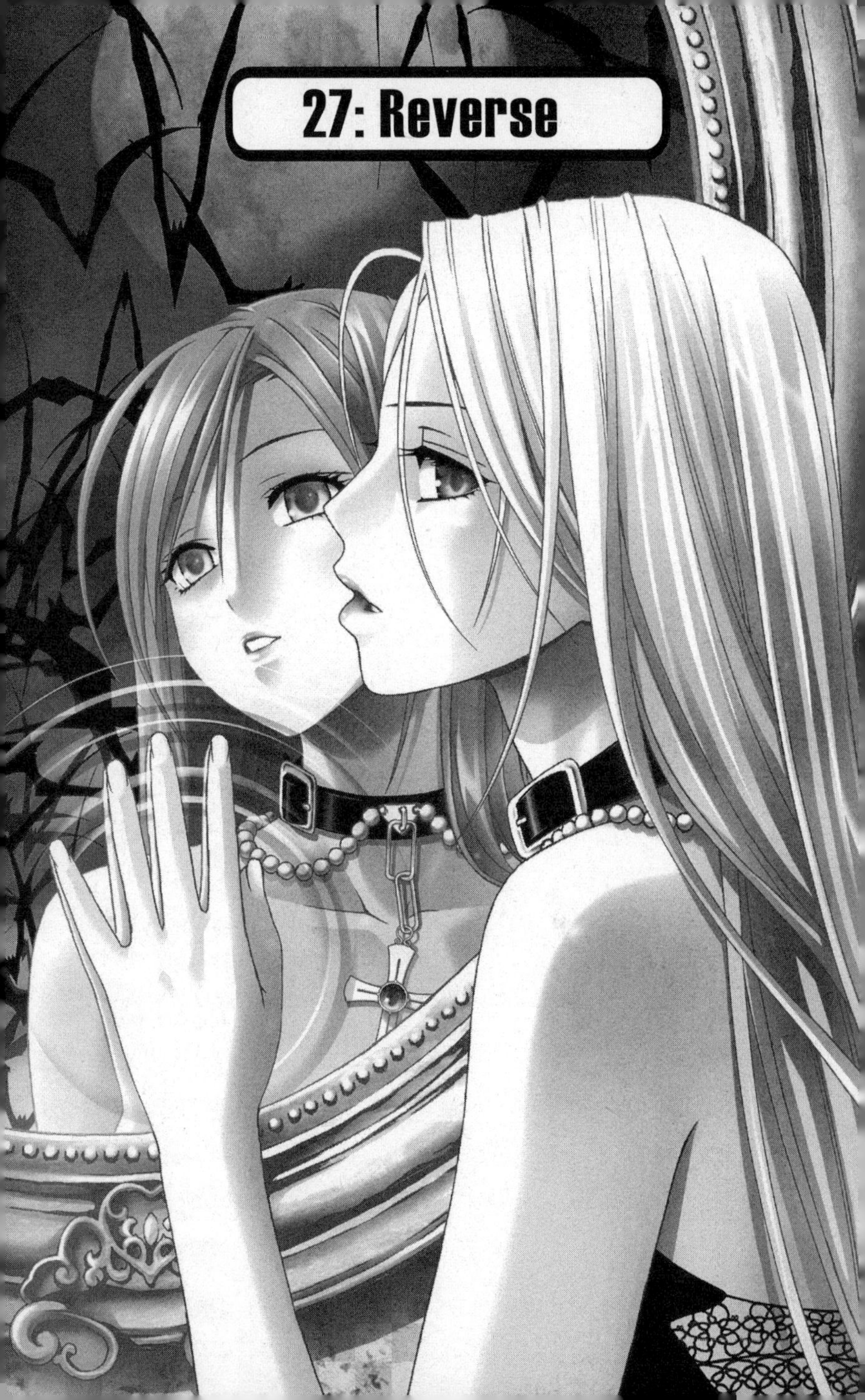
27: Reverse

# ROSARIO+VAMPIRE

## SeasonII

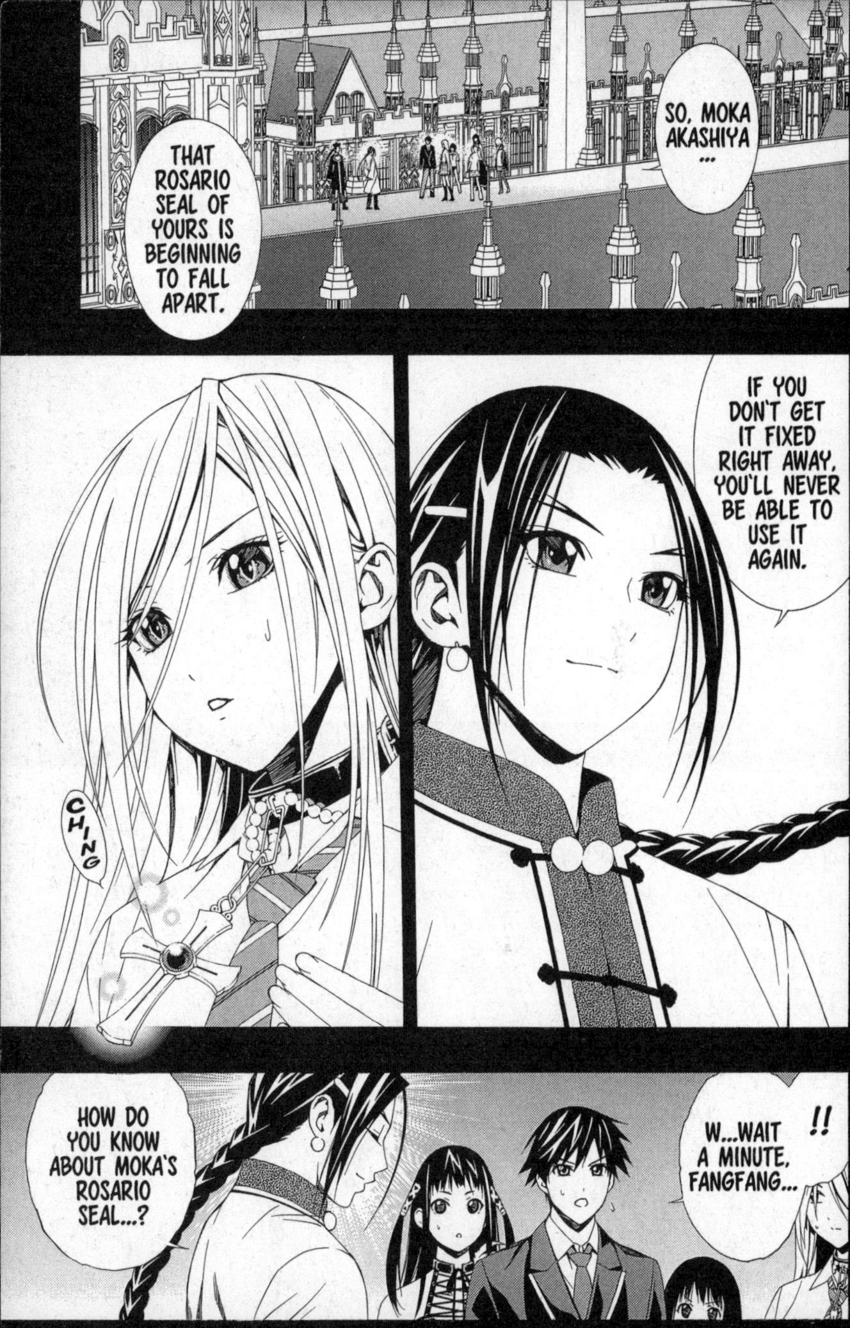
SO, MOKA AKASHIYA ...
THAT ROSARIO SEAL OF YOURS IS BEGINNING TO FALL APART.
IF YOU DON'T GET IT FIXED RIGHT AWAY, YOU'LL NEVER BE ABLE TO USE IT AGAIN.
CHING
!!
W...WAIT A MINUTE, FANGFANG...
HOW DO YOU KNOW ABOUT MOKA'S ROSARIO SEAL...?

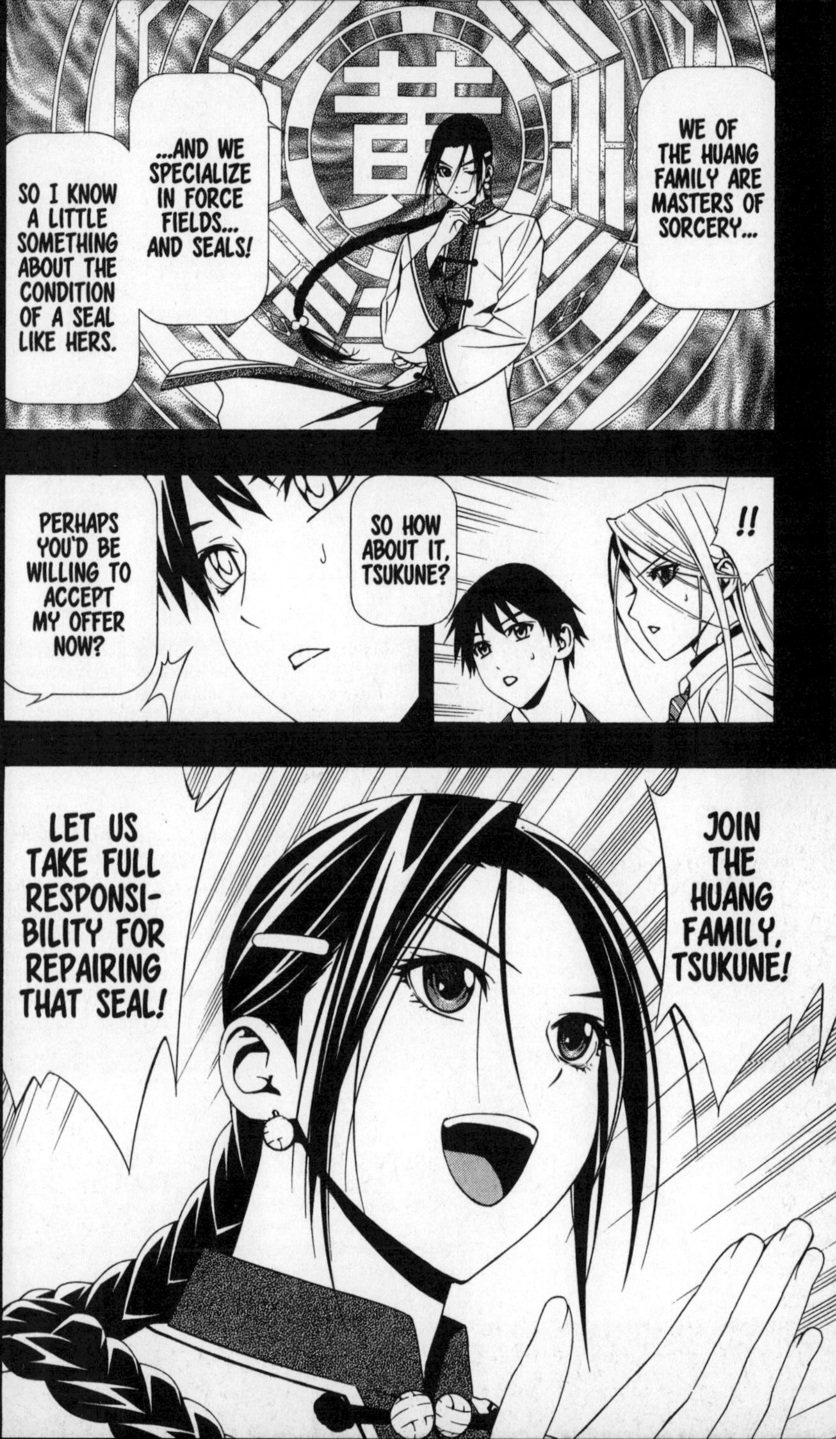
WE OF THE HUANG FAMILY ARE MASTERS OF SORCERY...
...AND WE SPECIALIZE IN FORCE FIELDS... AND SEALS!
SO I KNOW A LITTLE SOMETHING ABOUT THE CONDITION OF A SEAL LIKE HERS.
!!
SO HOW ABOUT IT, TSUKUNE?
PERHAPS YOU'D BE WILLING TO ACCEPT MY OFFER NOW?
JOIN THE HUANG FAMILY, TSUKUNE!
LET US TAKE FULL RESPONSI-BILITY FOR REPAIRING THAT SEAL!

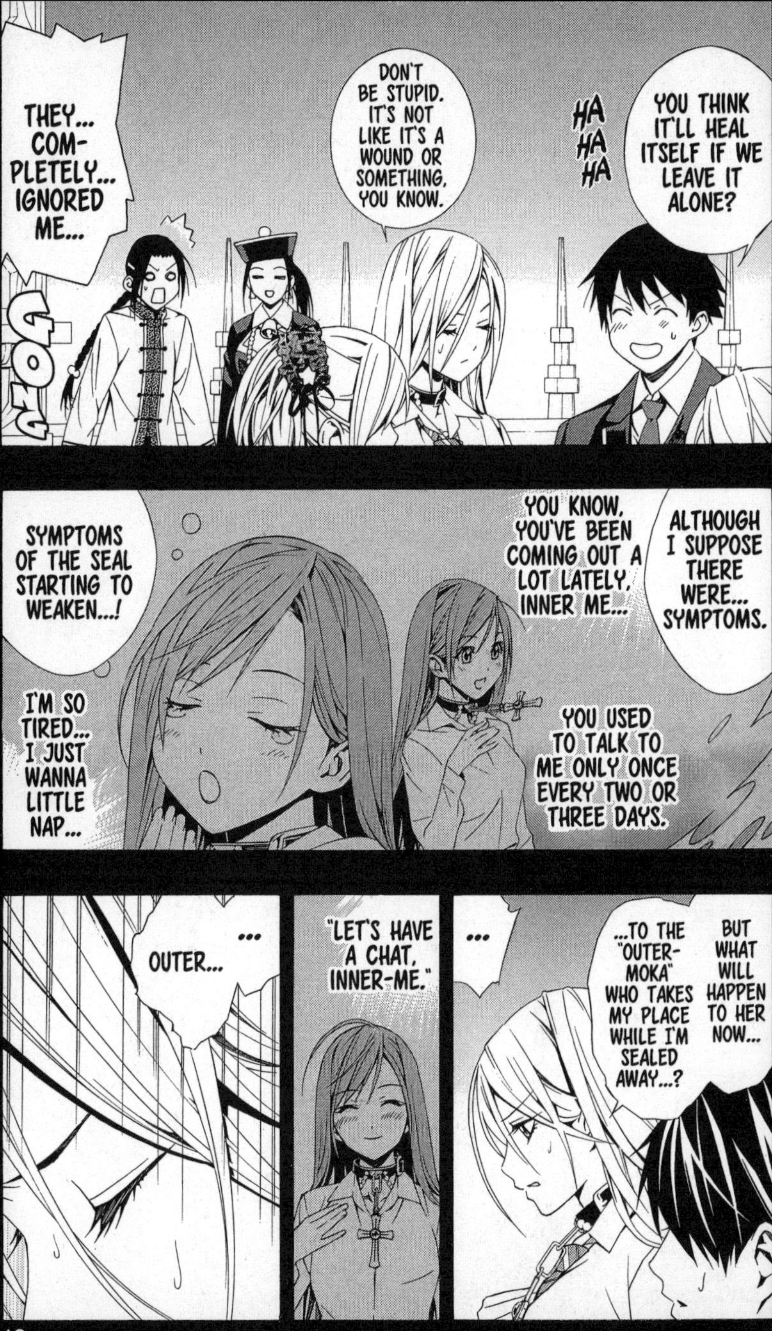
YOU THINK IT'LL HEAL ITSELF IF WE LEAVE IT ALONE?
HA HA HA
DON'T BE STUPID. IT'S NOT LIKE IT'S A WOUND OR SOMETHING, YOU KNOW.
THEY... COM-PLETELY... IGNORED ME...
GONG
ALTHOUGH I SUPPOSE THERE WERE... SYMPTOMS.
YOU KNOW, YOU'VE BEEN COMING OUT A LOT LATELY, INNER ME...
YOU USED TO TALK TO ME ONLY ONCE EVERY TWO OR THREE DAYS.
SYMPTOMS OF THE SEAL STARTING TO WEAKEN...!
I'M SO TIRED... I JUST WANNA LITTLE NAP...
BUT WHAT WILL HAPPEN TO HER NOW...
...TO THE "OUTER-MOKA" WHO TAKES MY PLACE WHILE I'M SEALED AWAY...?
...
"LET'S HAVE A CHAT, INNER-ME."
...
OUTER...

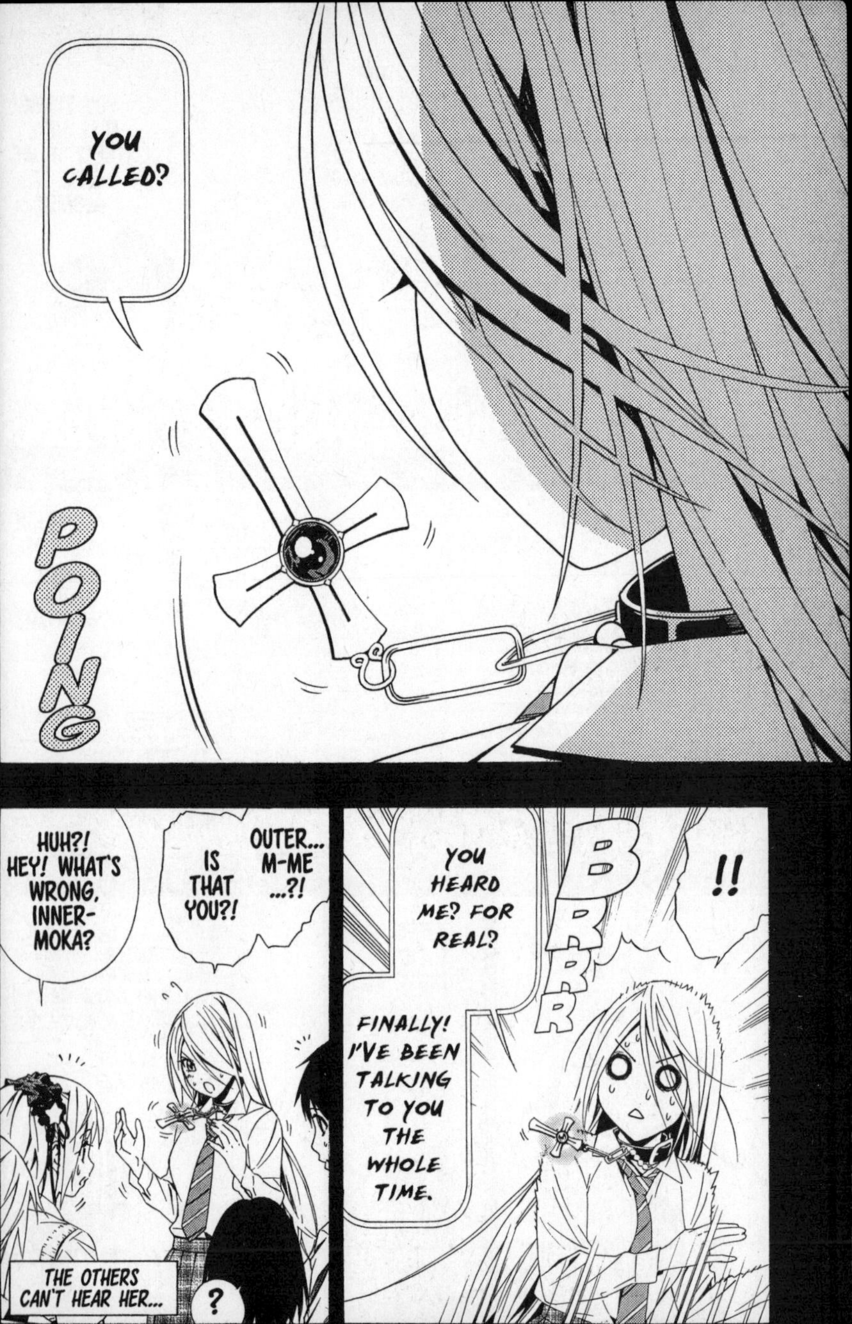
YOU CALLED?
POING
!!
BRRRR
YOU HEARD ME? FOR REAL?
FINALLY! I'VE BEEN TALKING TO YOU THE WHOLE TIME.
OUTER... M-ME ...?!
IS THAT YOU?!
HUH?! HEY! WHAT'S WRONG, INNER-MOKA?
THE OTHERS CAN'T HEAR HER...
?

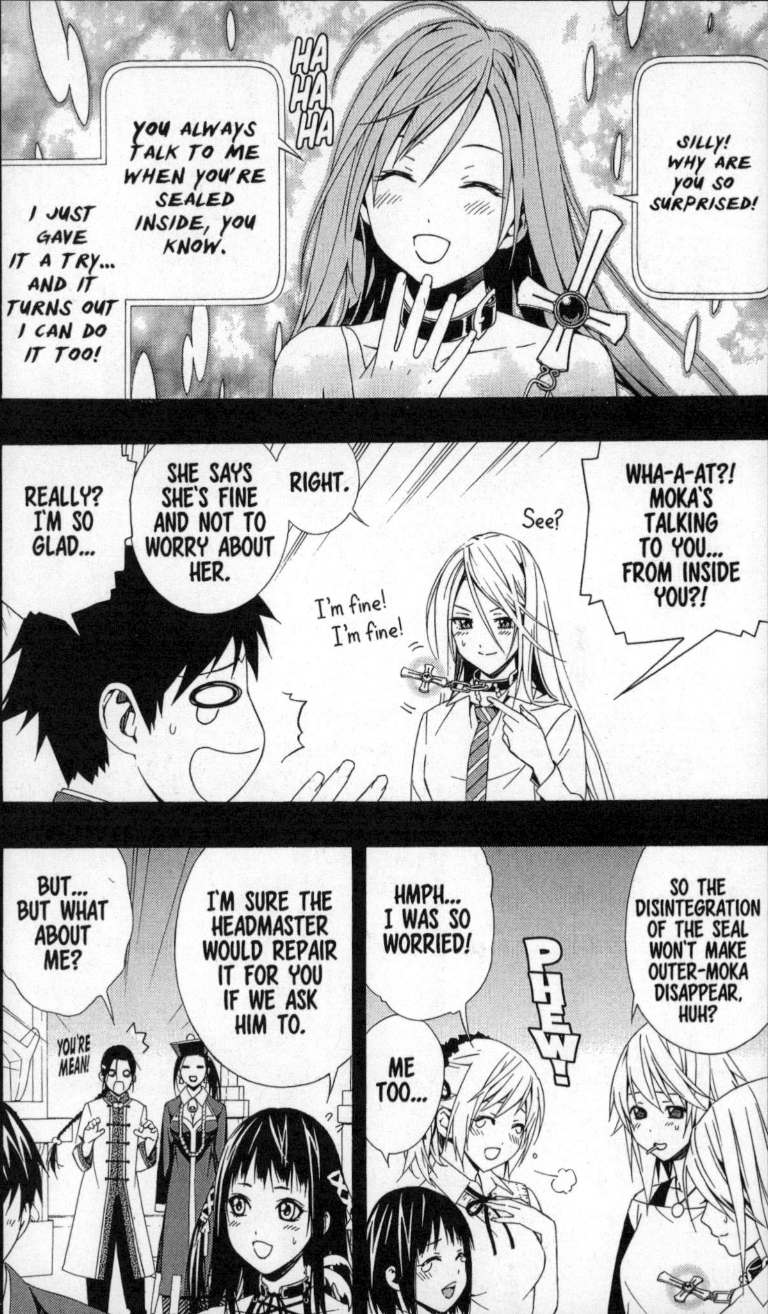

SILLY! WHY ARE YOU SO SURPRISED!
HA HA HA
YOU ALWAYS TALK TO ME WHEN YOU'RE SEALED INSIDE, YOU KNOW.
I JUST GAVE IT A TRY... AND IT TURNS OUT I CAN DO IT TOO!
WHA-A-AT?! MOKA'S TALKING TO YOU... FROM INSIDE YOU?!
See?
I'm fine! I'm fine!
RIGHT.
SHE SAYS SHE'S FINE AND NOT TO WORRY ABOUT HER.
REALLY? I'M SO GLAD...
SO THE DISINTEGRATION OF THE SEAL WON'T MAKE OUTER-MOKA DISAPPEAR, HUH?
PHEW!
HMPH... I WAS SO WORRIED!
ME TOO...
I'M SURE THE HEADMASTER WOULD REPAIR IT FOR YOU IF WE ASK HIM TO.
BUT... BUT WHAT ABOUT ME?
YOU'RE MEAN!

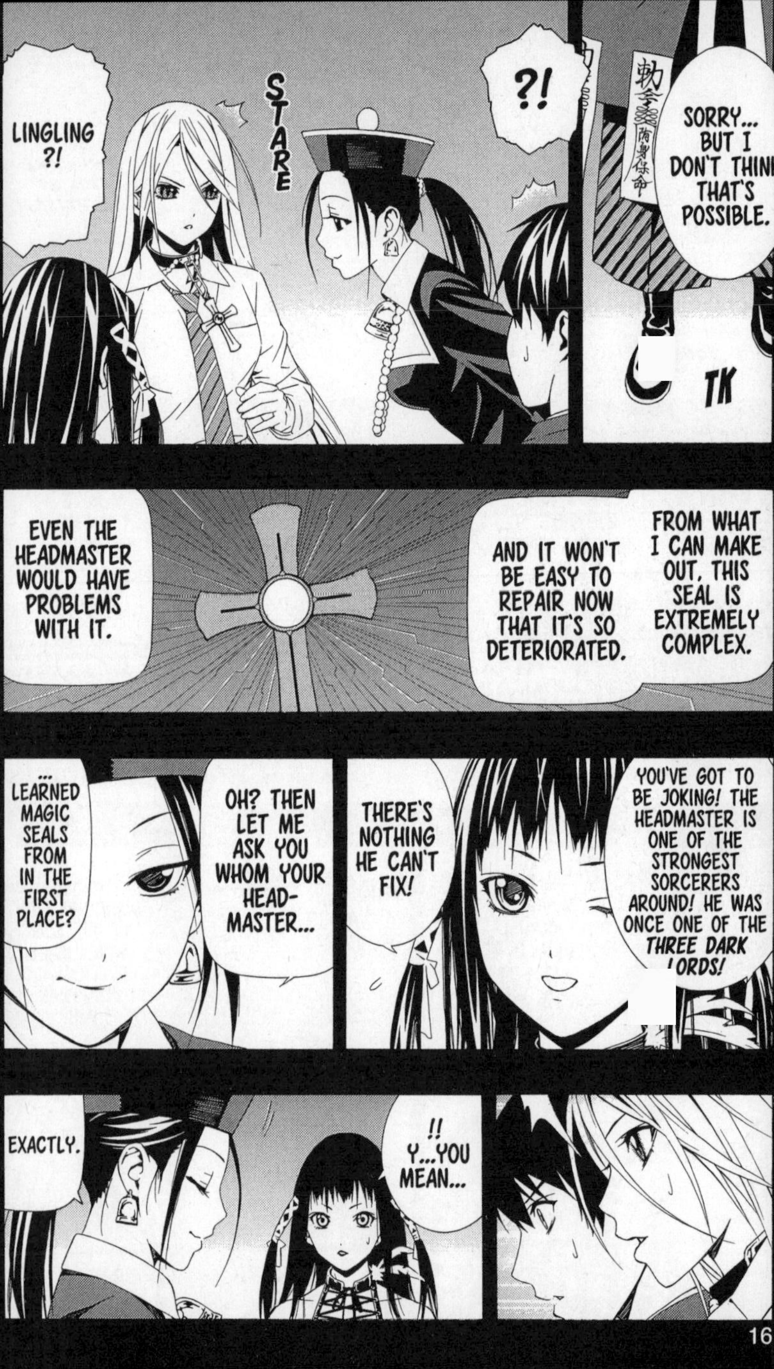
SORRY... BUT I DON'T THINK THAT'S POSSIBLE.
TK
?!
STARE
LINGLING ?!
FROM WHAT I CAN MAKE OUT, THIS SEAL IS EXTREMELY COMPLEX.
AND IT WON'T BE EASY TO REPAIR NOW THAT IT'S SO DETERIORATED.
EVEN THE HEADMASTER WOULD HAVE PROBLEMS WITH IT.
YOU'VE GOT TO BE JOKING! THE HEADMASTER IS ONE OF THE STRONGEST SORCERERS AROUND! HE WAS ONCE ONE OF THE *THREE DARK LORDS!*
THERE'S NOTHING HE CAN'T FIX!
OH? THEN LET ME ASK YOU WHOM YOUR HEAD-MASTER...
...LEARNED MAGIC SEALS FROM IN THE FIRST PLACE?
!! Y...YOU MEAN...
EXACTLY.

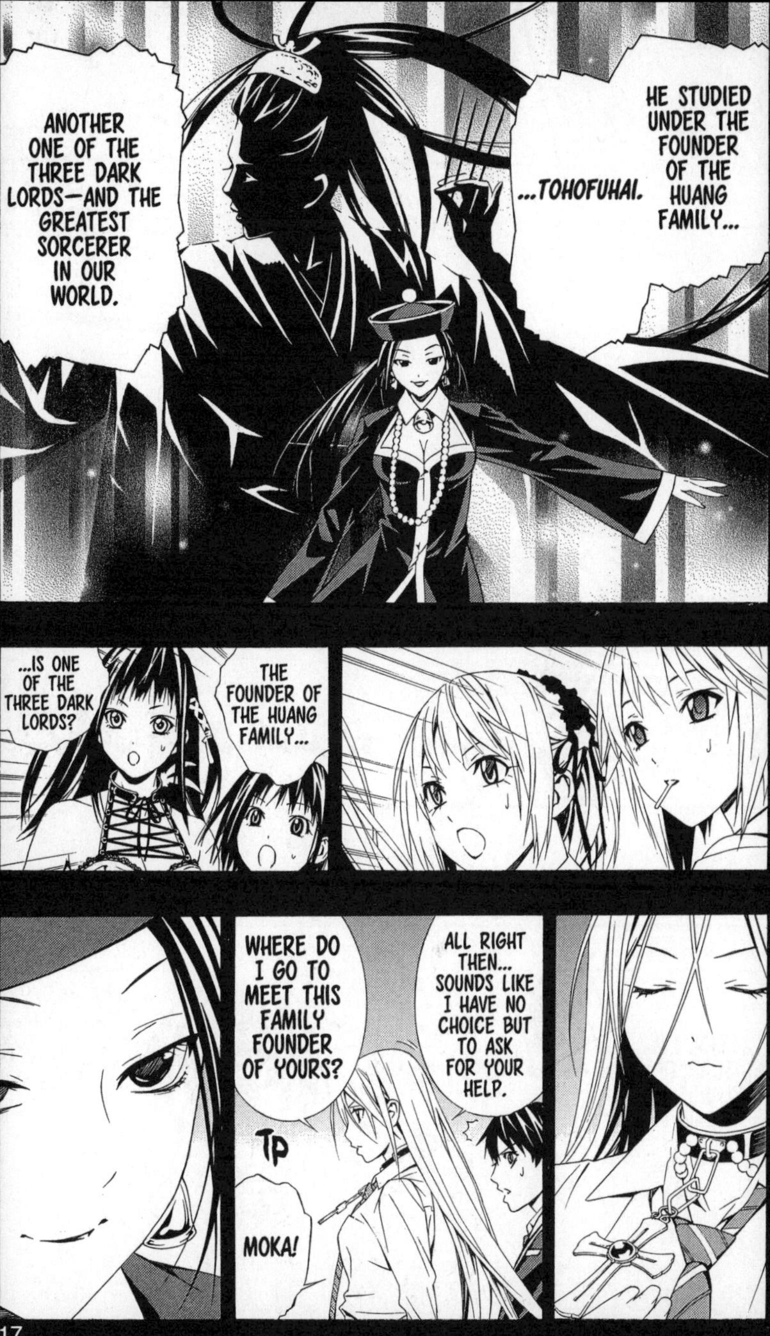
HE STUDIED UNDER THE FOUNDER OF THE HUANG FAMILY...
...TOHOFUHAI.
ANOTHER ONE OF THE THREE DARK LORDS—AND THE GREATEST SORCERER IN OUR WORLD.
THE FOUNDER OF THE HUANG FAMILY...
...IS ONE OF THE THREE DARK LORDS?
ALL RIGHT THEN... SOUNDS LIKE I HAVE NO CHOICE BUT TO ASK FOR YOUR HELP.
WHERE DO I GO TO MEET THIS FAMILY FOUNDER OF YOURS?
TP
MOKA!

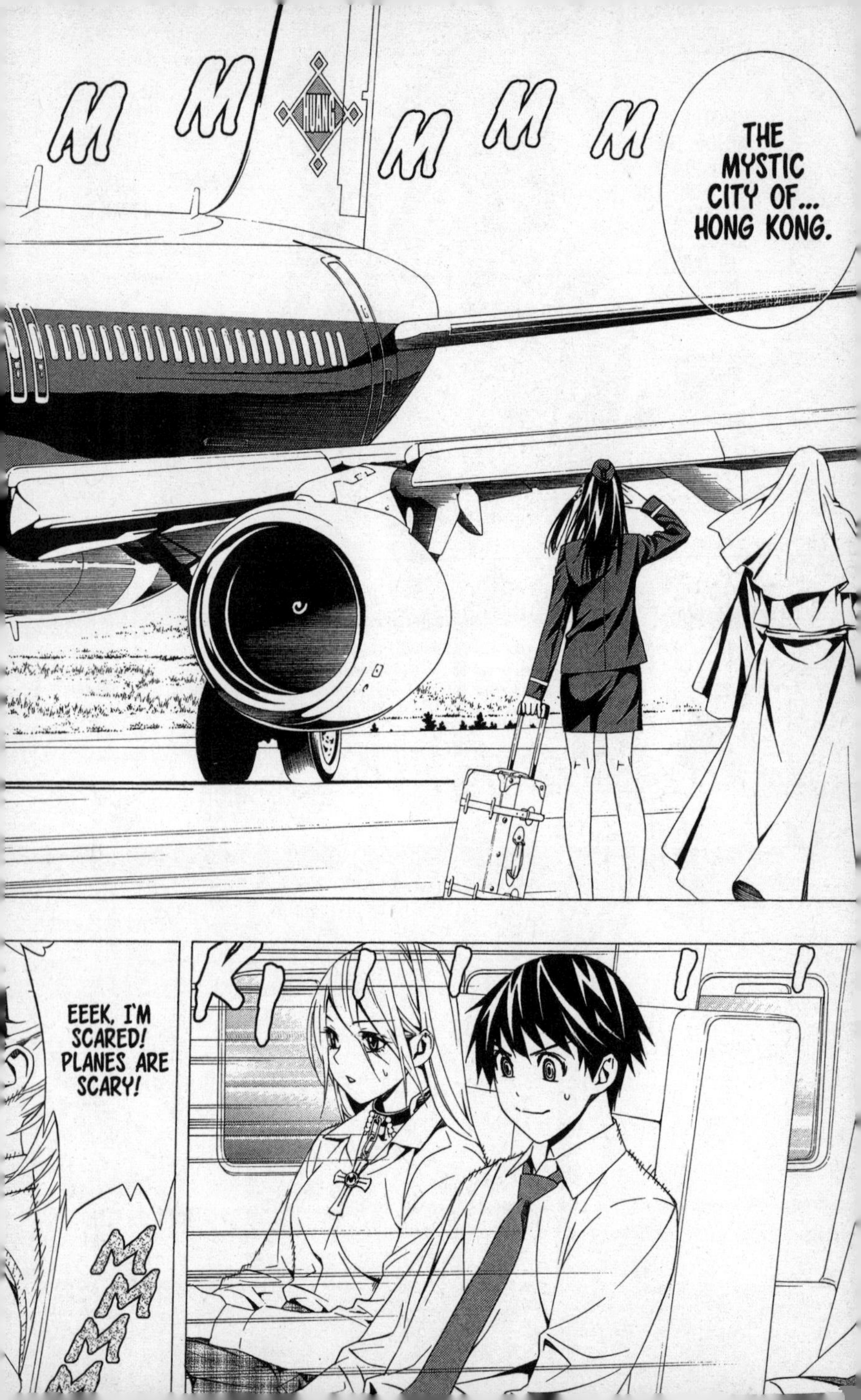
MMMMM
HUANG
THE MYSTIC CITY OF... HONG KONG.
EEEK, I'M SCARED! PLANES ARE SCARY!
MMMM

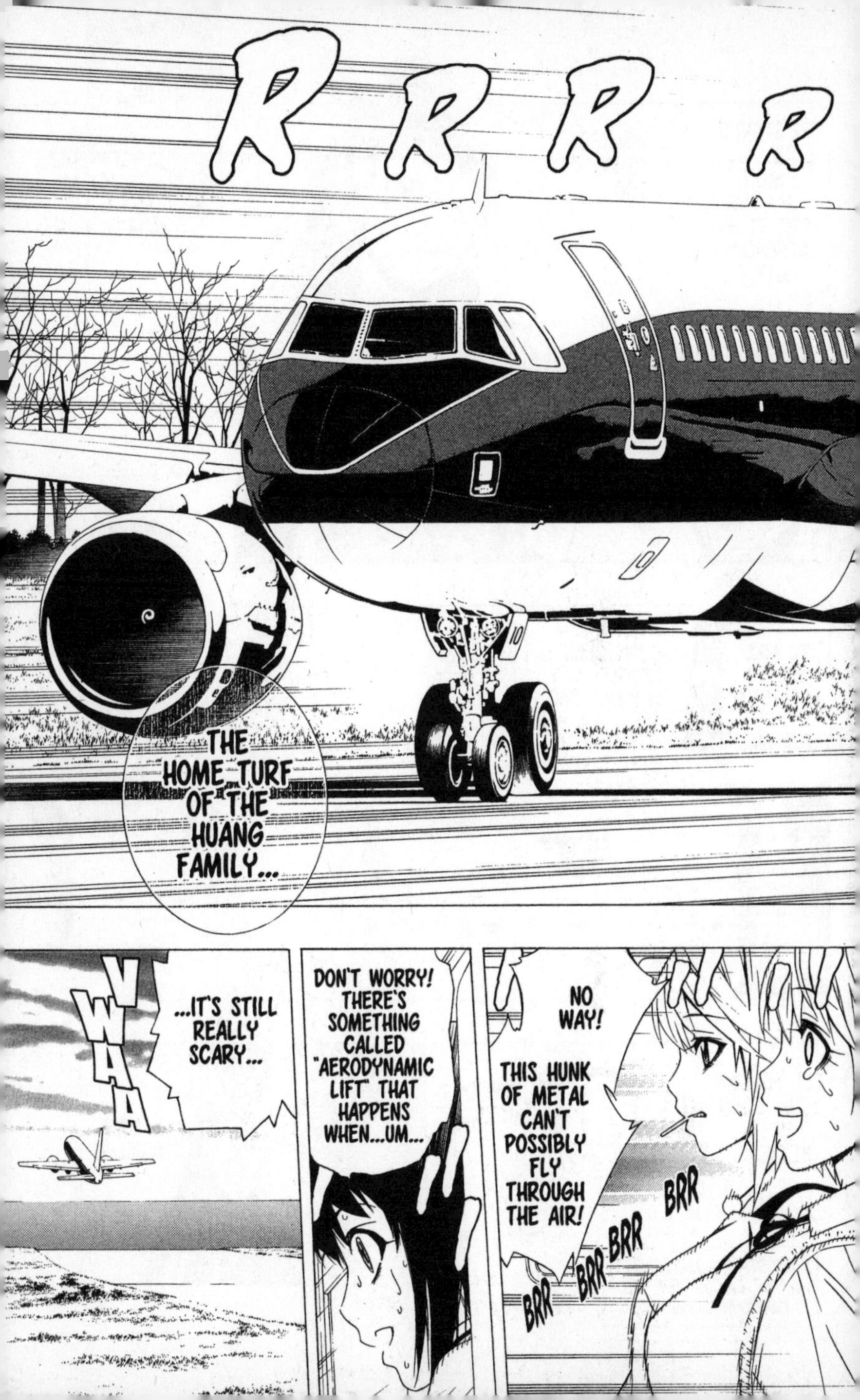
RRRR
THE HOME TURF OF THE HUANG FAMILY...
NO WAY!
THIS HUNK OF METAL CAN'T POSSIBLY FLY THROUGH THE AIR!
BRR BRR BRR BRR
DON'T WORRY! THERE'S SOMETHING CALLED "AERODYNAMIC LIFT" THAT HAPPENS WHEN...UM...
VWAA
...IT'S STILL REALLY SCARY...

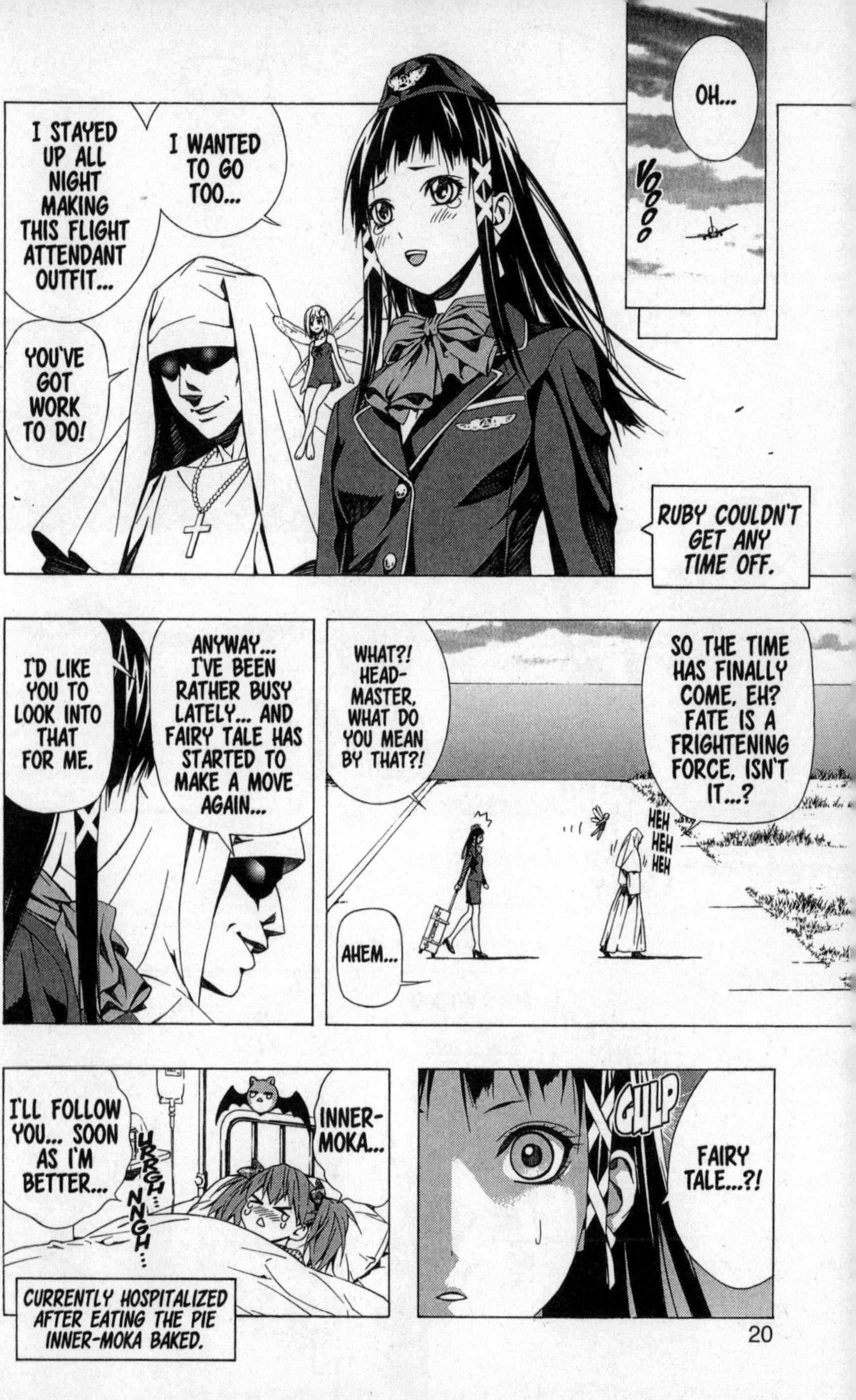
OH...
VOOOO
I WANTED TO GO TOO...
I STAYED UP ALL NIGHT MAKING THIS FLIGHT ATTENDANT OUTFIT...
YOU'VE GOT WORK TO DO!
RUBY COULDN'T GET ANY TIME OFF.
SO THE TIME HAS FINALLY COME, EH? FATE IS A FRIGHTENING FORCE, ISN'T IT...?
HEH HEH HEH
WHAT?! HEAD-MASTER, WHAT DO YOU MEAN BY THAT?!
AHEM...
ANYWAY... I'VE BEEN RATHER BUSY LATELY... AND FAIRY TALE HAS STARTED TO MAKE A MOVE AGAIN...
I'D LIKE YOU TO LOOK INTO THAT FOR ME.
GULP
FAIRY TALE...?!
INNER-MOKA...
I'LL FOLLOW YOU... SOON AS I'M BETTER...
URRGH...
NNGH...
CURRENTLY HOSPITALIZED AFTER EATING THE PIE INNER-MOKA BAKED.

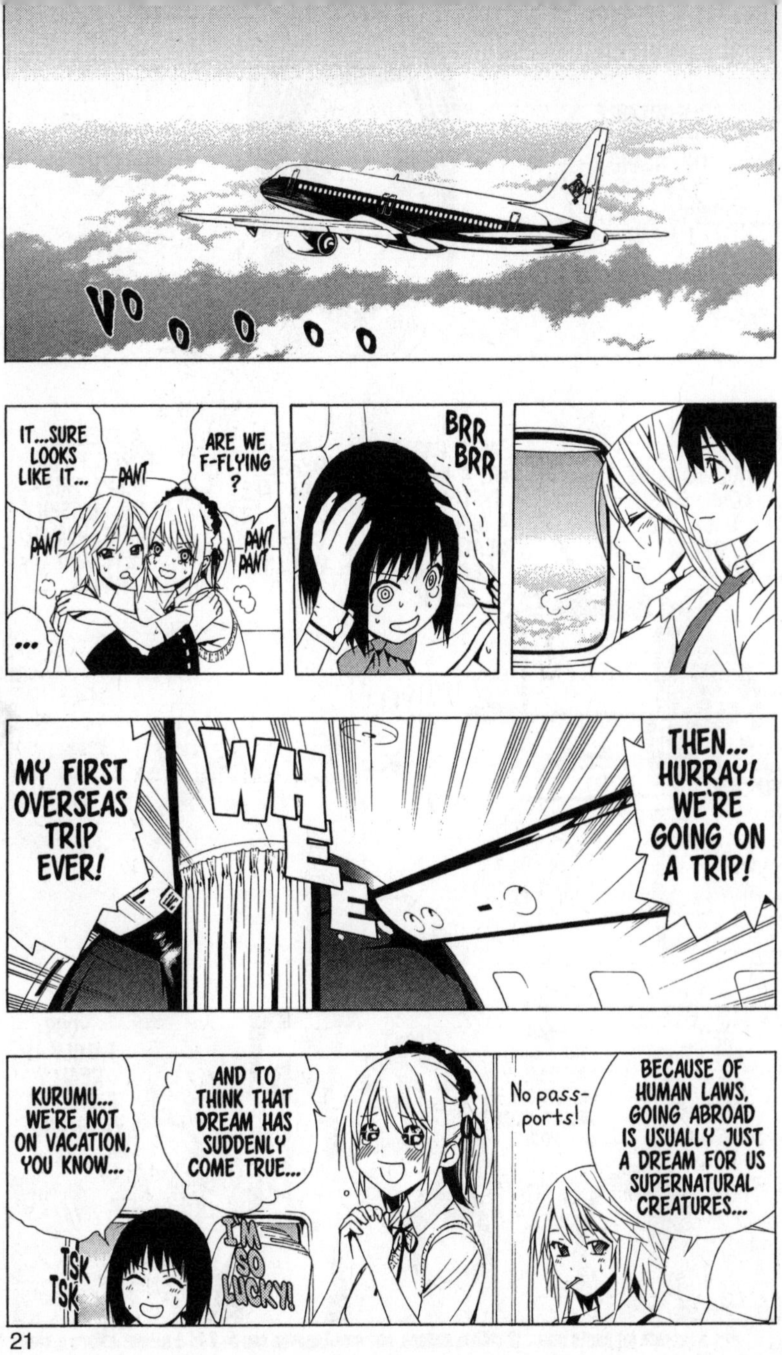
VOOOOO
BRR BRR
ARE WE F-FLYING?
IT...SURE LOOKS LIKE IT...
PANT
PANT
PANT PANT
...
THEN... HURRAY! WE'RE GOING ON A TRIP!
WHEEE
MY FIRST OVERSEAS TRIP EVER!
BECAUSE OF HUMAN LAWS, GOING ABROAD IS USUALLY JUST A DREAM FOR US SUPERNATURAL CREATURES...
No pass-ports!
AND TO THINK THAT DREAM HAS SUDDENLY COME TRUE...
I'M SO LUCKY!
KURUMU... WE'RE NOT ON VACATION, YOU KNOW...
TSK TSK

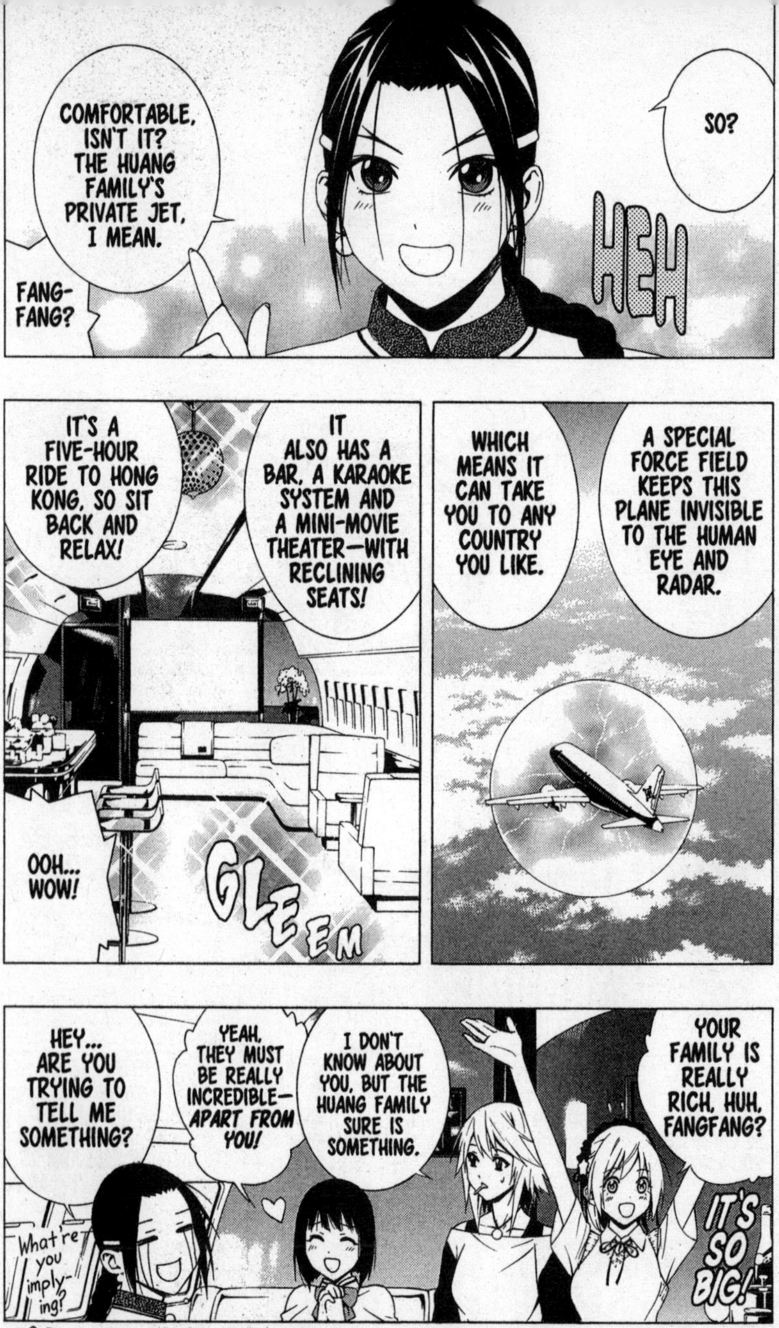
SO?
HEH
COMFORTABLE, ISN'T IT? THE HUANG FAMILY'S PRIVATE JET, I MEAN.
FANG-FANG?
A SPECIAL FORCE FIELD KEEPS THIS PLANE INVISIBLE TO THE HUMAN EYE AND RADAR.
WHICH MEANS IT CAN TAKE YOU TO ANY COUNTRY YOU LIKE.
IT ALSO HAS A BAR, A KARAOKE SYSTEM AND A MINI-MOVIE THEATER—WITH RECLINING SEATS!
IT'S A FIVE-HOUR RIDE TO HONG KONG, SO SIT BACK AND RELAX!
GLEEM
OOH... WOW!
YOUR FAMILY IS REALLY RICH, HUH, FANGFANG?
IT'S SO BIG!
I DON'T KNOW ABOUT YOU, BUT THE HUANG FAMILY SURE IS SOMETHING.
YEAH, THEY MUST BE REALLY INCREDIBLE—APART FROM YOU!
HEY... ARE YOU TRYING TO TELL ME SOMETHING?
What're you implying?

**Trivia** A private jet costs about 12 million dollars, and maintenance can be 2 to 4 million dollars a year.

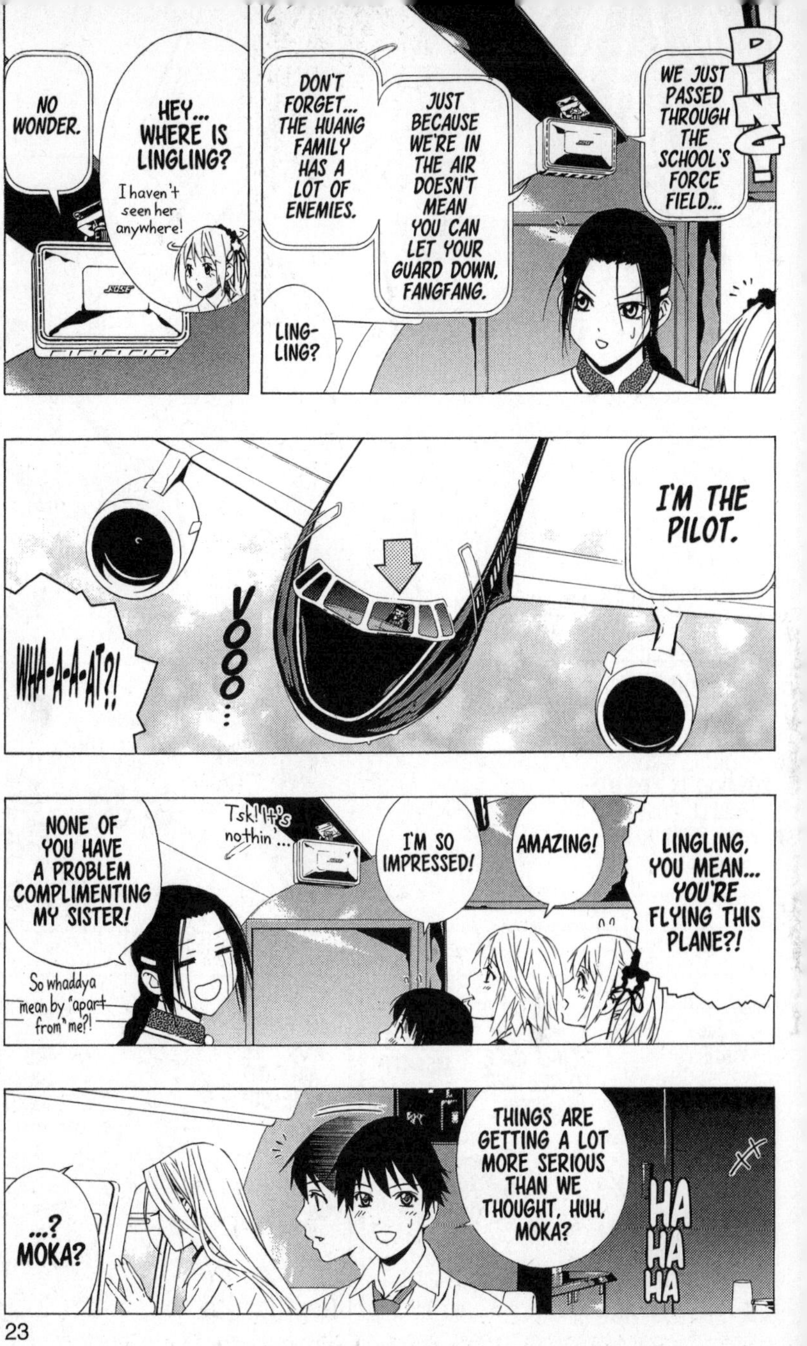
DING!
WE JUST PASSED THROUGH THE SCHOOL'S FORCE FIELD...
JUST BECAUSE WE'RE IN THE AIR DOESN'T MEAN YOU CAN LET YOUR GUARD DOWN, FANGFANG.
DON'T FORGET... THE HUANG FAMILY HAS A LOT OF ENEMIES.
LING-LING?
HEY... WHERE IS LINGLING?
I haven't seen her anywhere!
NO WONDER.
I'M THE PILOT.
VOOO...
WHA-A-A-AT?!
LINGLING, YOU MEAN... YOU'RE FLYING THIS PLANE?!
AMAZING!
I'M SO IMPRESSED!
Tsk! It's nothin'...
NONE OF YOU HAVE A PROBLEM COMPLIMENTING MY SISTER!
So whaddya mean by "apart from" me?!
HA HA HA
THINGS ARE GETTING A LOT MORE SERIOUS THAN WE THOUGHT, HUH, MOKA?
...? MOKA?

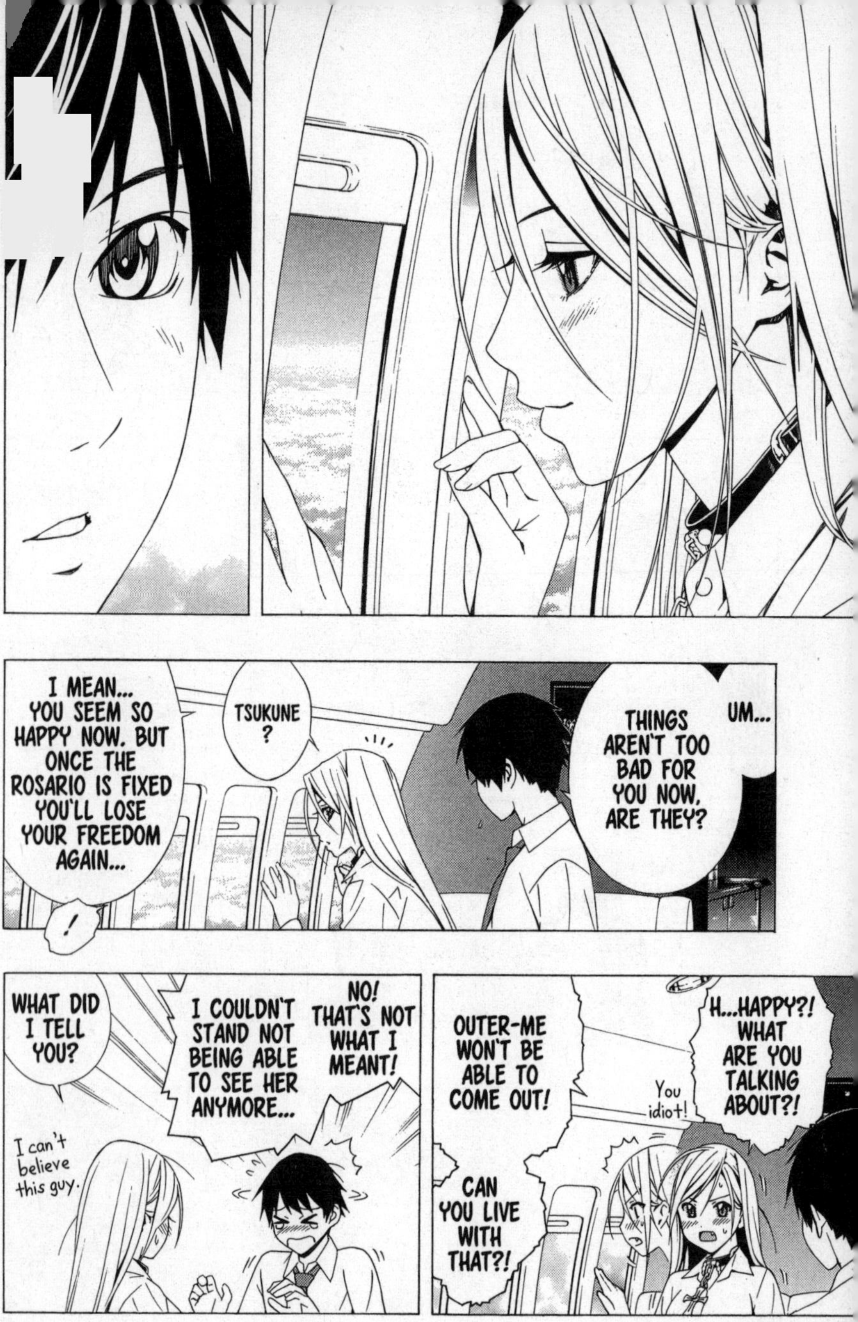
UM...
THINGS AREN'T TOO BAD FOR YOU NOW, ARE THEY?
TSUKUNE?
I MEAN... YOU SEEM SO HAPPY NOW. BUT ONCE THE ROSARIO IS FIXED YOU'LL LOSE YOUR FREEDOM AGAIN...
!
H...HAPPY?! WHAT ARE YOU TALKING ABOUT?!
You idiot!
OUTER-ME WON'T BE ABLE TO COME OUT!
CAN YOU LIVE WITH THAT?!
NO! THAT'S NOT WHAT I MEANT!
I COULDN'T STAND NOT BEING ABLE TO SEE HER ANYMORE...
WHAT DID I TELL YOU?
I can't believe this guy.

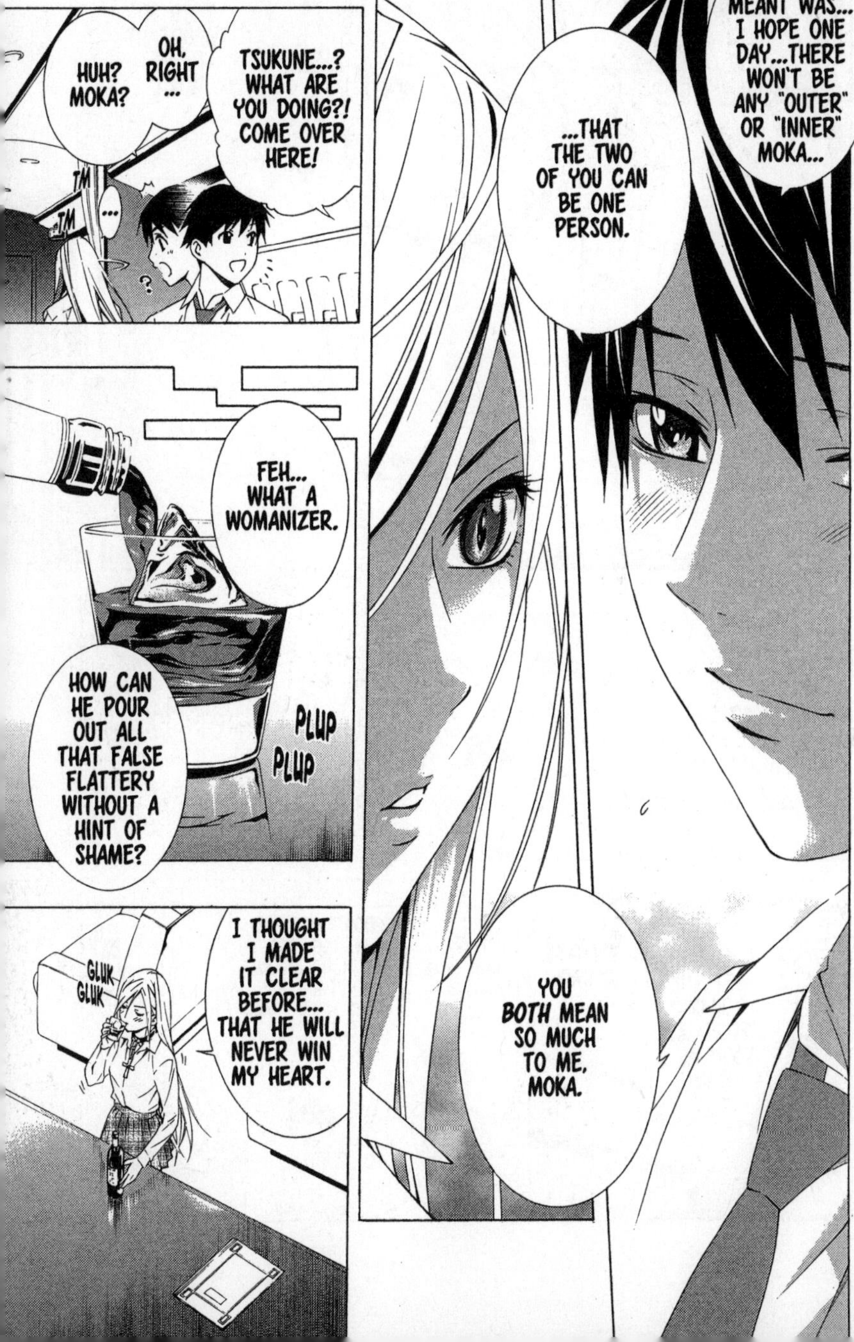
ALL I MEANT WAS... I HOPE ONE DAY...THERE WON'T BE ANY "OUTER" OR "INNER" MOKA...
...THAT THE TWO OF YOU CAN BE ONE PERSON.
YOU BOTH MEAN SO MUCH TO ME, MOKA.
TSUKUNE...? WHAT ARE YOU DOING?! COME OVER HERE!
OH, RIGHT ...
HUH? MOKA?
TM TM
...
?
FEH... WHAT A WOMANIZER.
PLUP PLUP
HOW CAN HE POUR OUT ALL THAT FALSE FLATTERY WITHOUT A HINT OF SHAME?
I THOUGHT I MADE IT CLEAR BEFORE... THAT HE WILL NEVER WIN MY HEART.
GLUK GLUK

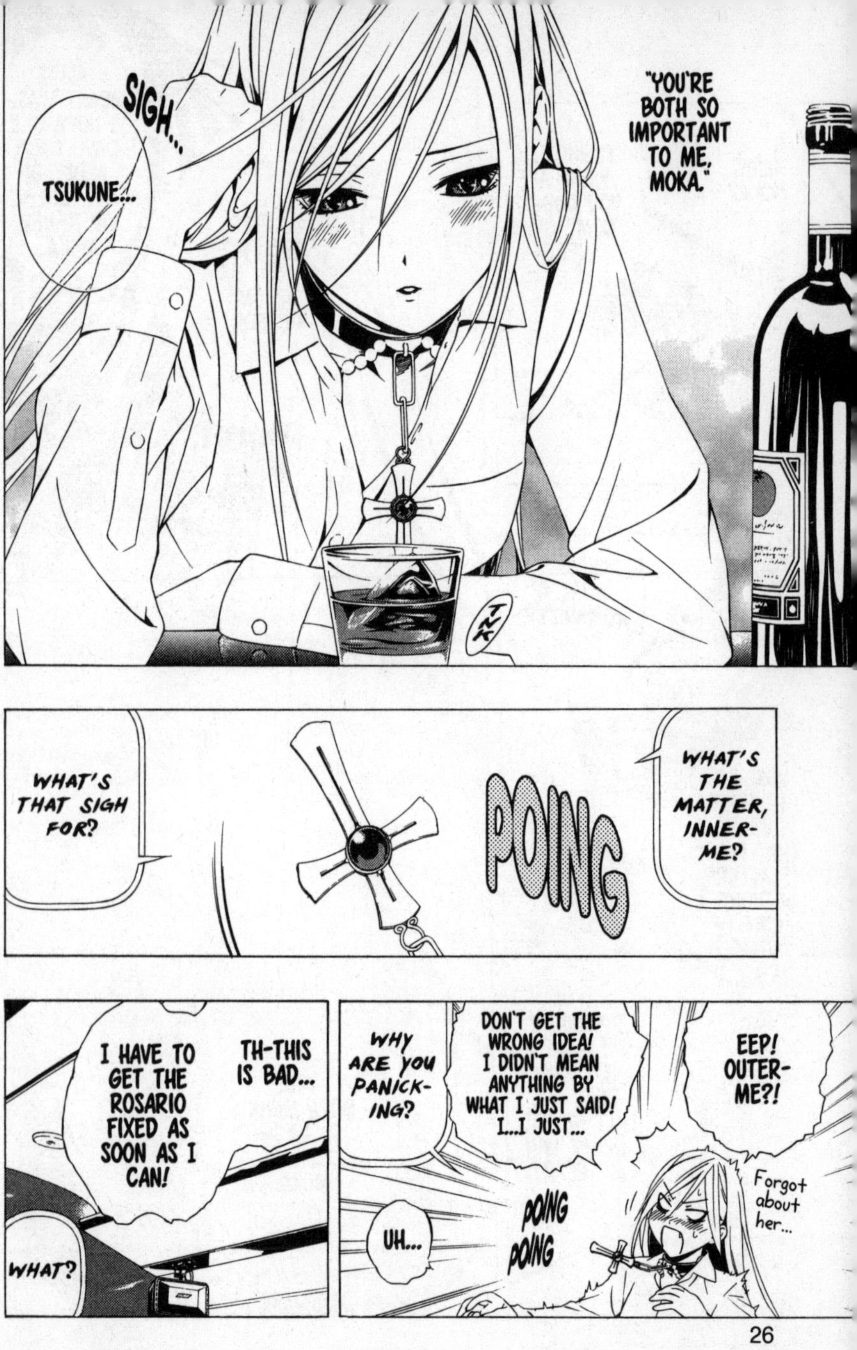
"YOU'RE BOTH SO IMPORTANT TO ME, MOKA."
SIGH...
TSUKUNE...
TNK
WHAT'S THE MATTER, INNER-ME?
POING
WHAT'S THAT SIGH FOR?
EEP! OUTER-ME?!
Forgot about her...
DON'T GET THE WRONG IDEA! I DIDN'T MEAN ANYTHING BY WHAT I JUST SAID! I...I JUST...
WHY ARE YOU PANICK-ING?
POING POING
UH...
TH-THIS IS BAD...
I HAVE TO GET THE ROSARIO FIXED AS SOON AS I CAN!
WHAT?

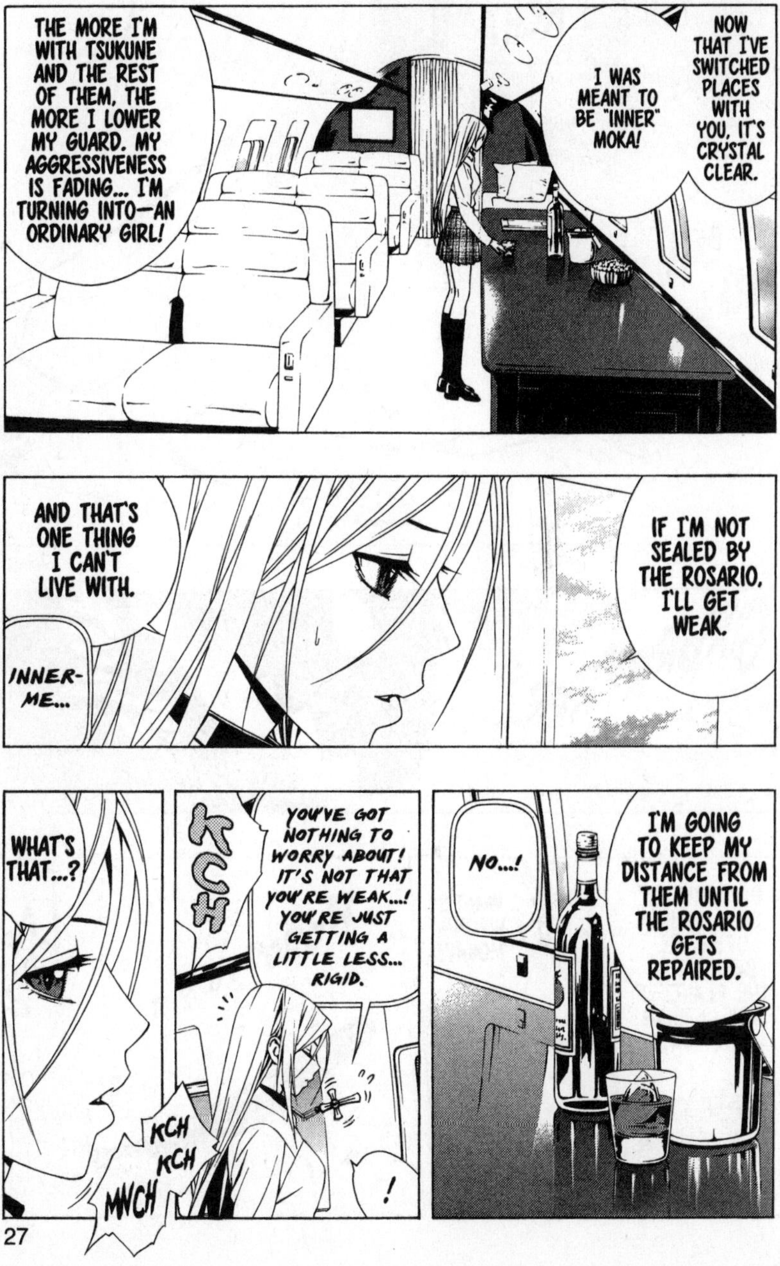
NOW THAT I'VE SWITCHED PLACES WITH YOU, IT'S CRYSTAL CLEAR.
I WAS MEANT TO BE "INNER" MOKA!
THE MORE I'M WITH TSUKUNE AND THE REST OF THEM, THE MORE I LOWER MY GUARD. MY AGGRESSIVENESS IS FADING... I'M TURNING INTO—AN ORDINARY GIRL!
IF I'M NOT SEALED BY THE ROSARIO, I'LL GET WEAK.
AND THAT'S ONE THING I CAN'T LIVE WITH.
INNER-ME...
I'M GOING TO KEEP MY DISTANCE FROM THEM UNTIL THE ROSARIO GETS REPAIRED.
NO...!
YOU'VE GOT NOTHING TO WORRY ABOUT! IT'S NOT THAT YOU'RE WEAK...! YOU'RE JUST GETTING A LITTLE LESS... RIGID.
KCH
!
WHAT'S THAT...?
KCH
KCH
MNCH

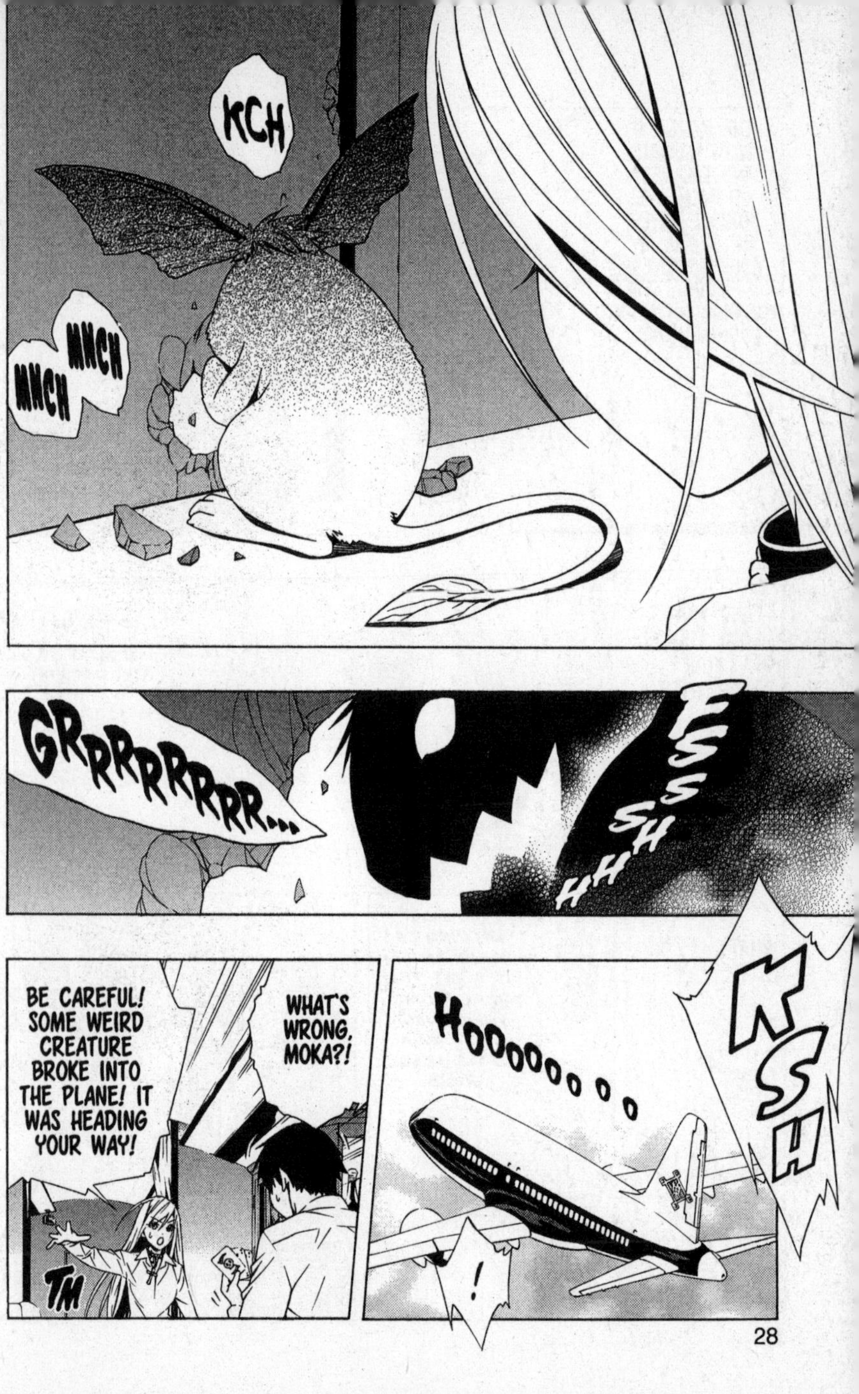
KCH
MNCH
MNCH
FSSSHHHH
GRRRRRRRR...
KSH
HOOOOOOO O O
!
WHAT'S WRONG, MOKA?!
BE CAREFUL! SOME WEIRD CREATURE BROKE INTO THE PLANE! IT WAS HEADING YOUR WAY!
TM

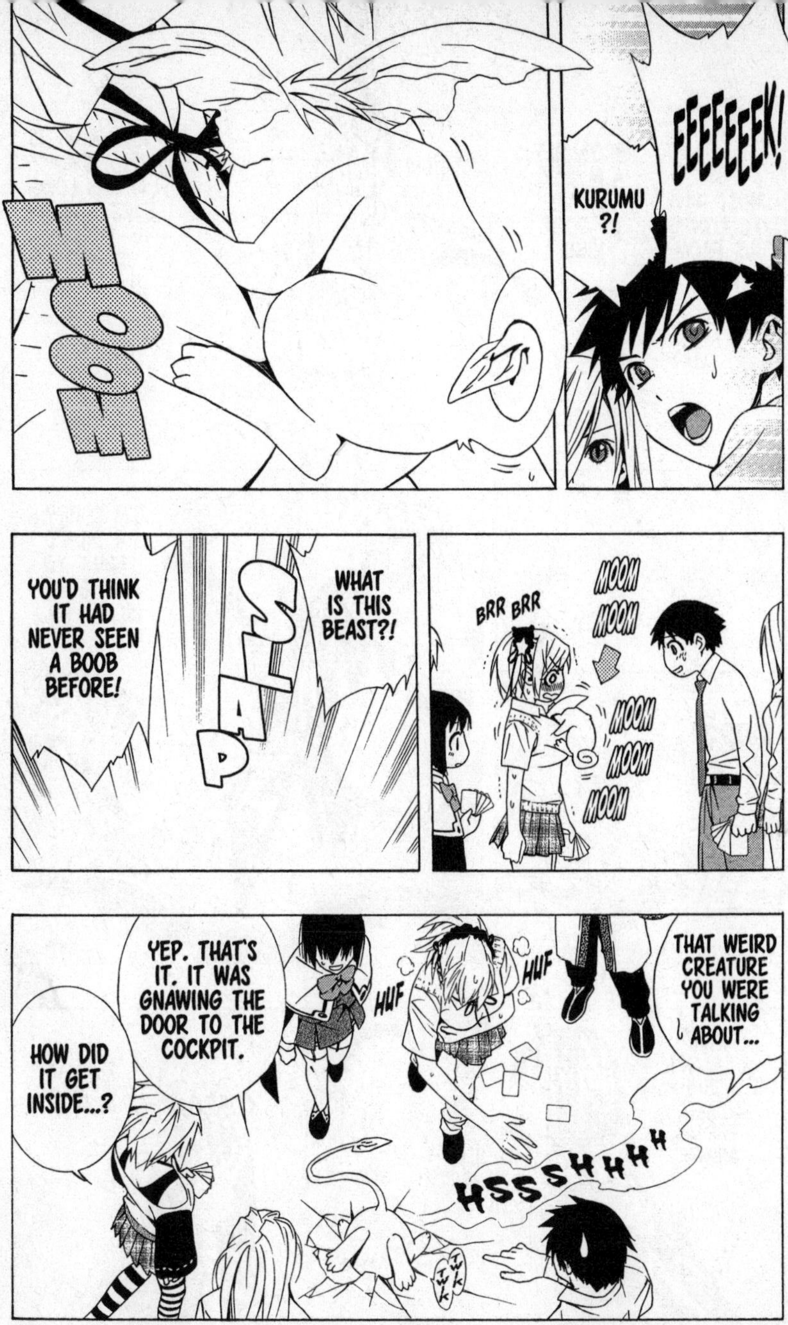
EEEEEEEK!
KURUMU ?!
MOOM
MOOM MOOM
BRR BRR
MOOM MOOM MOOM
WHAT IS THIS BEAST?!
SLAP
YOU'D THINK IT HAD NEVER SEEN A BOOB BEFORE!
THAT WEIRD CREATURE YOU WERE TALKING ABOUT...
HUF HUF
YEP. THAT'S IT. IT WAS GNAWING THE DOOR TO THE COCKPIT.
HOW DID IT GET INSIDE...?
HSSSHHHHH
TWK TWK

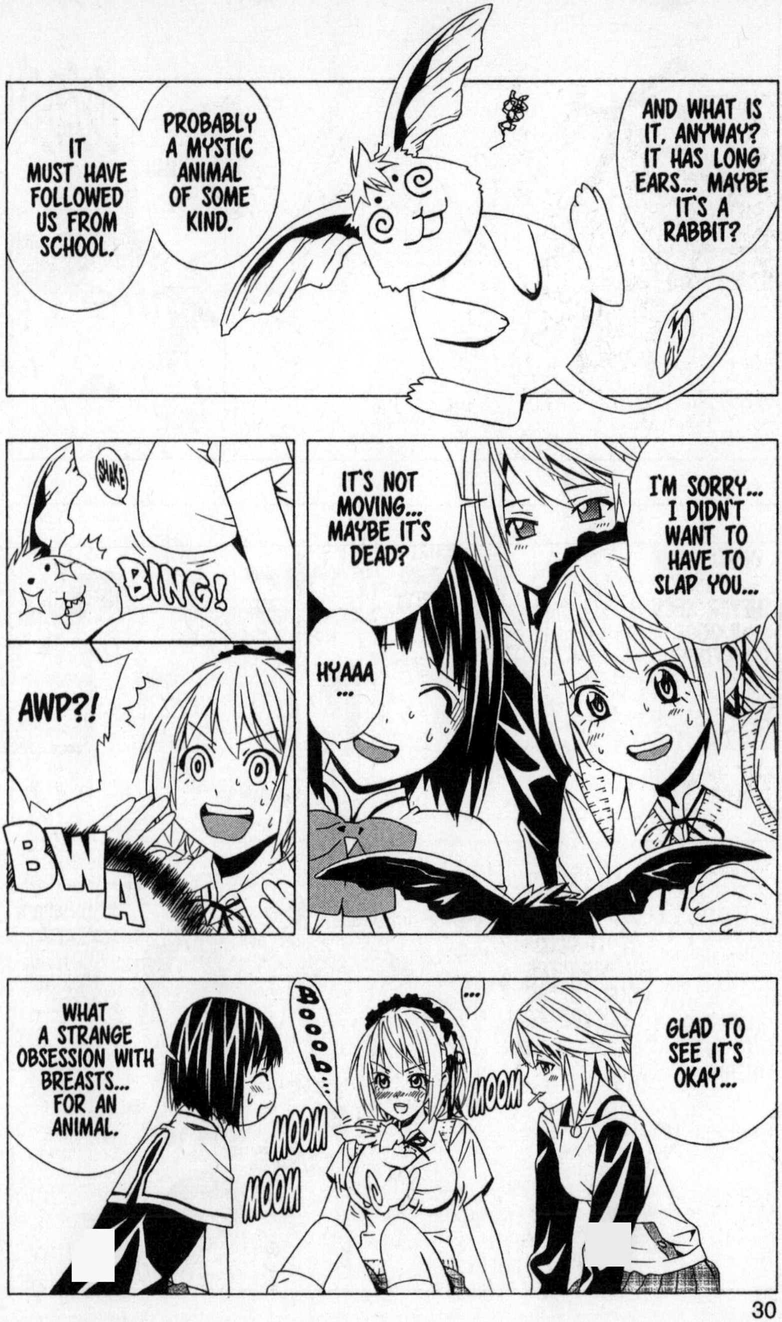
AND WHAT IS IT, ANYWAY? IT HAS LONG EARS... MAYBE IT'S A RABBIT?
PROBABLY A MYSTIC ANIMAL OF SOME KIND.
IT MUST HAVE FOLLOWED US FROM SCHOOL.
I'M SORRY... I DIDN'T WANT TO HAVE TO SLAP YOU...
IT'S NOT MOVING... MAYBE IT'S DEAD?
HYAAA...
SHAKE
BING!
AWP?!
BWA
GLAD TO SEE IT'S OKAY...
...
MOOM
Boooob...
MOOM
MOOM
WHAT A STRANGE OBSESSION WITH BREASTS... FOR AN ANIMAL.

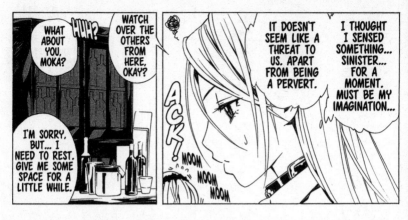

I THOUGHT I SENSED SOMETHING... SINISTER... FOR A MOMENT. MUST BE MY IMAGINATION...
IT DOESN'T SEEM LIKE A THREAT TO US. APART FROM BEING A PERVERT.
ACK!
MOOM MOOM MOOM
WATCH OVER THE OTHERS FROM HERE, OKAY?
HUH?
WHAT ABOUT YOU, MOKA?
I'M SORRY, BUT... I NEED TO REST. GIVE ME SOME SPACE FOR A LITTLE WHILE.
WHAT?! BUT THERE'S SO MUCH FUN STUFF TO DO!
WE COULD SING KARAOKE!
Or play cards!
How about Old Maid?
WHIP
DIDN'T YOU HEAR ME? DON'T COME AFTER ME, TSUKUNE.
SHK
MOKA...?
Oh...
INNER-ME...

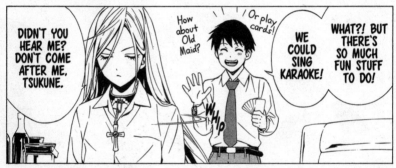

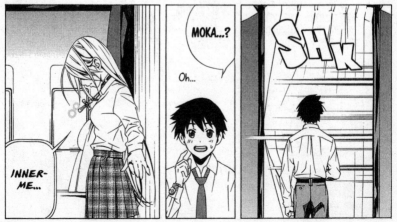

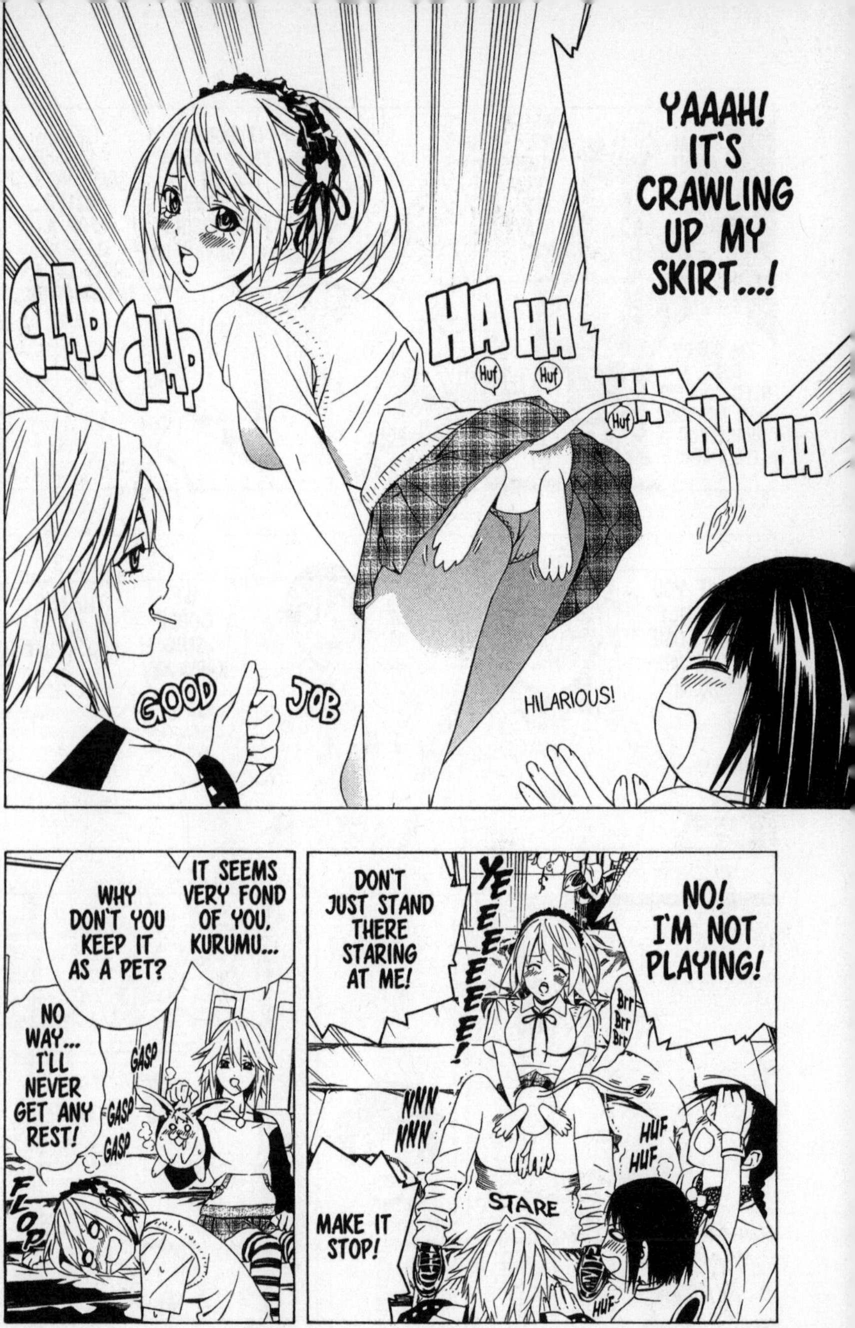
YAAAH! IT'S CRAWLING UP MY SKIRT...!
HA HA HA HA HA HA
Huf
Huf
Huf
HILARIOUS!
CLAP CLAP
GOOD JOB
NO! I'M NOT PLAYING!
YEEEEEEE!
DON'T JUST STAND THERE STARING AT ME!
Brr Brr Brr
NNN NNN
HUF HUF
STARE
MAKE IT STOP!
HUF
IT SEEMS VERY FOND OF YOU, KURUMU...
WHY DON'T YOU KEEP IT AS A PET?
NO WAY... I'LL NEVER GET ANY REST!
GASP
GASP GASP
FLOP

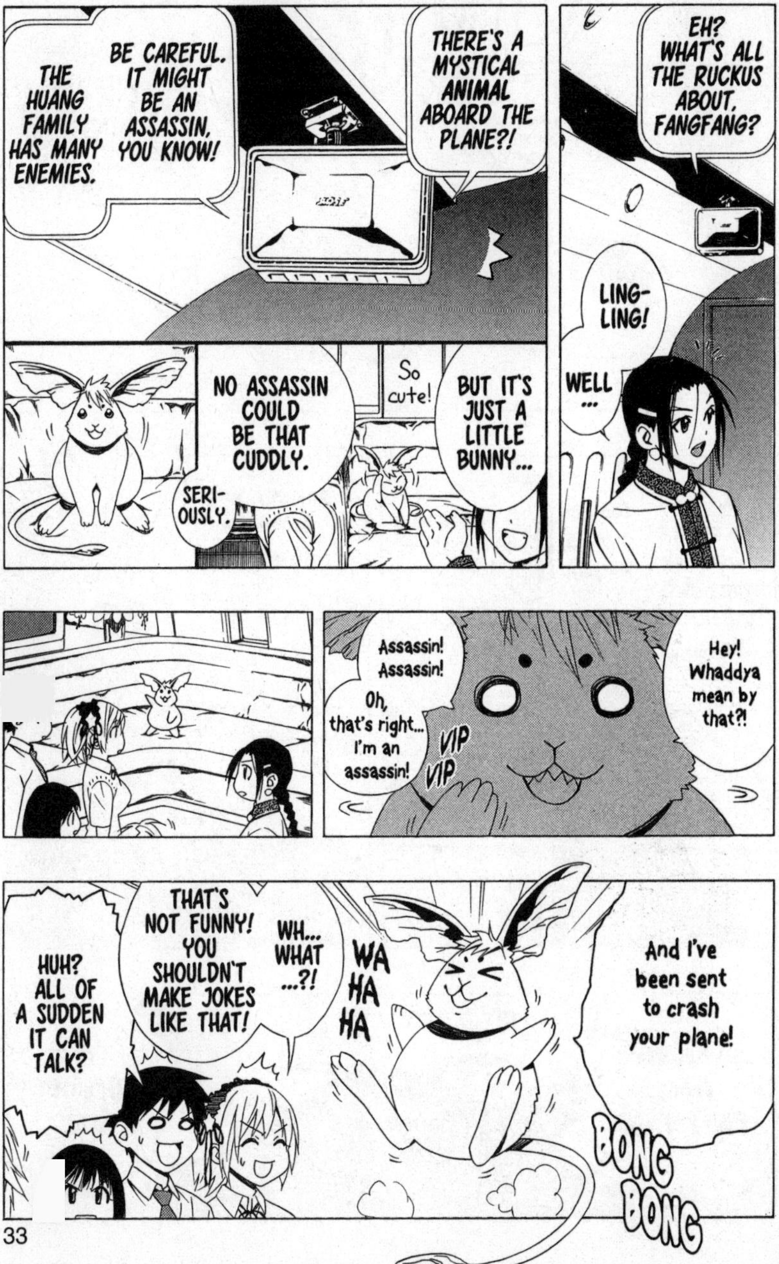
EH? WHAT'S ALL THE RUCKUS ABOUT, FANGFANG?
LING-LING!
WELL ...
THERE'S A MYSTICAL ANIMAL ABOARD THE PLANE?!
BE CAREFUL. IT MIGHT BE AN ASSASSIN, YOU KNOW!
THE HUANG FAMILY HAS MANY ENEMIES.
BUT IT'S JUST A LITTLE BUNNY...
So cute!
NO ASSASSIN COULD BE THAT CUDDLY.
SERI-OUSLY.
Hey! Whaddya mean by that?!
Assassin! Assassin!
Oh, that's right... I'm an assassin!
VIP VIP
And I've been sent to crash your plane!
WA HA HA
BONG BONG
WH... WHAT ...?!
THAT'S NOT FUNNY! YOU SHOULDN'T MAKE JOKES LIKE THAT!
HUH? ALL OF A SUDDEN IT CAN TALK?

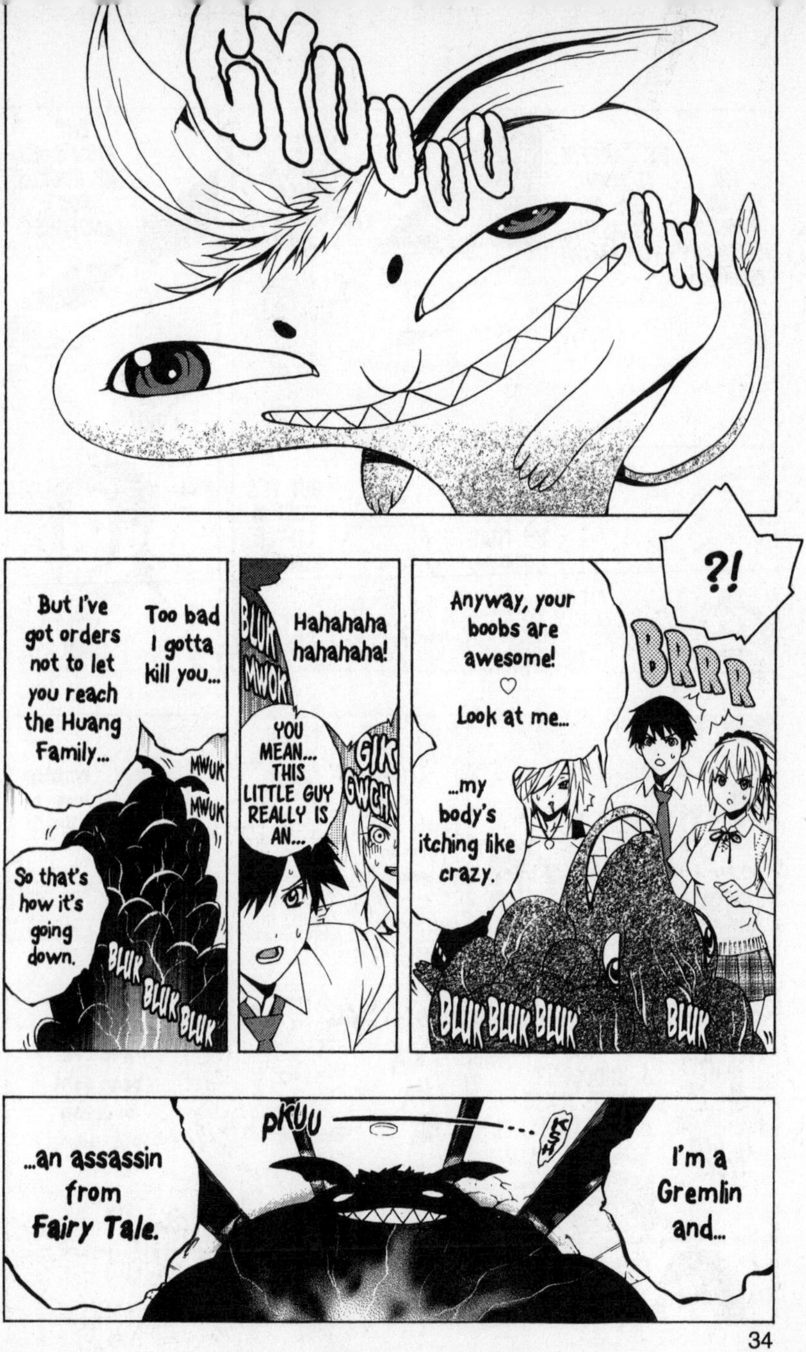
GYOOOOOON
?!
BRRR
Anyway, your boobs are awesome! ♡
Look at me...
...my body's itching like crazy.
BLUK BLUK BLUK
BLUK
BLUK MWOK
Hahahaha hahahaha!
GIK GWCH
YOU MEAN... THIS LITTLE GUY REALLY IS AN...
Too bad I gotta kill you...
But I've got orders not to let you reach the Huang Family...
MWUK MWUK
So that's how it's going down.
BLUK BLUK BLUK
PKUU
KSH
I'm a Gremlin and...
...an assassin from Fairy Tale.

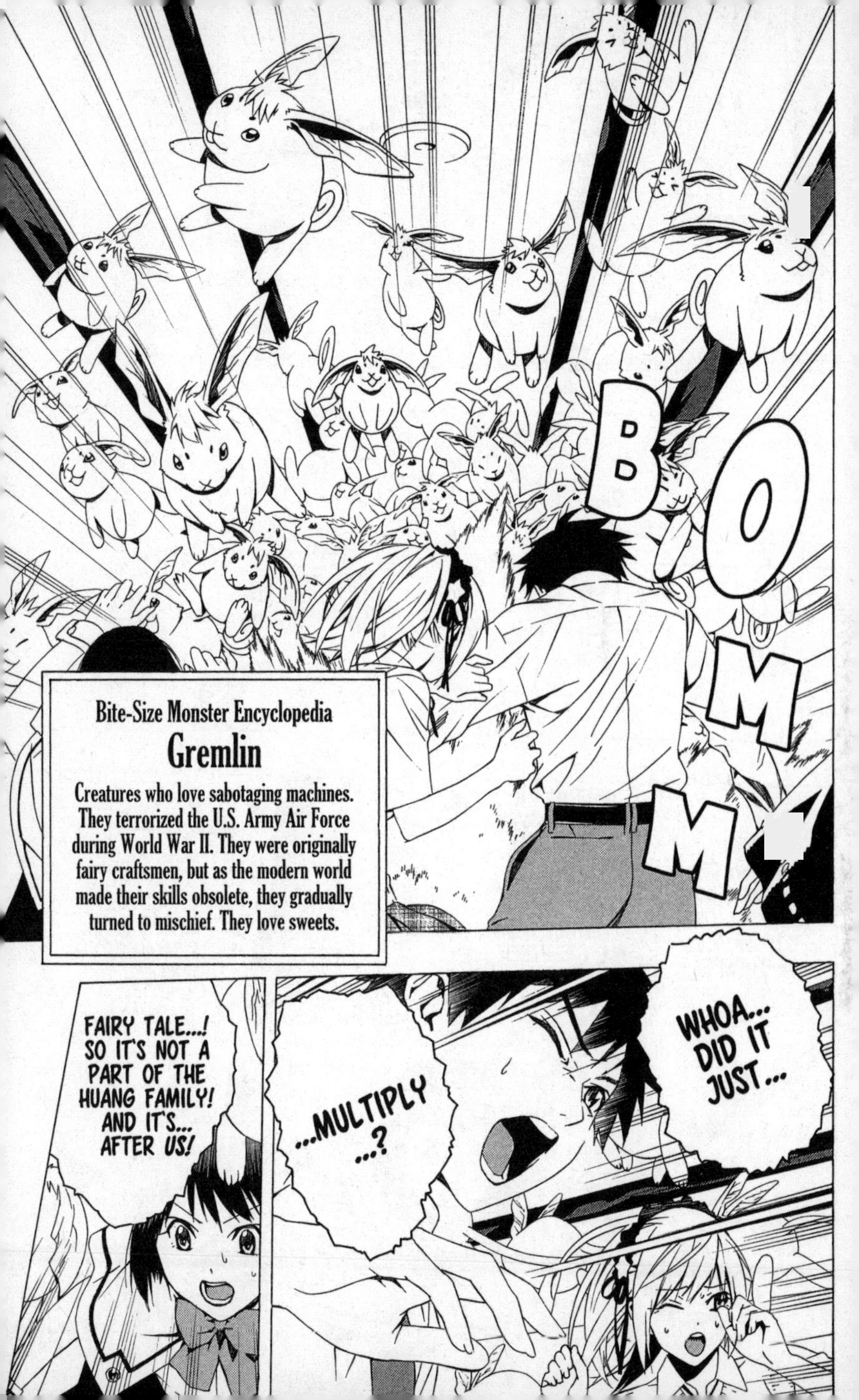
BOMMM
Bite-Size Monster Encyclopedia
Gremlin
Creatures who love sabotaging machines. They terrorized the U.S. Army Air Force during World War II. They were originally fairy craftsmen, but as the modern world made their skills obsolete, they gradually turned to mischief. They love sweets.
WHOA... DID IT JUST...
...MULTIPLY ...?
FAIRY TALE...! SO IT'S NOT A PART OF THE HUANG FAMILY! AND IT'S... AFTER US!

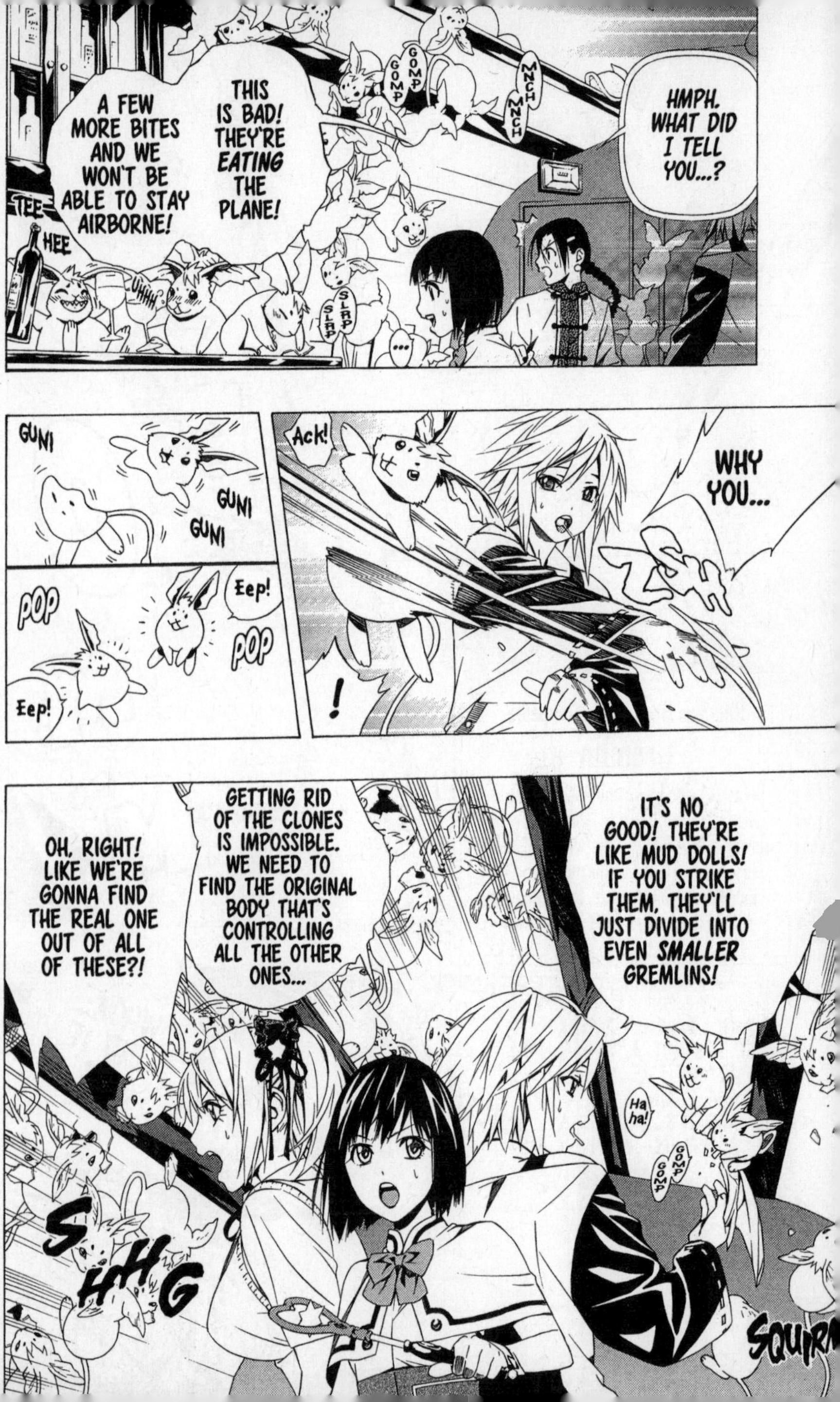
HMPH. WHAT DID I TELL YOU...?
MNCH MNCH
GOMP GOMP
THIS IS BAD! THEY'RE EATING THE PLANE!
A FEW MORE BITES AND WE WON'T BE ABLE TO STAY AIRBORNE!
SLRP SLRP
...
UHHH
TEE HEE
WHY YOU...
Ack!
!
GUNI
GUNI
GUNI
Eep!
POP
POP
Eep!
IT'S NO GOOD! THEY'RE LIKE MUD DOLLS! IF YOU STRIKE THEM, THEY'LL JUST DIVIDE INTO EVEN SMALLER GREMLINS!
GETTING RID OF THE CLONES IS IMPOSSIBLE. WE NEED TO FIND THE ORIGINAL BODY THAT'S CONTROLLING ALL THE OTHER ONES...
OH, RIGHT! LIKE WE'RE GONNA FIND THE REAL ONE OUT OF ALL OF THESE?!
Ha ha!
GOMP GOMP
SQUIRM
SHG

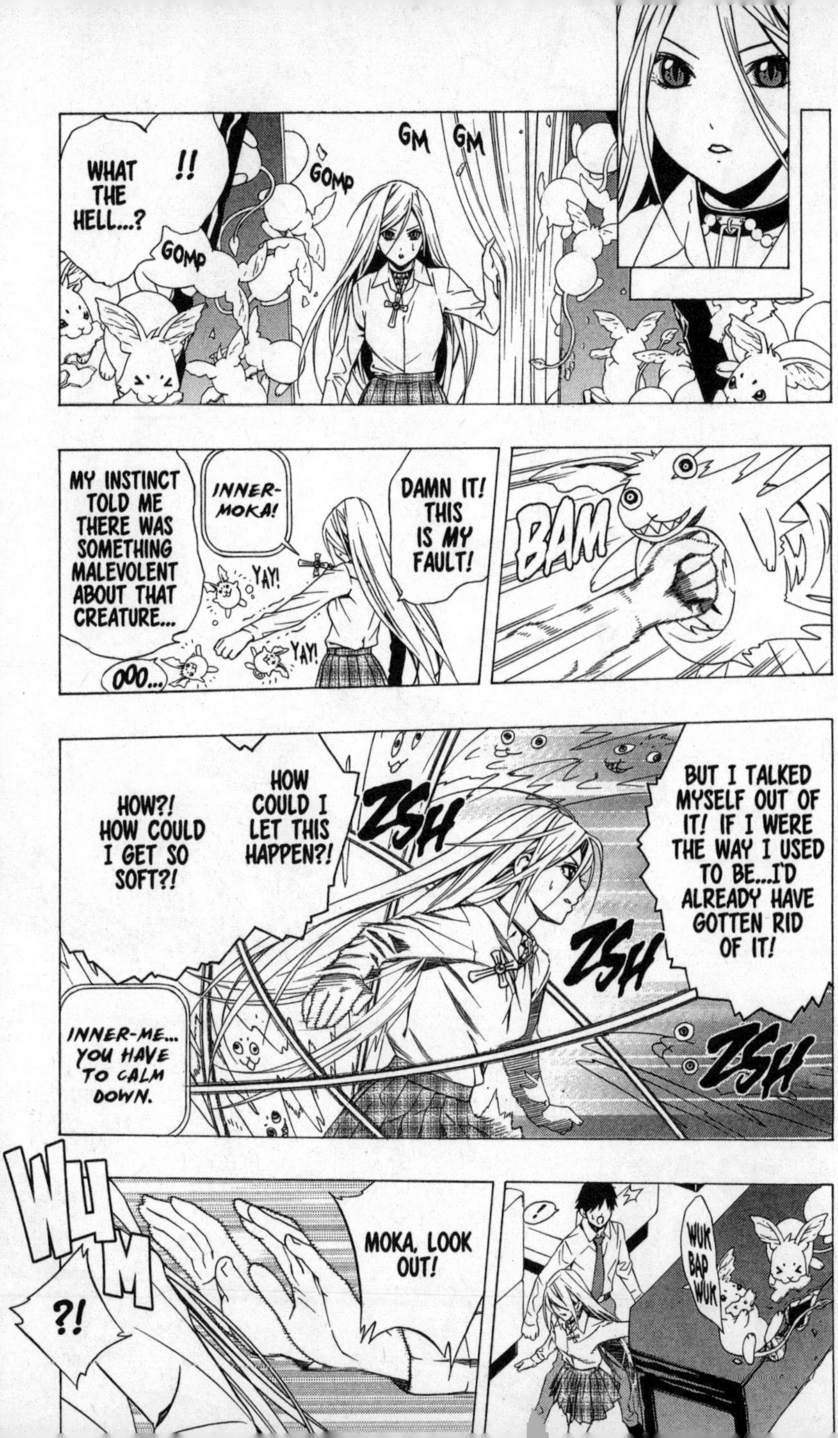
GM GM
GOMP
!!
WHAT THE HELL...?
GOMP
BAM
DAMN IT! THIS IS MY FAULT!
INNER-MOKA!
MY INSTINCT TOLD ME THERE WAS SOMETHING MALEVOLENT ABOUT THAT CREATURE...
YAY!
YAY!
OOO...
BUT I TALKED MYSELF OUT OF IT! IF I WERE THE WAY I USED TO BE...I'D ALREADY HAVE GOTTEN RID OF IT!
ZSH
HOW COULD I LET THIS HAPPEN?!
HOW?! HOW COULD I GET SO SOFT?!
ZSH
ZSH
INNER-ME... YOU HAVE TO CALM DOWN.
!
WUK BAP WUK
MOKA, LOOK OUT!
WUM
?!

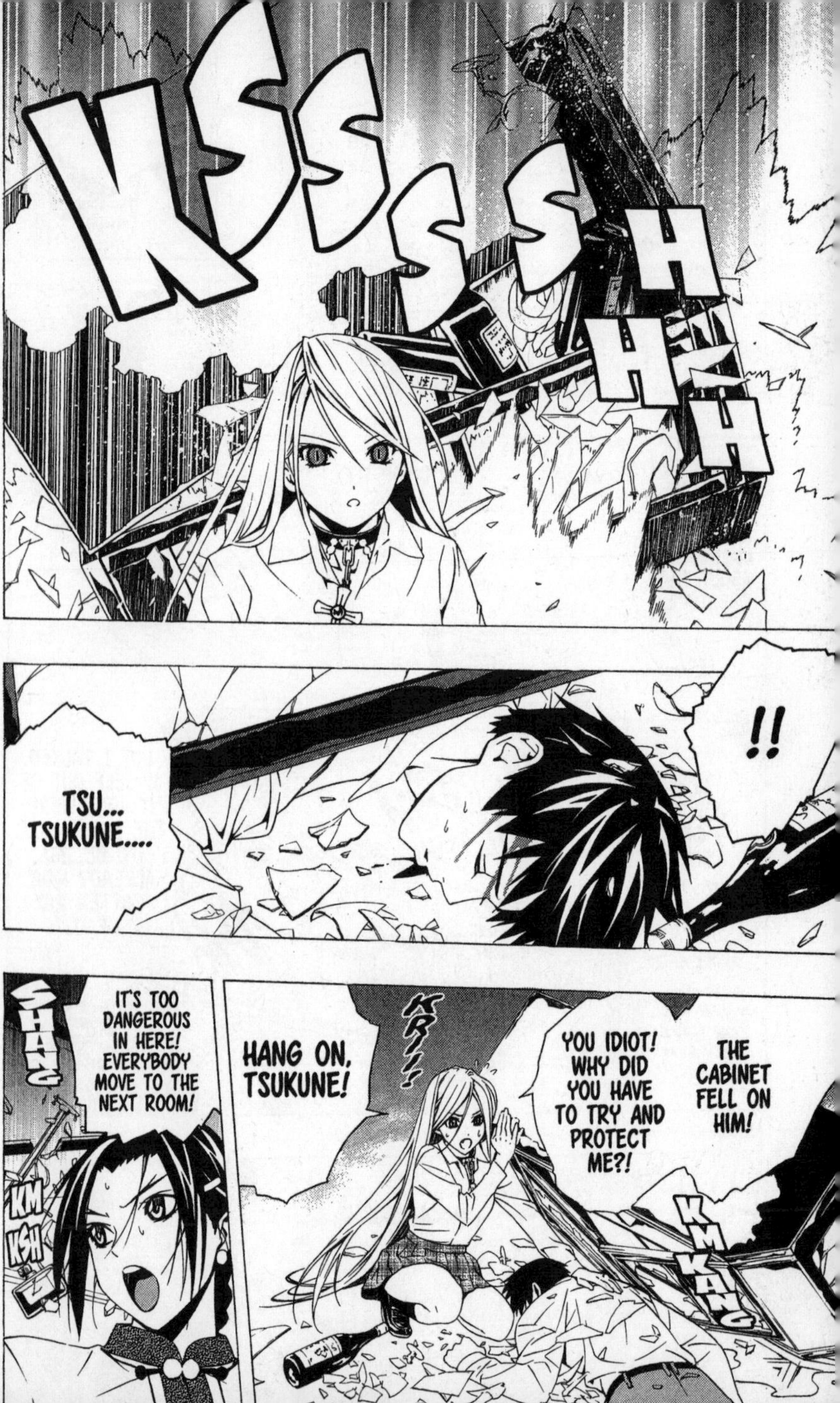
KSSSSH
HHH
!!
TSU... TSUKUNE....
THE CABINET FELL ON HIM!
YOU IDIOT! WHY DID YOU HAVE TO TRY AND PROTECT ME?!
KRI!
HANG ON, TSUKUNE!
KMKANG
IT'S TOO DANGEROUS IN HERE! EVERYBODY MOVE TO THE NEXT ROOM!
SHANG
KM KSH

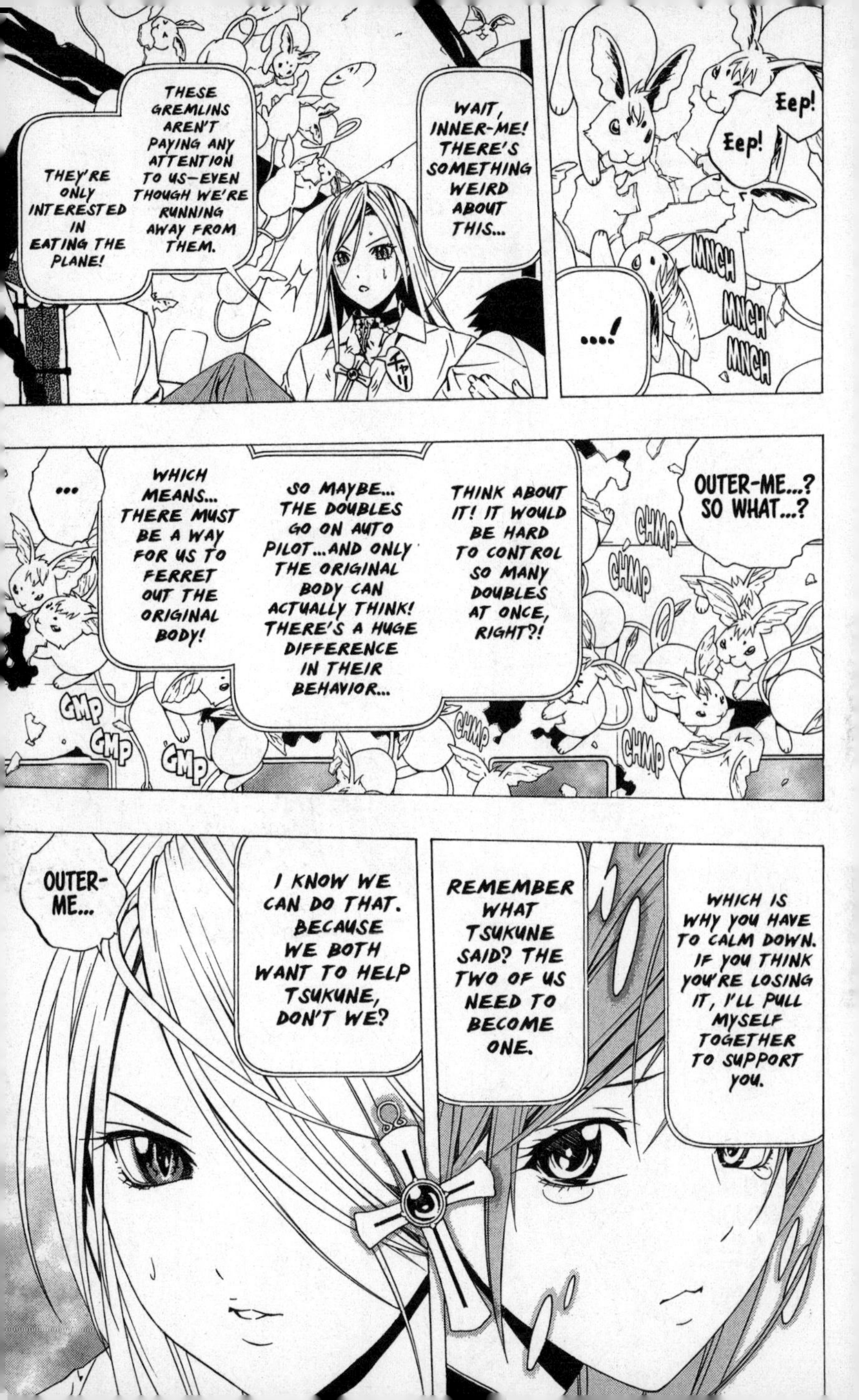
Eep!
Eep!
MNCH
MNCH
MNCH
....!
WAIT, INNER-ME! THERE'S SOMETHING WEIRD ABOUT THIS...
THESE GREMLINS AREN'T PAYING ANY ATTENTION TO US—EVEN THOUGH WE'RE RUNNING AWAY FROM THEM.
THEY'RE ONLY INTERESTED IN EATING THE PLANE!
OUTER-ME...? SO WHAT...?
CHMP
CHMP
THINK ABOUT IT! IT WOULD BE HARD TO CONTROL SO MANY DOUBLES AT ONCE, RIGHT?!
SO MAYBE... THE DOUBLES GO ON AUTO PILOT...AND ONLY THE ORIGINAL BODY CAN ACTUALLY THINK! THERE'S A HUGE DIFFERENCE IN THEIR BEHAVIOR...
WHICH MEANS... THERE MUST BE A WAY FOR US TO FERRET OUT THE ORIGINAL BODY!
...
CHMP
CHMP
GMP
GMP
GMP
WHICH IS WHY YOU HAVE TO CALM DOWN. IF YOU THINK YOU'RE LOSING IT, I'LL PULL MYSELF TOGETHER TO SUPPORT YOU.
REMEMBER WHAT TSUKUNE SAID? THE TWO OF US NEED TO BECOME ONE.
I KNOW WE CAN DO THAT. BECAUSE WE BOTH WANT TO HELP TSUKUNE, DON'T WE?
OUTER-ME...

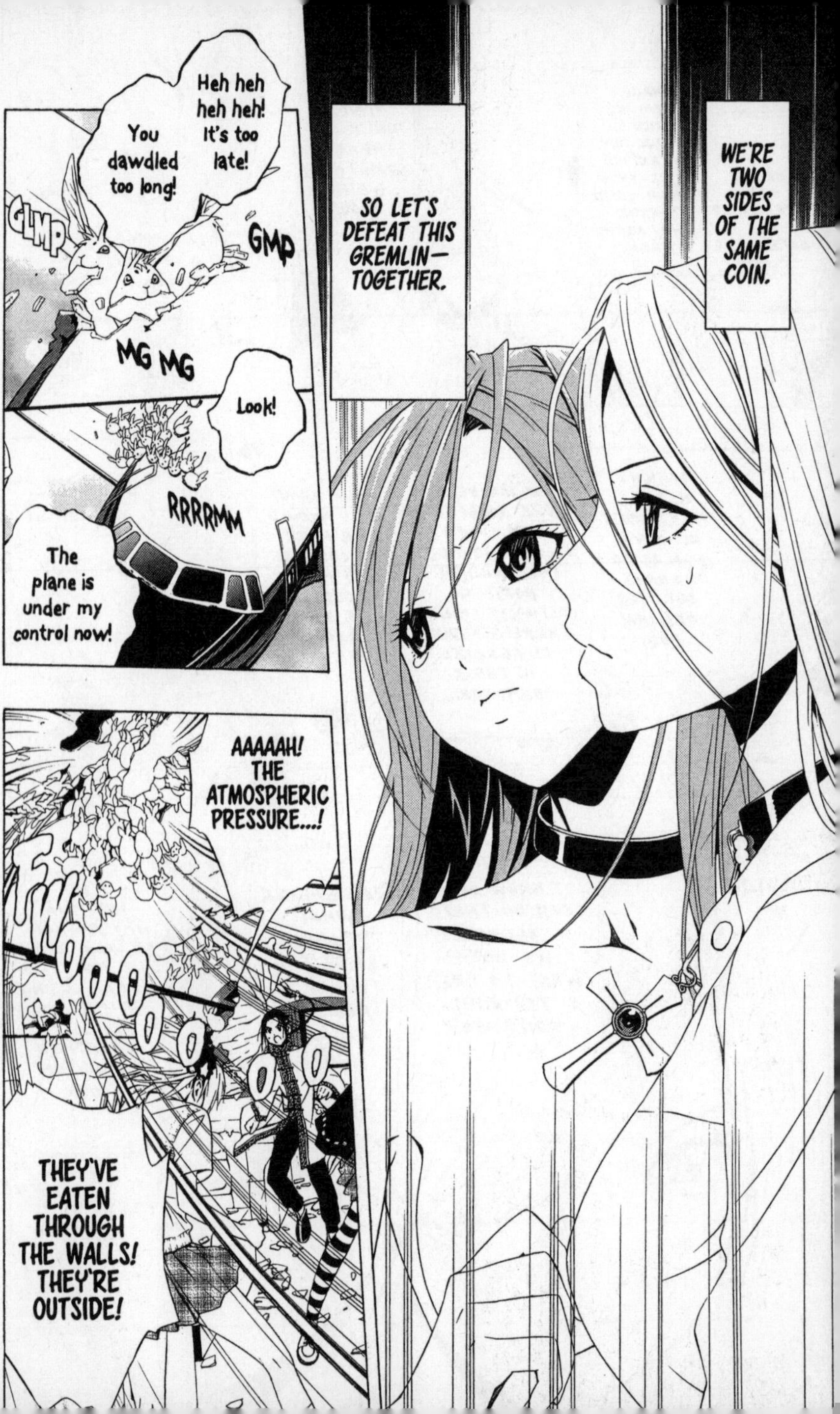
WE'RE TWO SIDES OF THE SAME COIN.
SO LET'S DEFEAT THIS GREMLIN—TOGETHER.
Heh heh heh heh! It's too late!
You dawdled too long!
GLMP
GMP
MG MG
Look!
RRRRMM
The plane is under my control now!
AAAAAH! THE ATMOSPHERIC PRESSURE...!
FWOOOOOOO
THEY'VE EATEN THROUGH THE WALLS! THEY'RE OUTSIDE!

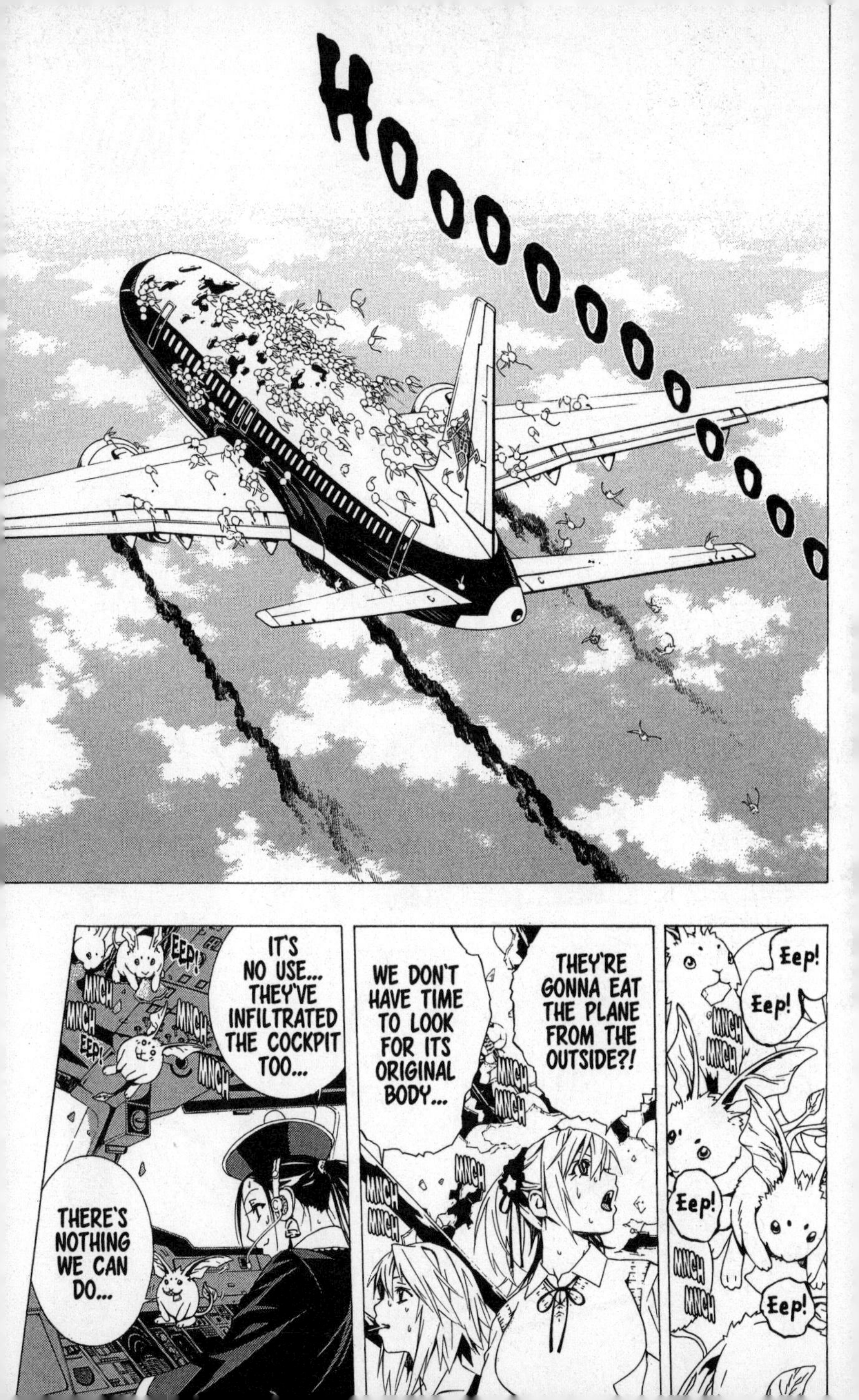
HOOOOOOOOOOOO
Eep!
Eep!
MNCH MNCH
Eep!
MNCH MNCH
Eep!
THEY'RE GONNA EAT THE PLANE FROM THE OUTSIDE?!
MNCH MNCH
WE DON'T HAVE TIME TO LOOK FOR ITS ORIGINAL BODY...
MNCH
MNCH MNCH
IT'S NO USE... THEY'VE INFILTRATED THE COCKPIT TOO...
EEP!
MNCH
MNCH MNCH
EEP!
MNCH
THERE'S NOTHING WE CAN DO...

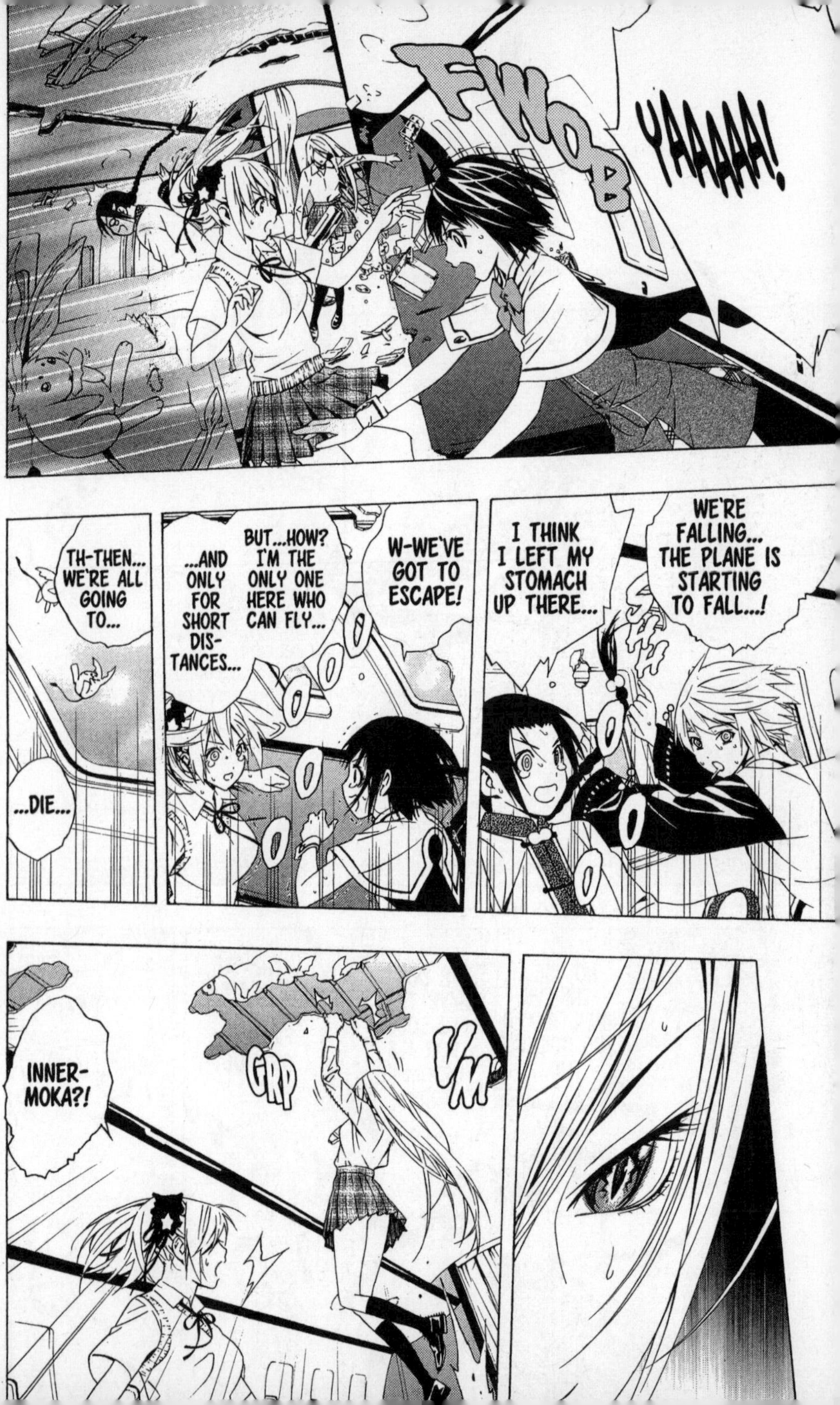
YAAAAA!
FWOB
WE'RE FALLING... THE PLANE IS STARTING TO FALL...!
I THINK I LEFT MY STOMACH UP THERE...
W-WE'VE GOT TO ESCAPE!
BUT...HOW? I'M THE ONLY ONE HERE WHO CAN FLY...
...AND ONLY FOR SHORT DIS-TANCES...
TH-THEN... WE'RE ALL GOING TO...
...DIE...
VM
GRP
INNER-MOKA?!

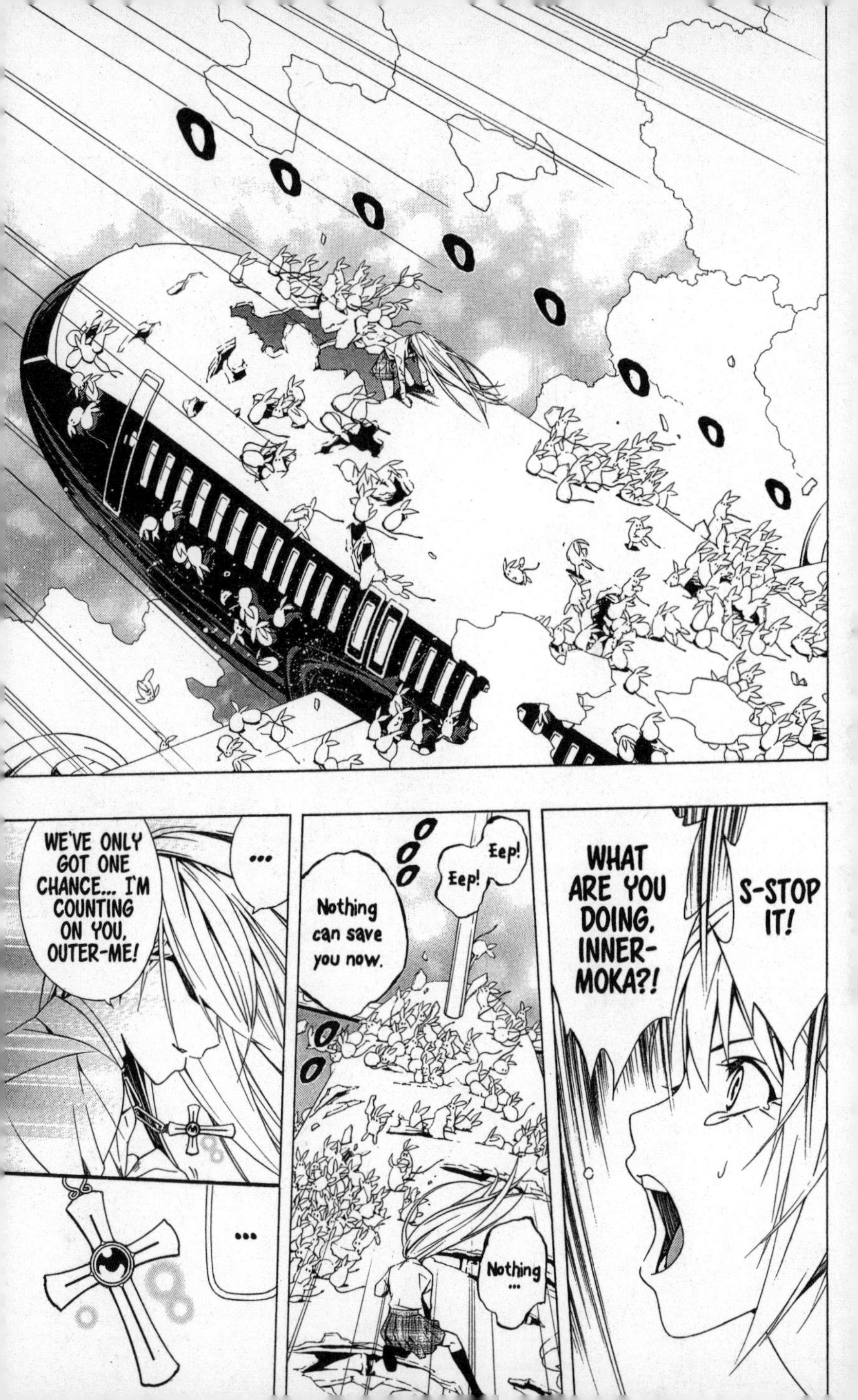
S-STOP IT!
WHAT ARE YOU DOING, INNER-MOKA?!
Eep!
Eep!
Nothing can save you now.
Nothing ...
...
WE'VE ONLY GOT ONE CHANCE... I'M COUNTING ON YOU, OUTER-ME!
...

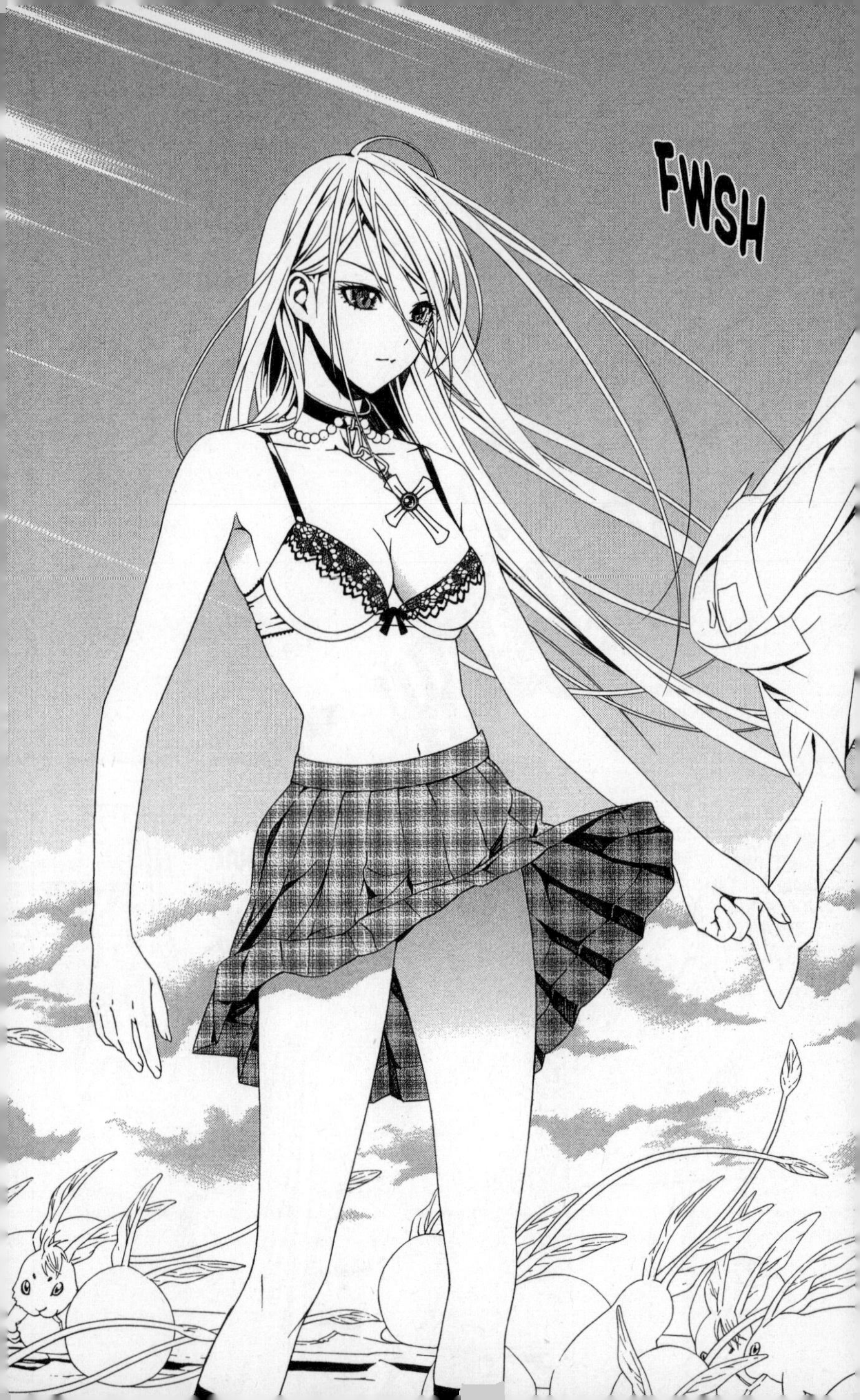
FWSH

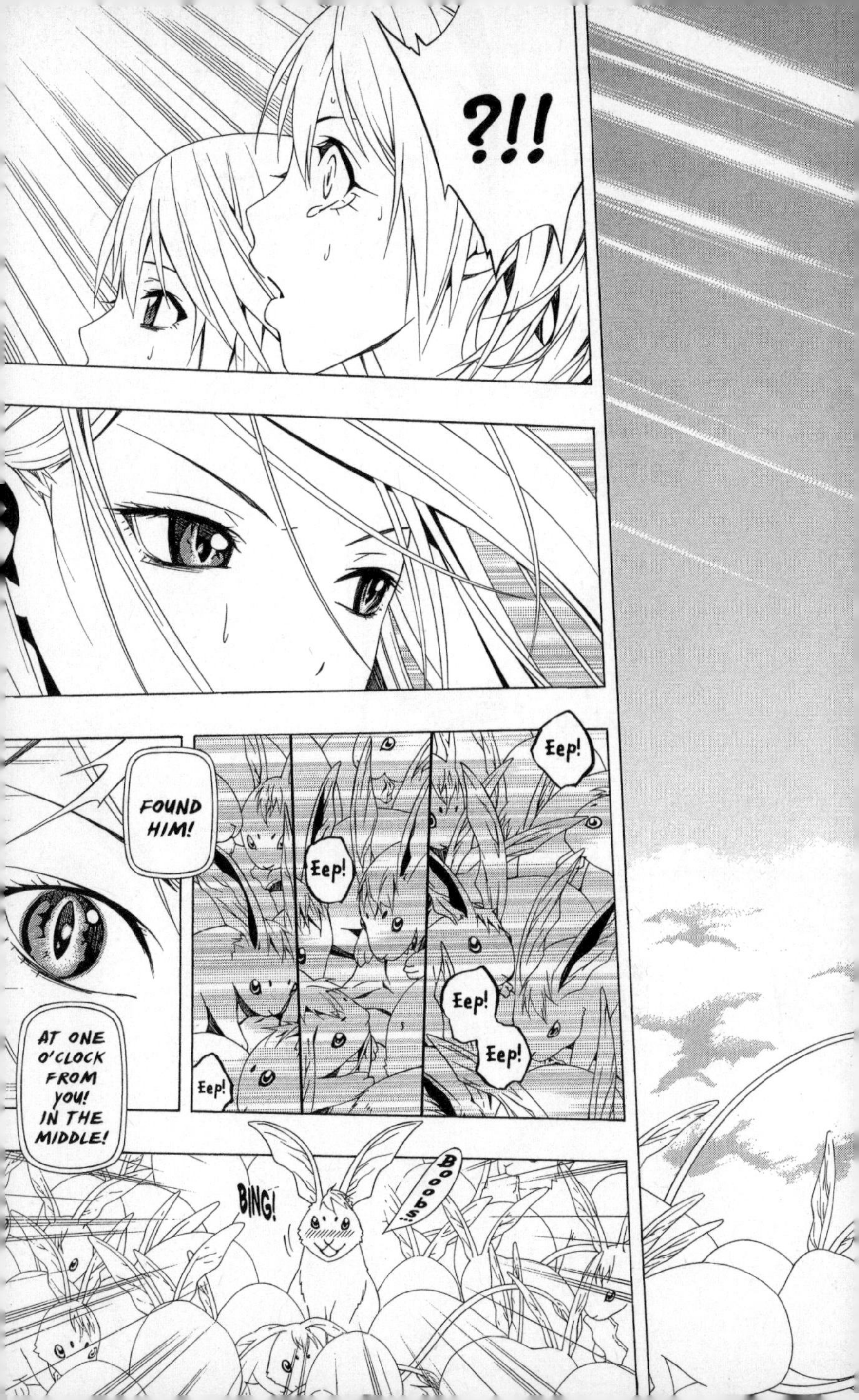
?!!
Eep!
Eep!
Eep!
Eep!
Eep!
FOUND HIM!
AT ONE O'CLOCK FROM YOU! IN THE MIDDLE!
BING!
Booobs!!

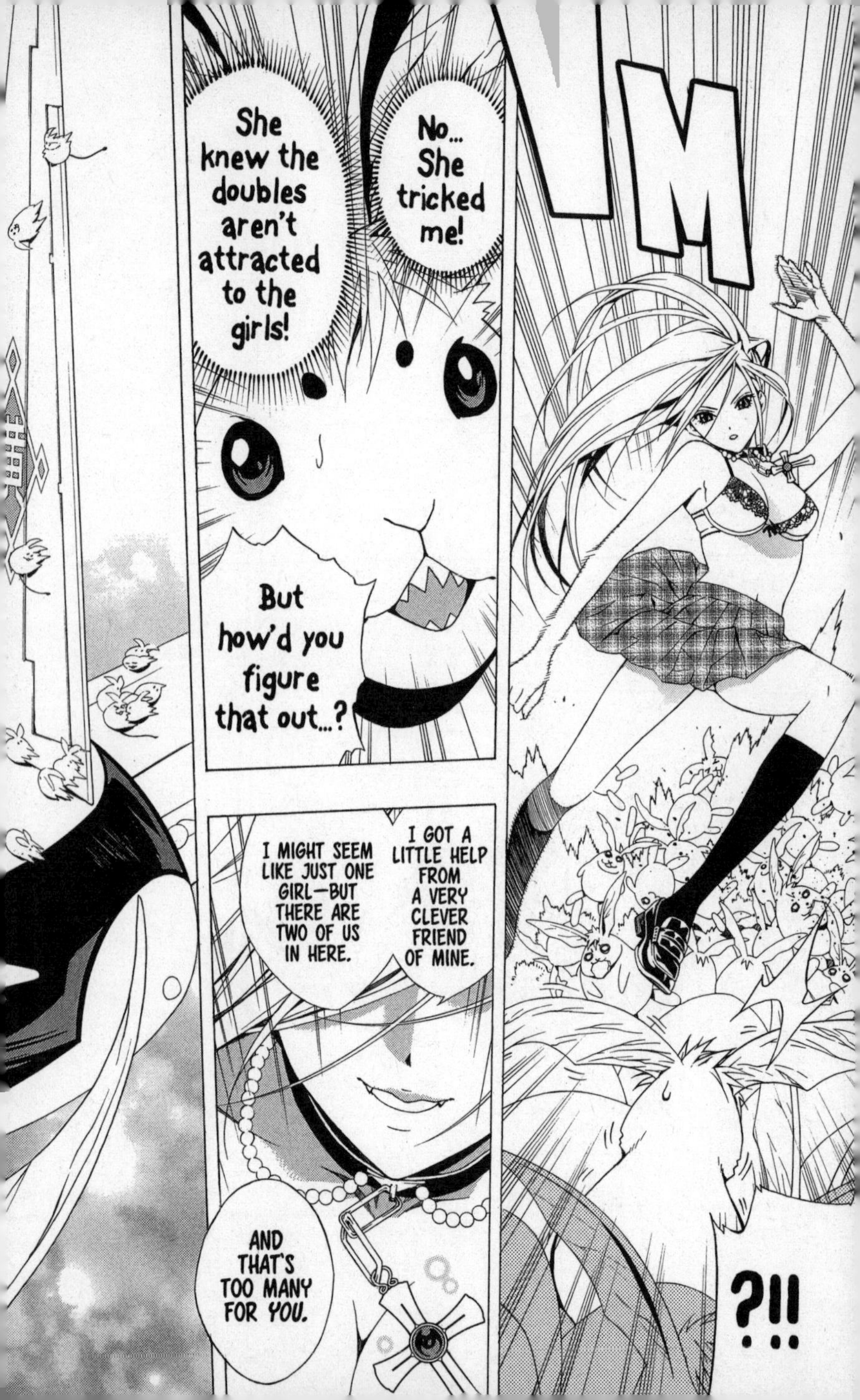

M
?!!
No... She tricked me!
She knew the doubles aren't attracted to the girls!
But how'd you figure that out...?
I GOT A LITTLE HELP FROM A VERY CLEVER FRIEND OF MINE.
I MIGHT SEEM LIKE JUST ONE GIRL—BUT THERE ARE TWO OF US IN HERE.
AND THAT'S TOO MANY FOR YOU.

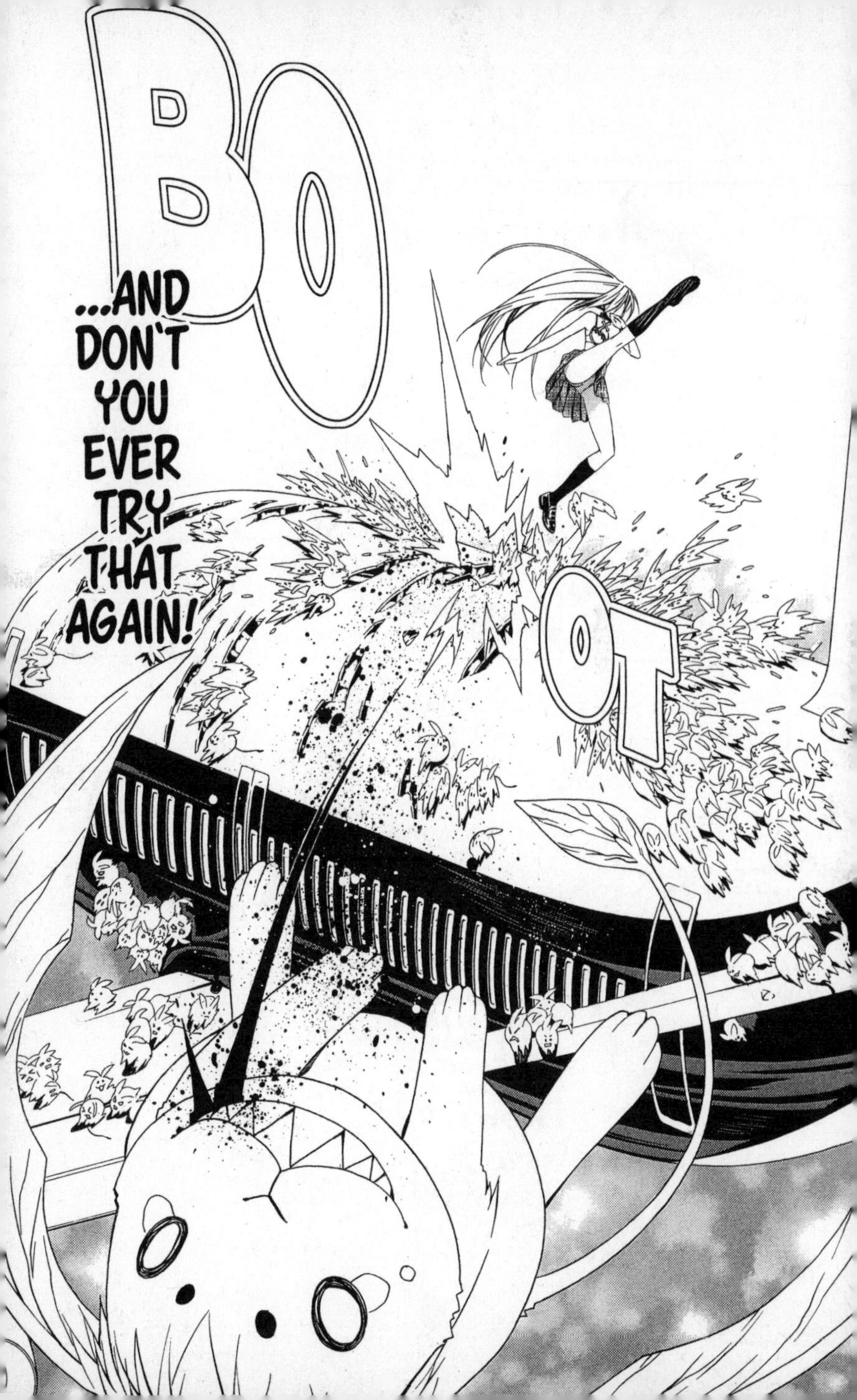
BOOT
...AND DON'T YOU EVER TRY THAT AGAIN!

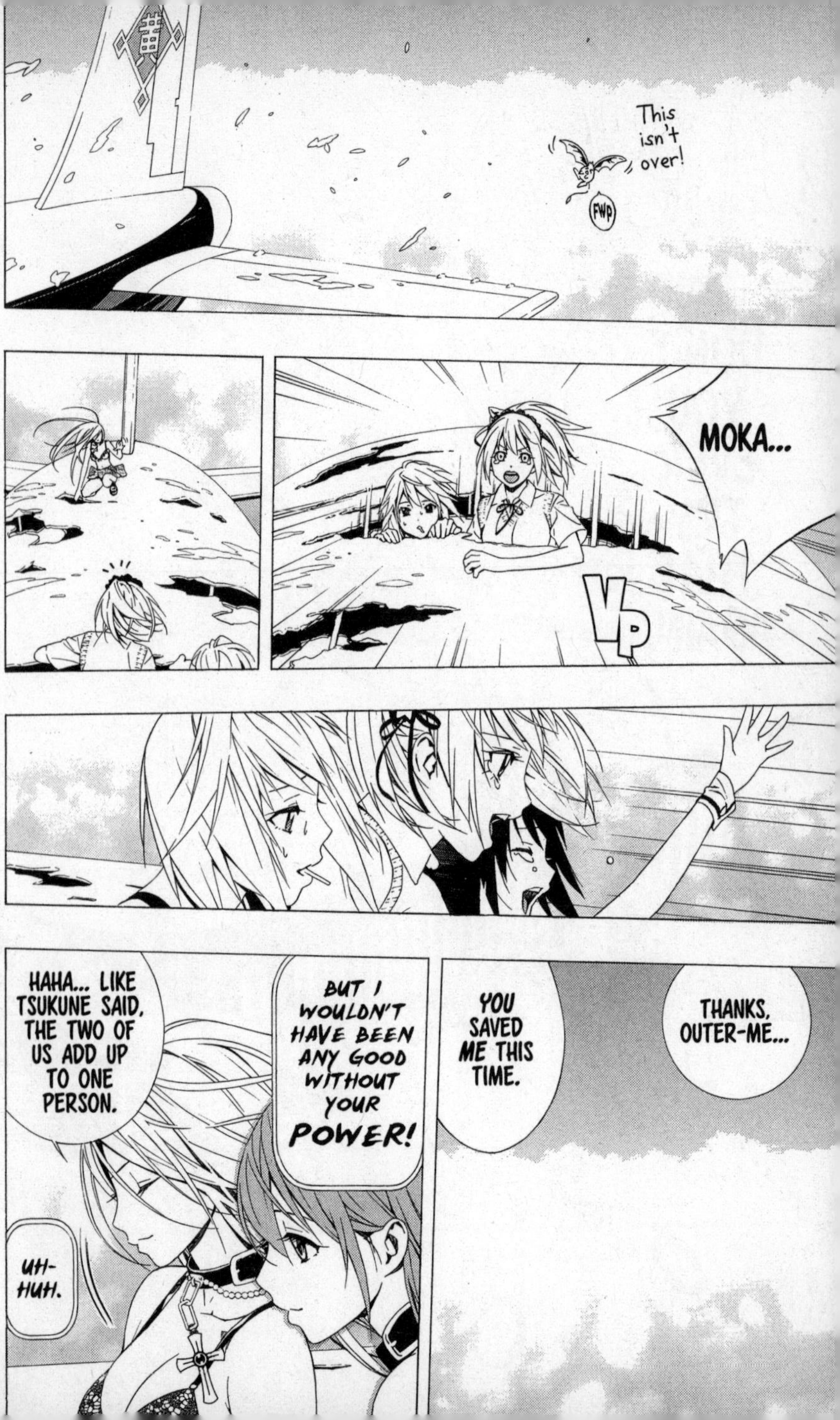
This isn't over!
FWP
MOKA...
VP
THANKS, OUTER-ME...
YOU SAVED ME THIS TIME.
BUT I WOULDN'T HAVE BEEN ANY GOOD WITHOUT YOUR POWER!
HAHA... LIKE TSUKUNE SAID, THE TWO OF US ADD UP TO ONE PERSON.
UH-HUH.

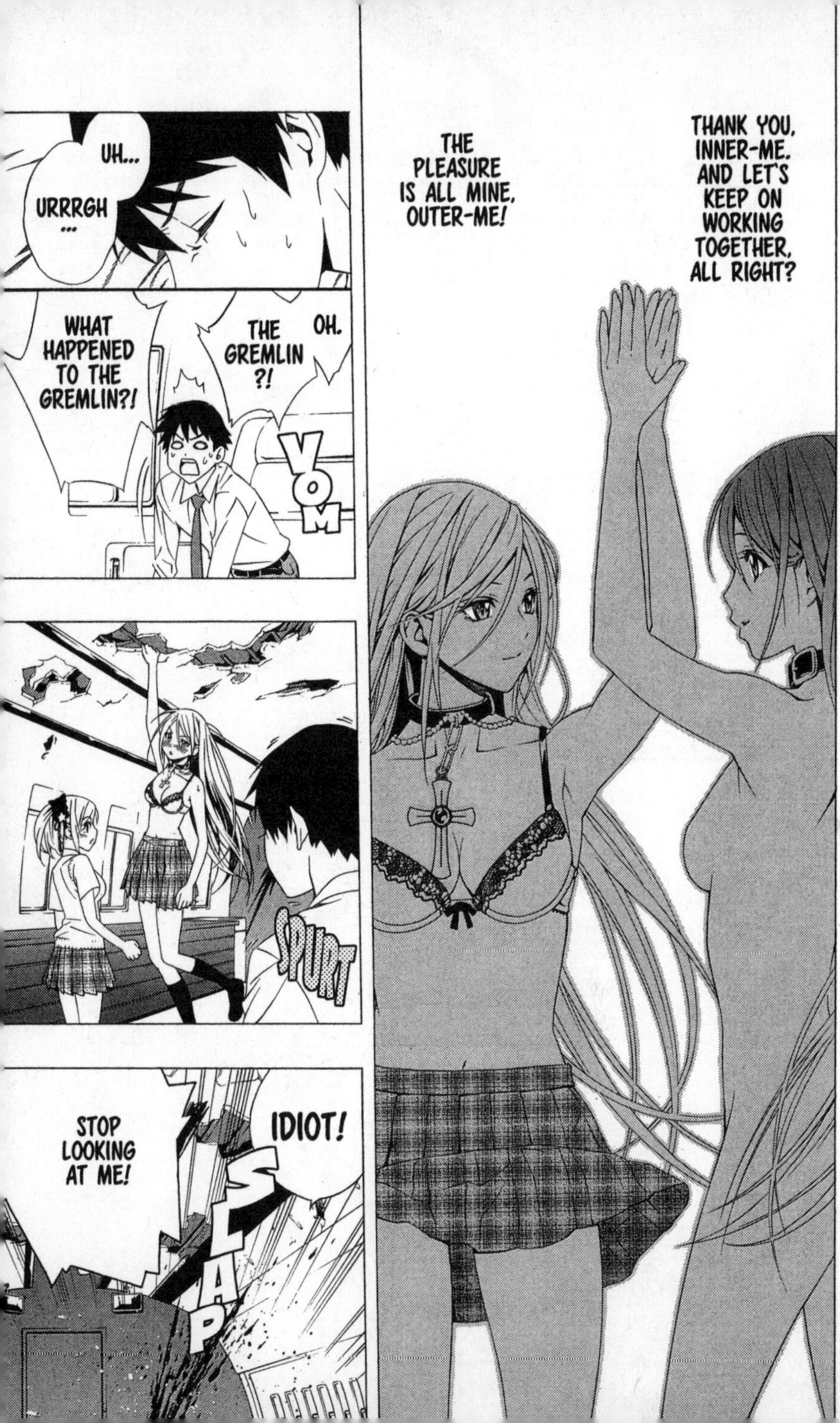
THANK YOU, INNER-ME. AND LET'S KEEP ON WORKING TOGETHER, ALL RIGHT?
THE PLEASURE IS ALL MINE, OUTER-ME!
UH...
URRRGH ...
OH.
THE GREMLIN ?!
WHAT HAPPENED TO THE GREMLIN?!
VOM
SPURT
IDIOT!
STOP LOOKING AT ME!
SLAP

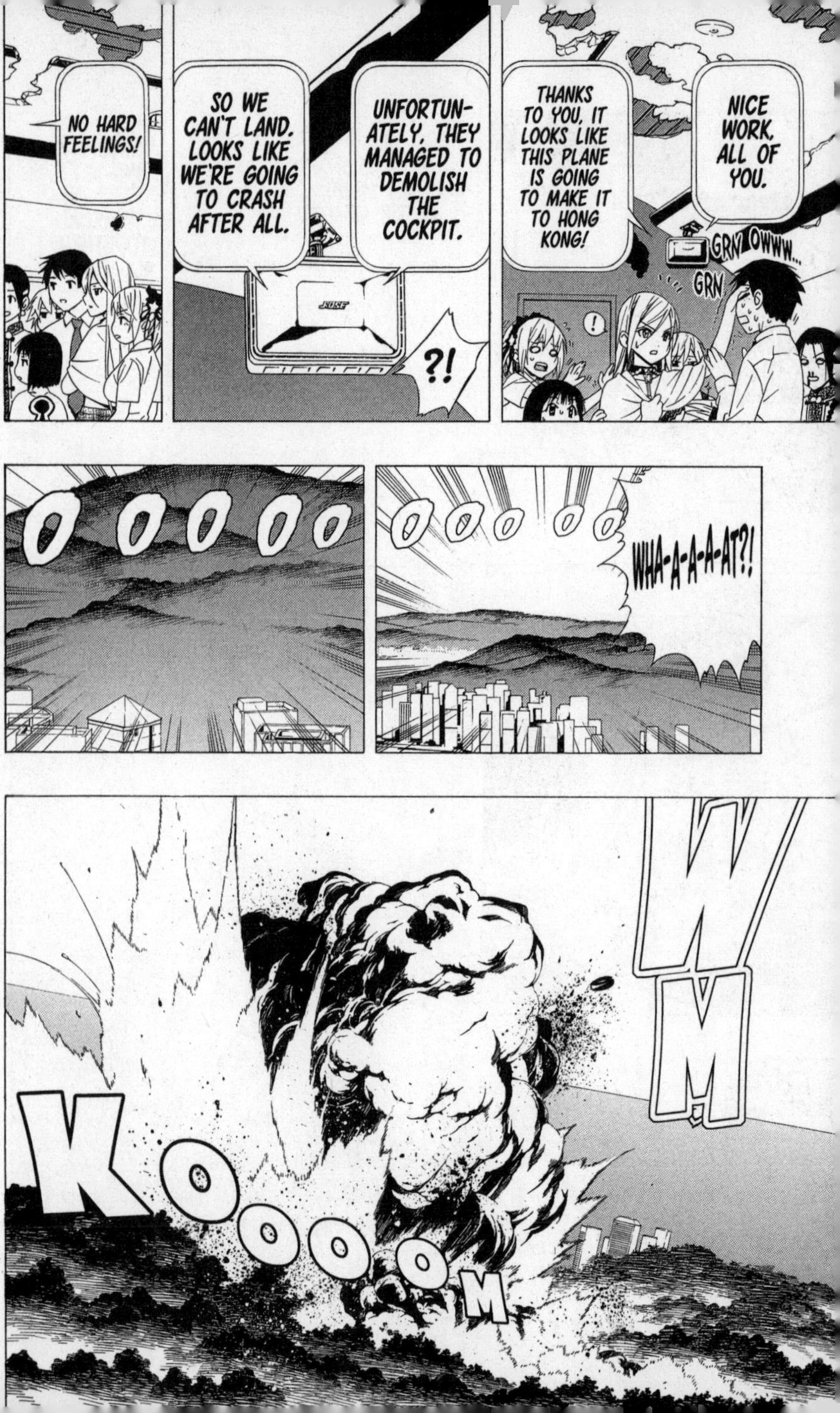
NICE WORK, ALL OF YOU.
THANKS TO YOU, IT LOOKS LIKE THIS PLANE IS GOING TO MAKE IT TO HONG KONG!
GRN OWWW...
GRN
!
UNFORTUN-ATELY, THEY MANAGED TO DEMOLISH THE COCKPIT.
SO WE CAN'T LAND. LOOKS LIKE WE'RE GOING TO CRASH AFTER ALL.
?!
NO HARD FEELINGS!
O O O O O
WHA-A-A-AT?!
O O O O O
WM
KO.O.O.O.OM

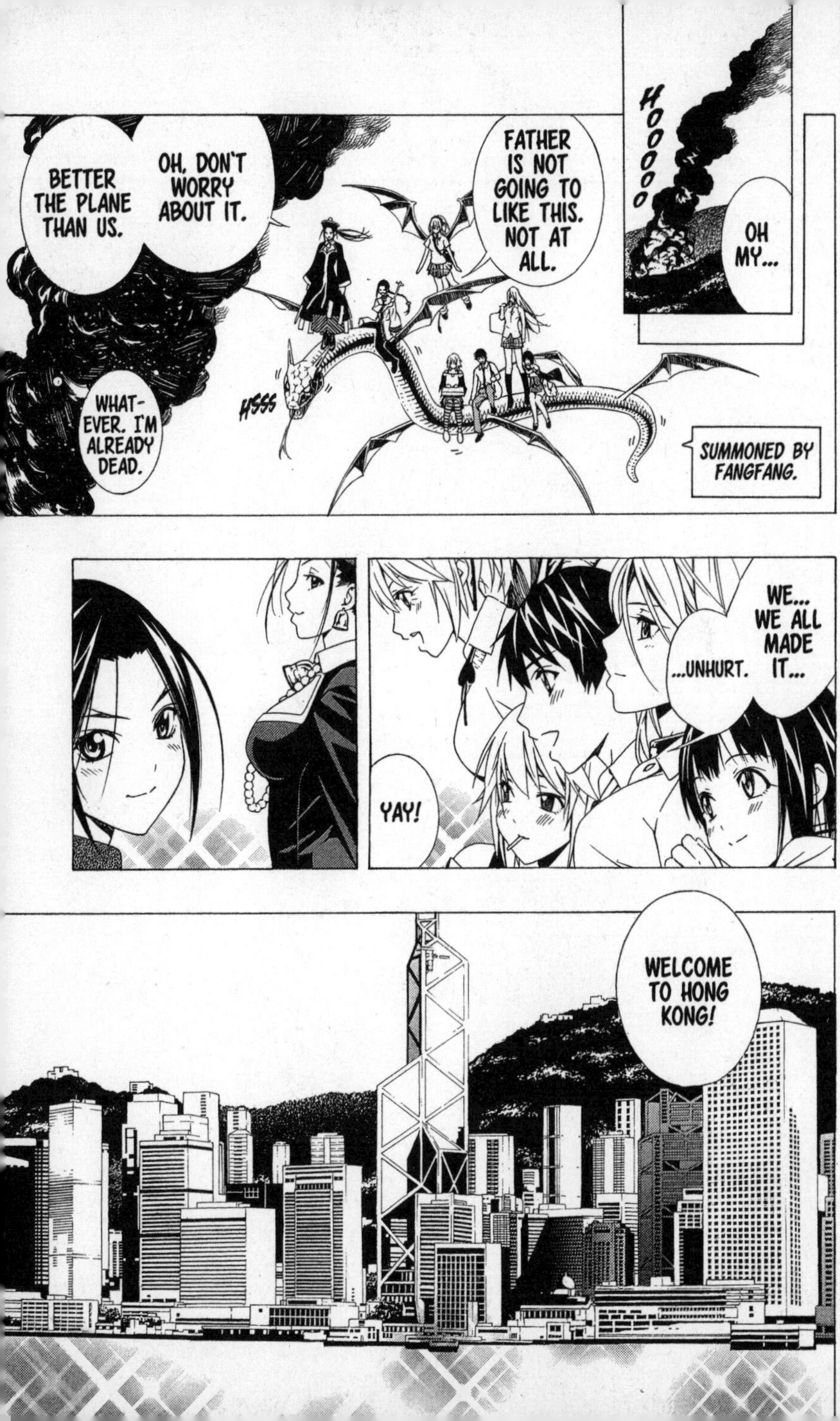
HOOOOOO
OH MY...
FATHER IS NOT GOING TO LIKE THIS. NOT AT ALL.
OH, DON'T WORRY ABOUT IT.
BETTER THE PLANE THAN US.
SUMMONED BY FANGFANG.
HSSS
WHAT-EVER. I'M ALREADY DEAD.
WE... WE ALL MADE IT...
...UNHURT.
YAY!
WELCOME TO HONG KONG!

# 28: Home Sweet Home

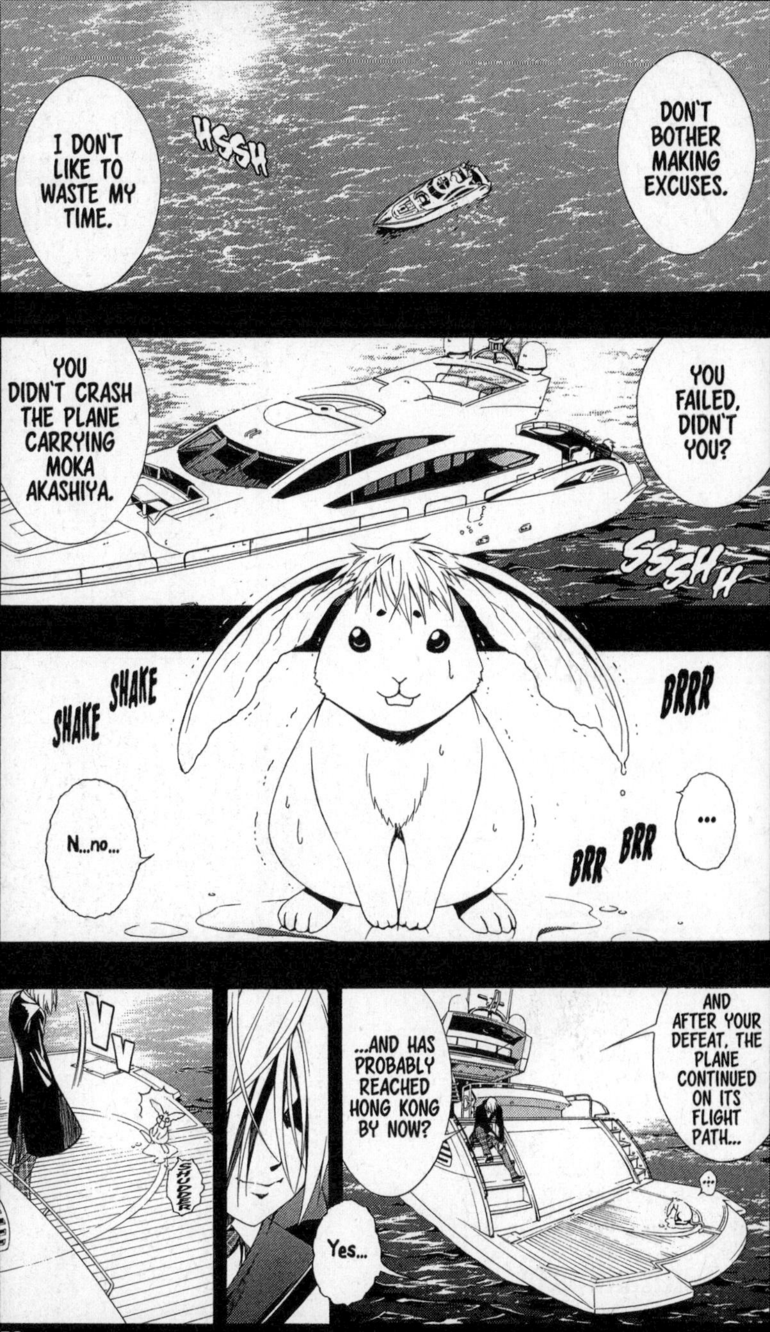
DON'T BOTHER MAKING EXCUSES.
HSSH
I DON'T LIKE TO WASTE MY TIME.
YOU FAILED, DIDN'T YOU?
SSSHH
YOU DIDN'T CRASH THE PLANE CARRYING MOKA AKASHIYA.
BRRR
...
BRR BRR
SHAKE SHAKE
N...no...
AND AFTER YOUR DEFEAT, THE PLANE CONTINUED ON ITS FLIGHT PATH...
...
...AND HAS PROBABLY REACHED HONG KONG BY NOW?
Yes...
VV
SHUDDER

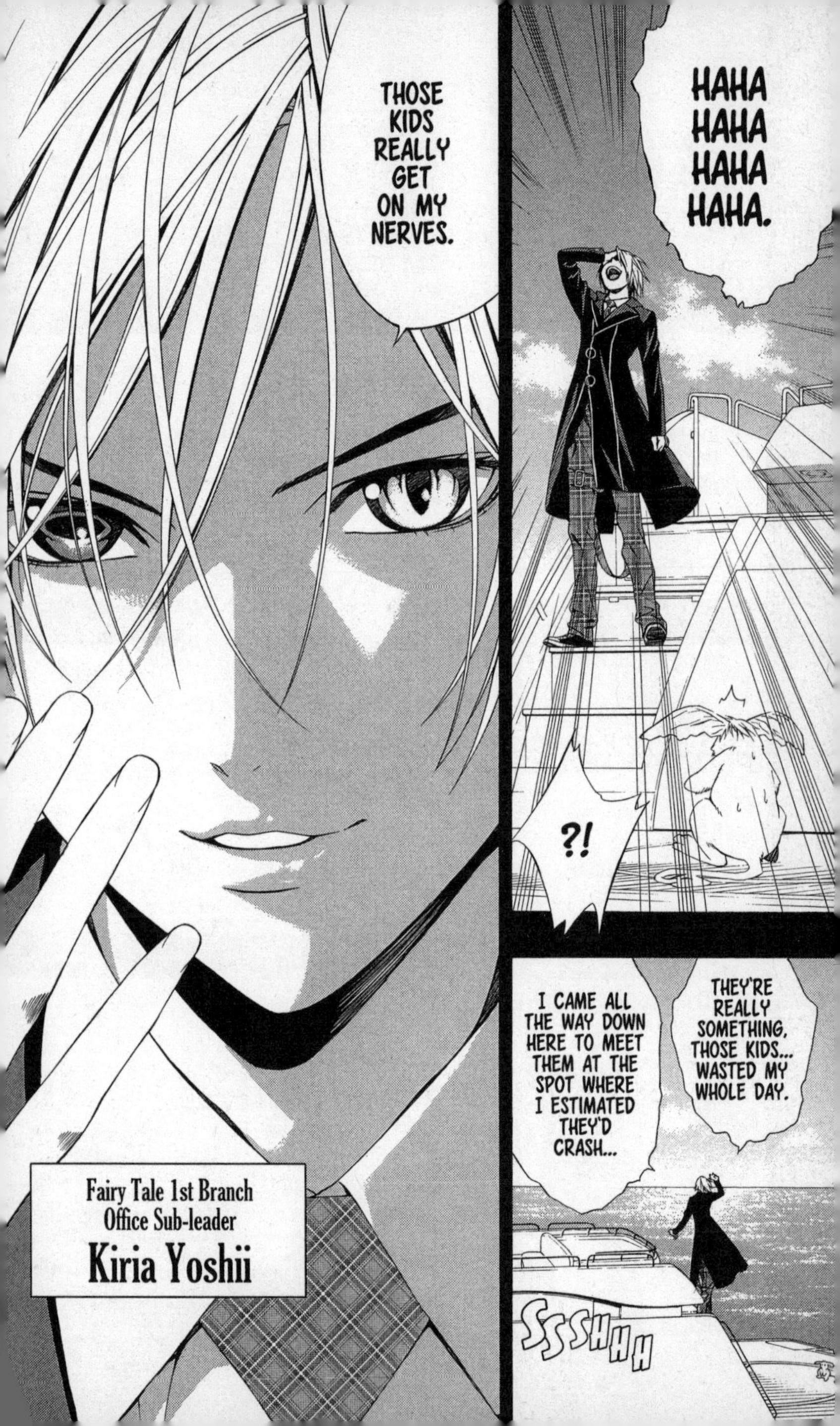
HAHA HAHA HAHA HAHA.
?!
THEY'RE REALLY SOMETHING, THOSE KIDS... WASTED MY WHOLE DAY.
I CAME ALL THE WAY DOWN HERE TO MEET THEM AT THE SPOT WHERE I ESTIMATED THEY'D CRASH...
SSSHHHH
THOSE KIDS REALLY GET ON MY NERVES.
Fairy Tale 1st Branch Office Sub-leader
Kiria Yoshii

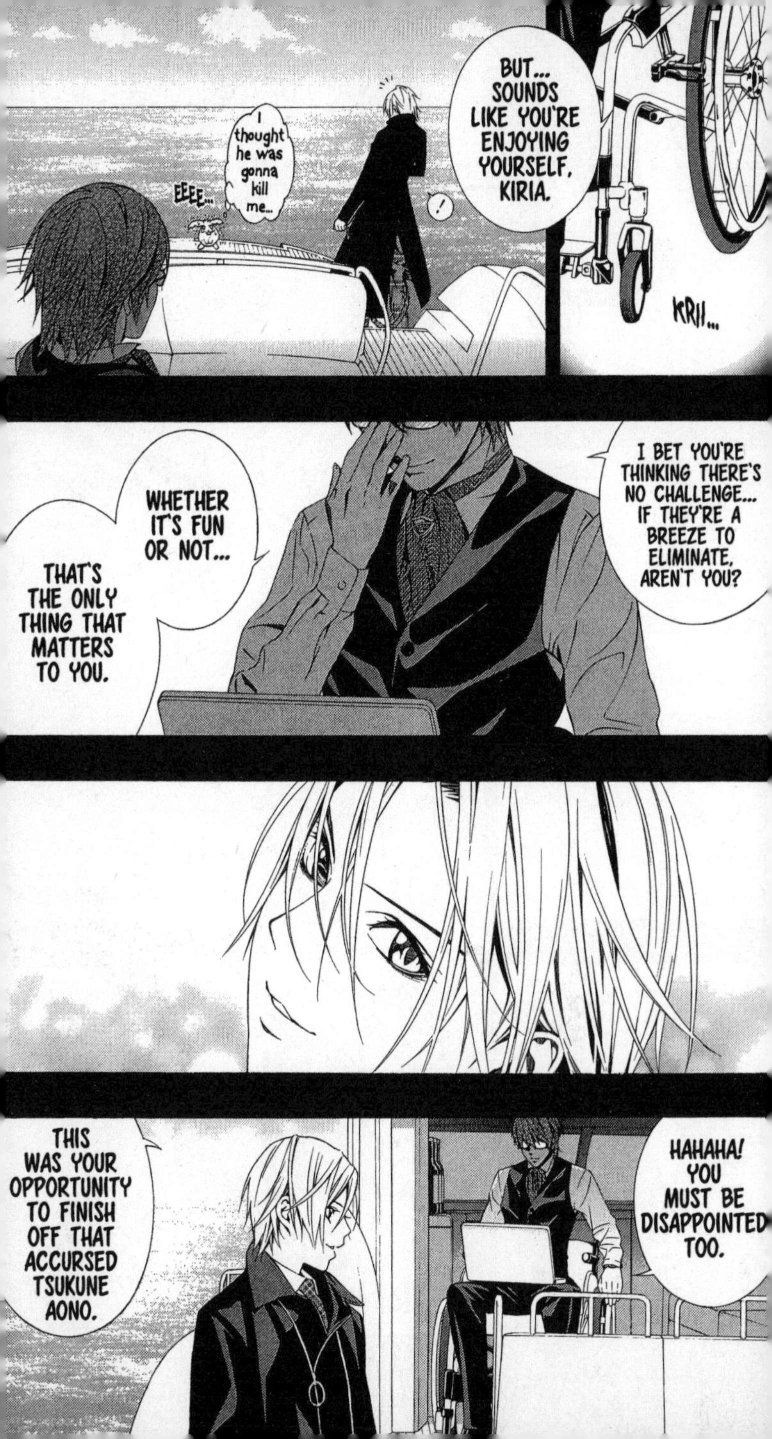
BUT... SOUNDS LIKE YOU'RE ENJOYING YOURSELF, KIRIA.
KRII...
!
I thought he was gonna kill me...
EEEE...
I BET YOU'RE THINKING THERE'S NO CHALLENGE... IF THEY'RE A BREEZE TO ELIMINATE, AREN'T YOU?
WHETHER IT'S FUN OR NOT...
THAT'S THE ONLY THING THAT MATTERS TO YOU.
HAHAHA! YOU MUST BE DISAPPOINTED TOO.
THIS WAS YOUR OPPORTUNITY TO FINISH OFF THAT ACCURSED TSUKUNE AONO.

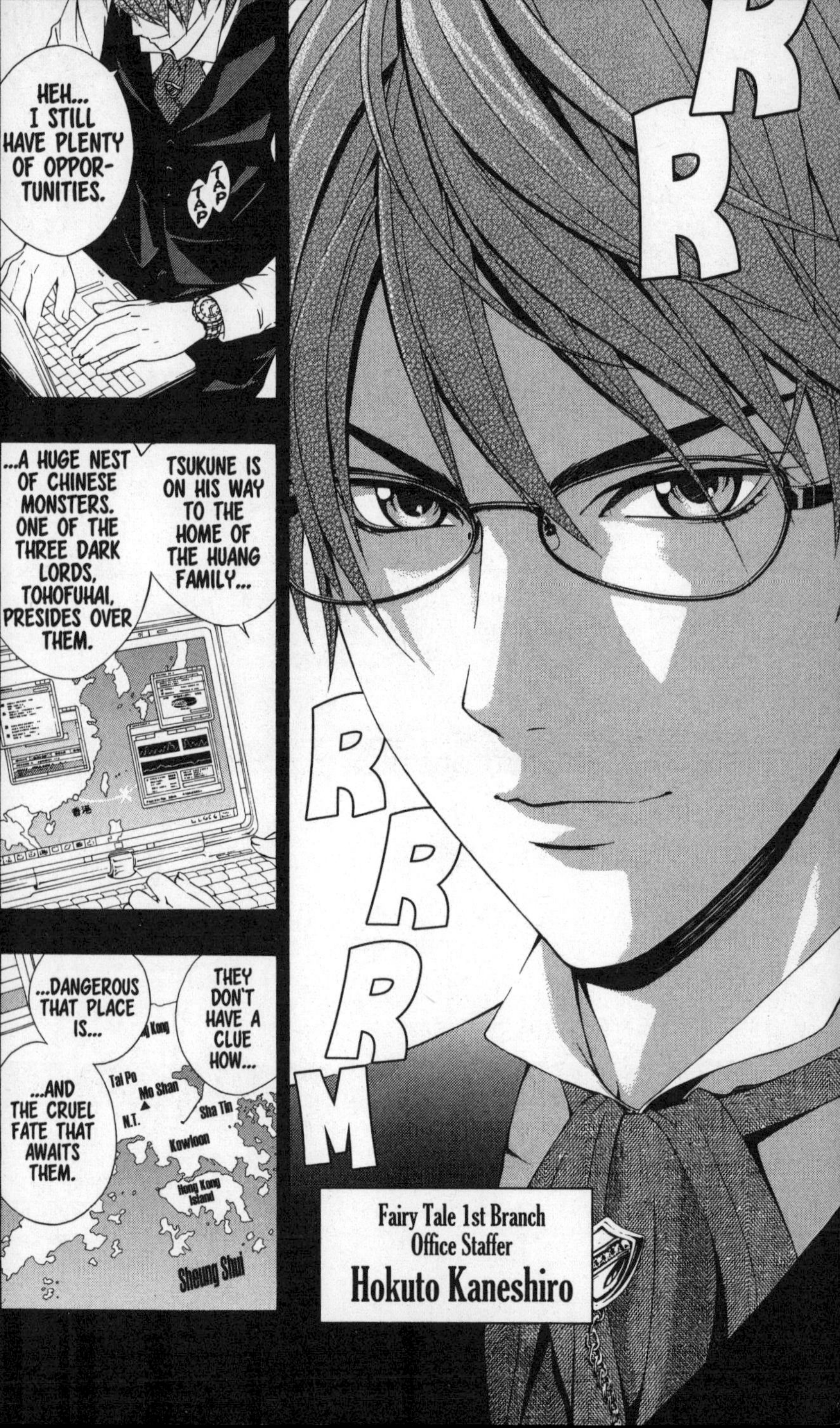
RRR
RRRRM
Fairy Tale 1st Branch Office Staffer
Hokuto Kaneshiro
HEH... I STILL HAVE PLENTY OF OPPOR-TUNITIES.
TAP TAP
TSUKUNE IS ON HIS WAY TO THE HOME OF THE HUANG FAMILY...
...A HUGE NEST OF CHINESE MONSTERS. ONE OF THE THREE DARK LORDS, TOHOFUHAI, PRESIDES OVER THEM.
香港
THEY DON'T HAVE A CLUE HOW...
...DANGEROUS THAT PLACE IS...
...AND THE CRUEL FATE THAT AWAITS THEM.
Tai Po
Mo Shan
N.T.
Sha Tin
Kowloon
Hong Kong Island
Sheung Shui

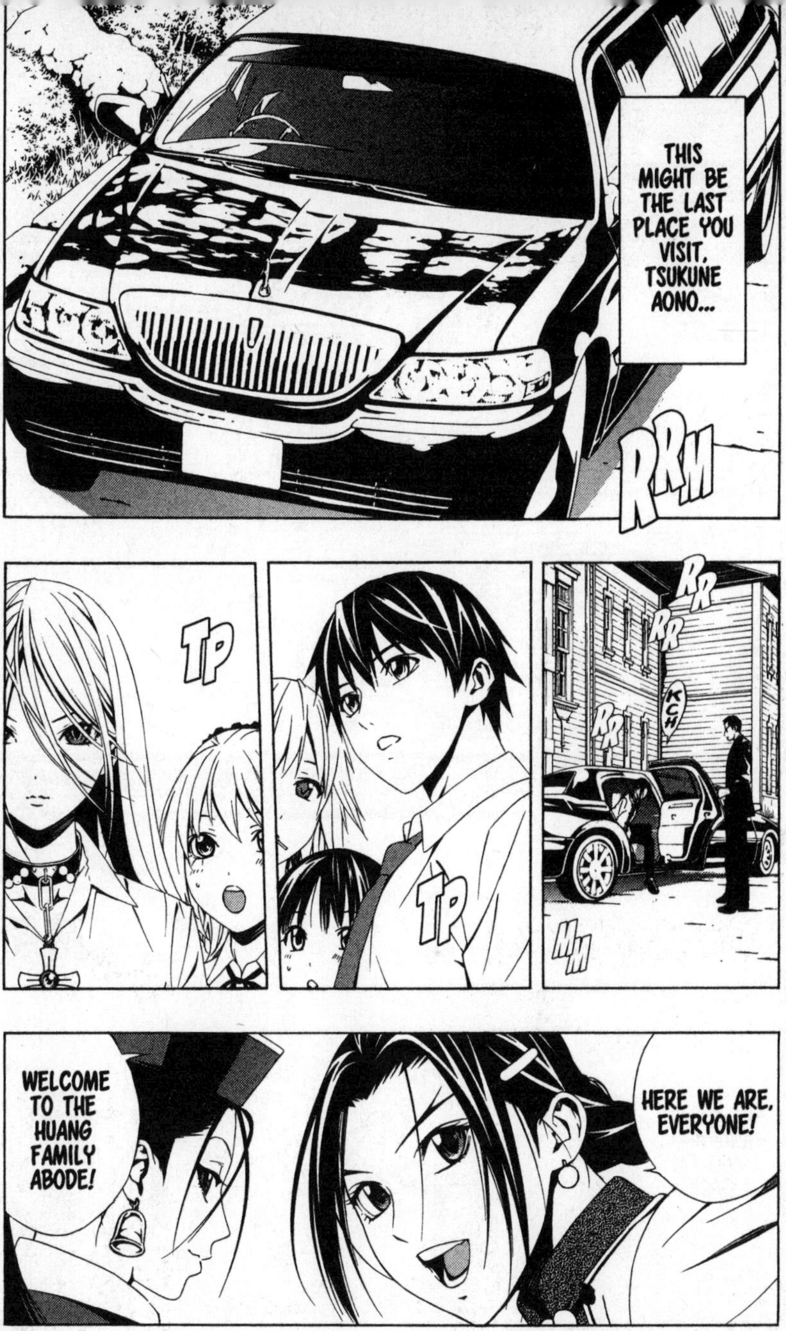
THIS MIGHT BE THE LAST PLACE YOU VISIT, TSUKUNE AONO...
RRM
RR
RR
KCH
RR
MM
TP
TP
HERE WE ARE, EVERYONE!
WELCOME TO THE HUANG FAMILY ABODE!

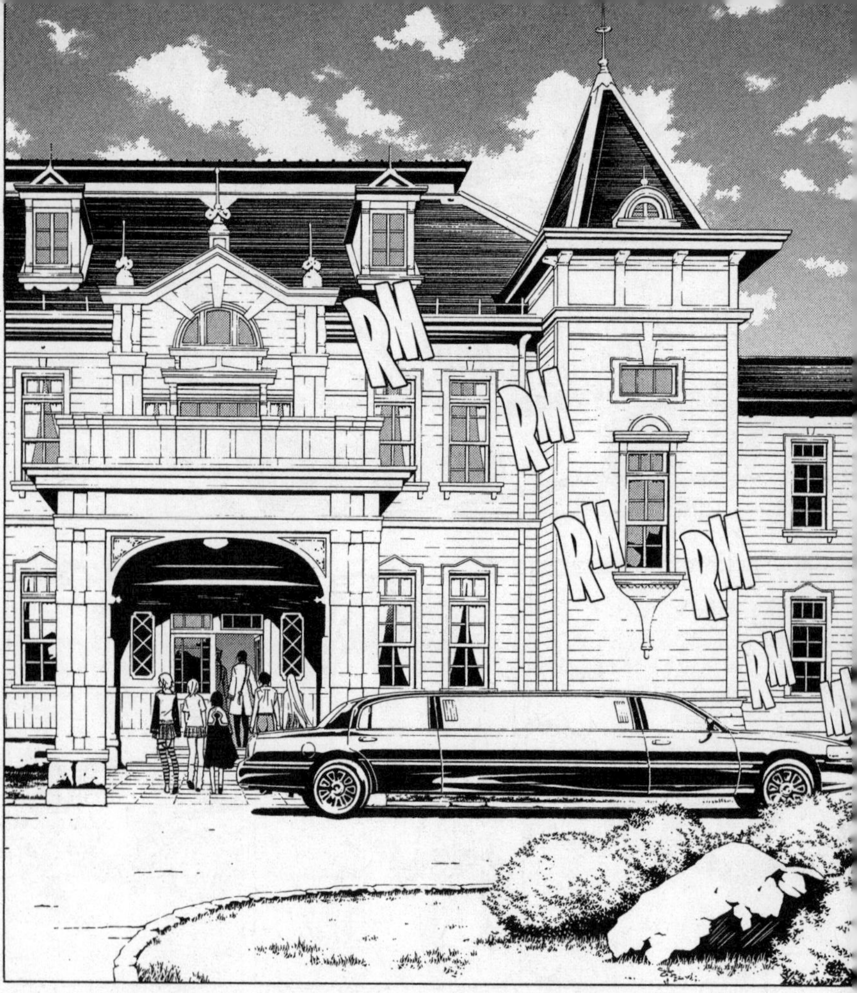
RM
RM
RM
RM
RM
M

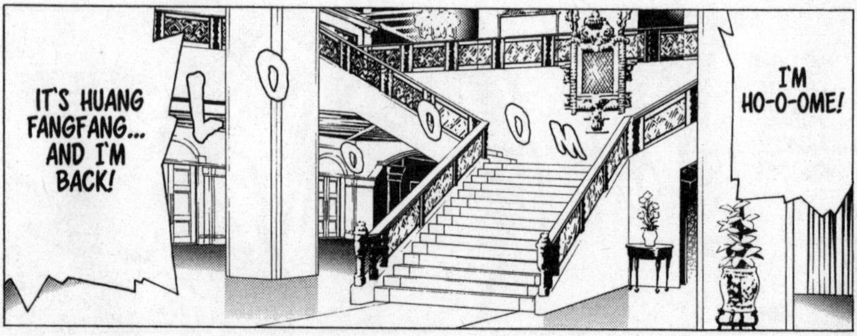
I'M HO-O-OME!
LOOOOM
IT'S HUANG FANGFANG... AND I'M BACK!

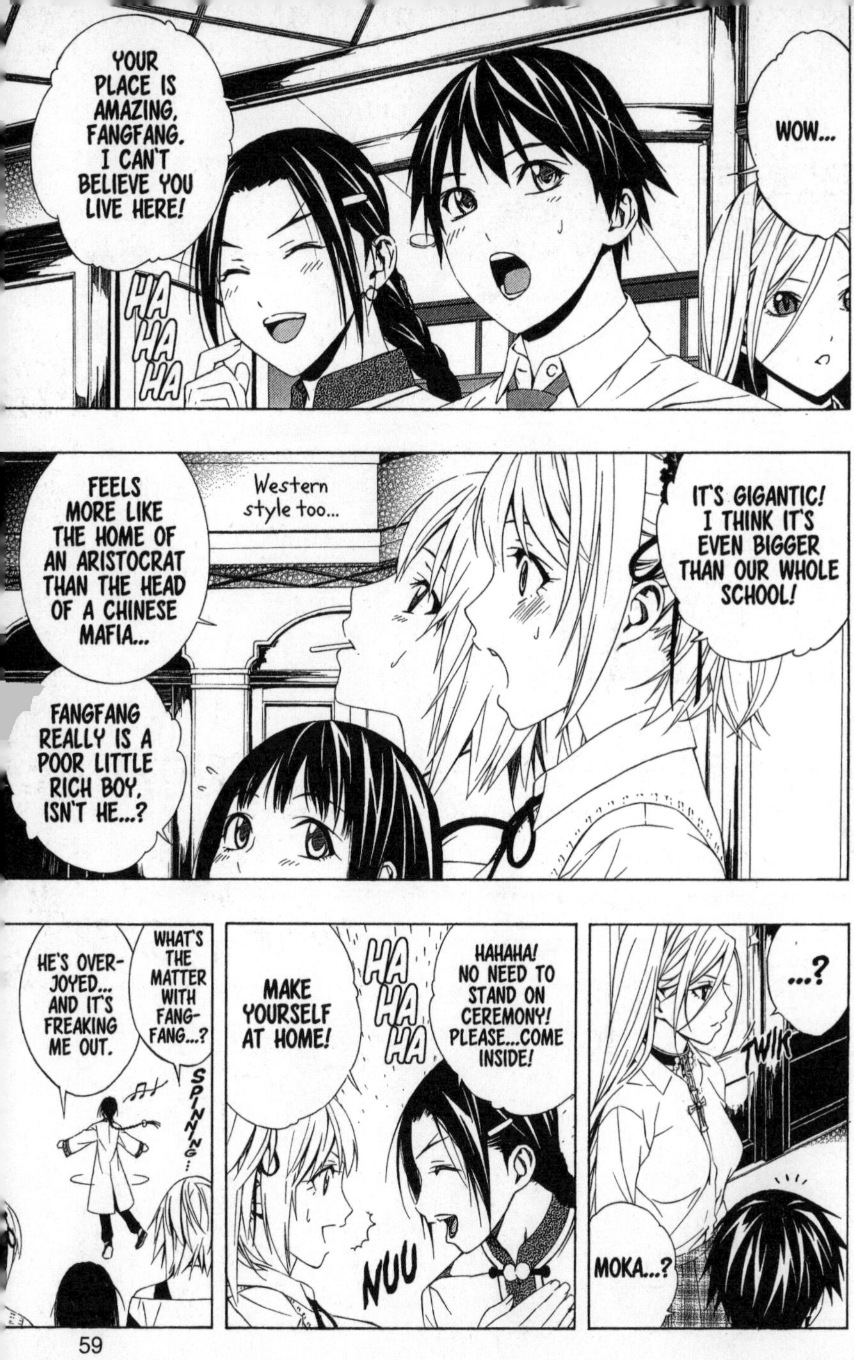
WOW...
YOUR PLACE IS AMAZING, FANGFANG. I CAN'T BELIEVE YOU LIVE HERE!
HA HA HA
IT'S GIGANTIC! I THINK IT'S EVEN BIGGER THAN OUR WHOLE SCHOOL!
Western style too...
FEELS MORE LIKE THE HOME OF AN ARISTOCRAT THAN THE HEAD OF A CHINESE MAFIA...
FANGFANG REALLY IS A POOR LITTLE RICH BOY, ISN'T HE...?
...?
TWIK
MOKA...?
HAHAHA! NO NEED TO STAND ON CEREMONY! PLEASE...COME INSIDE!
HA HA HA
MAKE YOURSELF AT HOME!
NUU
WHAT'S THE MATTER WITH FANG-FANG...?
HE'S OVER-JOYED... AND IT'S FREAKING ME OUT.
SPINNING...

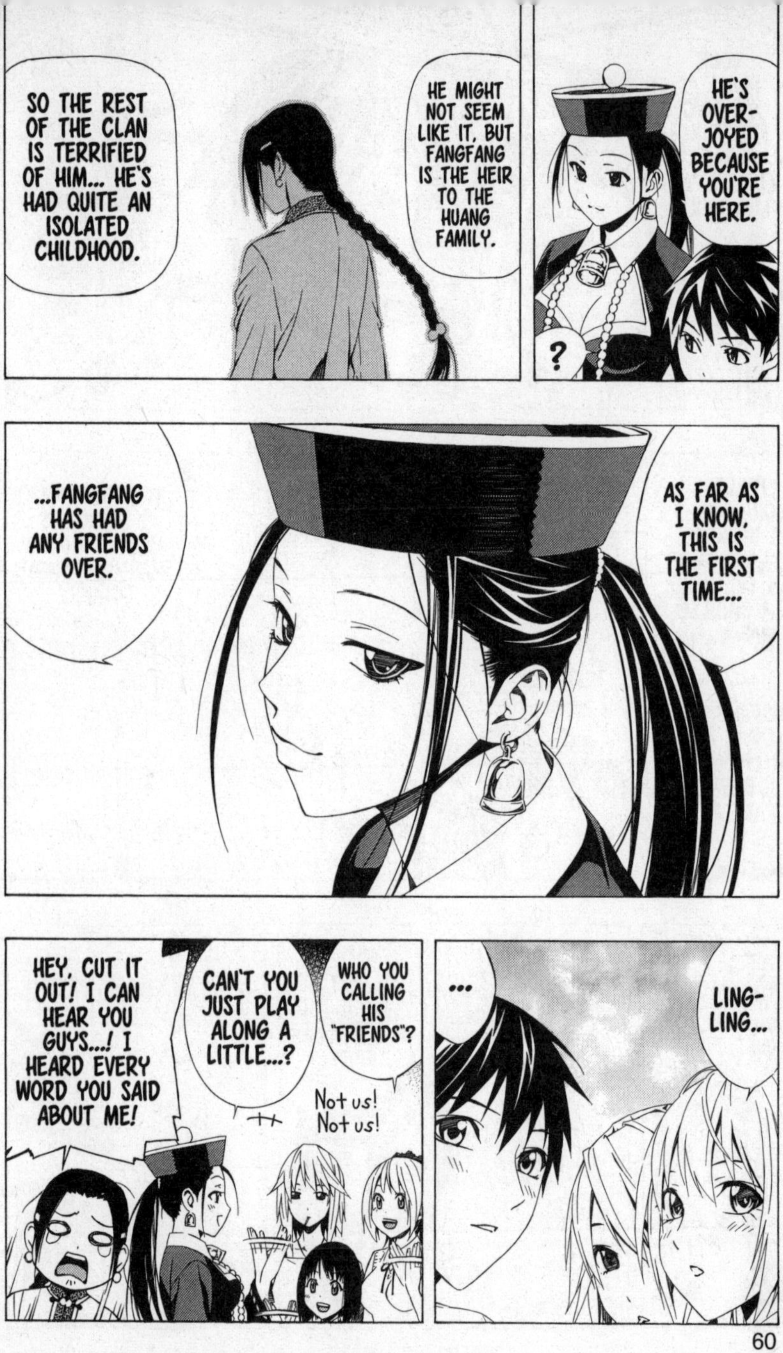
HE'S OVER-JOYED BECAUSE YOU'RE HERE.
?
HE MIGHT NOT SEEM LIKE IT, BUT FANGFANG IS THE HEIR TO THE HUANG FAMILY.
SO THE REST OF THE CLAN IS TERRIFIED OF HIM... HE'S HAD QUITE AN ISOLATED CHILDHOOD.
AS FAR AS I KNOW, THIS IS THE FIRST TIME...
...FANGFANG HAS HAD ANY FRIENDS OVER.
LING-LING...
...
WHO YOU CALLING HIS "FRIENDS"?
CAN'T YOU JUST PLAY ALONG A LITTLE...?
HEY, CUT IT OUT! I CAN HEAR YOU GUYS...! I HEARD EVERY WORD YOU SAID ABOUT ME!
Not us! Not us!

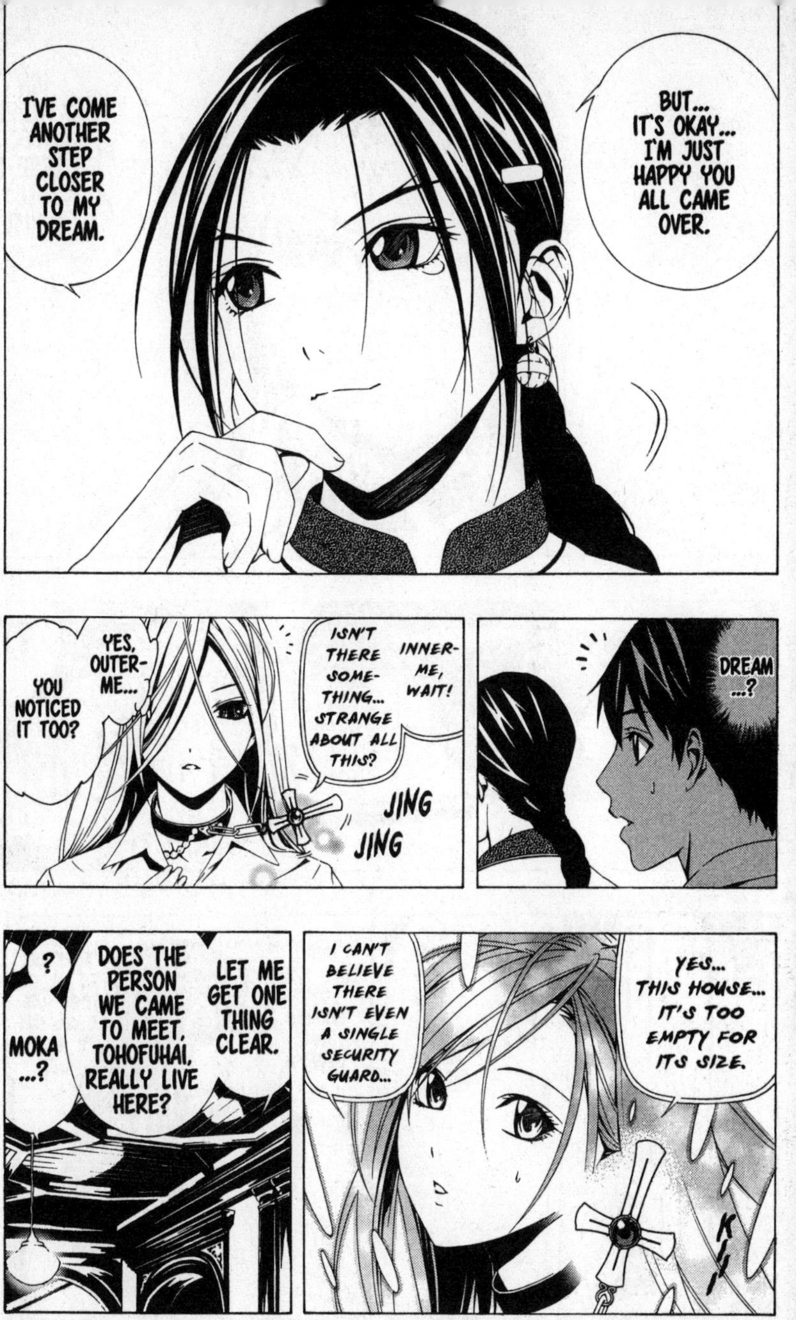

BUT... IT'S OKAY... I'M JUST HAPPY YOU ALL CAME OVER.
I'VE COME ANOTHER STEP CLOSER TO MY DREAM.
DREAM ...?
INNER-ME, WAIT!
ISN'T THERE SOME-THING... STRANGE ABOUT ALL THIS?
JING
JING
YES, OUTER-ME...
YOU NOTICED IT TOO?
YES... THIS HOUSE... IT'S TOO EMPTY FOR ITS SIZE.
I CAN'T BELIEVE THERE ISN'T EVEN A SINGLE SECURITY GUARD...
KIII
LET ME GET ONE THING CLEAR.
DOES THE PERSON WE CAME TO MEET, TOHOFUHAI, REALLY LIVE HERE?
?
MOKA ...?

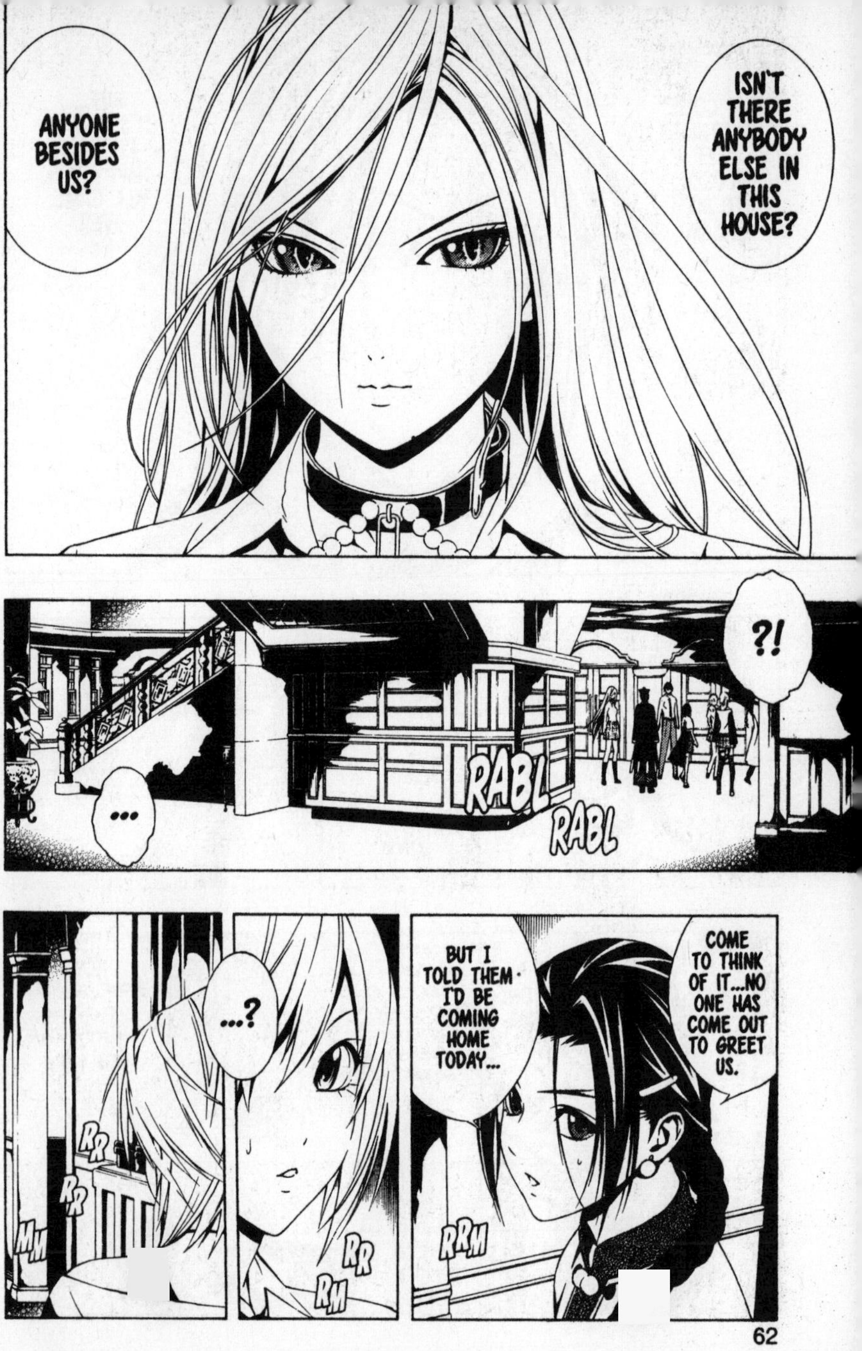
ISN'T THERE ANYBODY ELSE IN THIS HOUSE?
ANYONE BESIDES US?
?!
RABL
RABL
...
COME TO THINK OF IT...NO ONE HAS COME OUT TO GREET US.
BUT I TOLD THEM I'D BE COMING HOME TODAY...
RRM
...?
RR
RM
RR
RR
MM

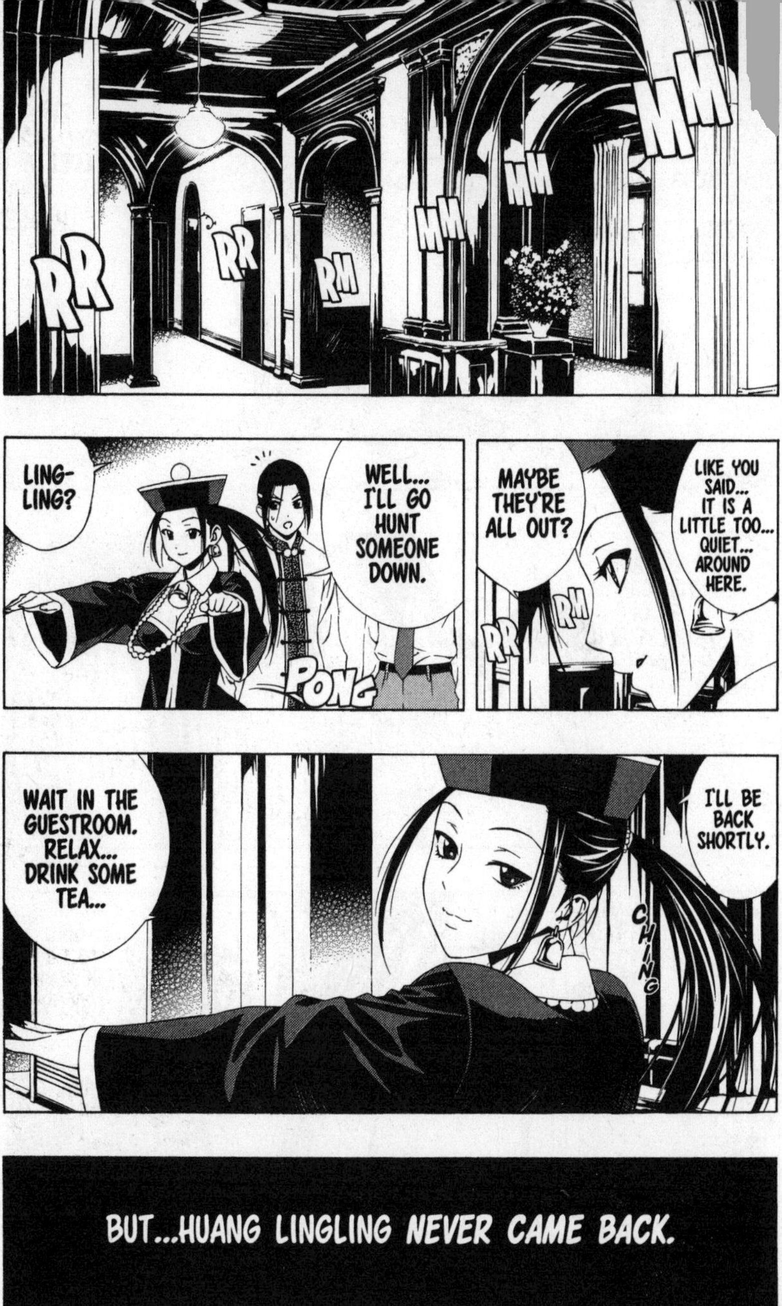
RR RR RM MM MM MM
LIKE YOU SAID... IT IS A LITTLE TOO... QUIET... AROUND HERE.
MAYBE THEY'RE ALL OUT?
RR RM
WELL... I'LL GO HUNT SOMEONE DOWN.
LING-LING?
PONG
I'LL BE BACK SHORTLY.
WAIT IN THE GUESTROOM. RELAX... DRINK SOME TEA...
CHING
BUT...HUANG LINGLING *NEVER CAME BACK.*

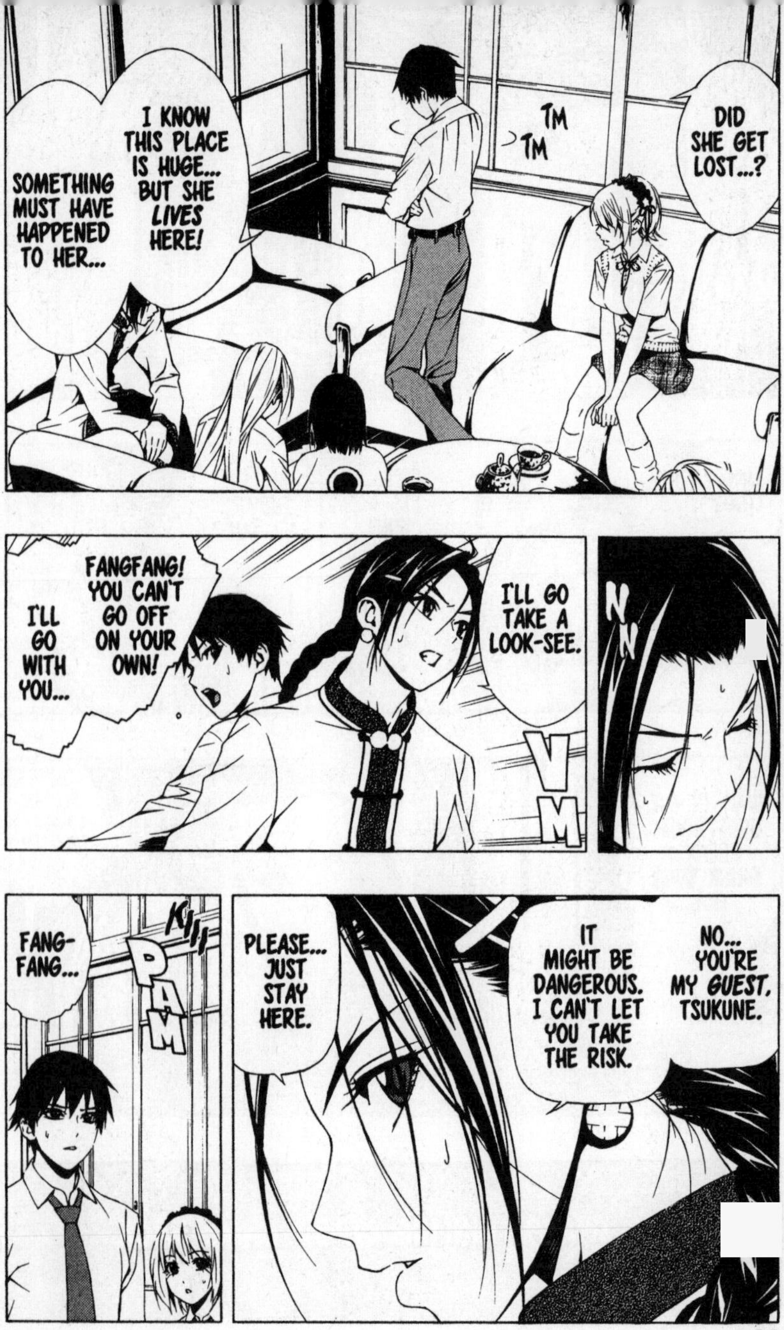
DID SHE GET LOST...?
TM TM
I KNOW THIS PLACE IS HUGE... BUT SHE *LIVES* HERE!
SOMETHING MUST HAVE HAPPENED TO HER...
NN
I'LL GO TAKE A LOOK-SEE.
VM
FANGFANG! YOU CAN'T GO OFF ON YOUR OWN!
I'LL GO WITH YOU...
NO... YOU'RE MY *GUEST*, TSUKUNE.
IT MIGHT BE DANGEROUS. I CAN'T LET YOU TAKE THE RISK.
PLEASE... JUST STAY HERE.
KIII
PAM
FANG-FANG...

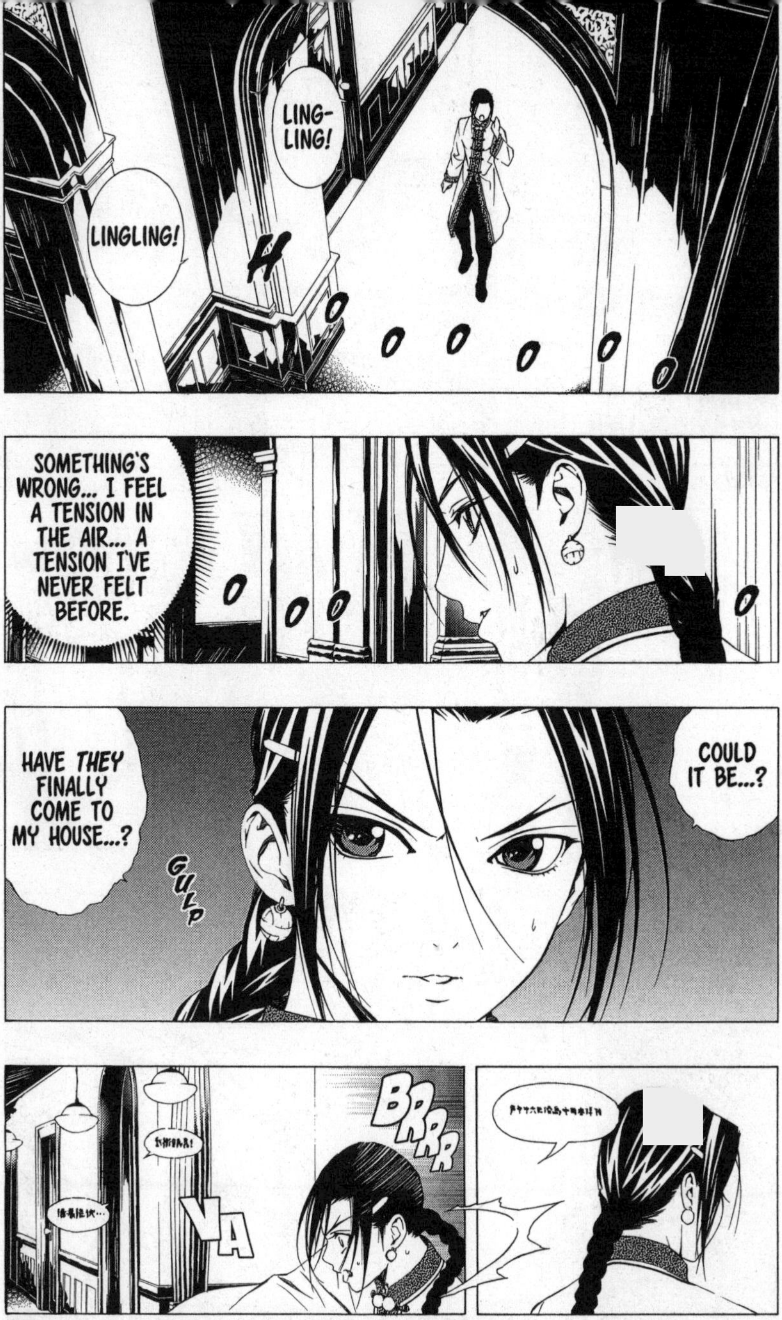
LING-LING!
LINGLING!
SOMETHING'S WRONG... I FEEL A TENSION IN THE AIR... A TENSION I'VE NEVER FELT BEFORE.
COULD IT BE...?
HAVE THEY FINALLY COME TO MY HOUSE...?
GULP
BRRR
VA

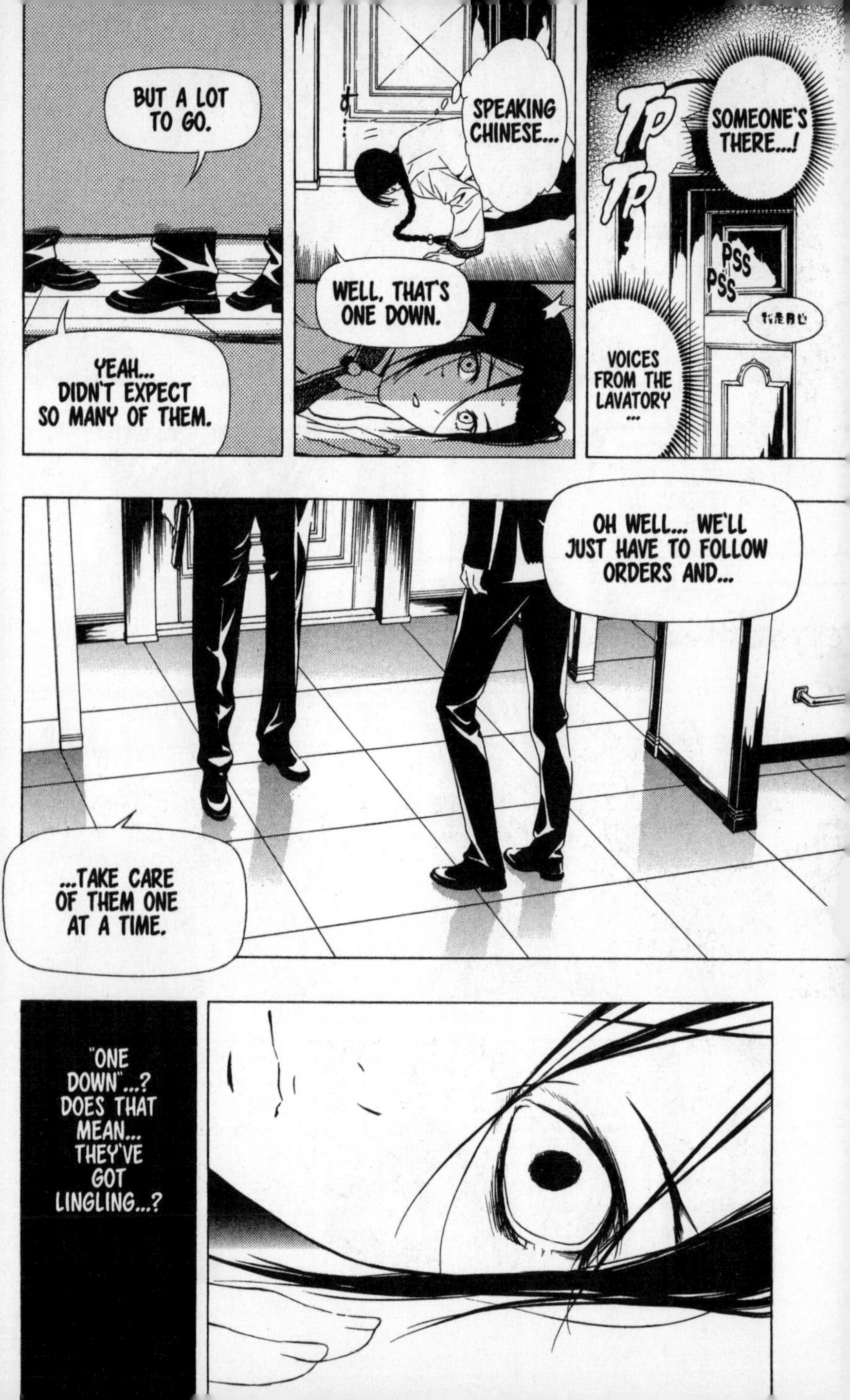
SOMEONE'S THERE...!
TP TP
PSS PSS
VOICES FROM THE LAVATORY...
SPEAKING CHINESE...
WELL, THAT'S ONE DOWN.
BUT A LOT TO GO.
YEAH... DIDN'T EXPECT SO MANY OF THEM.
OH WELL... WE'LL JUST HAVE TO FOLLOW ORDERS AND...
...TAKE CARE OF THEM ONE AT A TIME.
"ONE DOWN"...? DOES THAT MEAN... THEY'VE GOT LINGLING...?

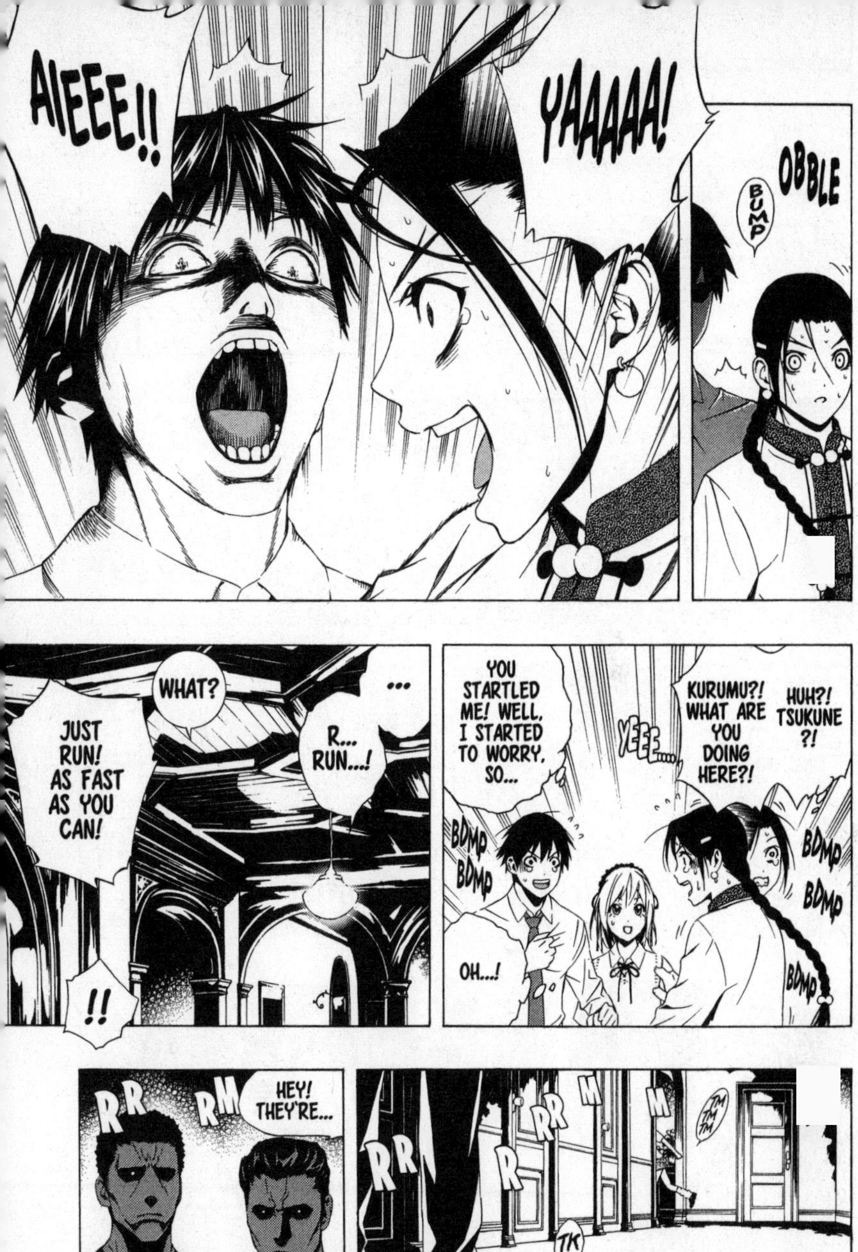
BUMP
OBBLE
YAAAAA!
AIEEE!!
HUH?! TSUKUNE?!
KURUMU?! WHAT ARE YOU DOING HERE?!
YEEE....
YOU STARTLED ME! WELL, I STARTED TO WORRY, SO...
BDMP BDMP
BDMP
BDMP BDMP
OH...!
...
R... RUN...!
WHAT?
JUST RUN! AS FAST AS YOU CAN!
!!
TM TM TM
M M
RRR
R
RR
TK...
HEY! THEY'RE...
RR RM
...

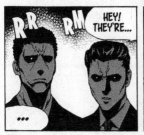

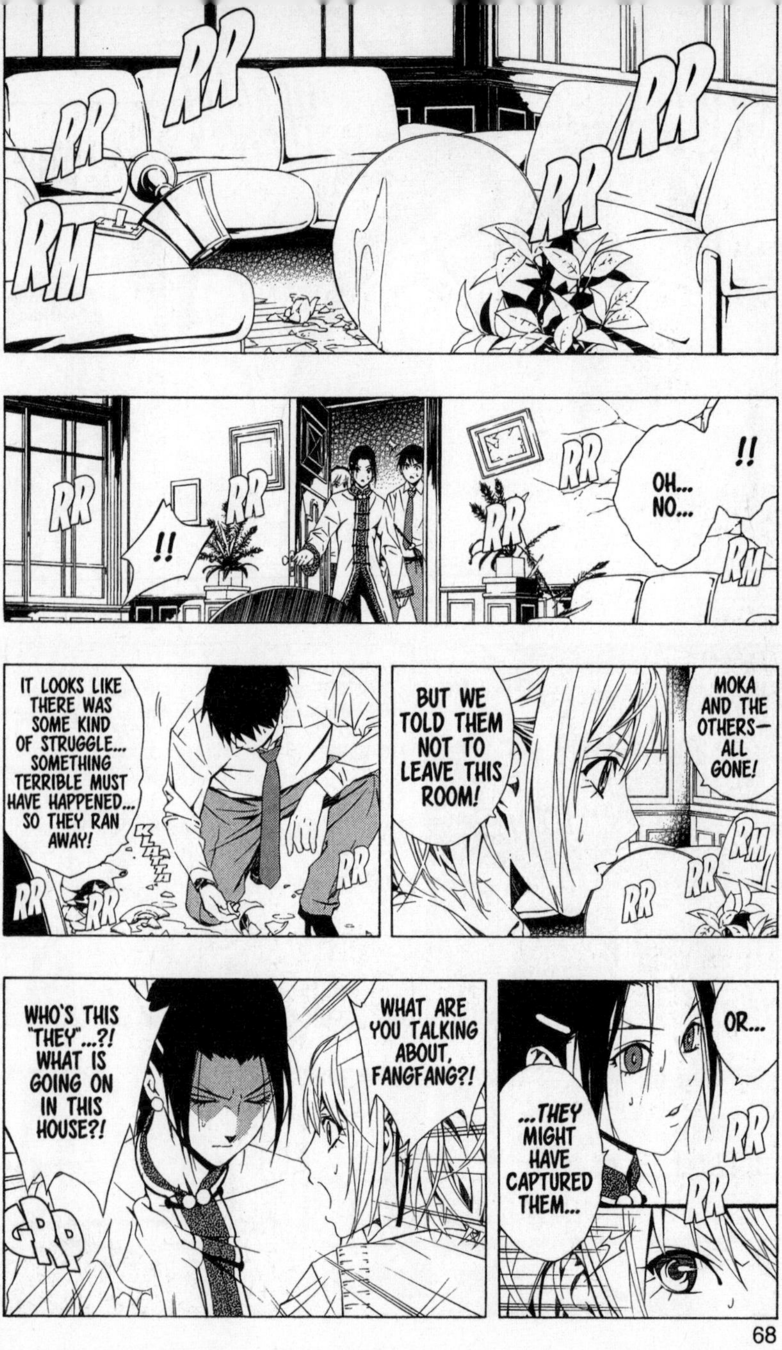
RR
RR
RR
RR
RM
!!
OH... NO...
RR
RM
RR
RR
!!
MOKA AND THE OTHERS— ALL GONE!
BUT WE TOLD THEM NOT TO LEAVE THIS ROOM!
RM
RR
RR
IT LOOKS LIKE THERE WAS SOME KIND OF STRUGGLE... SOMETHING TERRIBLE MUST HAVE HAPPENED... SO THEY RAN AWAY!
RR
RR
RR
OR...
...THEY MIGHT HAVE CAPTURED THEM...
RR
RR
WHAT ARE YOU TALKING ABOUT, FANGFANG?!
WHO'S THIS "THEY"...?! WHAT IS GOING ON IN THIS HOUSE?!
GRP

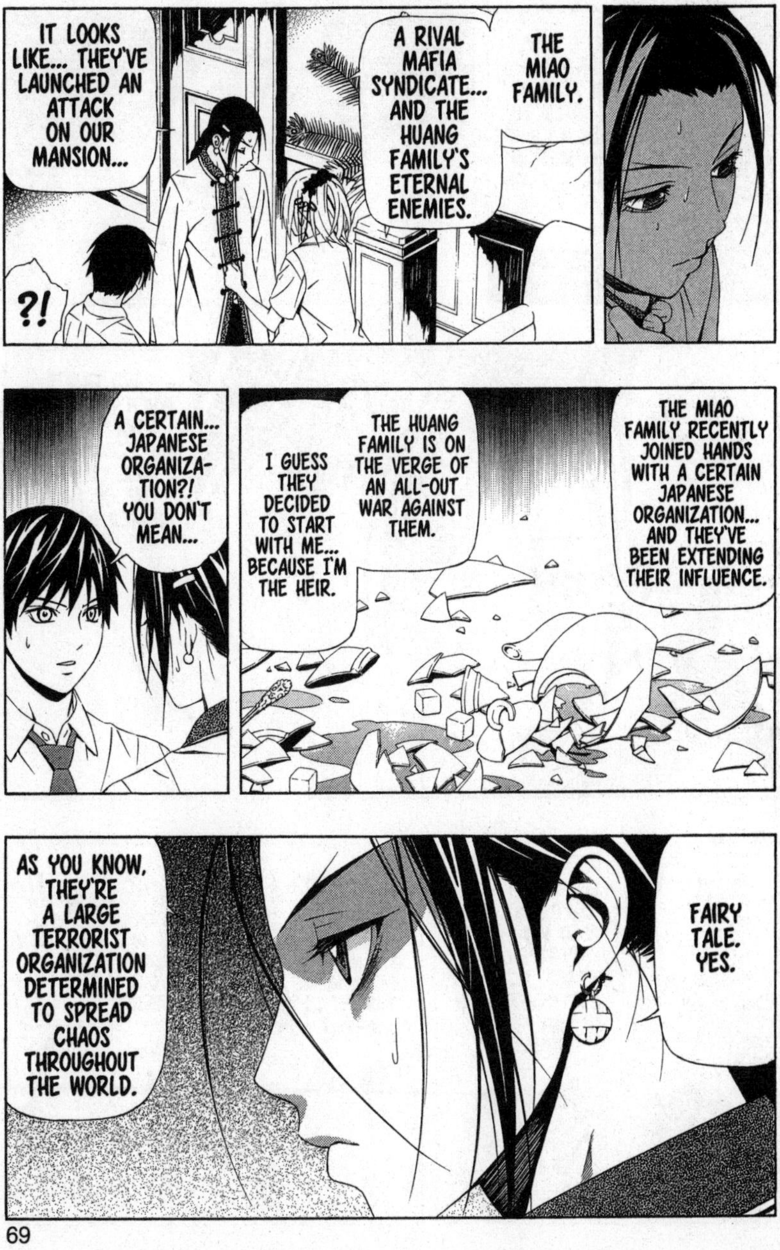
THE MIAO FAMILY.
A RIVAL MAFIA SYNDICATE... AND THE HUANG FAMILY'S ETERNAL ENEMIES.
IT LOOKS LIKE... THEY'VE LAUNCHED AN ATTACK ON OUR MANSION...
?!
THE MIAO FAMILY RECENTLY JOINED HANDS WITH A CERTAIN JAPANESE ORGANIZATION... AND THEY'VE BEEN EXTENDING THEIR INFLUENCE.
THE HUANG FAMILY IS ON THE VERGE OF AN ALL-OUT WAR AGAINST THEM.
I GUESS THEY DECIDED TO START WITH ME... BECAUSE I'M THE HEIR.
A CERTAIN... JAPANESE ORGANIZA-TION?! YOU DON'T MEAN...
FAIRY TALE. YES.
AS YOU KNOW, THEY'RE A LARGE TERRORIST ORGANIZATION DETERMINED TO SPREAD CHAOS THROUGHOUT THE WORLD.

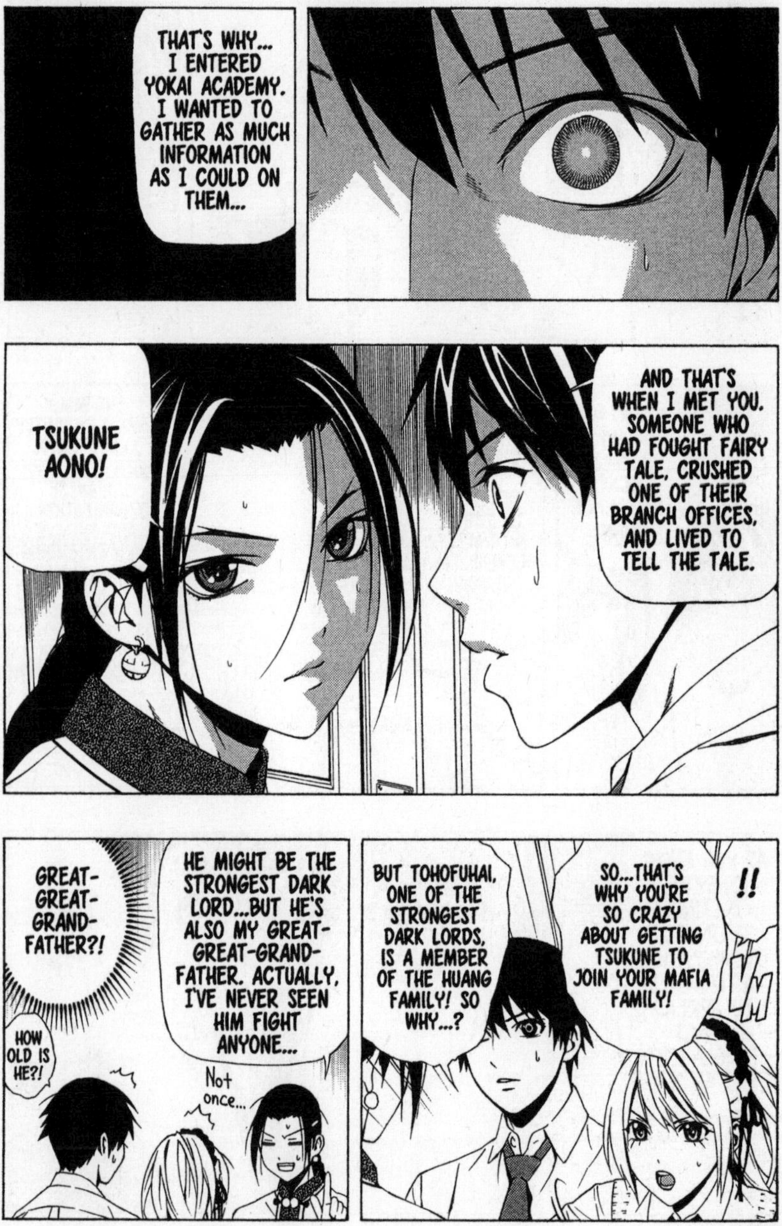
THAT'S WHY... I ENTERED YOKAI ACADEMY. I WANTED TO GATHER AS MUCH INFORMATION AS I COULD ON THEM...
AND THAT'S WHEN I MET YOU. SOMEONE WHO HAD FOUGHT FAIRY TALE, CRUSHED ONE OF THEIR BRANCH OFFICES, AND LIVED TO TELL THE TALE.
TSUKUNE AONO!
!!
VM
SO...THAT'S WHY YOU'RE SO CRAZY ABOUT GETTING TSUKUNE TO JOIN YOUR MAFIA FAMILY!
BUT TOHOFUHAI, ONE OF THE STRONGEST DARK LORDS, IS A MEMBER OF THE HUANG FAMILY! SO WHY...?
HE MIGHT BE THE STRONGEST DARK LORD...BUT HE'S ALSO MY GREAT-GREAT-GRAND-FATHER. ACTUALLY, I'VE NEVER SEEN HIM FIGHT ANYONE...
GREAT-GREAT-GRAND-FATHER?!
Not once...
HOW OLD IS HE?!

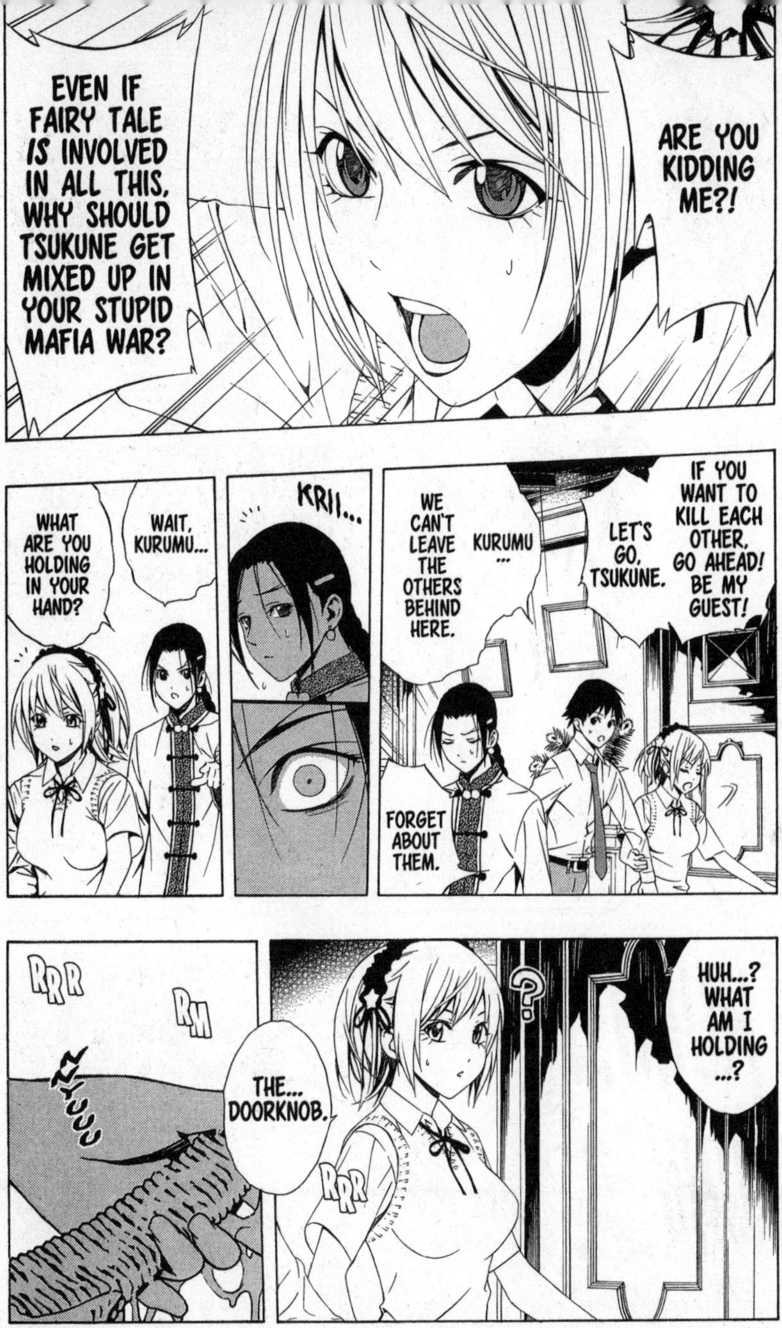
ARE YOU KIDDING ME?!
EVEN IF FAIRY TALE IS INVOLVED IN ALL THIS, WHY SHOULD TSUKUNE GET MIXED UP IN YOUR STUPID MAFIA WAR?
IF YOU WANT TO KILL EACH OTHER, GO AHEAD! BE MY GUEST!
LET'S GO, TSUKUNE.
KURUMU ...
WE CAN'T LEAVE THE OTHERS BEHIND HERE.
FORGET ABOUT THEM.
KRII...
WAIT, KURUMU...
WHAT ARE YOU HOLDING IN YOUR HAND?
HUH...? WHAT AM I HOLDING ...?
THE... DOORKNOB.
RRR
RRR
RM
NYUUU

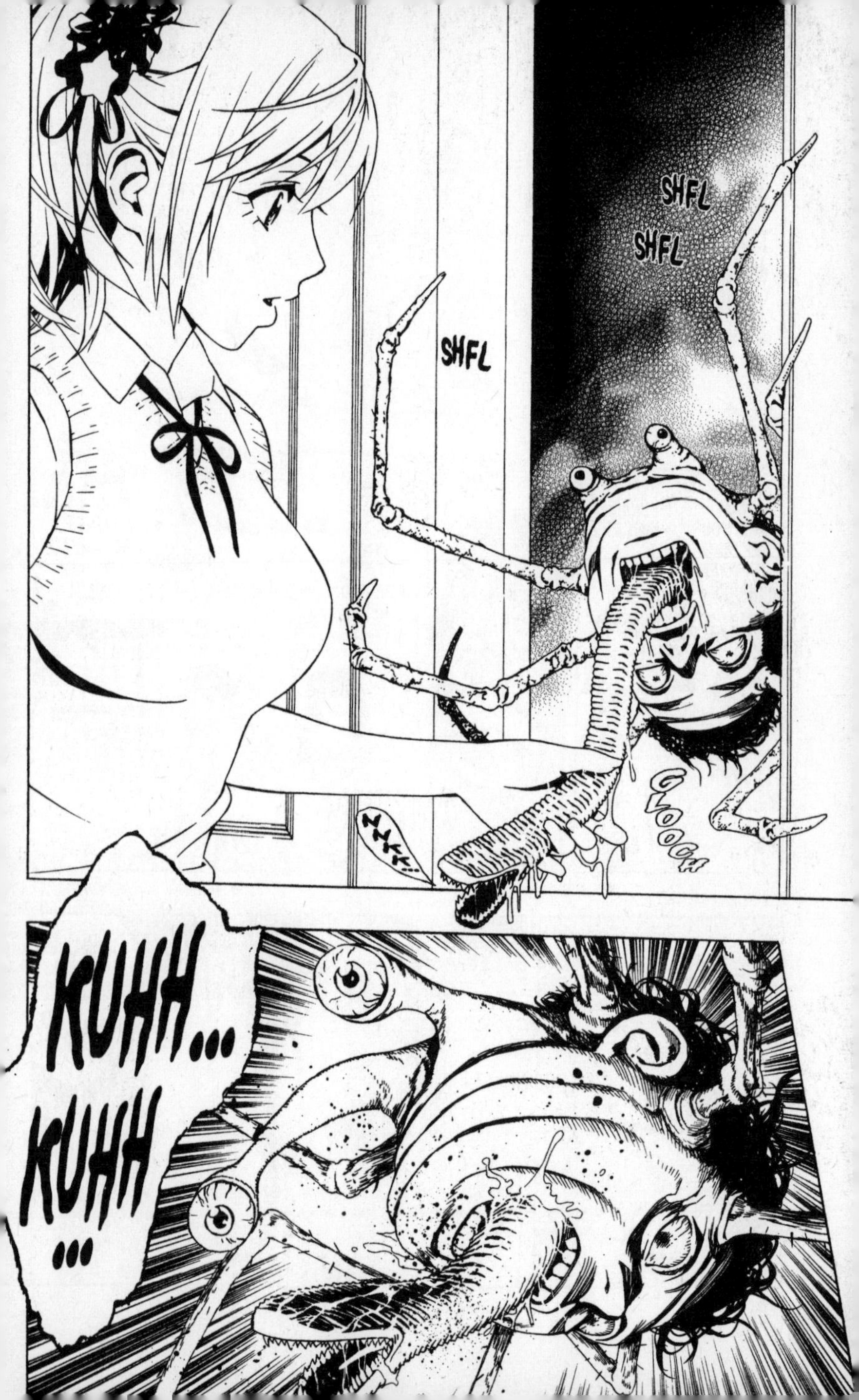
SHFL
SHFL
SHFL
GLOOCH
HNKK...
KUHH... KUHH...

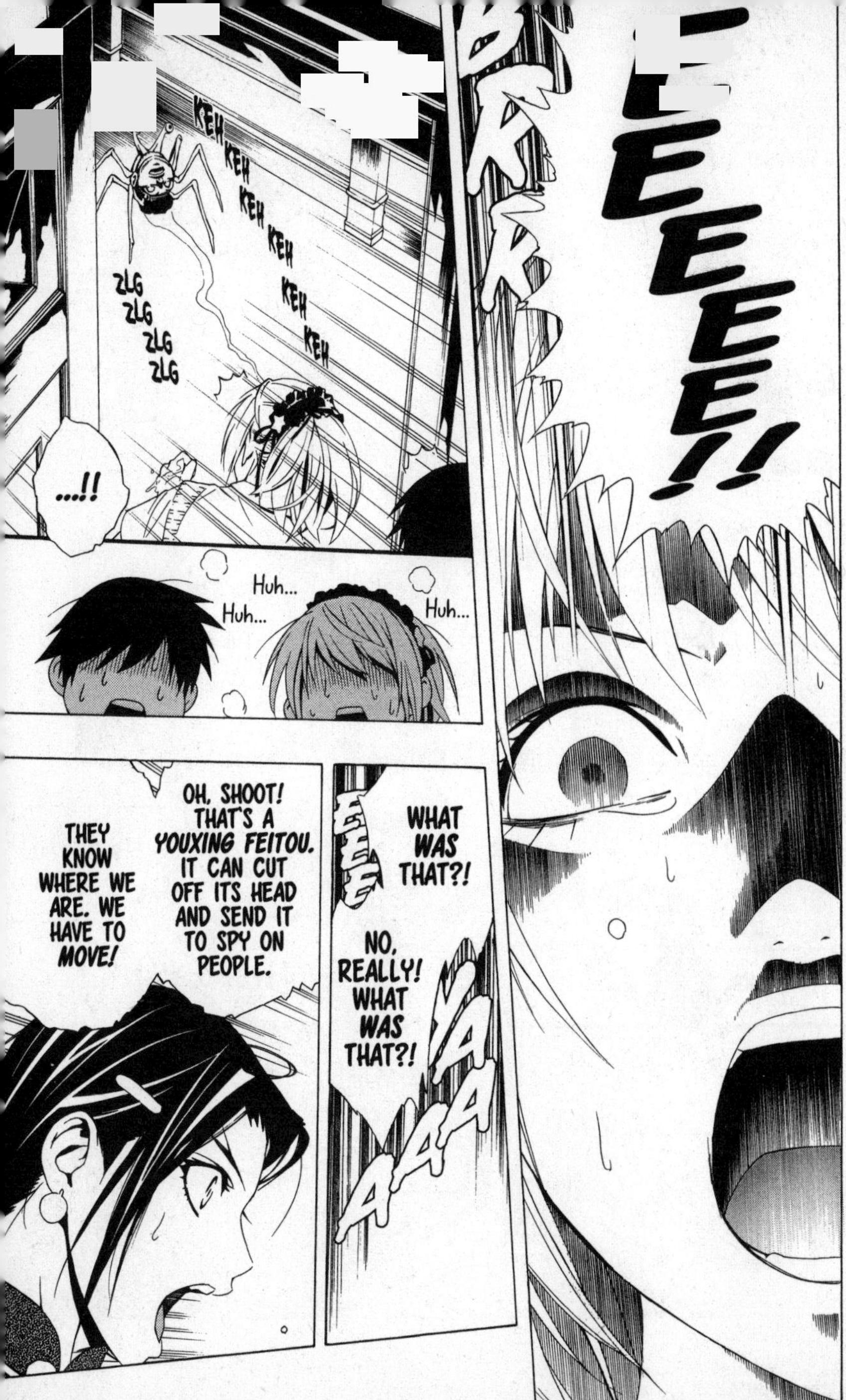
EEEEEE!!
KEH KEH KEH KEH KEH KEH
ZLG ZLG ZLG ZLG
...!!
Huh...
Huh...
Huh...
WHAT WAS THAT?!
NO, REALLY! WHAT WAS THAT?!
OH, SHOOT! THAT'S A YOUXING FEITOU. IT CAN CUT OFF ITS HEAD AND SEND IT TO SPY ON PEOPLE.
THEY KNOW WHERE WE ARE. WE HAVE TO MOVE!

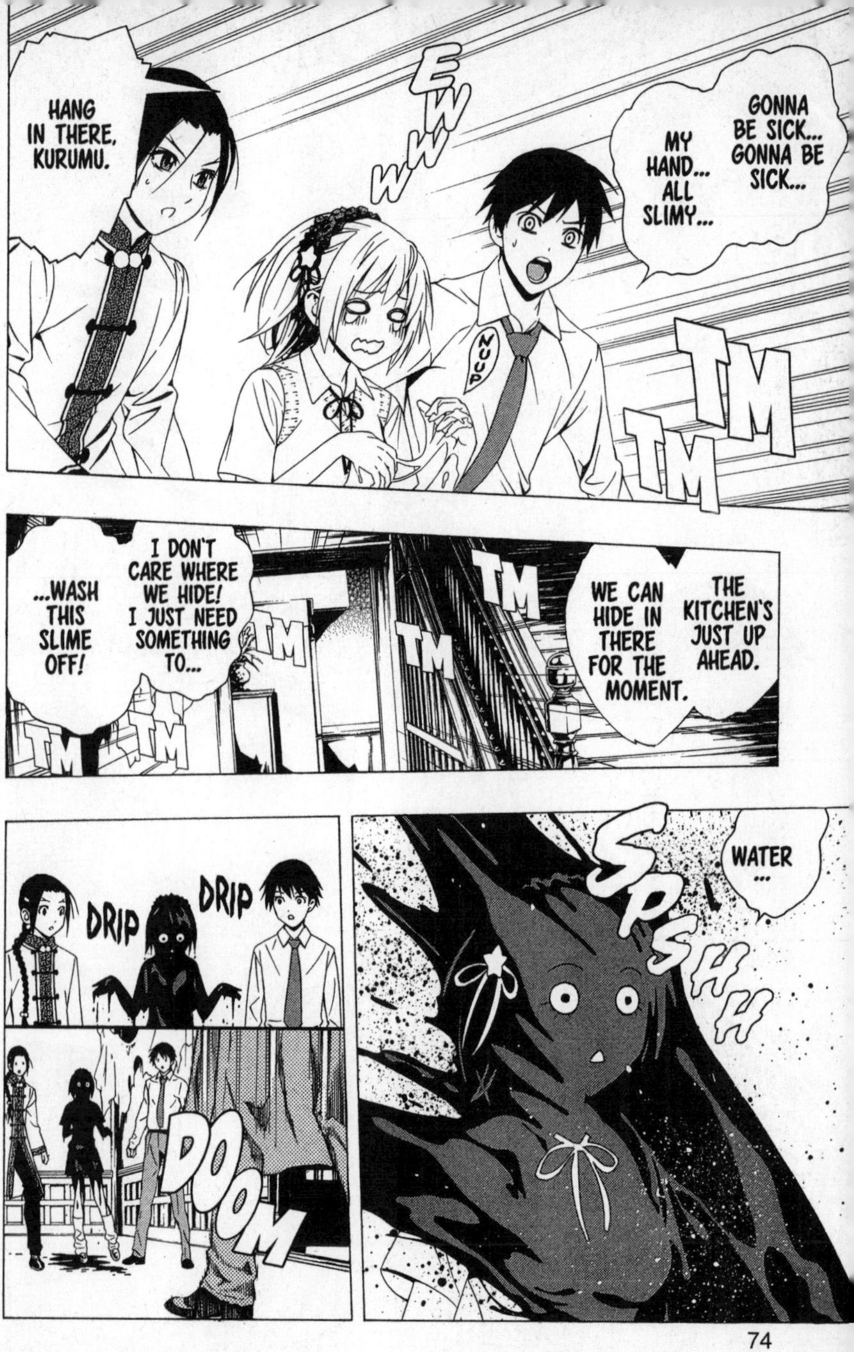
GONNA BE SICK... GONNA BE SICK...
MY HAND... ALL SLIMY...
TM TM
NUUP
EWWWW
HANG IN THERE, KURUMU.
THE KITCHEN'S JUST UP AHEAD.
WE CAN HIDE IN THERE FOR THE MOMENT.
TM
TM
TM
I DON'T CARE WHERE WE HIDE! I JUST NEED SOMETHING TO...
...WASH THIS SLIME OFF!
TM TM
WATER ...
SPSHH
DRIP
DRIP
DOOOM

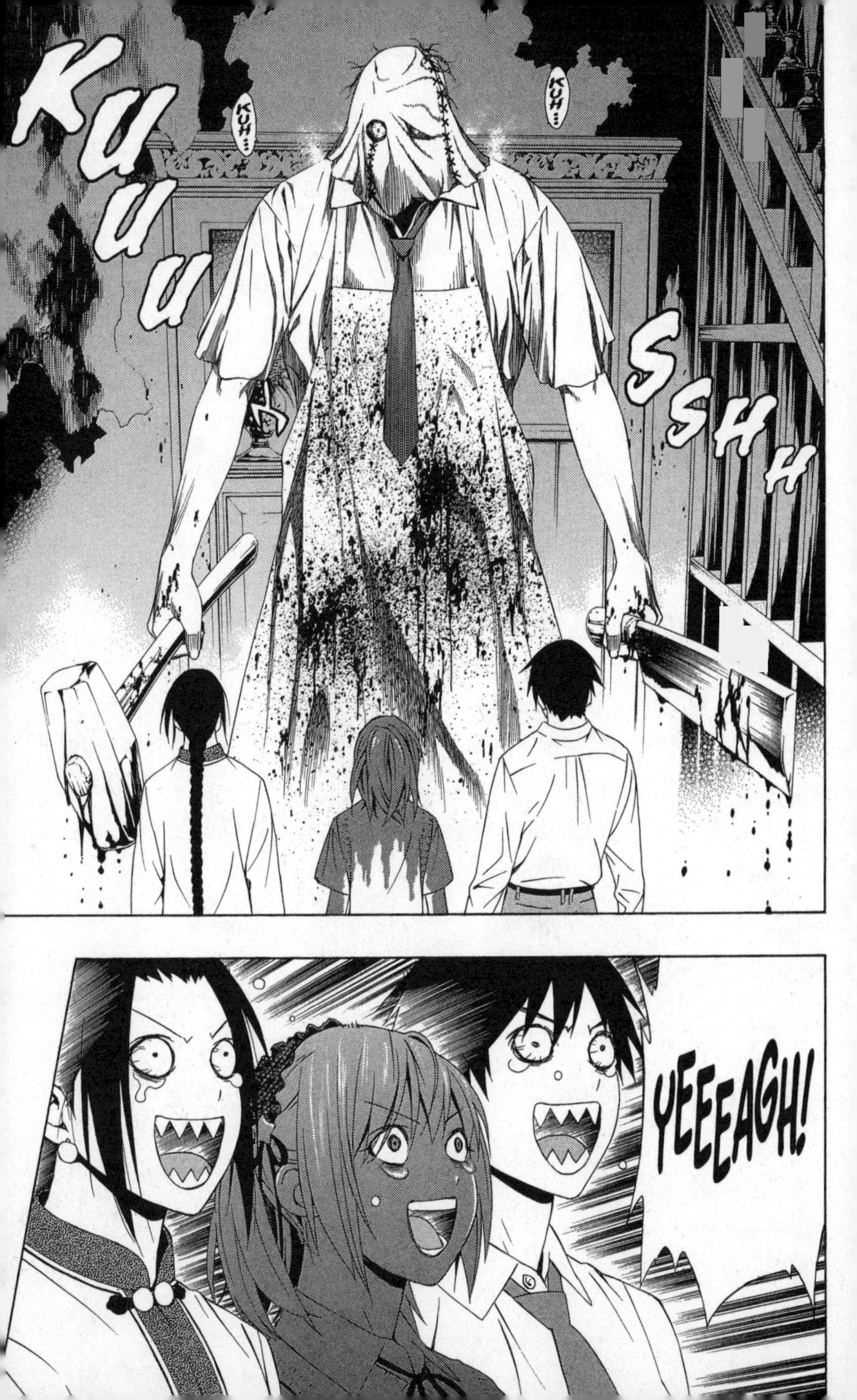
KUH...
SSHH
KUH...
KUUUU
YEEEAGH!

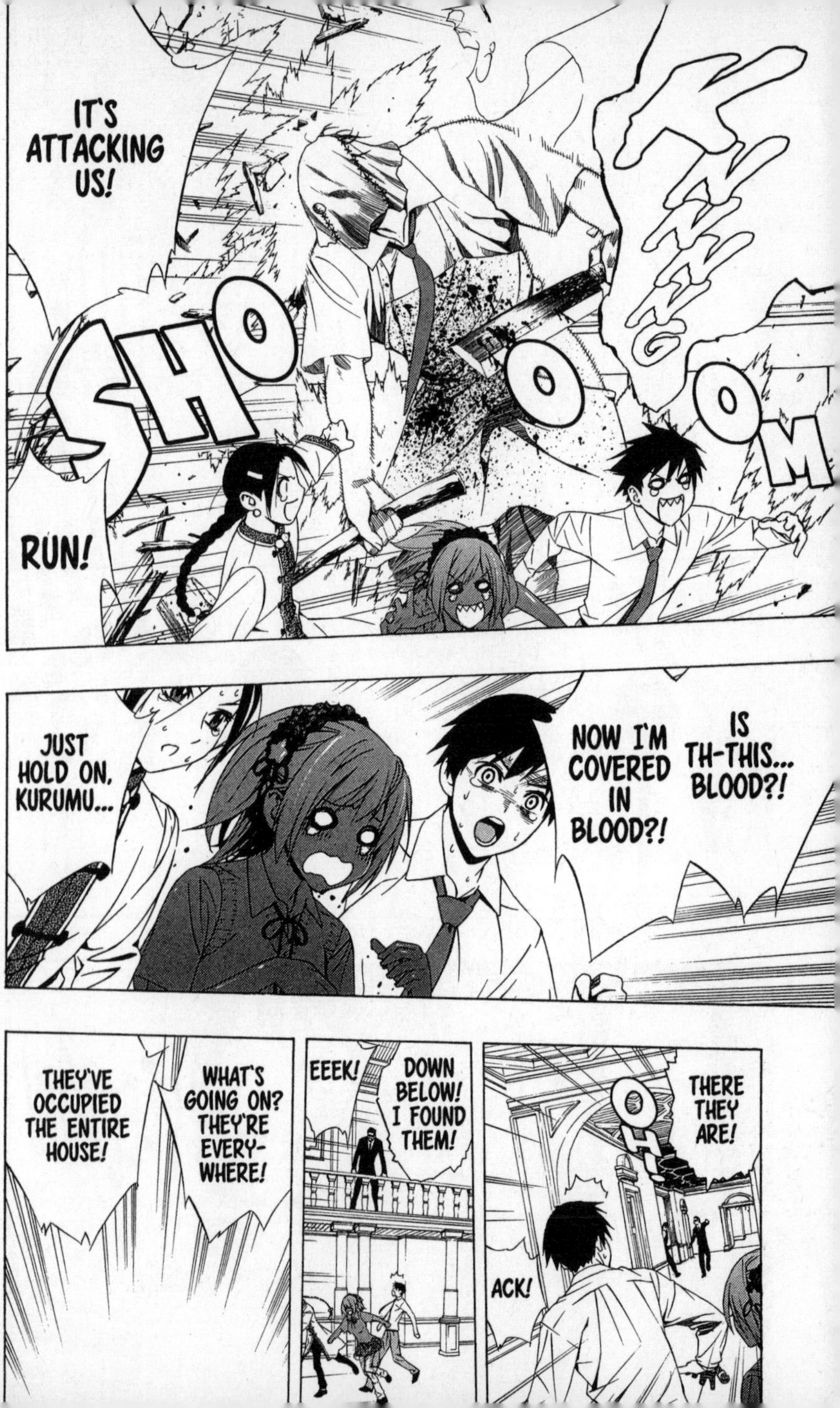
SHOOOOM
IT'S ATTACKING US!
RUN!
IS TH-THIS... BLOOD?!
NOW I'M COVERED IN BLOOD?!
JUST HOLD ON, KURUMU...
THERE THEY ARE!
ACK!
DOWN BELOW! I FOUND THEM!
EEEK!
WHAT'S GOING ON? THEY'RE EVERY-WHERE!
THEY'VE OCCUPIED THE ENTIRE HOUSE!

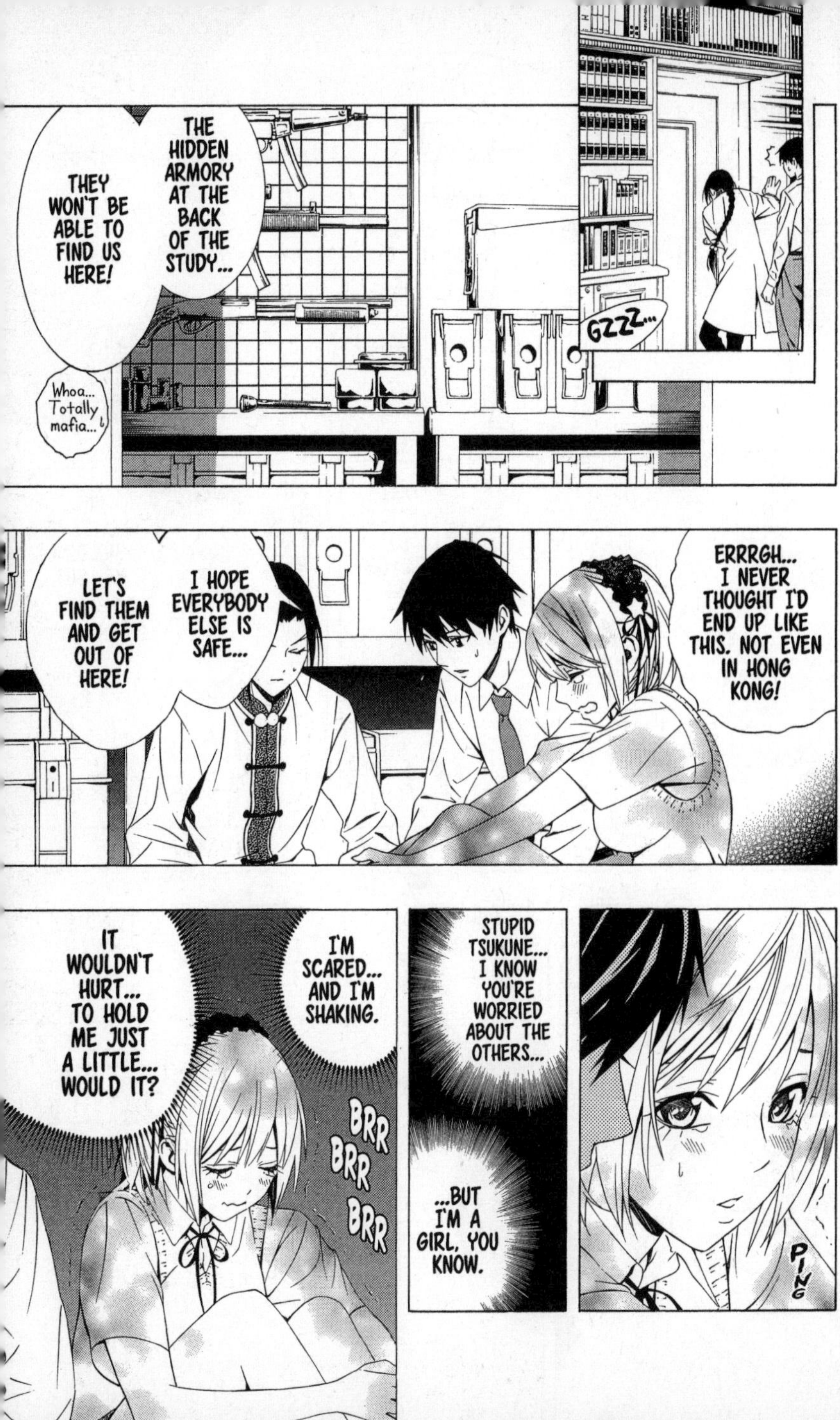

GZZZ...
THE HIDDEN ARMORY AT THE BACK OF THE STUDY...
THEY WON'T BE ABLE TO FIND US HERE!
Whoa... Totally mafia...
ERRRGH... I NEVER THOUGHT I'D END UP LIKE THIS. NOT EVEN IN HONG KONG!
I HOPE EVERYBODY ELSE IS SAFE...
LET'S FIND THEM AND GET OUT OF HERE!
PING
STUPID TSUKUNE... I KNOW YOU'RE WORRIED ABOUT THE OTHERS...
...BUT I'M A GIRL, YOU KNOW.
I'M SCARED... AND I'M SHAKING.
IT WOULDN'T HURT... TO HOLD ME JUST A LITTLE... WOULD IT?
BRR BRR BRR

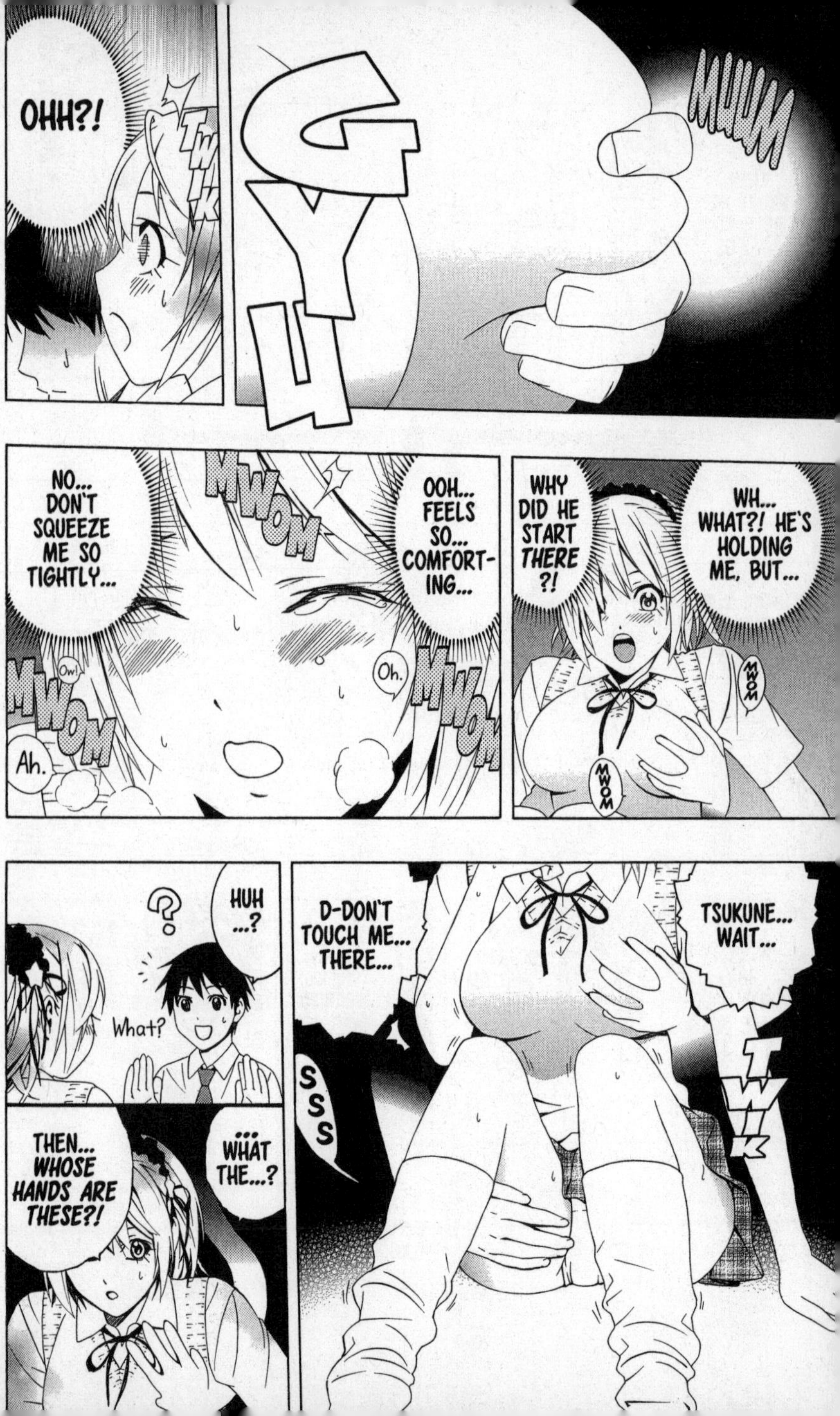
MUUM
GYU
OHH?!
TWIK
WH... WHAT?! HE'S HOLDING ME, BUT...
WHY DID HE START THERE?!
MWOM
MWOM
OOH... FEELS SO... COMFORTING...
MWOM
NO... DON'T SQUEEZE ME SO TIGHTLY...
Oh.
MWOM
Ow!
Ah.
TSUKUNE... WAIT...
D-DON'T TOUCH ME... THERE...
TWIK
SSS
HUH...?
?
What?
...WHAT THE...?
THEN... WHOSE HANDS ARE THESE?!

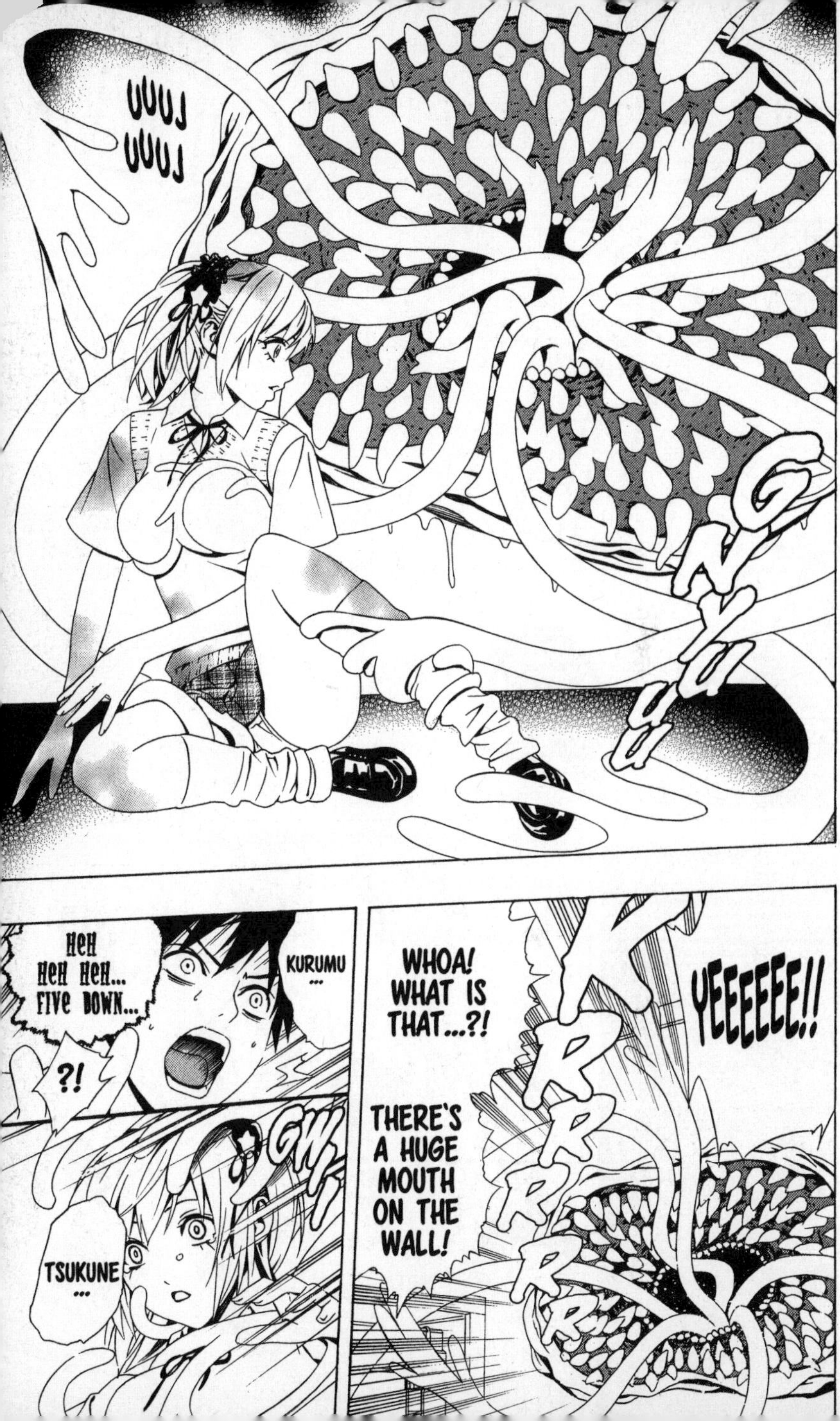

GNYUUUU
UUUJ
UUUJ
YEEEEEE!!
WHOA! WHAT IS THAT...?!
THERE'S A HUGE MOUTH ON THE WALL!
RRRRR
KURUMU ...
HEH HEH HEH... FIVE DOWN...
?!
GW!
TSUKUNE ...

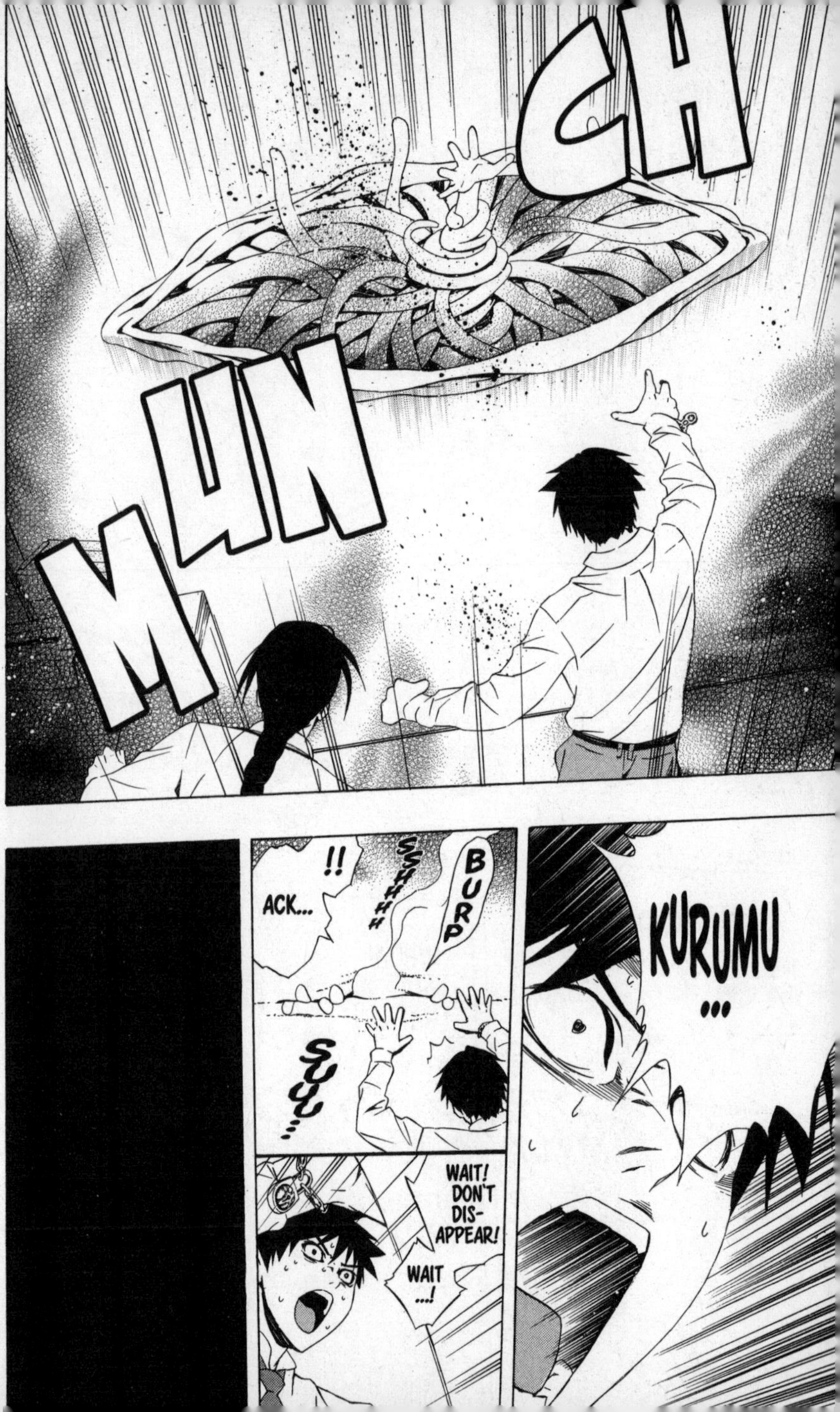

MUNCH
KURUMU ...
BURP
SSHHHH
!!
ACK...
SUUU...
WAIT! DON'T DIS-APPEAR!
WAIT ...!

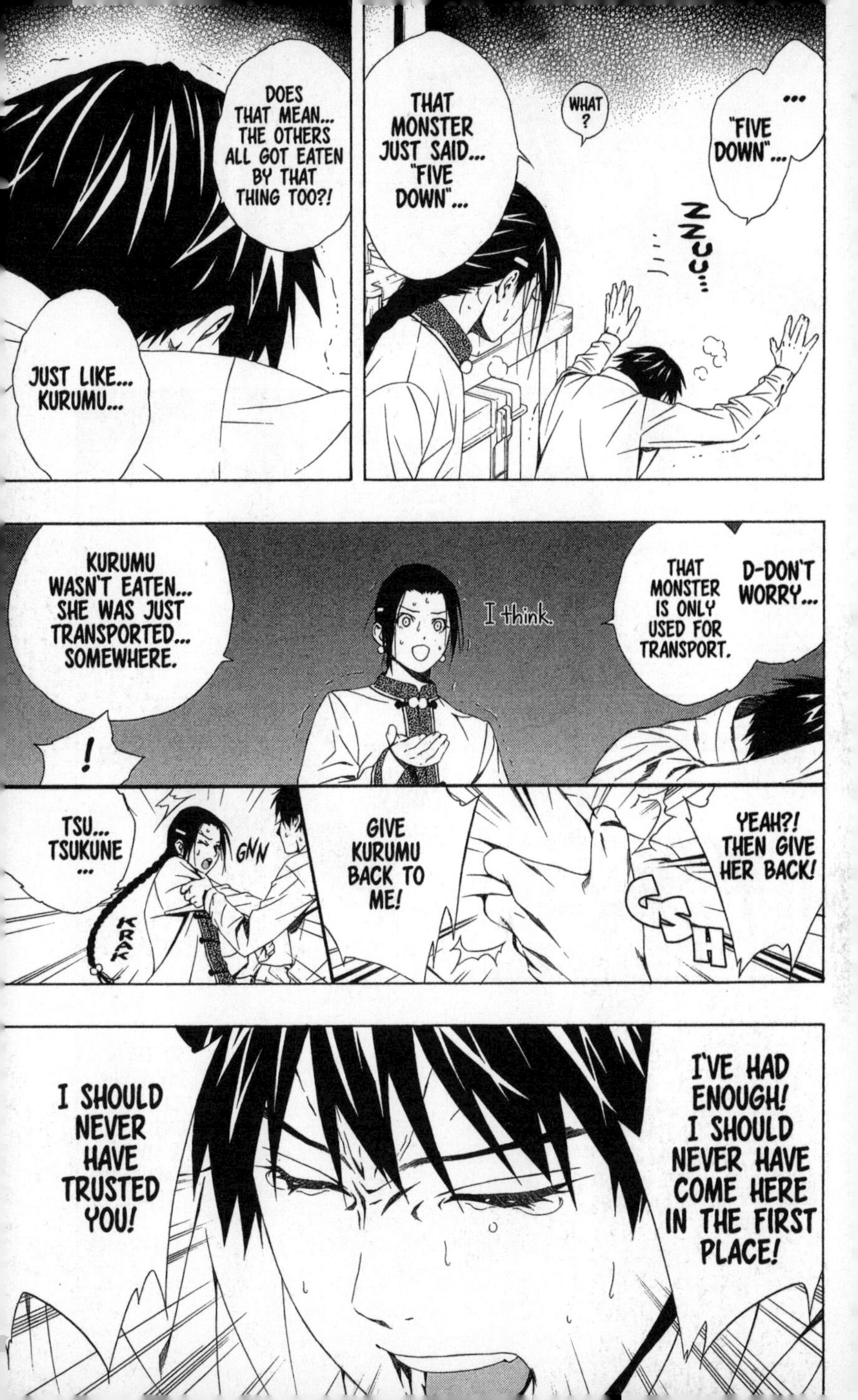
..."FIVE DOWN"...
WHAT?
THAT MONSTER JUST SAID... "FIVE DOWN"...
ZZUU...
DOES THAT MEAN... THE OTHERS ALL GOT EATEN BY THAT THING TOO?!
JUST LIKE... KURUMU...
D-DON'T WORRY...
THAT MONSTER IS ONLY USED FOR TRANSPORT.
I think.
KURUMU WASN'T EATEN... SHE WAS JUST TRANSPORTED... SOMEWHERE.
!
YEAH?! THEN GIVE HER BACK!
GSH
GIVE KURUMU BACK TO ME!
GNN
TSU... TSUKUNE...
KRAK
I'VE HAD ENOUGH! I SHOULD NEVER HAVE COME HERE IN THE FIRST PLACE!
I SHOULD NEVER HAVE TRUSTED YOU!

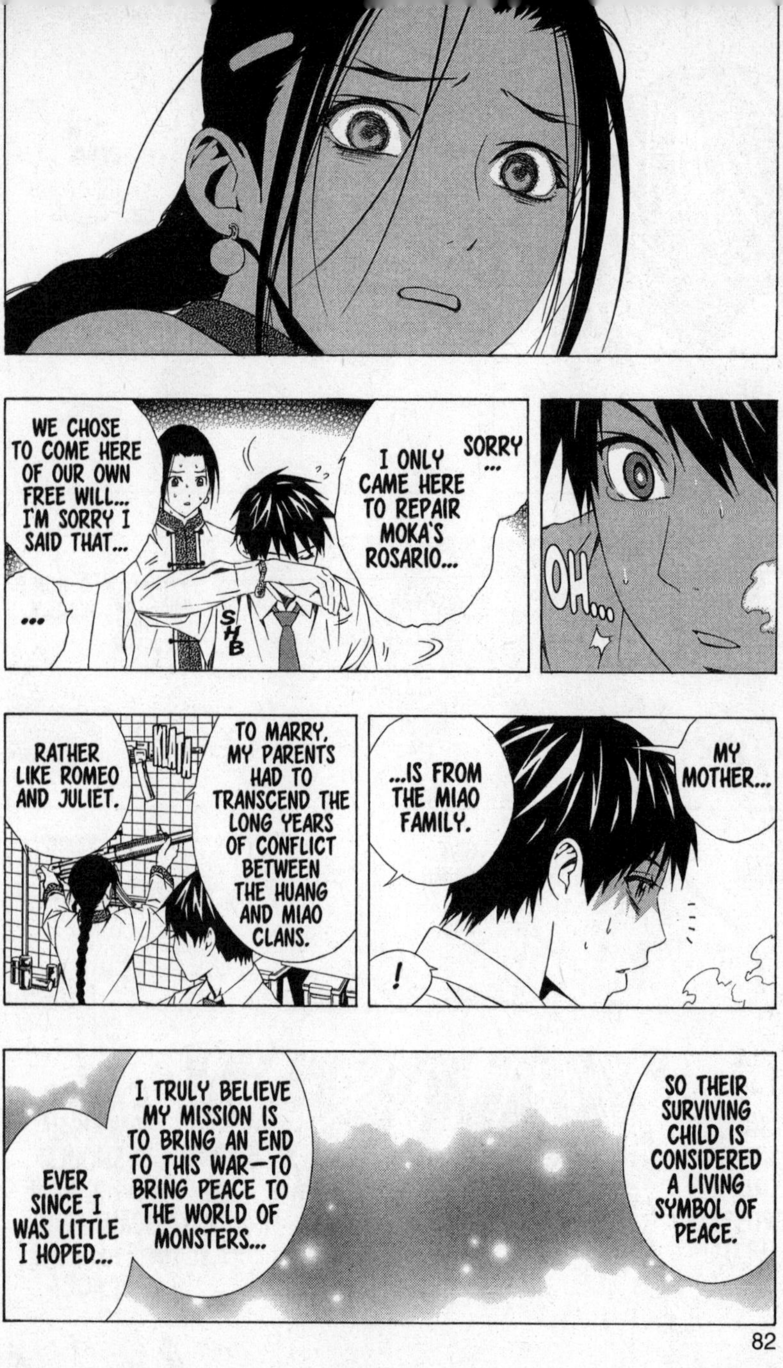
OH...
SORRY ...
I ONLY CAME HERE TO REPAIR MOKA'S ROSARIO...
SHB
WE CHOSE TO COME HERE OF OUR OWN FREE WILL... I'M SORRY I SAID THAT...
...
MY MOTHER...
...IS FROM THE MIAO FAMILY.
!
TO MARRY, MY PARENTS HAD TO TRANSCEND THE LONG YEARS OF CONFLICT BETWEEN THE HUANG AND MIAO CLANS.
RATHER LIKE ROMEO AND JULIET.
SO THEIR SURVIVING CHILD IS CONSIDERED A LIVING SYMBOL OF PEACE.
I TRULY BELIEVE MY MISSION IS TO BRING AN END TO THIS WAR—TO BRING PEACE TO THE WORLD OF MONSTERS...
EVER SINCE I WAS LITTLE I HOPED...

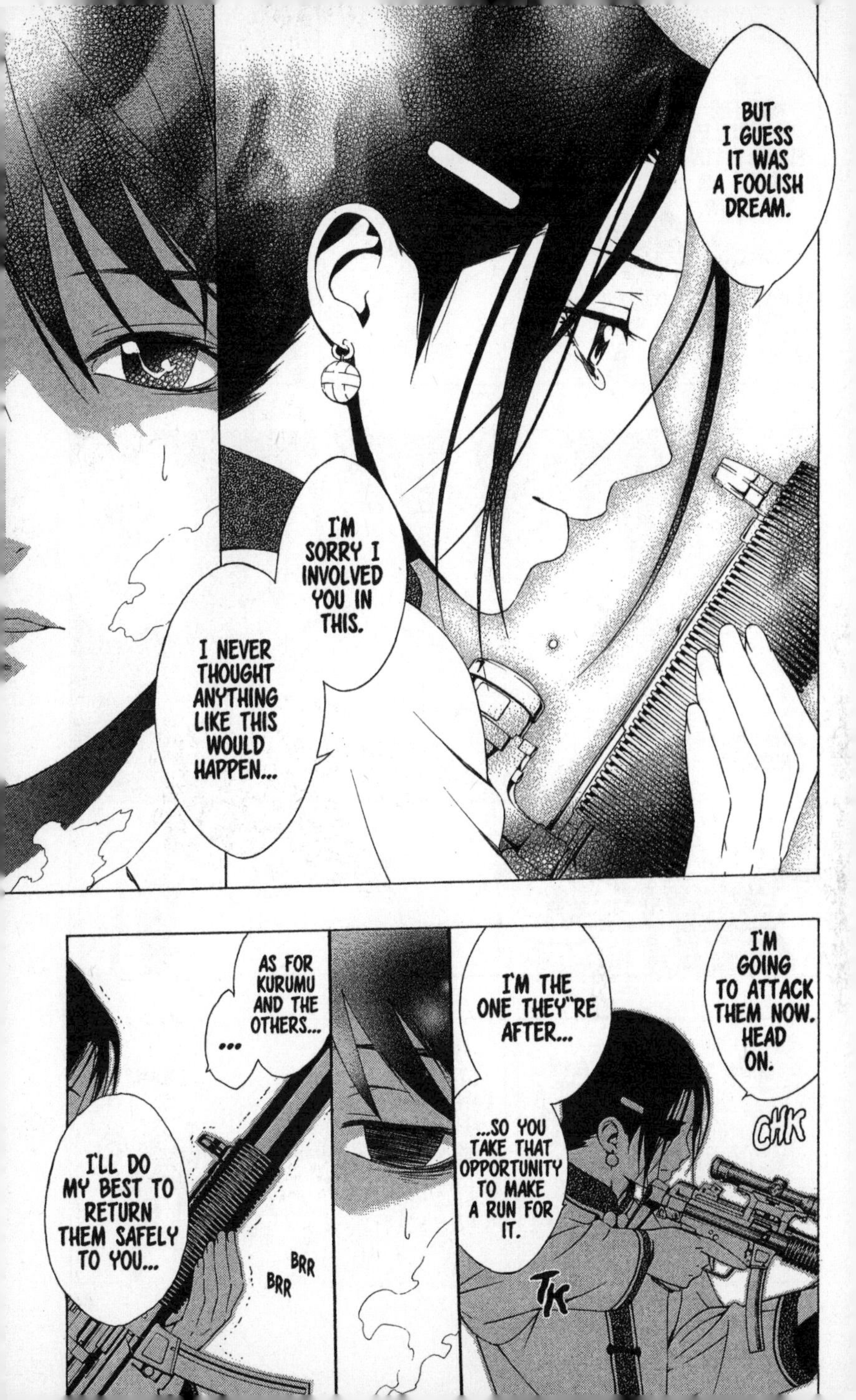
BUT I GUESS IT WAS A FOOLISH DREAM.
I'M SORRY I INVOLVED YOU IN THIS.
I NEVER THOUGHT ANYTHING LIKE THIS WOULD HAPPEN...
I'M GOING TO ATTACK THEM NOW. HEAD ON.
CHK
I'M THE ONE THEY'RE AFTER...
...SO YOU TAKE THAT OPPORTUNITY TO MAKE A RUN FOR IT.
TK
AS FOR KURUMU AND THE OTHERS...
...
I'LL DO MY BEST TO RETURN THEM SAFELY TO YOU...
BRR
BRR

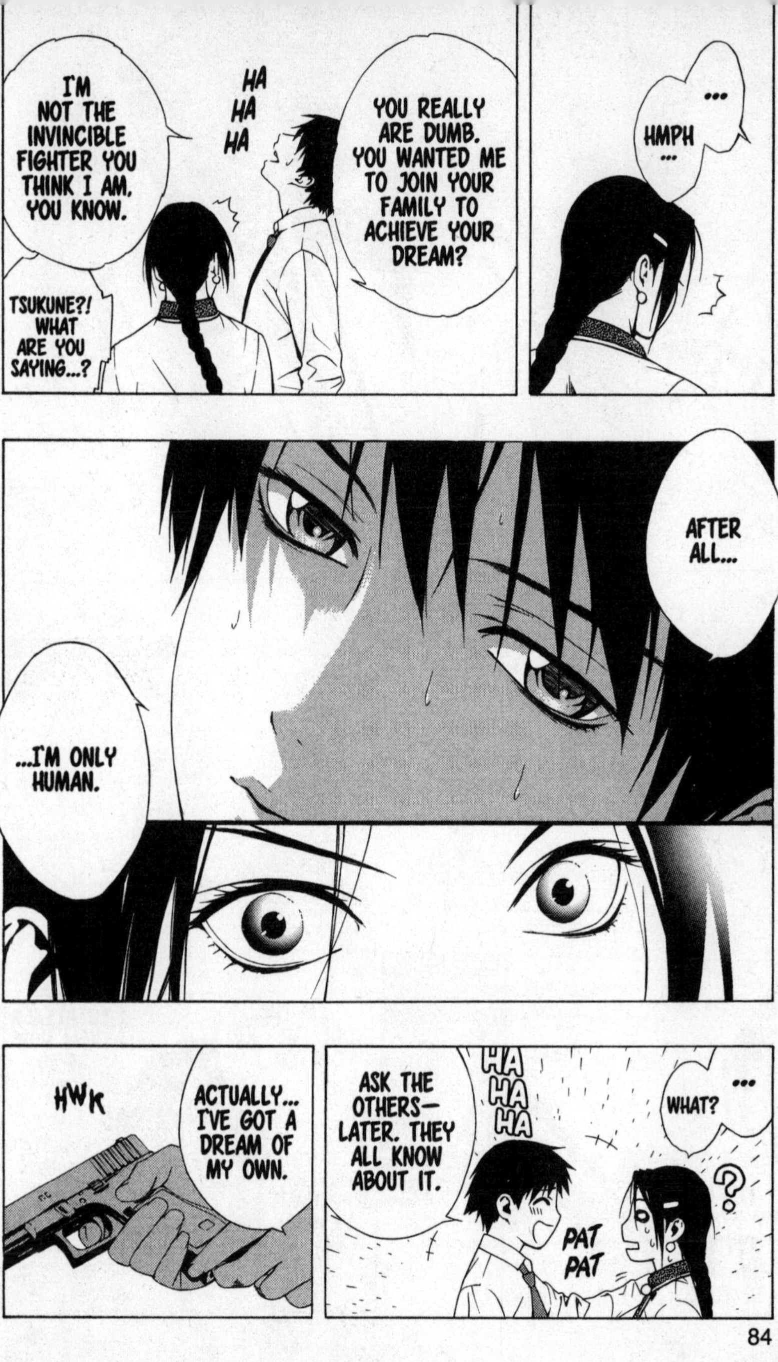
...
HMPH...
YOU REALLY ARE DUMB. YOU WANTED ME TO JOIN YOUR FAMILY TO ACHIEVE YOUR DREAM?
HA HA HA
I'M NOT THE INVINCIBLE FIGHTER YOU THINK I AM, YOU KNOW.
TSUKUNE?! WHAT ARE YOU SAYING...?
AFTER ALL...
...I'M ONLY HUMAN.
...
WHAT?
HA HA HA
ASK THE OTHERS— LATER. THEY ALL KNOW ABOUT IT.
PAT PAT
ACTUALLY... I'VE GOT A DREAM OF MY OWN.
HWK

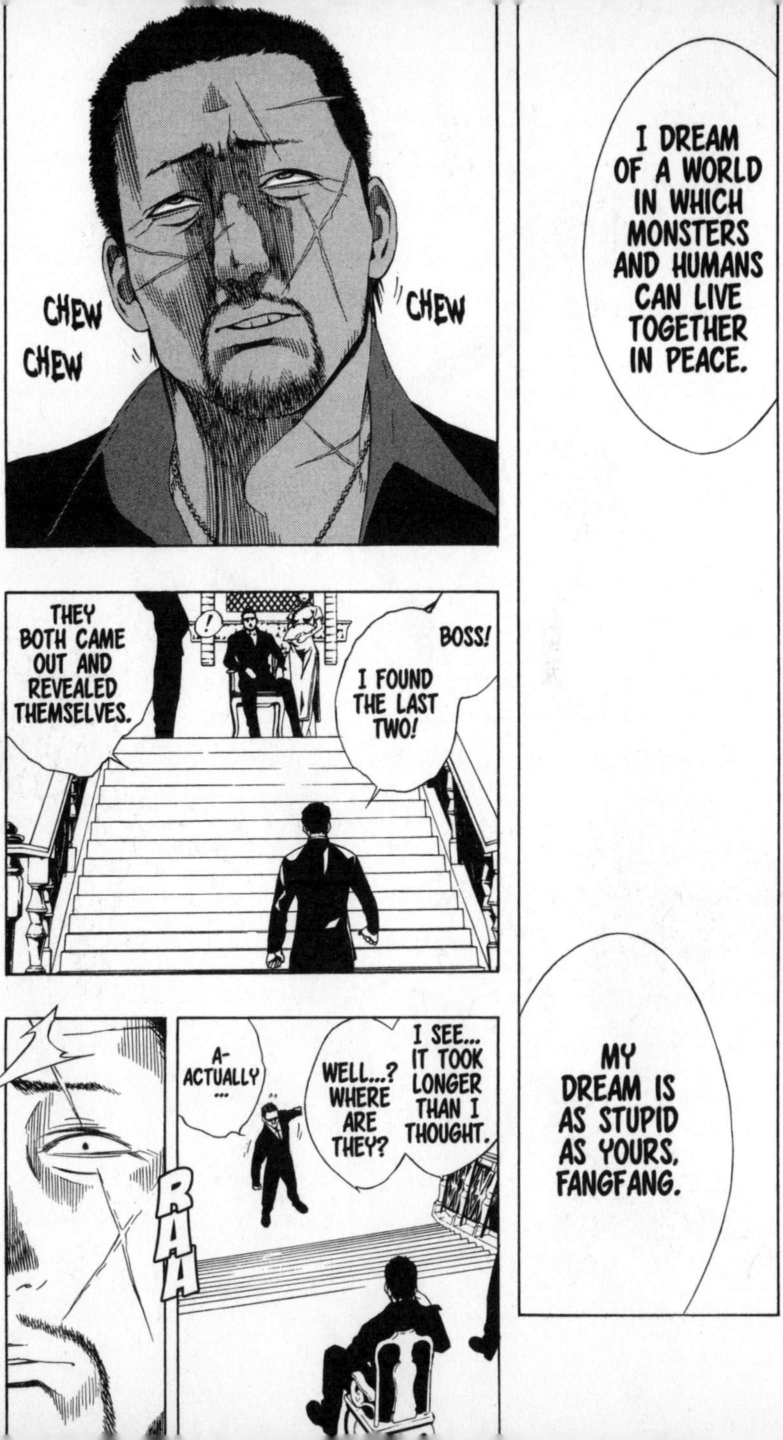

I DREAM OF A WORLD IN WHICH MONSTERS AND HUMANS CAN LIVE TOGETHER IN PEACE.
MY DREAM IS AS STUPID AS YOURS, FANGFANG.
CHEW
CHEW
CHEW
BOSS!
I FOUND THE LAST TWO!
THEY BOTH CAME OUT AND REVEALED THEMSELVES.
I SEE... IT TOOK LONGER THAN I THOUGHT.
WELL...? WHERE ARE THEY?
A-ACTUALLY...
RAA

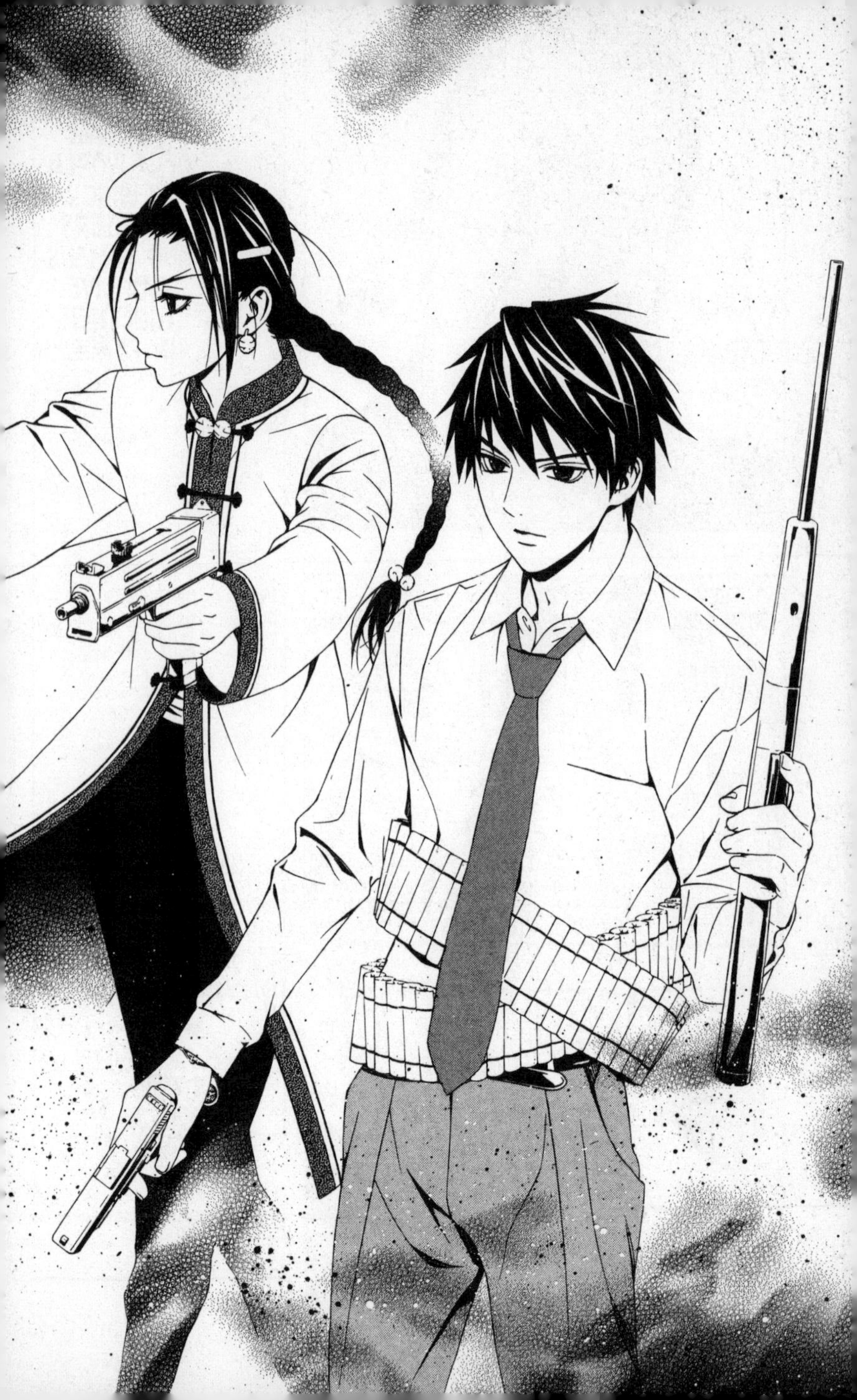

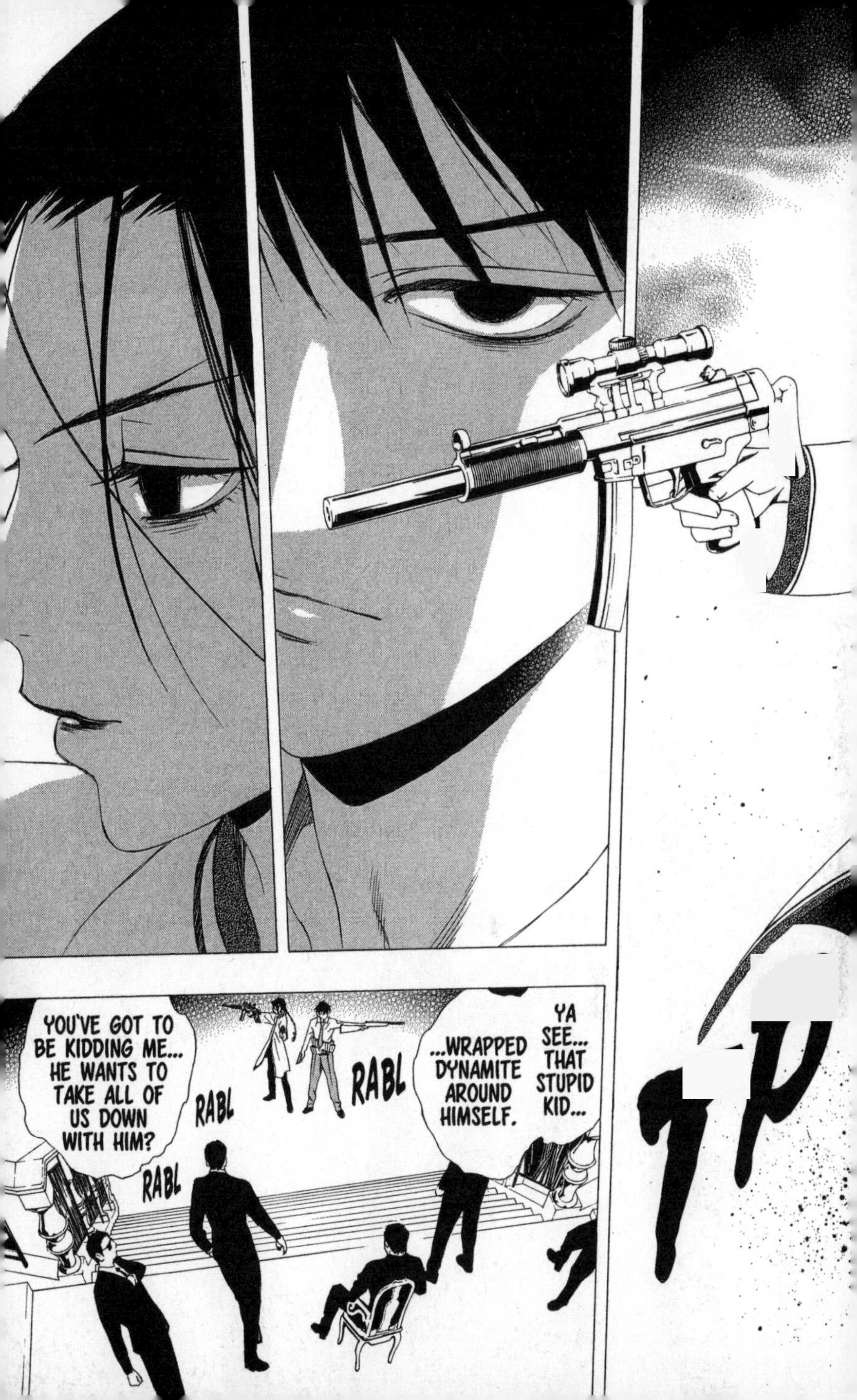
YA SEE... THAT STUPID KID...
...WRAPPED DYNAMITE AROUND HIMSELF.
RABL
YOU'VE GOT TO BE KIDDING ME... HE WANTS TO TAKE ALL OF US DOWN WITH HIM?
RABL
RABL

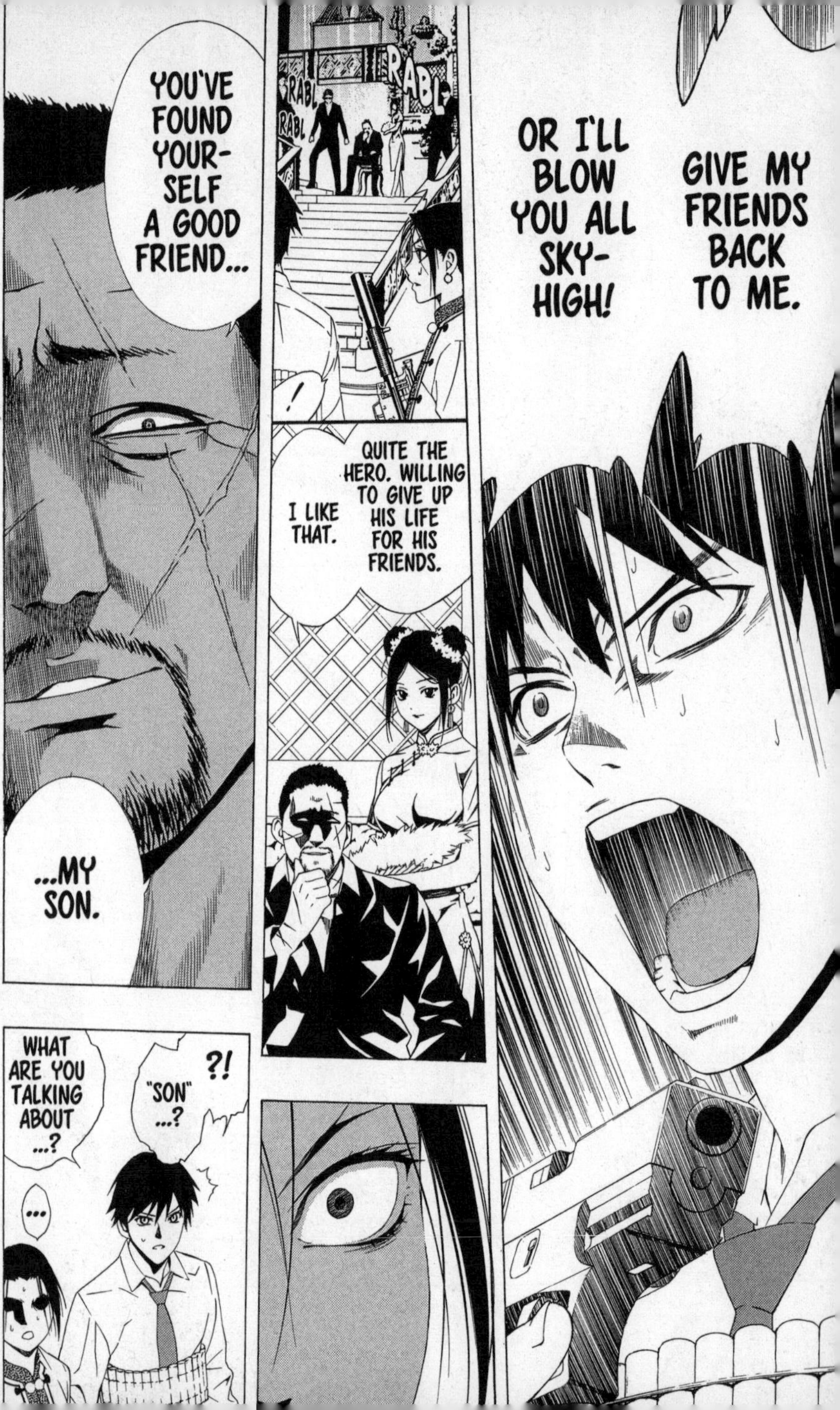
GIVE MY FRIENDS BACK TO ME.
OR I'LL BLOW YOU ALL SKY-HIGH!
RABL
RABL
RABL
!
QUITE THE HERO. WILLING TO GIVE UP HIS LIFE FOR HIS FRIENDS.
I LIKE THAT.
YOU'VE FOUND YOUR-SELF A GOOD FRIEND...
...MY SON.
?!
"SON" ...?
WHAT ARE YOU TALKING ABOUT ...?
...

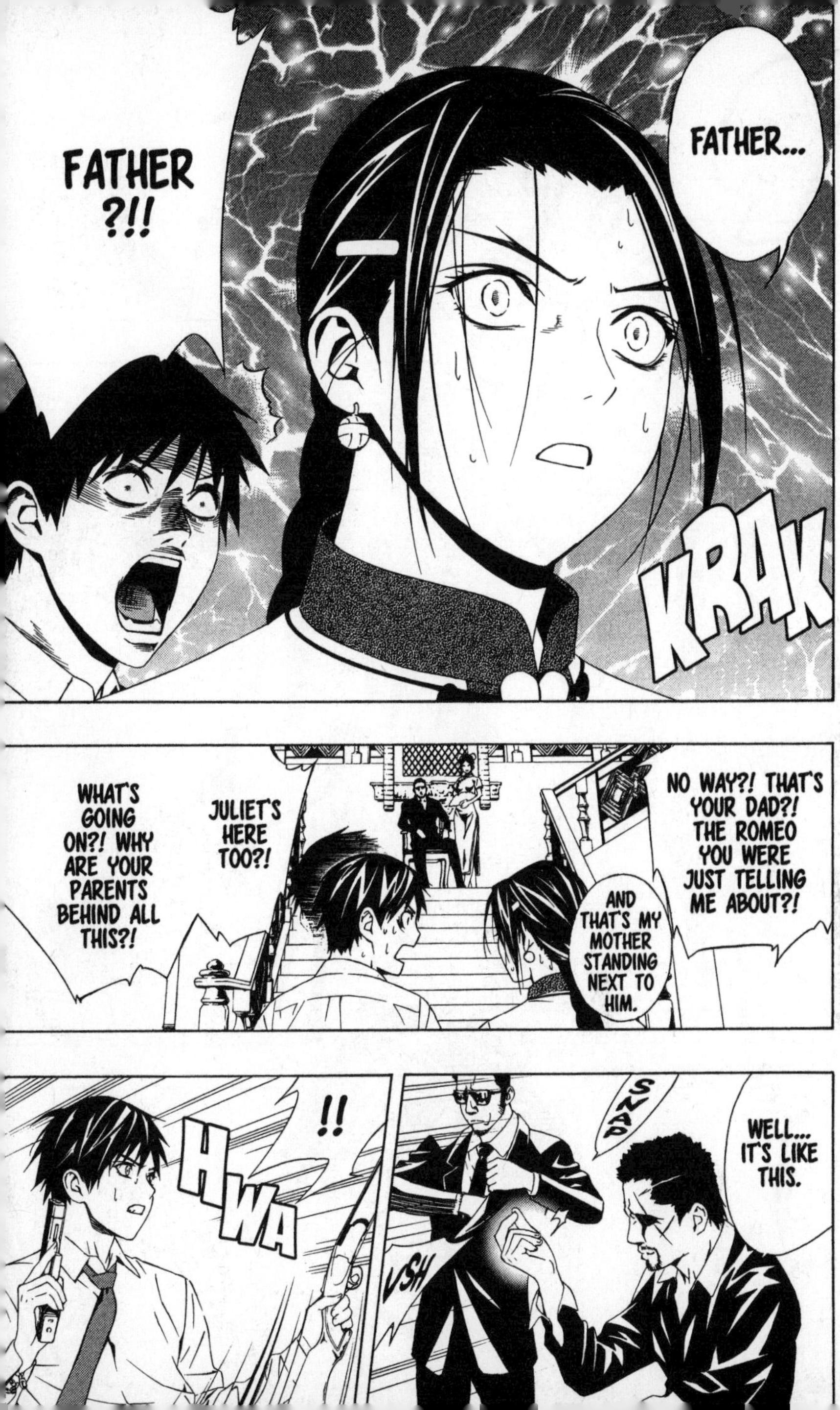
FATHER...
FATHER ?!!
KRAK
NO WAY?! THAT'S YOUR DAD?! THE ROMEO YOU WERE JUST TELLING ME ABOUT?!
AND THAT'S MY MOTHER STANDING NEXT TO HIM.
JULIET'S HERE TOO?!
WHAT'S GOING ON?! WHY ARE YOUR PARENTS BEHIND ALL THIS?!
WELL... IT'S LIKE THIS.
SNAP
VSH
!!
HWA

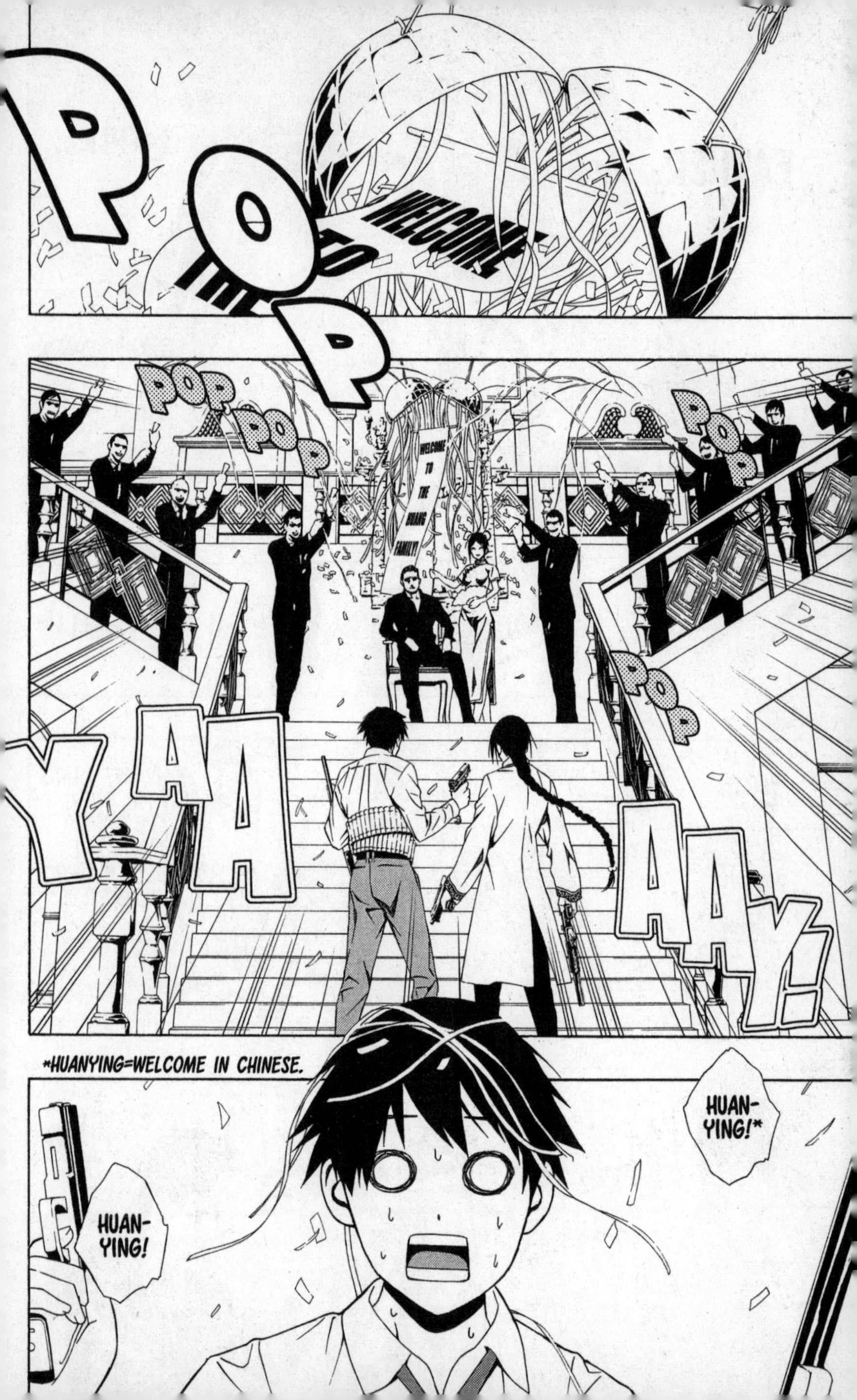
POP
WELCOME TO THE
WELCOME TO THE HUANG FAMILY!
POP
POP
POP
POP
YAAAAAY!
HUAN-YING!*
HUAN-YING!
*HUANYING=WELCOME IN CHINESE.

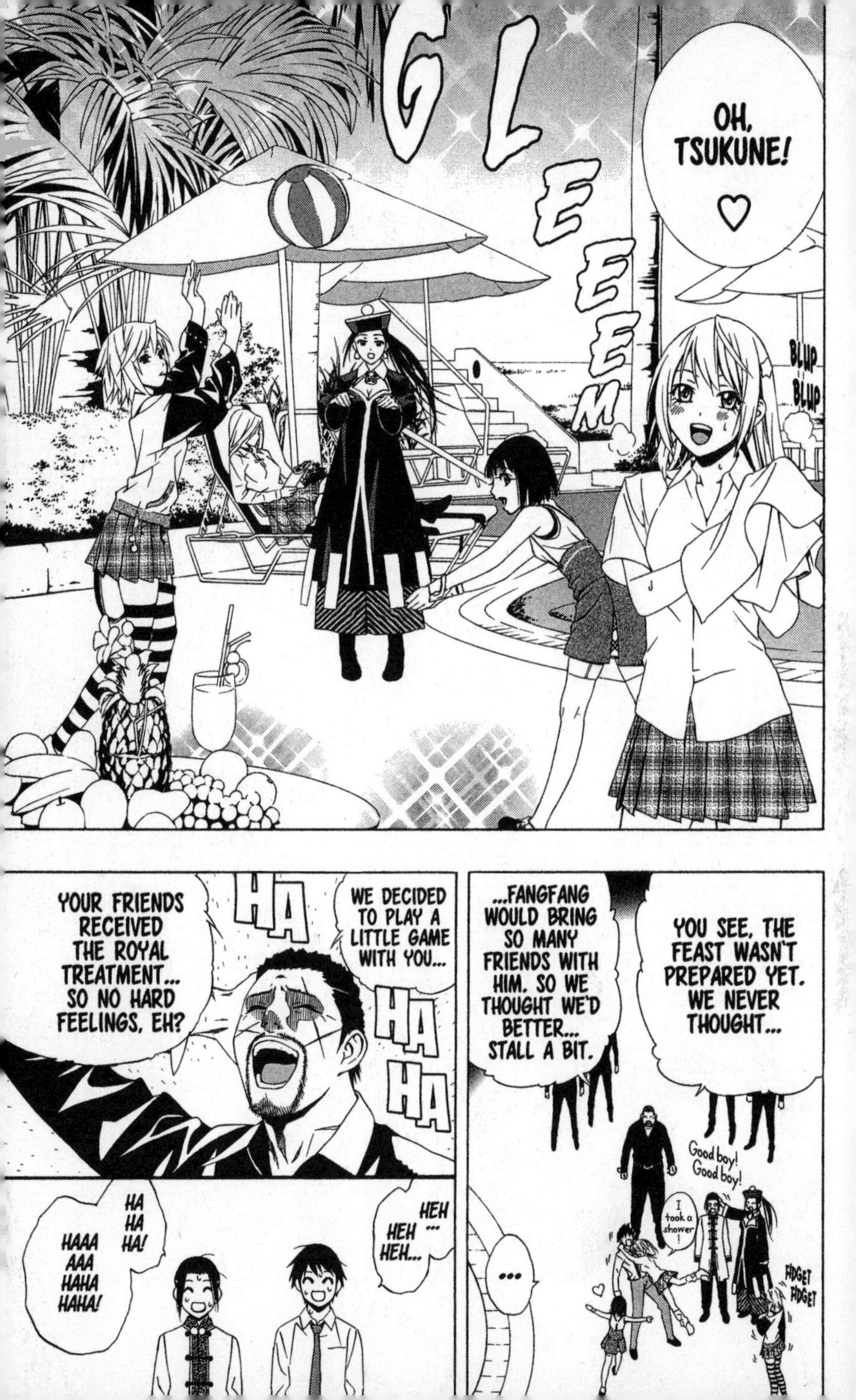
OH, TSUKUNE! ♡
BLUP BLUP
GLEEEEM
YOU SEE, THE FEAST WASN'T PREPARED YET. WE NEVER THOUGHT...
...FANGFANG WOULD BRING SO MANY FRIENDS WITH HIM. SO WE THOUGHT WE'D BETTER... STALL A BIT.
Good boy! Good boy!
I took a shower!
FIDGET FIDGET
...
WE DECIDED TO PLAY A LITTLE GAME WITH YOU...
HA HA HA
YOUR FRIENDS RECEIVED THE ROYAL TREATMENT... SO NO HARD FEELINGS, EH?
HEH... HEH HEH...
HA HA HA!
HAAA AAA HAHA HAHA!

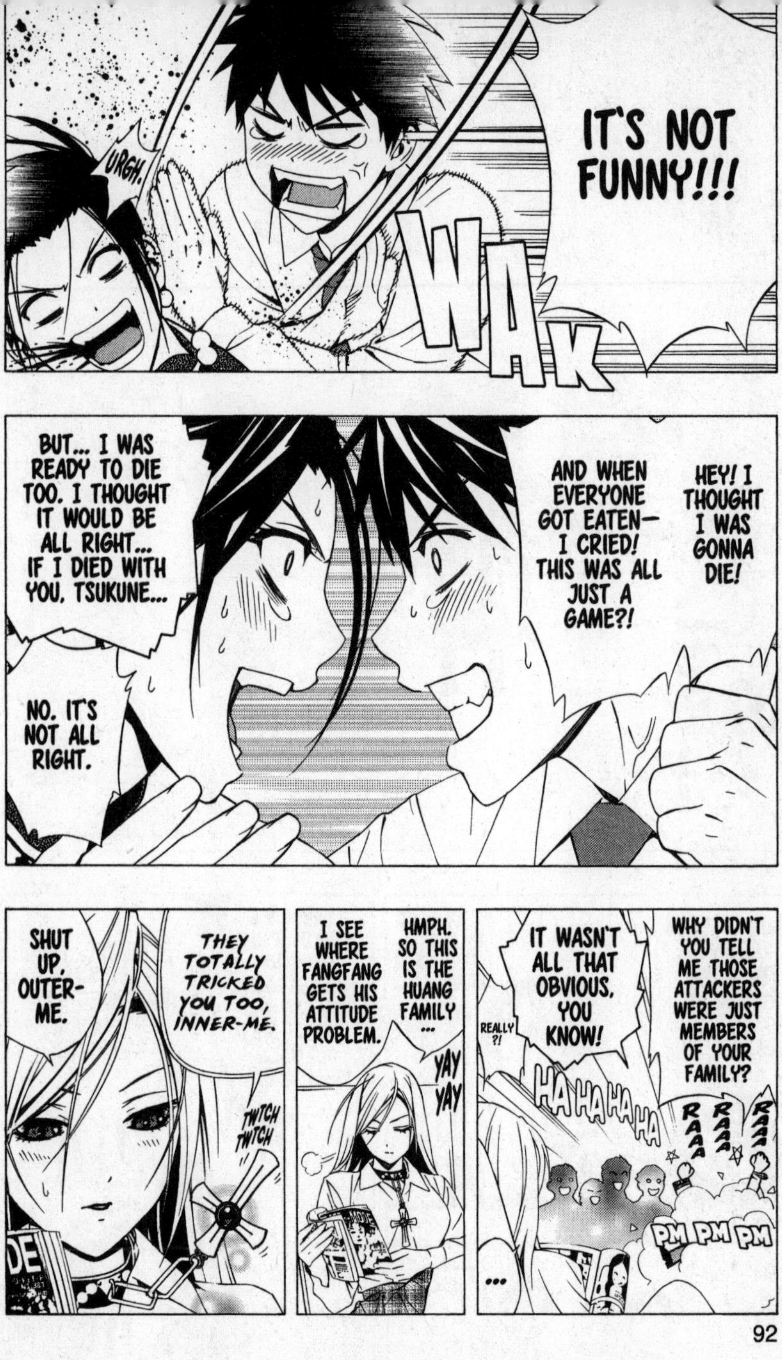
IT'S NOT FUNNY!!!
WAK
URGH.
HEY! I THOUGHT I WAS GONNA DIE!
AND WHEN EVERYONE GOT EATEN— I CRIED! THIS WAS ALL JUST A GAME?!
BUT... I WAS READY TO DIE TOO. I THOUGHT IT WOULD BE ALL RIGHT... IF I DIED WITH YOU, TSUKUNE...
NO. IT'S NOT ALL RIGHT.
WHY DIDN'T YOU TELL ME THOSE ATTACKERS WERE JUST MEMBERS OF YOUR FAMILY?
IT WASN'T ALL THAT OBVIOUS, YOU KNOW!
REALLY?!
HA HA HA HA HA
RAAA RAAA RAAA
PM PM PM
...
HMPH. SO THIS IS THE HUANG FAMILY...
I SEE WHERE FANGFANG GETS HIS ATTITUDE PROBLEM.
YAY YAY
THEY TOTALLY TRICKED YOU TOO, INNER-ME.
SHUT UP, OUTER-ME.
TWITCH TWITCH

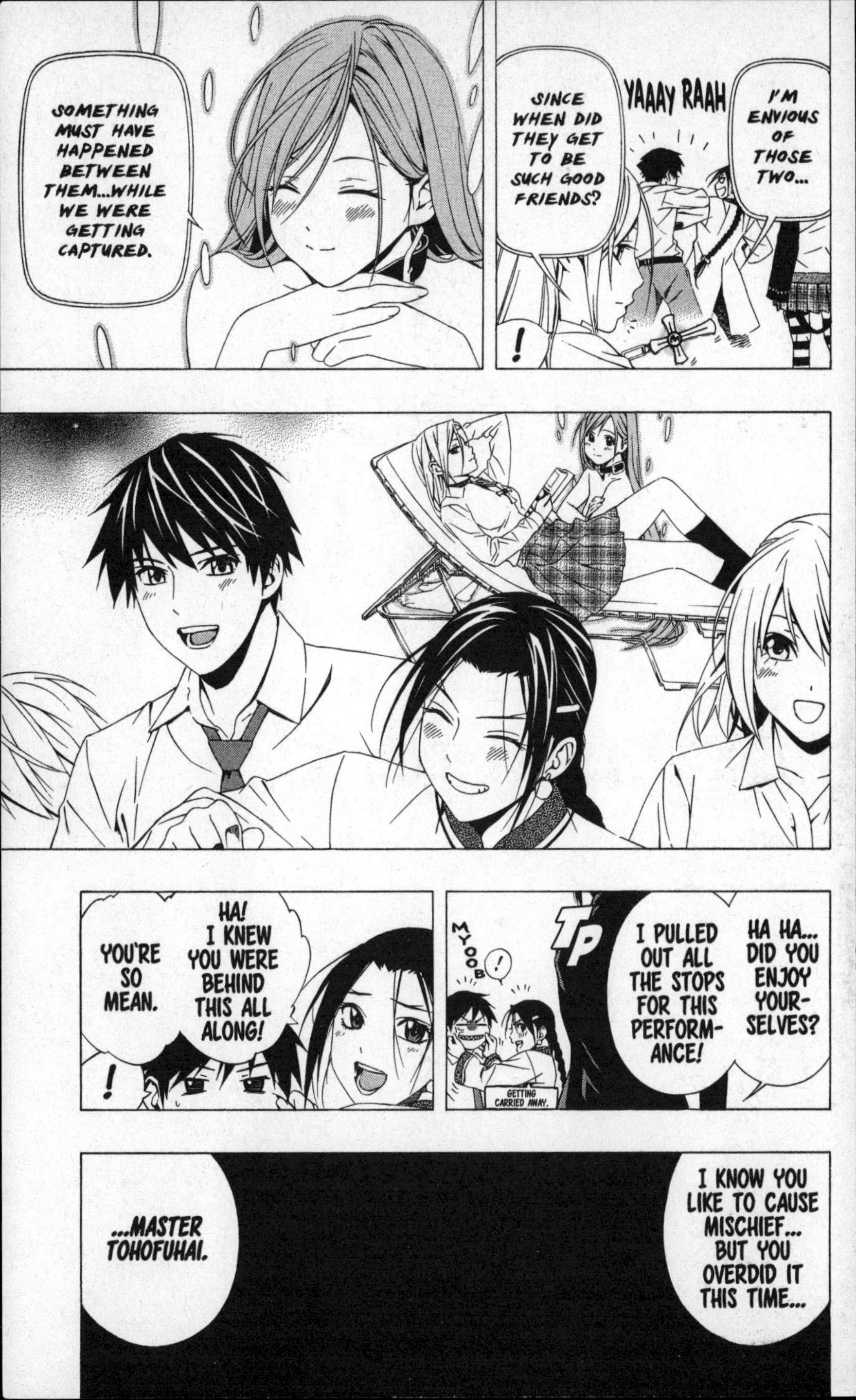
I'M ENVIOUS OF THOSE TWO...
YAAAY RAAH
SINCE WHEN DID THEY GET TO BE SUCH GOOD FRIENDS?
!
SOMETHING MUST HAVE HAPPENED BETWEEN THEM...WHILE WE WERE GETTING CAPTURED.
HA HA... DID YOU ENJOY YOUR-SELVES?
I PULLED OUT ALL THE STOPS FOR THIS PERFORM-ANCE!
TP
MYOOB
!
GETTING CARRIED AWAY.
HA! I KNEW YOU WERE BEHIND THIS ALL ALONG!
YOU'RE SO MEAN.
!
I KNOW YOU LIKE TO CAUSE MISCHIEF... BUT YOU OVERDID IT THIS TIME...
...MASTER TOHOFUHAI.

# 29: Repairing the Seal

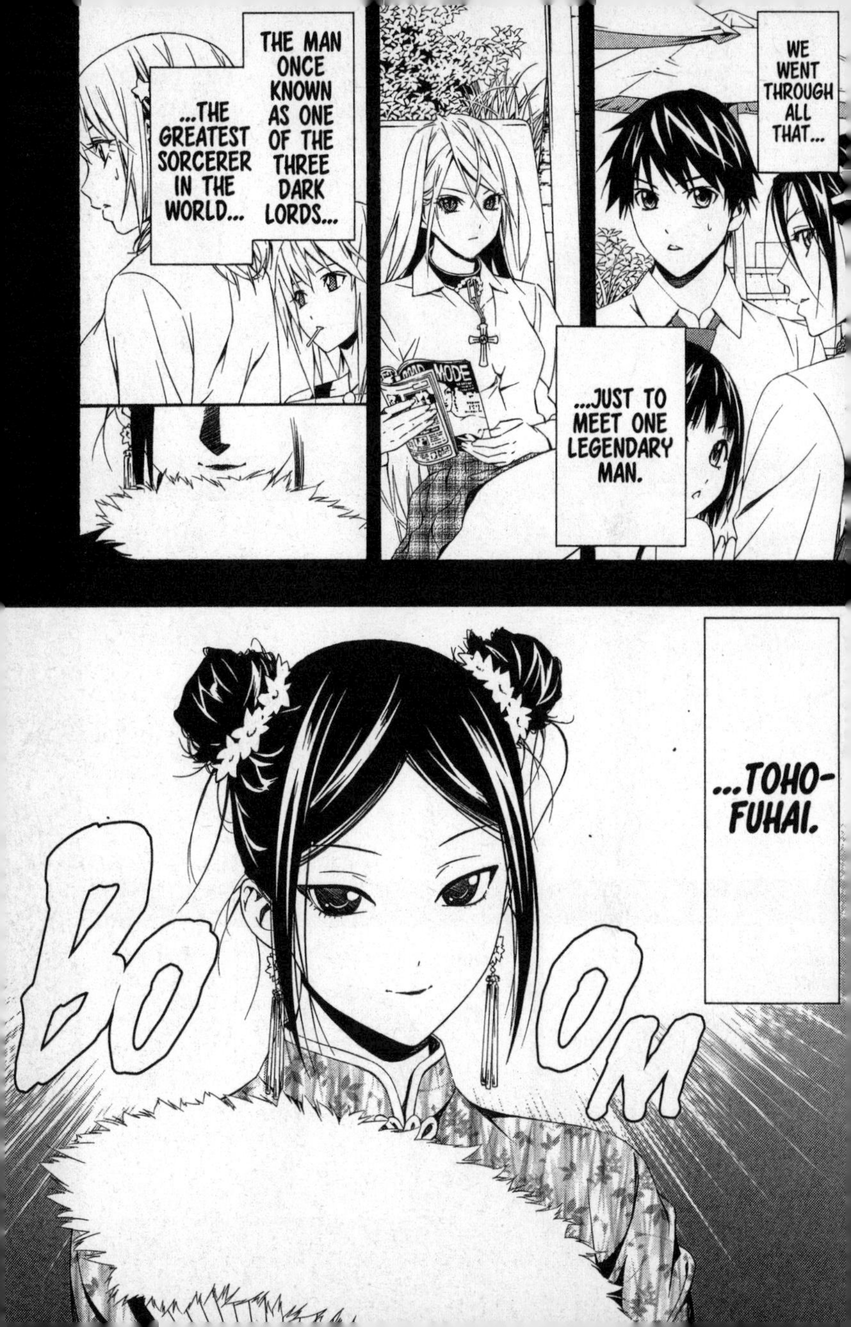
WE WENT THROUGH ALL THAT...
...JUST TO MEET ONE LEGENDARY MAN.
THE MAN ONCE KNOWN AS ONE OF THE THREE DARK LORDS...
...THE GREATEST SORCERER IN THE WORLD...
...TOHO-FUHAI.
BOOM

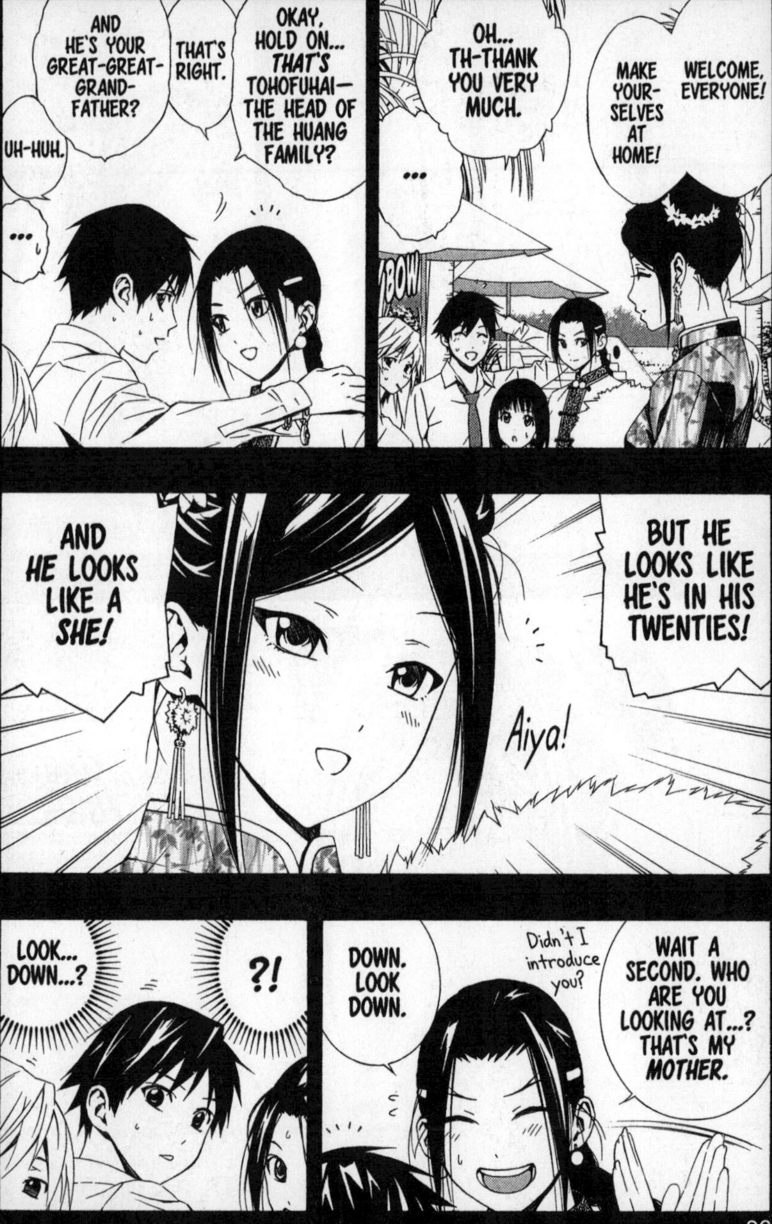
WELCOME, EVERYONE!
MAKE YOURSELVES AT HOME!
OH... TH-THANK YOU VERY MUCH.
...
BOW
OKAY, HOLD ON... *THAT'S* TOHOFUHAI— THE HEAD OF THE HUANG FAMILY?
THAT'S RIGHT.
AND HE'S YOUR GREAT-GREAT-GRANDFATHER?
UH-HUH.
...
BUT HE LOOKS LIKE HE'S IN HIS TWENTIES!
Aiya!
AND *HE* LOOKS LIKE A *SHE!*
WAIT A SECOND. WHO ARE YOU LOOKING AT...? THAT'S MY *MOTHER.*
Didn't I introduce you?
DOWN. LOOK DOWN.
?!
LOOK... DOWN...?

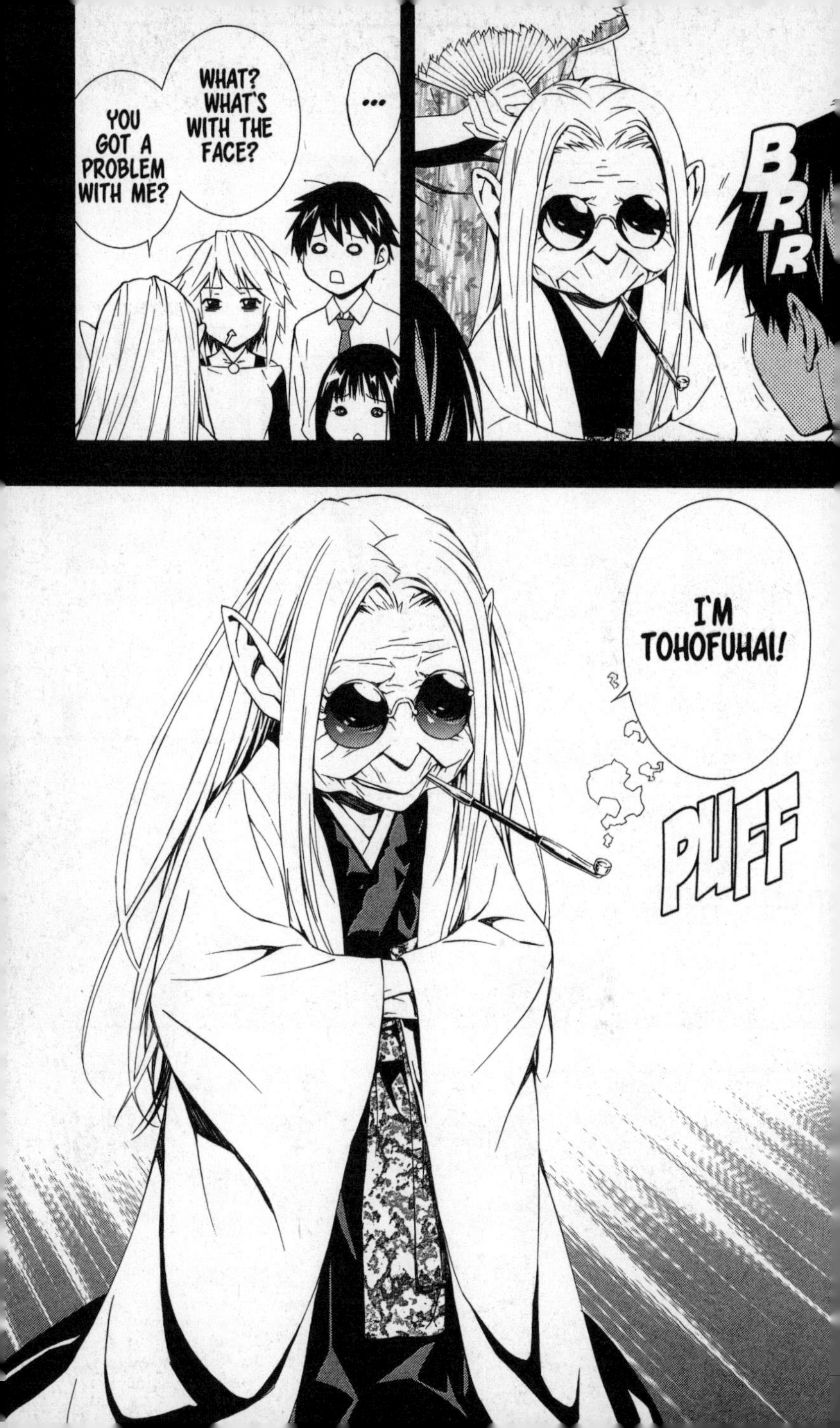
BRR
...
WHAT? WHAT'S WITH THE FACE?
YOU GOT A PROBLEM WITH ME?
I'M TOHOFUHAI!
PUFF

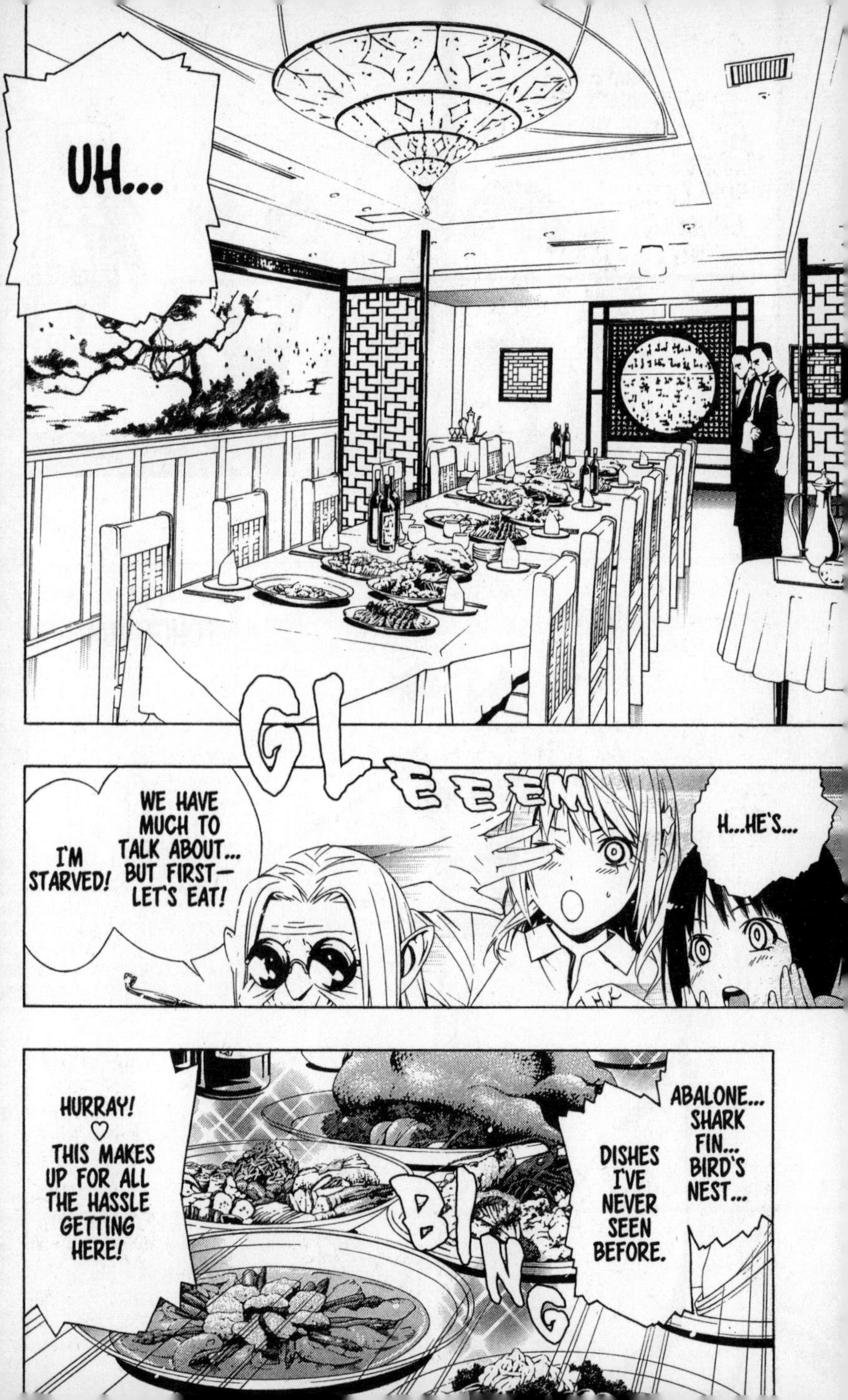
UH...
H...HE'S...
GLEEEEM
WE HAVE MUCH TO TALK ABOUT... BUT FIRST— LET'S EAT!
I'M STARVED!
ABALONE... SHARK FIN... BIRD'S NEST...
DISHES I'VE NEVER SEEN BEFORE.
BING
HURRAY! ♡ THIS MAKES UP FOR ALL THE HASSLE GETTING HERE!

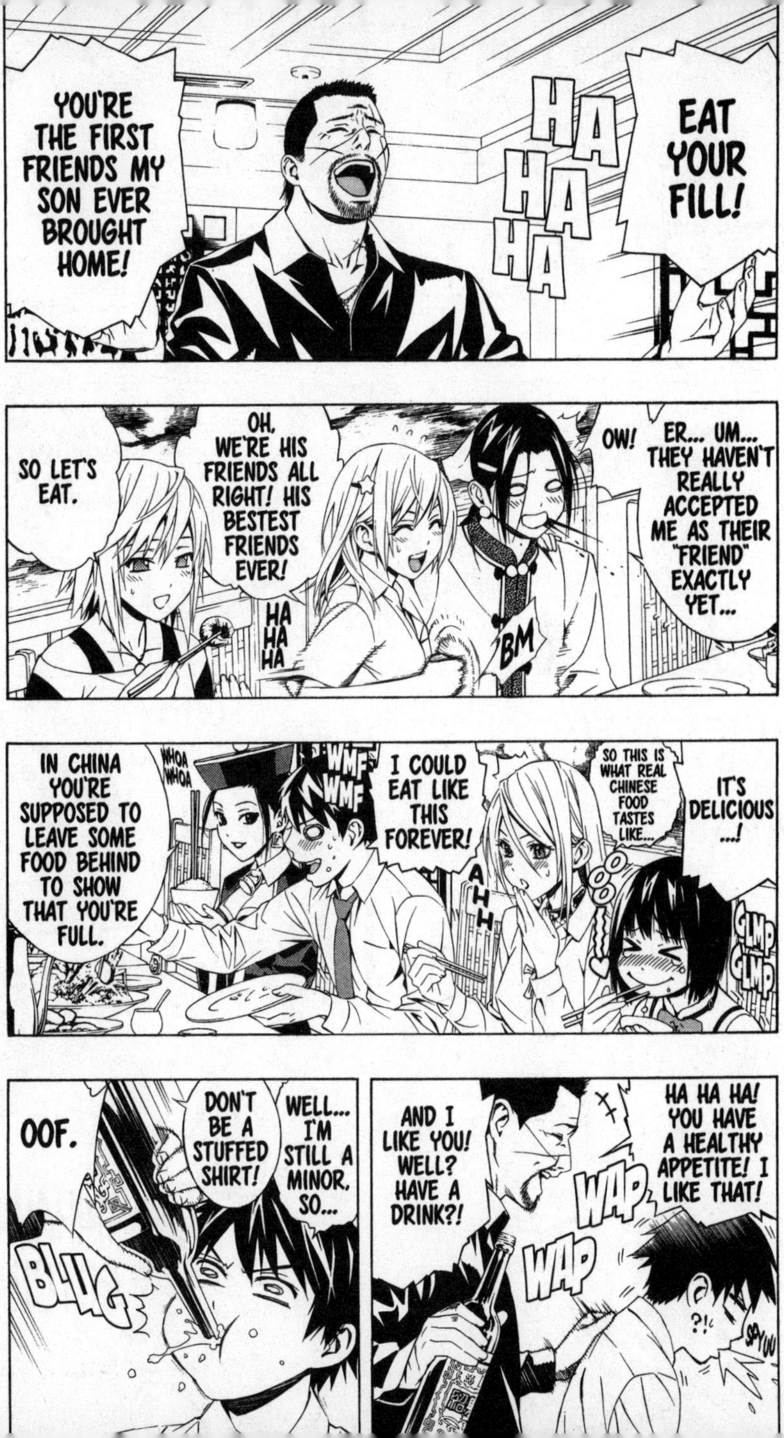
EAT YOUR FILL!
HA HA HA
YOU'RE THE FIRST FRIENDS MY SON EVER BROUGHT HOME!
ER... UM... THEY HAVEN'T REALLY ACCEPTED ME AS THEIR "FRIEND" EXACTLY YET...
OW!
BM
OH, WE'RE HIS FRIENDS ALL RIGHT! HIS BESTEST FRIENDS EVER!
HA HA HA
SO LET'S EAT.
IT'S DELICIOUS ...!
SO THIS IS WHAT REAL CHINESE FOOD TASTES LIKE...
GLMP GLMP
AHH
I COULD EAT LIKE THIS FOREVER!
WMF WMF
WHOA WHOA
IN CHINA YOU'RE SUPPOSED TO LEAVE SOME FOOD BEHIND TO SHOW THAT YOU'RE FULL.
HA HA HA! YOU HAVE A HEALTHY APPETITE! I LIKE THAT!
AND I LIKE YOU! WELL? HAVE A DRINK?!
WAP
WAP
?!
SPYUU
WELL... I'M STILL A MINOR, SO...
DON'T BE A STUFFED SHIRT!
OOF.
BLUG

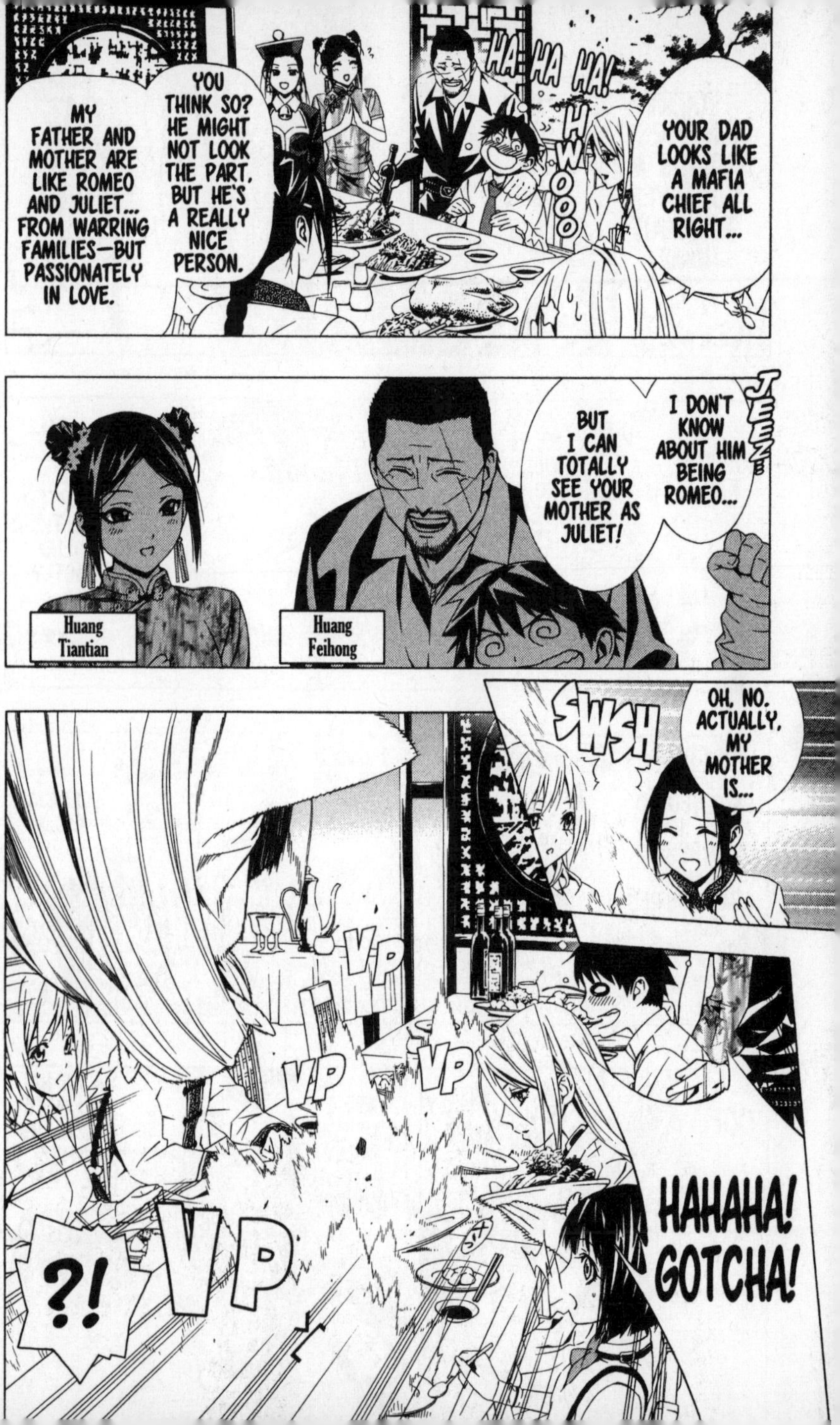
HA HA HA!
YOUR DAD LOOKS LIKE A MAFIA CHIEF ALL RIGHT...
HWOOOO
YOU THINK SO? HE MIGHT NOT LOOK THE PART, BUT HE'S A REALLY NICE PERSON.
MY FATHER AND MOTHER ARE LIKE ROMEO AND JULIET... FROM WARRING FAMILIES—BUT PASSIONATELY IN LOVE.
JEEZ
I DON'T KNOW ABOUT HIM BEING ROMEO...
BUT I CAN TOTALLY SEE YOUR MOTHER AS JULIET!
Huang Feihong
Huang Tiantian
OH, NO. ACTUALLY, MY MOTHER IS...
SWSH
VP
VP
VP
HAHAHA! GOTCHA!
VP
?!

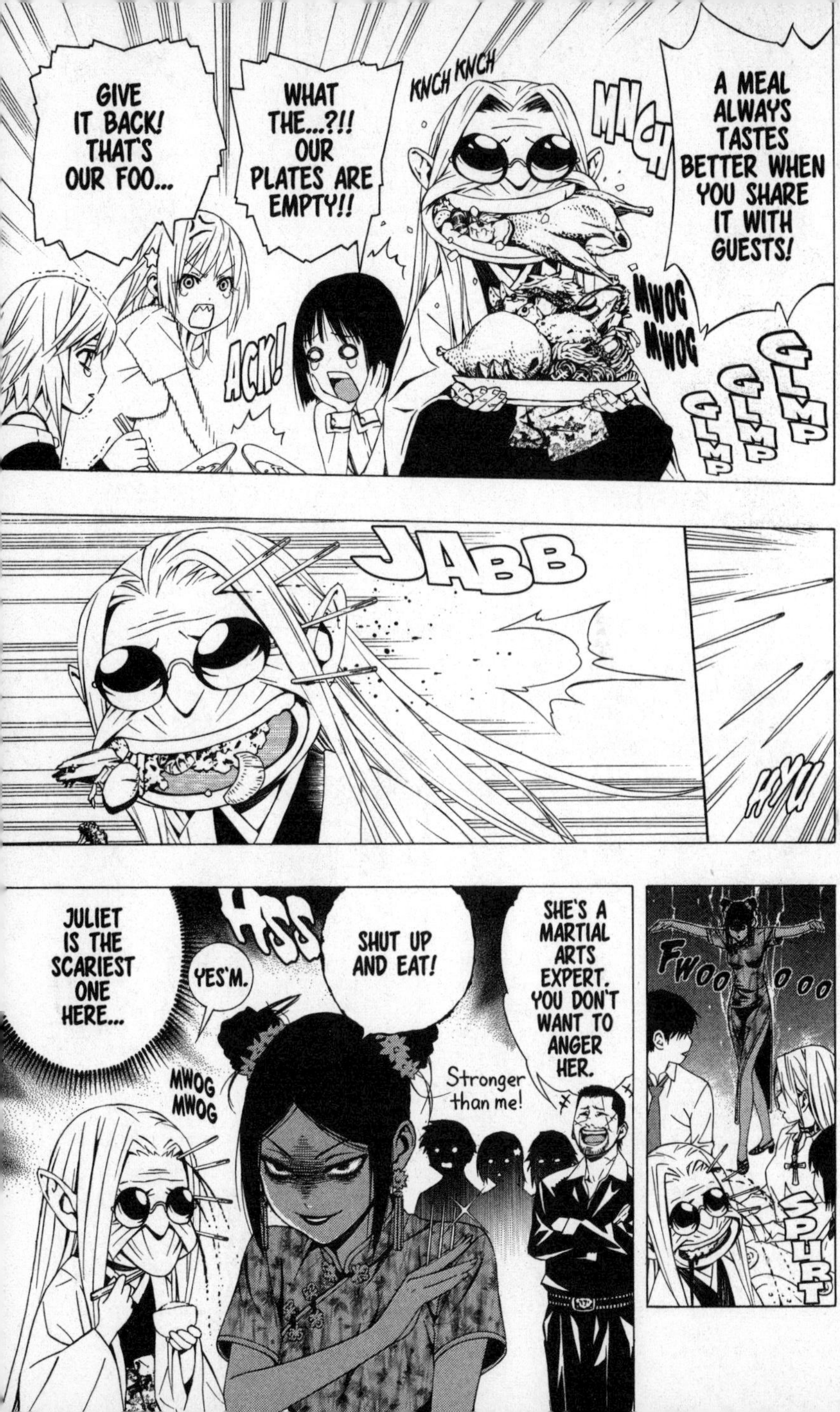
A MEAL ALWAYS TASTES BETTER WHEN YOU SHARE IT WITH GUESTS!
MNCH
KNCH KNCH
MWOG MWOG
GLMP GLMP GLMP
WHAT THE...?!! OUR PLATES ARE EMPTY!!
ACK!
GIVE IT BACK! THAT'S OUR FOO...
HYU
JABB
FWOOOOOO
SPURT
SHE'S A MARTIAL ARTS EXPERT. YOU DON'T WANT TO ANGER HER.
Stronger than me!
SHUT UP AND EAT!
HSS
YES'M.
JULIET IS THE SCARIEST ONE HERE...
MWOG MWOG

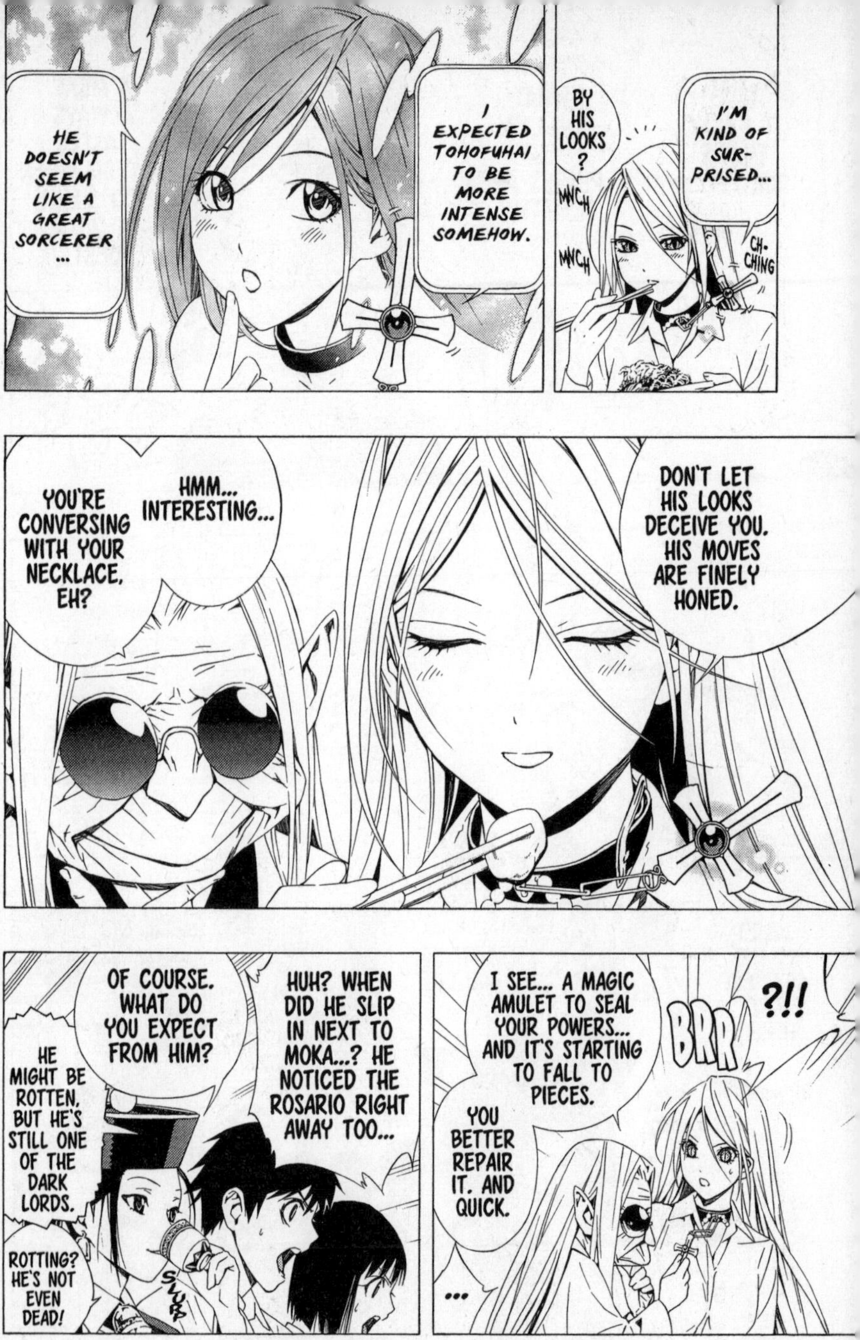
I'M KIND OF SUR-PRISED...
BY HIS LOOKS?
MNCH
MNCH
CH-CHING
I EXPECTED TOHOFUHAI TO BE MORE INTENSE SOMEHOW.
HE DOESN'T SEEM LIKE A GREAT SORCERER...
DON'T LET HIS LOOKS DECEIVE YOU. HIS MOVES ARE FINELY HONED.
HMM... INTERESTING...
YOU'RE CONVERSING WITH YOUR NECKLACE, EH?
?!!
BRR
I SEE... A MAGIC AMULET TO SEAL YOUR POWERS... AND IT'S STARTING TO FALL TO PIECES.
YOU BETTER REPAIR IT. AND QUICK.
...
HUH? WHEN DID HE SLIP IN NEXT TO MOKA...? HE NOTICED THE ROSARIO RIGHT AWAY TOO...
OF COURSE. WHAT DO YOU EXPECT FROM HIM?
HE MIGHT BE ROTTEN, BUT HE'S STILL ONE OF THE DARK LORDS.
ROTTING? HE'S NOT EVEN DEAD!
SLURP

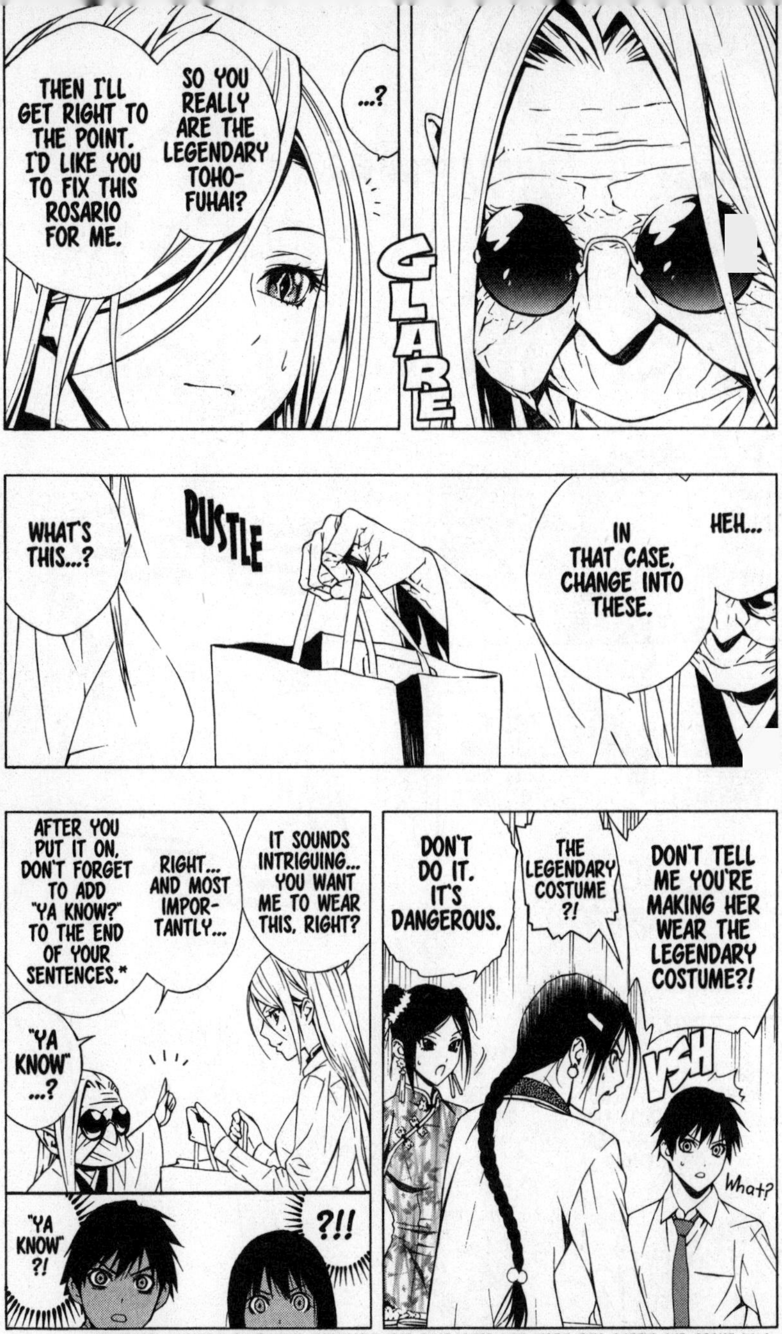
GLARE
...?
SO YOU REALLY ARE THE LEGENDARY TOHO-FUHAI?
THEN I'LL GET RIGHT TO THE POINT. I'D LIKE YOU TO FIX THIS ROSARIO FOR ME.
HEH...
IN THAT CASE, CHANGE INTO THESE.
RUSTLE
WHAT'S THIS...?
DON'T TELL ME YOU'RE MAKING HER WEAR THE LEGENDARY COSTUME?!
THE LEGENDARY COSTUME?!
DON'T DO IT. IT'S DANGEROUS.
VSH
What?
IT SOUNDS INTRIGUING... YOU WANT ME TO WEAR THIS, RIGHT?
RIGHT... AND MOST IMPORTANTLY...
AFTER YOU PUT IT ON, DON'T FORGET TO ADD "YA KNOW?" TO THE END OF YOUR SENTENCES.*
"YA KNOW" ...?
?!!
"YA KNOW" ?!



*IN URUSEI YATSURA, BY RUMIKO TAKAHASHI, THE CHARACTER LUM WORE THIS OUTFIT AND SPOKE IN A SENDAI DIALECT, ADDING "-CHA" OR "-DACCHA" TO HER LINES, WHICH ROUGHLY TRANSLATES AS "YA KNOW?"

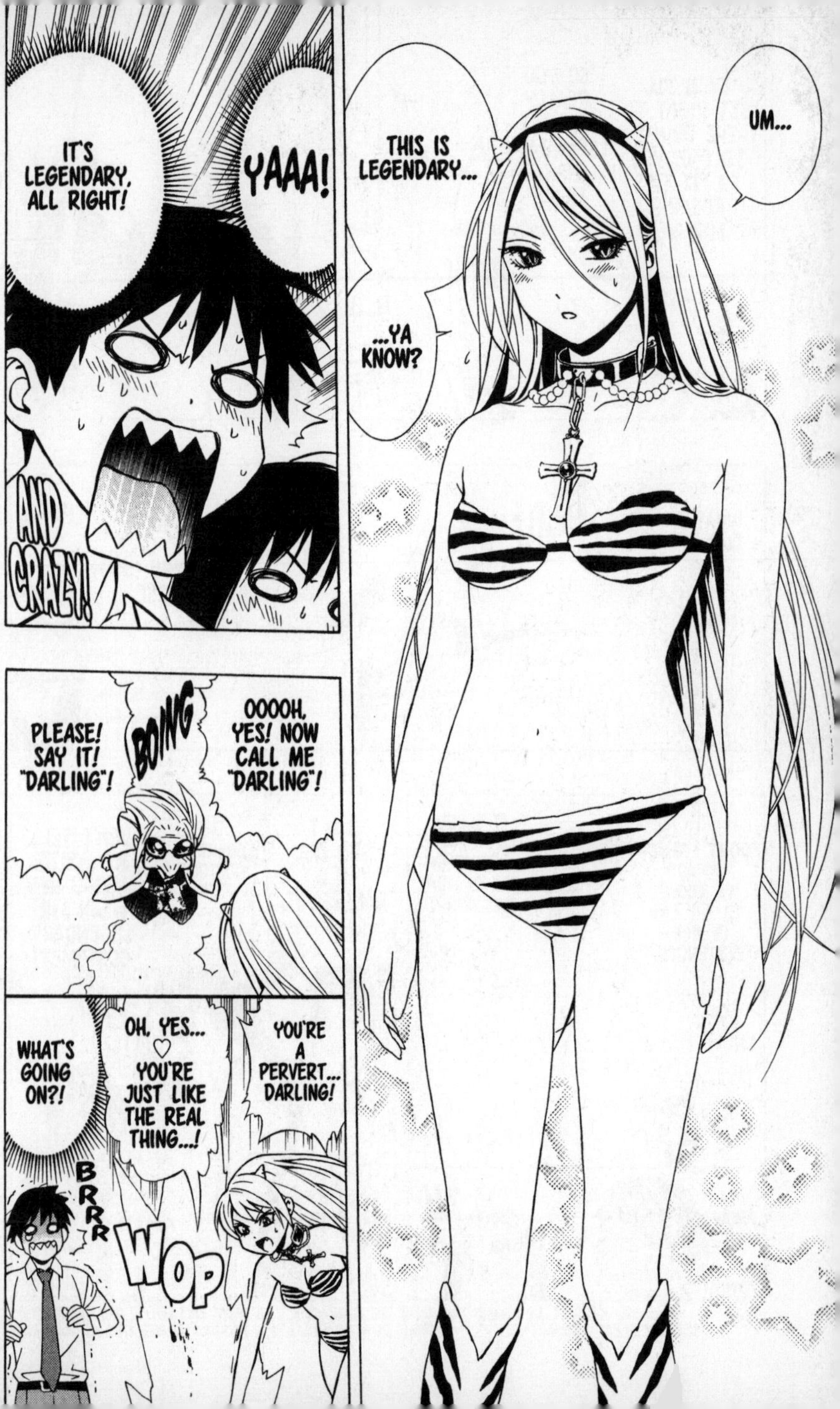
UM...
THIS IS LEGENDARY...
...YA KNOW?
YAAA!
IT'S LEGENDARY, ALL RIGHT!
AND CRAZY!
OOOOH, YES! NOW CALL ME "DARLING"!
BOING
PLEASE! SAY IT! "DARLING"!
YOU'RE A PERVERT... DARLING!
OH, YES... ♡ YOU'RE JUST LIKE THE REAL THING...!
WHAT'S GOING ON?!
BRRR
WOP

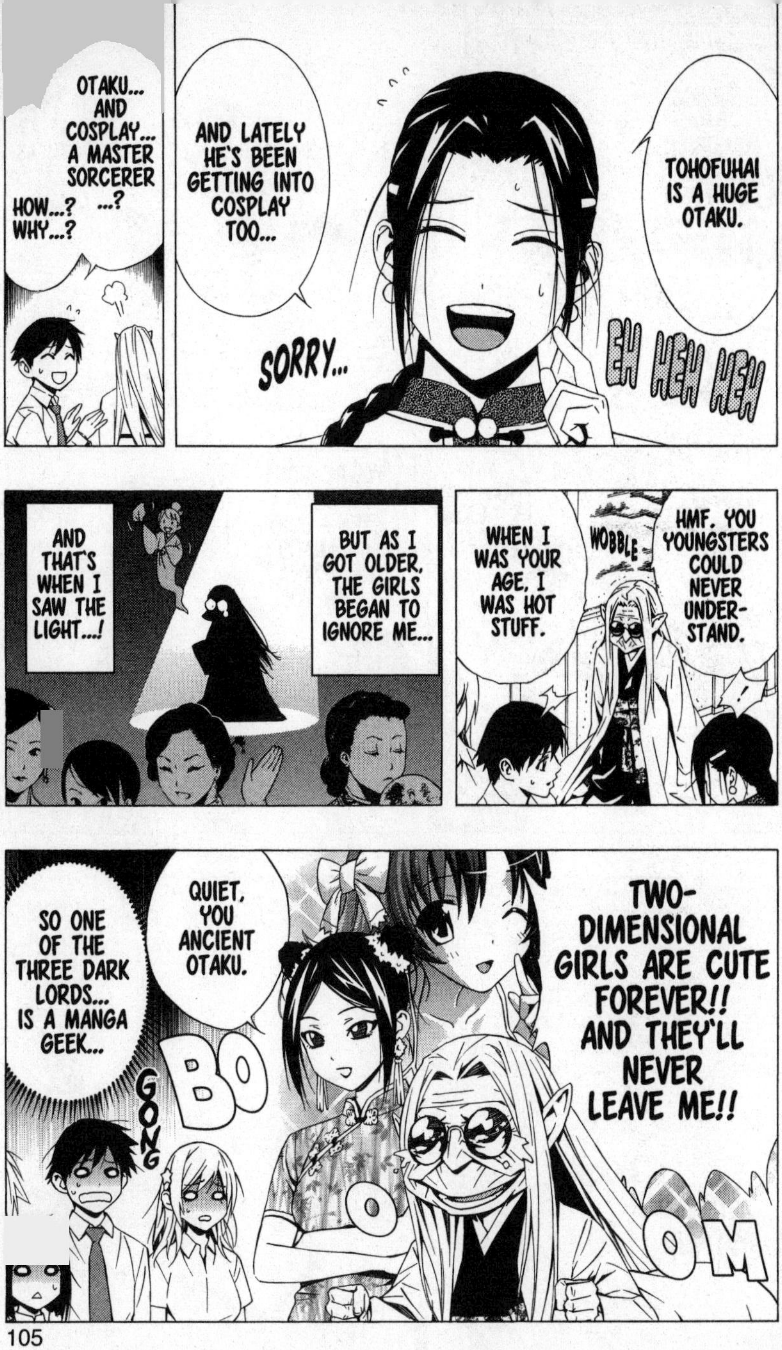
TOHOFUHAI IS A HUGE OTAKU.
EH HEH HEH
AND LATELY HE'S BEEN GETTING INTO COSPLAY TOO...
SORRY...
OTAKU... AND COSPLAY... A MASTER SORCERER ...?
HOW...? WHY...?
HMF. YOU YOUNGSTERS COULD NEVER UNDER-STAND.
WOBBLE
WHEN I WAS YOUR AGE, I WAS HOT STUFF.
BUT AS I GOT OLDER, THE GIRLS BEGAN TO IGNORE ME...
AND THAT'S WHEN I SAW THE LIGHT...!
TWO-DIMENSIONAL GIRLS ARE CUTE FOREVER!! AND THEY'LL NEVER LEAVE ME!!
BOOOM
QUIET, YOU ANCIENT OTAKU.
GONG
SO ONE OF THE THREE DARK LORDS... IS A MANGA GEEK...

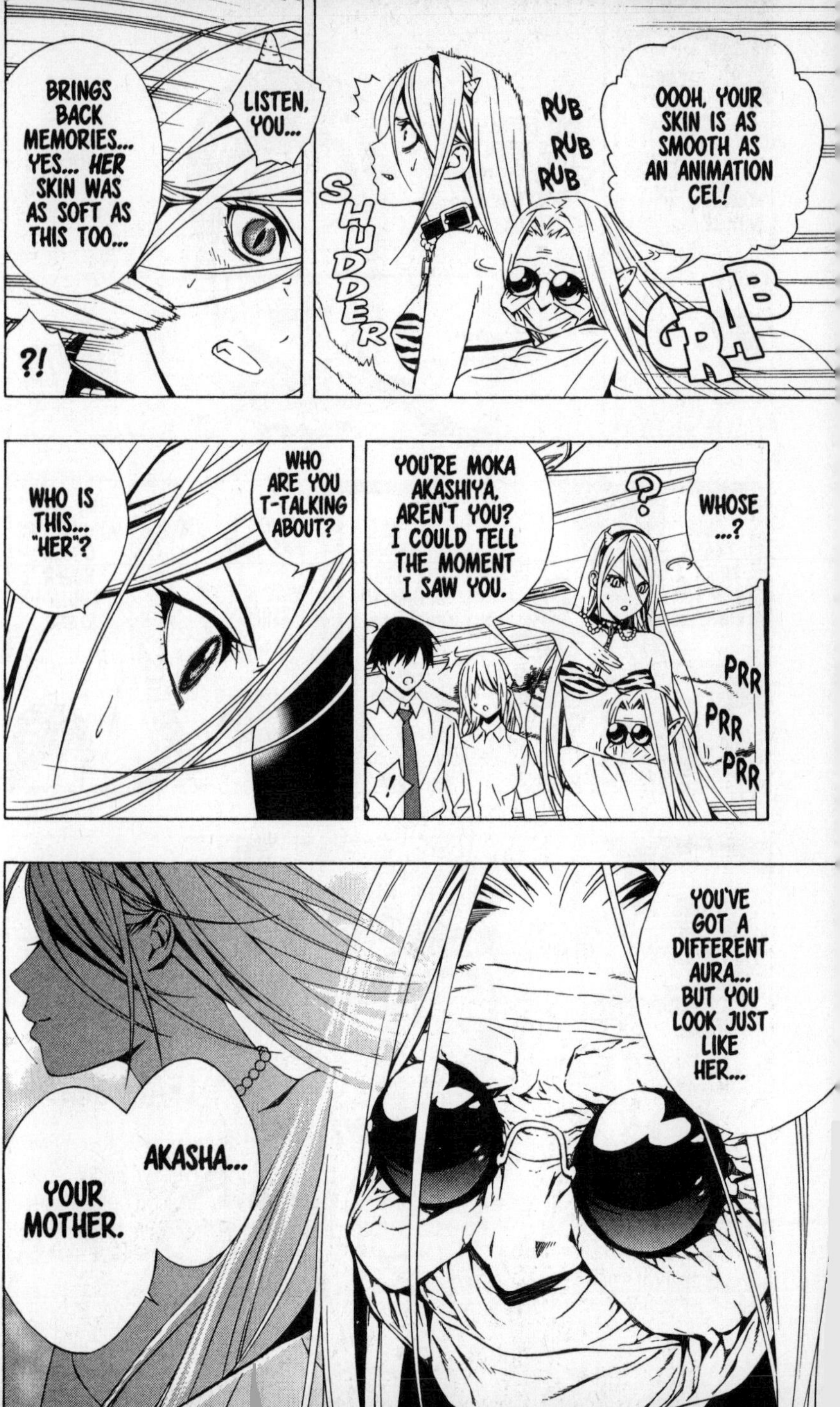
OOOH, YOUR SKIN IS AS SMOOTH AS AN ANIMATION CEL!
RUB RUB RUB
GRAB
SHUDDER
LISTEN, YOU...
BRINGS BACK MEMORIES... YES... HER SKIN WAS AS SOFT AS THIS TOO...
?!
WHOSE ...?
?
YOU'RE MOKA AKASHIYA, AREN'T YOU? I COULD TELL THE MOMENT I SAW YOU.
PRR PRR PRR
!
WHO ARE YOU T-TALKING ABOUT?
WHO IS THIS... "HER"?
YOU'VE GOT A DIFFERENT AURA... BUT YOU LOOK JUST LIKE HER...
AKASHA...
YOUR MOTHER.

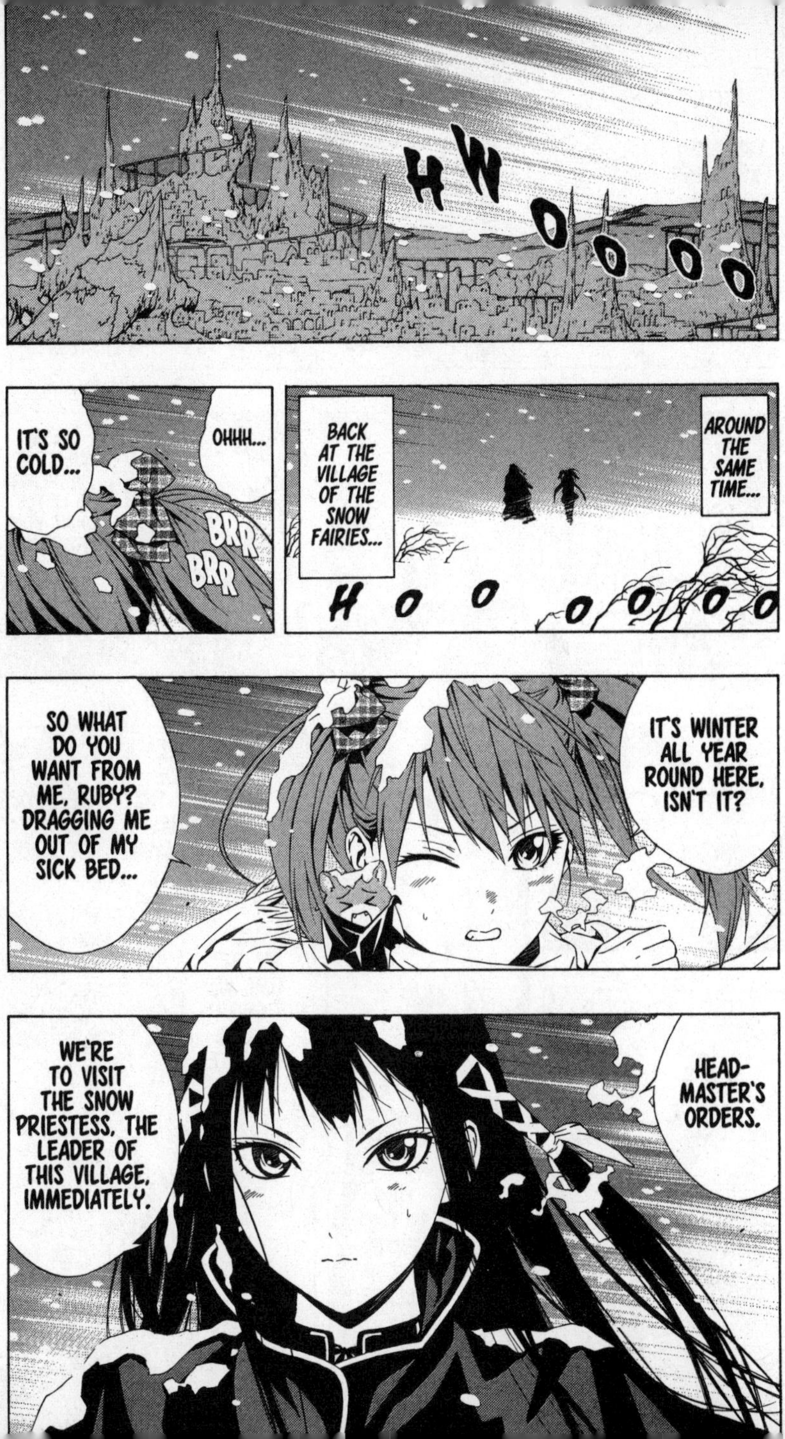
HWOOOOO
AROUND THE SAME TIME...
BACK AT THE VILLAGE OF THE SNOW FAIRIES...
HOOOOOOO
OHHH...
IT'S SO COLD...
BRR BRR
IT'S WINTER ALL YEAR ROUND HERE, ISN'T IT?
SO WHAT DO YOU WANT FROM ME, RUBY? DRAGGING ME OUT OF MY SICK BED...
HEAD-MASTER'S ORDERS.
WE'RE TO VISIT THE SNOW PRIESTESS, THE LEADER OF THIS VILLAGE, IMMEDIATELY.

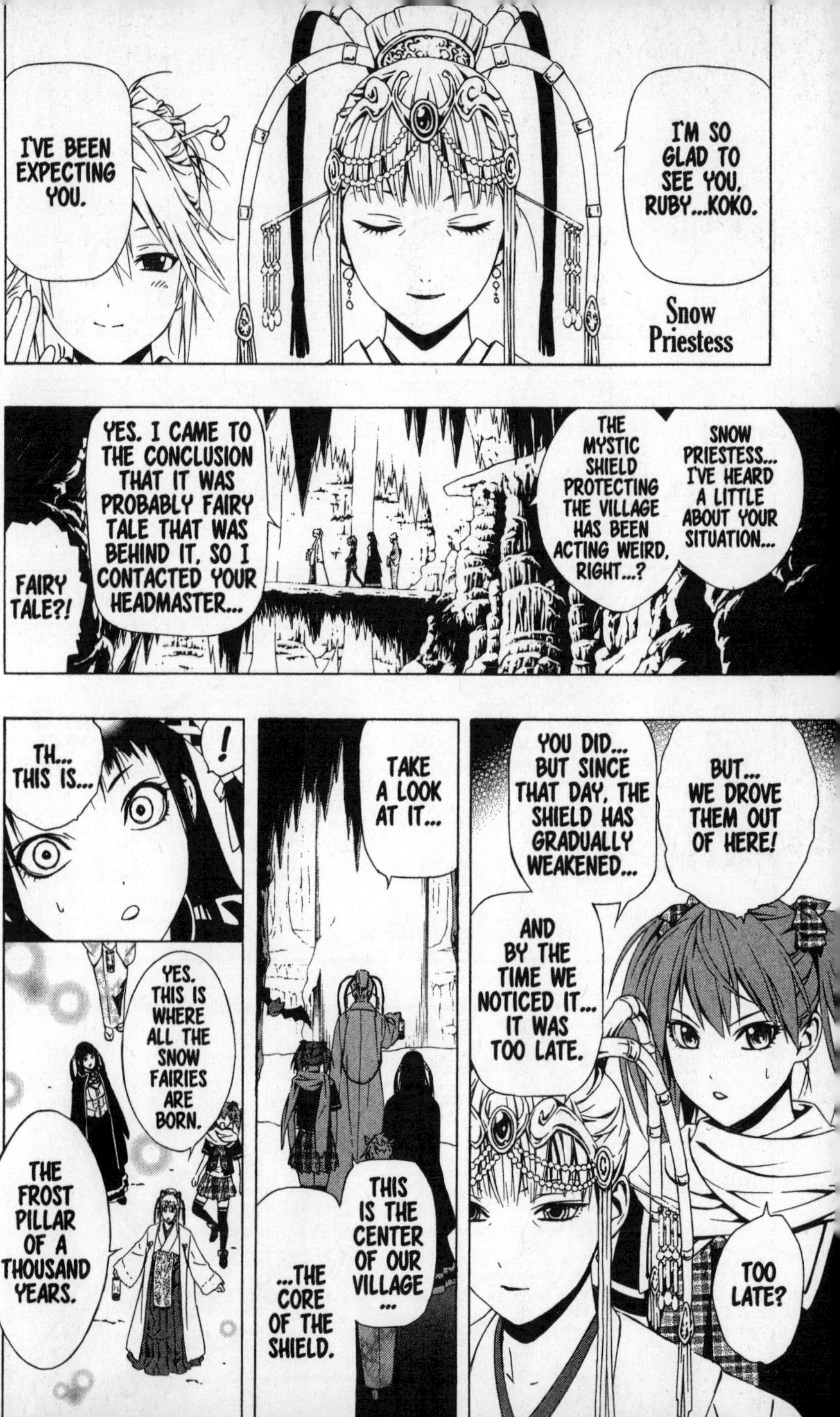
I'M SO GLAD TO SEE YOU, RUBY...KOKO.
I'VE BEEN EXPECTING YOU.
Snow Priestess
SNOW PRIESTESS... I'VE HEARD A LITTLE ABOUT YOUR SITUATION...
THE MYSTIC SHIELD PROTECTING THE VILLAGE HAS BEEN ACTING WEIRD, RIGHT...?
YES. I CAME TO THE CONCLUSION THAT IT WAS PROBABLY FAIRY TALE THAT WAS BEHIND IT, SO I CONTACTED YOUR HEADMASTER...
FAIRY TALE?!
BUT... WE DROVE THEM OUT OF HERE!
YOU DID... BUT SINCE THAT DAY, THE SHIELD HAS GRADUALLY WEAKENED...
AND BY THE TIME WE NOTICED IT... IT WAS TOO LATE.
TOO LATE?
TAKE A LOOK AT IT...
THIS IS THE CENTER OF OUR VILLAGE...
...THE CORE OF THE SHIELD.
!
TH... THIS IS...
YES. THIS IS WHERE ALL THE SNOW FAIRIES ARE BORN.
THE FROST PILLAR OF A THOUSAND YEARS.

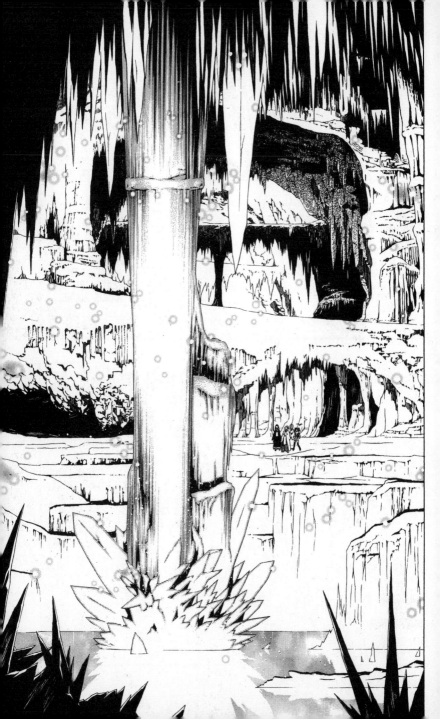

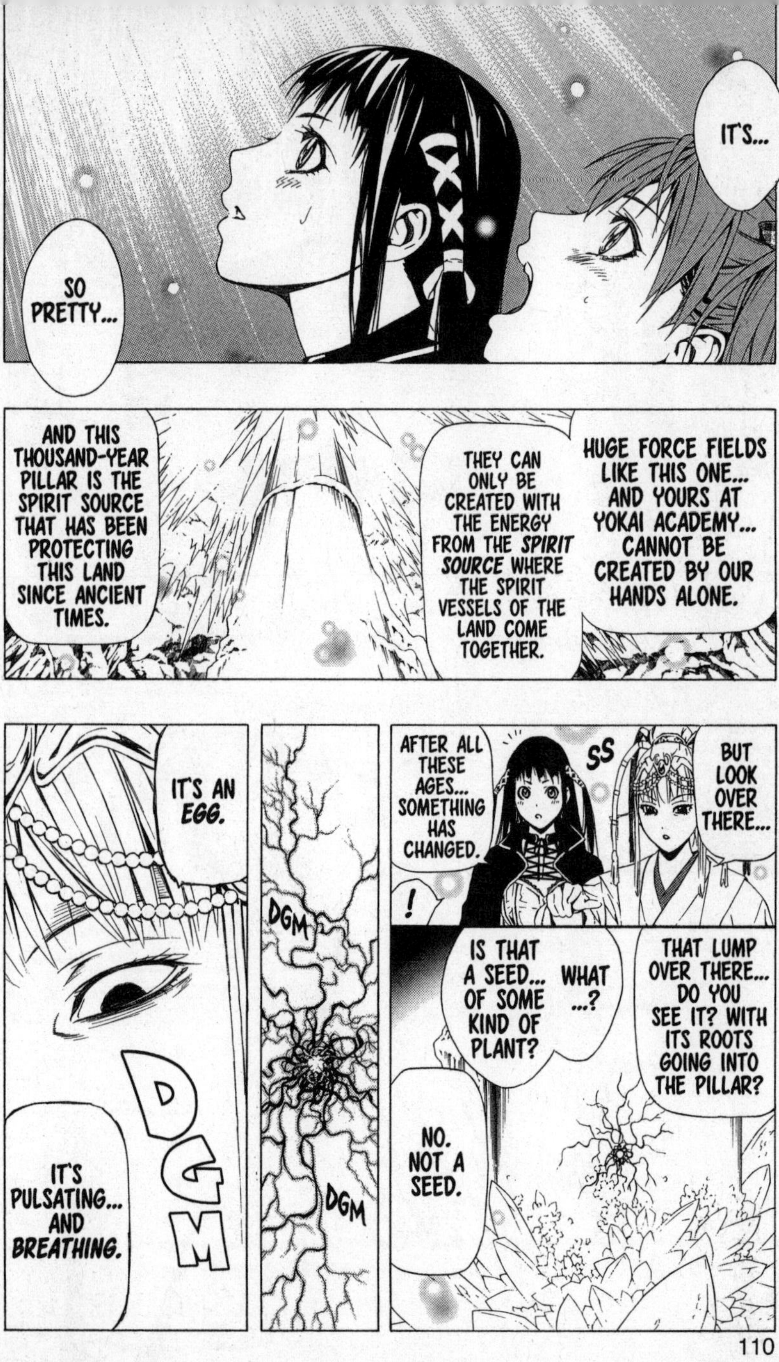
IT'S...
SO PRETTY...
HUGE FORCE FIELDS LIKE THIS ONE... AND YOURS AT YOKAI ACADEMY... CANNOT BE CREATED BY OUR HANDS ALONE.
THEY CAN ONLY BE CREATED WITH THE ENERGY FROM THE *SPIRIT SOURCE* WHERE THE SPIRIT VESSELS OF THE LAND COME TOGETHER.
AND THIS THOUSAND-YEAR PILLAR IS THE SPIRIT SOURCE THAT HAS BEEN PROTECTING THIS LAND SINCE ANCIENT TIMES.
BUT LOOK OVER THERE...
SS
AFTER ALL THESE AGES... SOMETHING HAS CHANGED.
!
THAT LUMP OVER THERE... DO YOU SEE IT? WITH ITS ROOTS GOING INTO THE PILLAR?
WHAT ...?
IS THAT A SEED... OF SOME KIND OF PLANT?
NO. NOT A SEED.
DGM
DGM
IT'S AN *EGG.*
DGM
IT'S PULSATING... AND *BREATHING.*

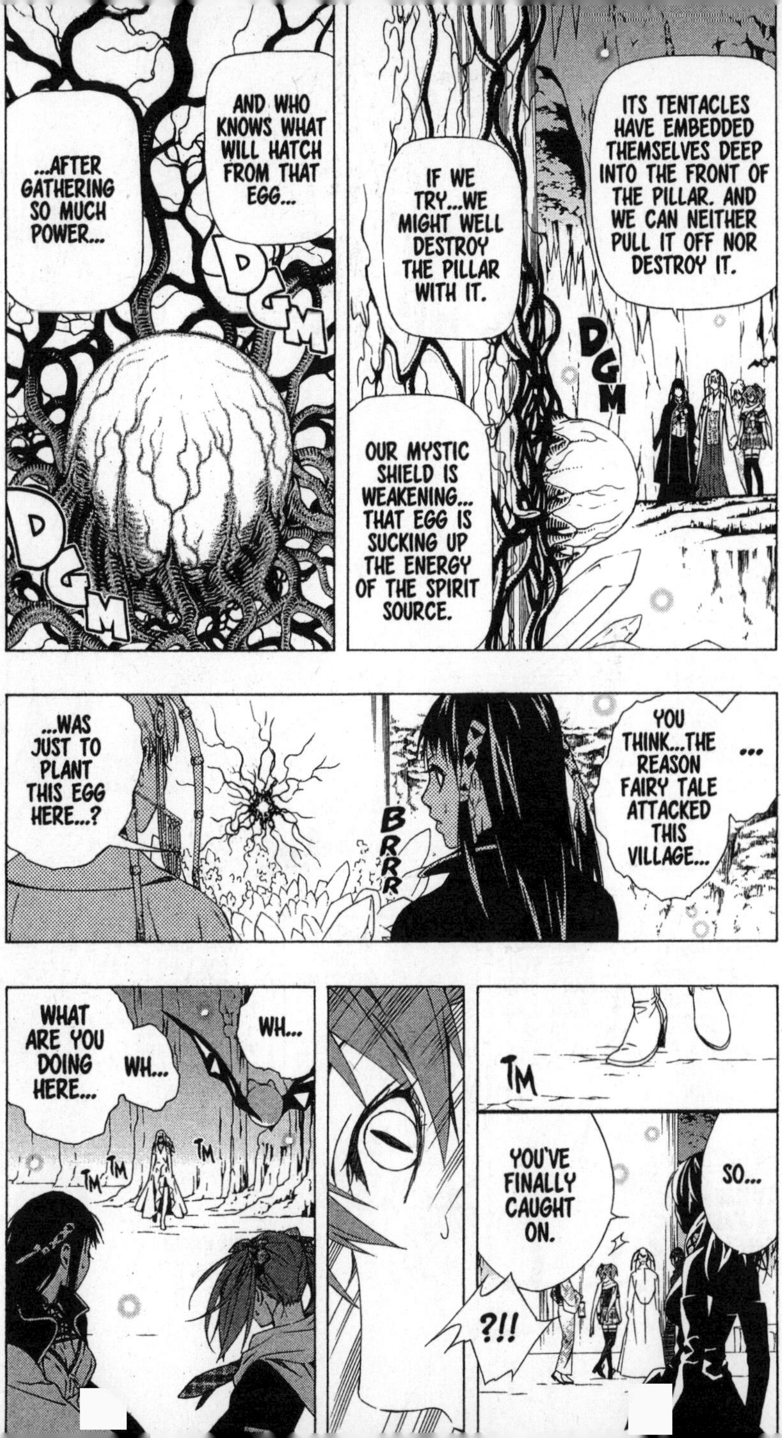
ITS TENTACLES HAVE EMBEDDED THEMSELVES DEEP INTO THE FRONT OF THE PILLAR. AND WE CAN NEITHER PULL IT OFF NOR DESTROY IT.
IF WE TRY...WE MIGHT WELL DESTROY THE PILLAR WITH IT.
DGM
OUR MYSTIC SHIELD IS WEAKENING... THAT EGG IS SUCKING UP THE ENERGY OF THE SPIRIT SOURCE.
AND WHO KNOWS WHAT WILL HATCH FROM THAT EGG...
...AFTER GATHERING SO MUCH POWER...
DGM
DGM
...
YOU THINK...THE REASON FAIRY TALE ATTACKED THIS VILLAGE...
BRRR
...WAS JUST TO PLANT THIS EGG HERE...?
TM
SO...
YOU'VE FINALLY CAUGHT ON.
?!!
WH...
WH...
WHAT ARE YOU DOING HERE...
TM
TM
TM

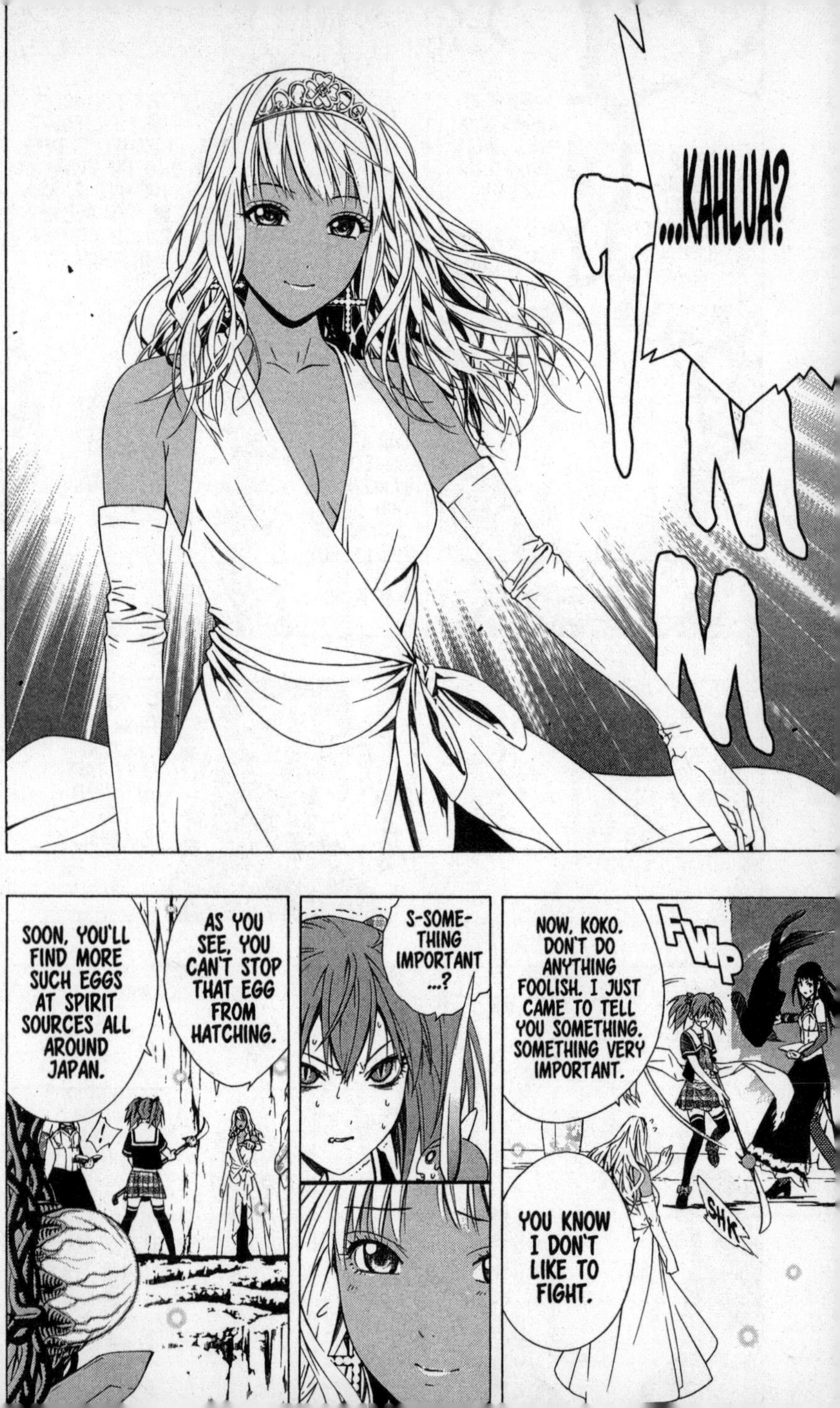
...KAHLUA?
FWP
NOW, KOKO. DON'T DO ANYTHING FOOLISH. I JUST CAME TO TELL YOU SOMETHING. SOMETHING VERY IMPORTANT.
SHK
YOU KNOW I DON'T LIKE TO FIGHT.
S-SOME-THING IMPORTANT ...?
AS YOU SEE, YOU CAN'T STOP THAT EGG FROM HATCHING.
SOON, YOU'LL FIND MORE SUCH EGGS AT SPIRIT SOURCES ALL AROUND JAPAN.

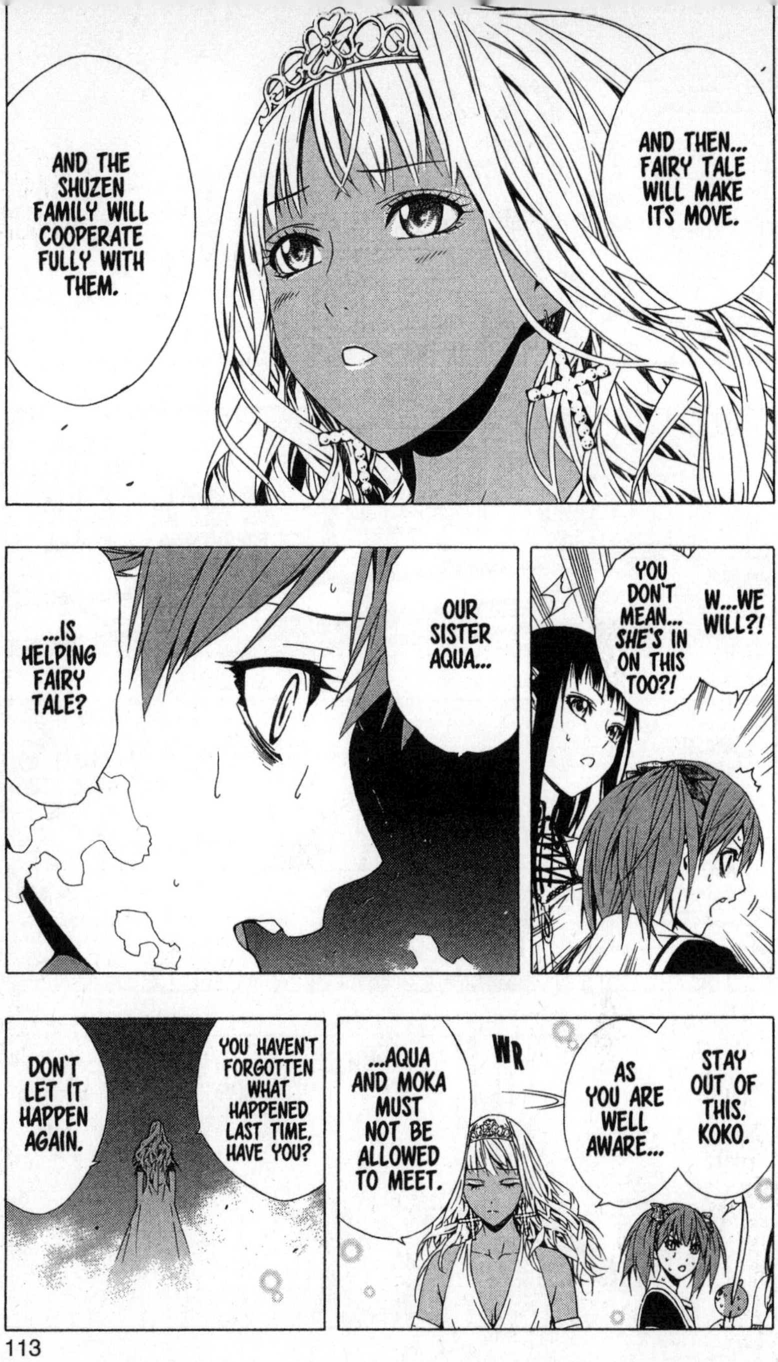
AND THEN... FAIRY TALE WILL MAKE ITS MOVE.
AND THE SHUZEN FAMILY WILL COOPERATE FULLY WITH THEM.
W...WE WILL?!
YOU DON'T MEAN... SHE'S IN ON THIS TOO?!
OUR SISTER AQUA...
...IS HELPING FAIRY TALE?
STAY OUT OF THIS, KOKO.
AS YOU ARE WELL AWARE...
WR
...AQUA AND MOKA MUST NOT BE ALLOWED TO MEET.
YOU HAVEN'T FORGOTTEN WHAT HAPPENED LAST TIME, HAVE YOU?
DON'T LET IT HAPPEN AGAIN.

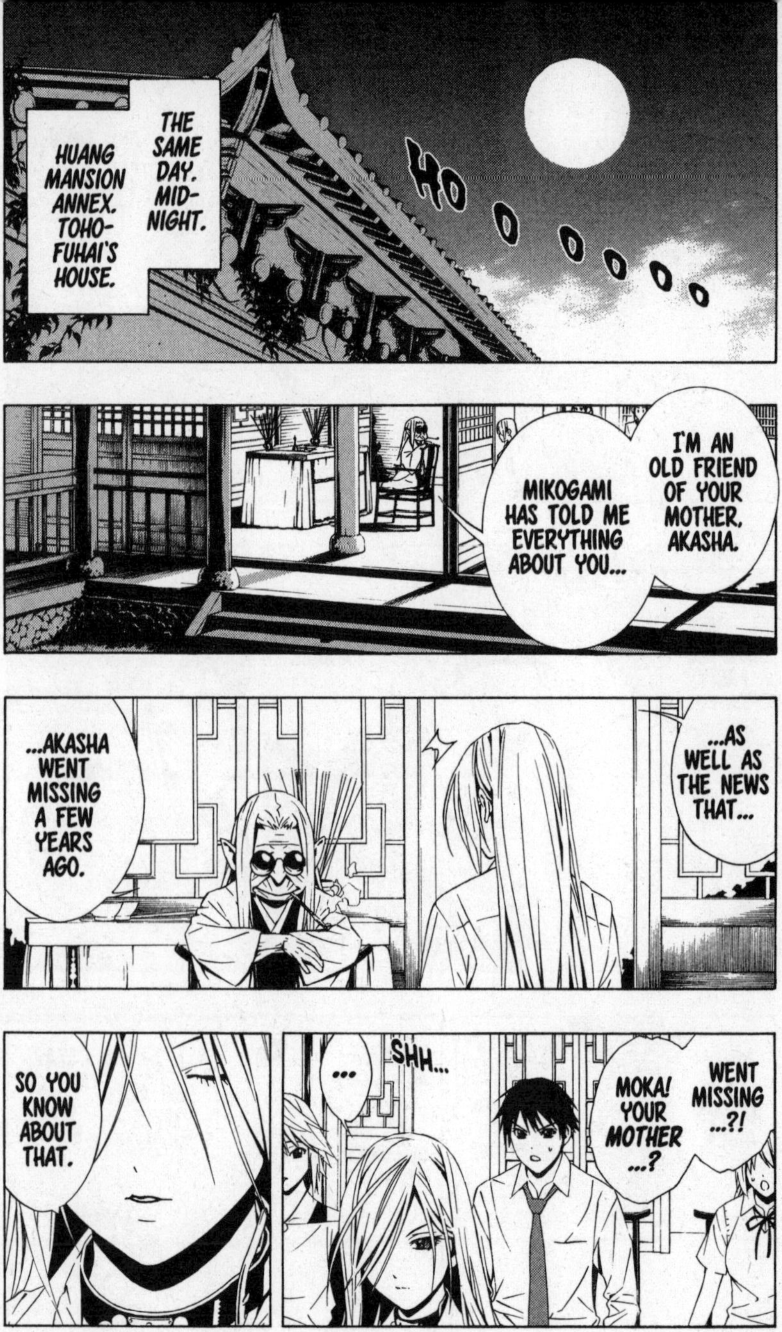
THE SAME DAY. MID-NIGHT.
HUANG MANSION ANNEX. TOHO-FUHAI'S HOUSE.
HOOOOOO
I'M AN OLD FRIEND OF YOUR MOTHER, AKASHA.
MIKOGAMI HAS TOLD ME EVERYTHING ABOUT YOU...
...AS WELL AS THE NEWS THAT...
...AKASHA WENT MISSING A FEW YEARS AGO.
WENT MISSING ...?!
MOKA! YOUR MOTHER ...?
SHH...
...
SO YOU KNOW ABOUT THAT.

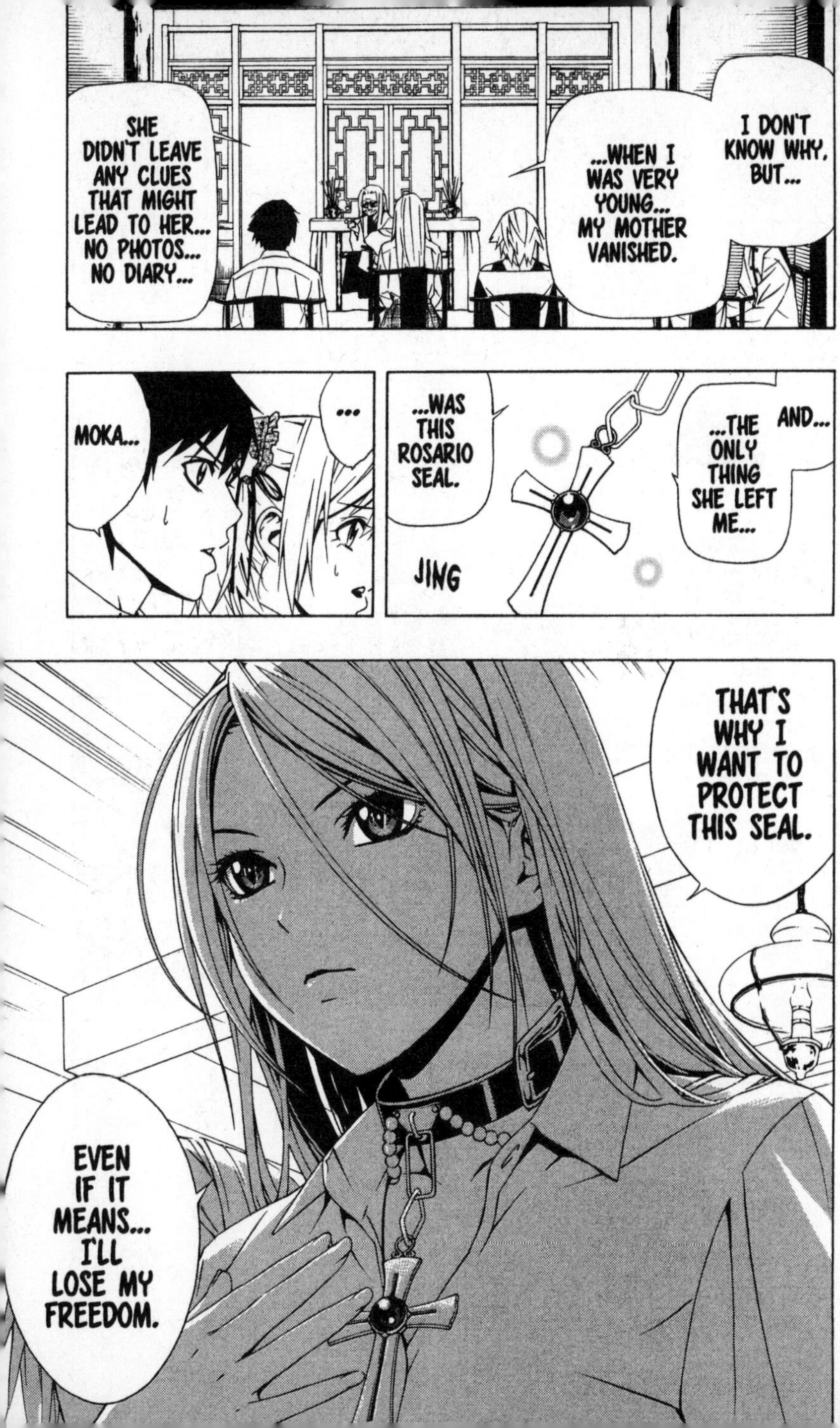
I DON'T KNOW WHY, BUT...
...WHEN I WAS VERY YOUNG... MY MOTHER VANISHED.
SHE DIDN'T LEAVE ANY CLUES THAT MIGHT LEAD TO HER... NO PHOTOS... NO DIARY...
AND...
...THE ONLY THING SHE LEFT ME...
...WAS THIS ROSARIO SEAL.
JING
...
MOKA...
THAT'S WHY I WANT TO PROTECT THIS SEAL.
EVEN IF IT MEANS... I'LL LOSE MY FREEDOM.

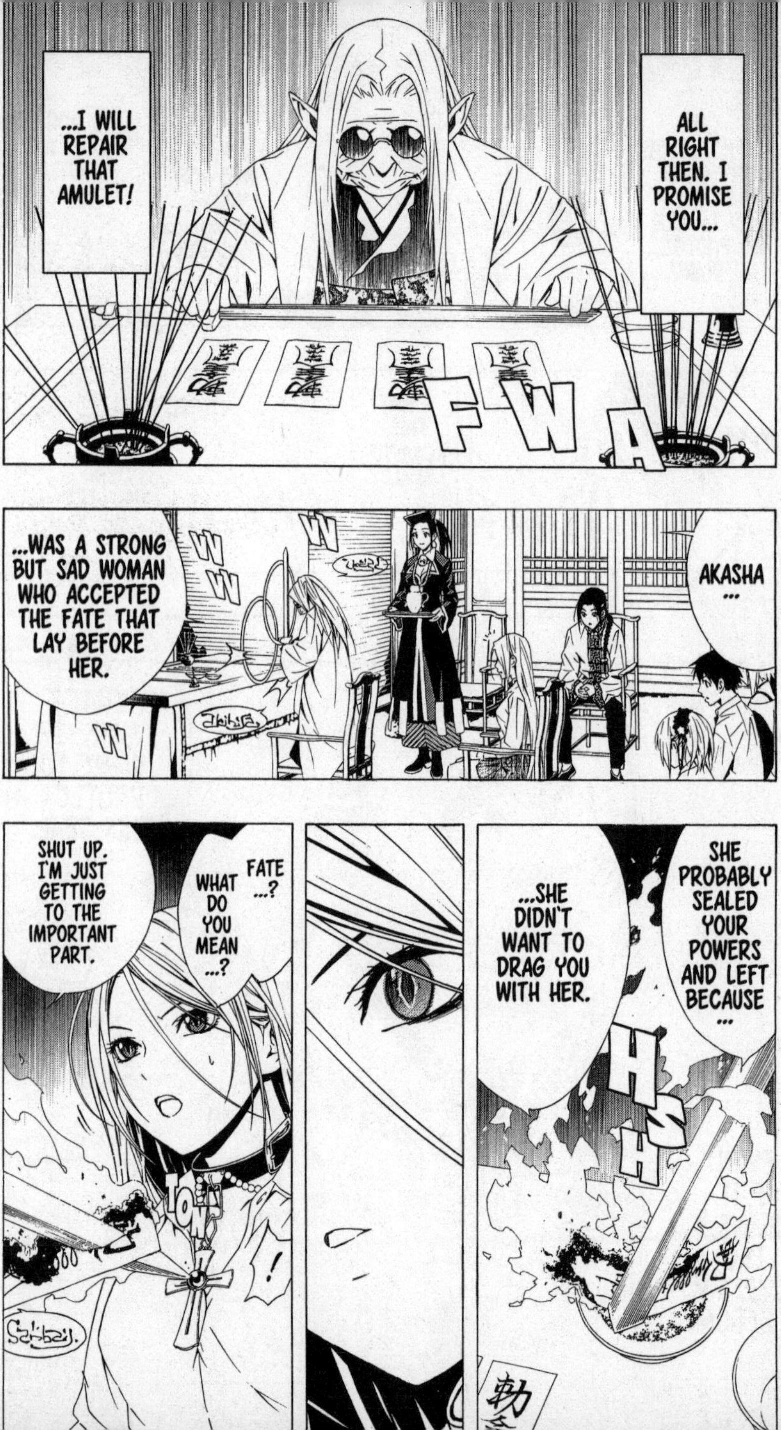
ALL RIGHT THEN. I PROMISE YOU...
...I WILL REPAIR THAT AMULET!
FWA
AKASHA ...
...WAS A STRONG BUT SAD WOMAN WHO ACCEPTED THE FATE THAT LAY BEFORE HER.
SHE PROBABLY SEALED YOUR POWERS AND LEFT BECAUSE ...
...SHE DIDN'T WANT TO DRAG YOU WITH HER.
HSH
FATE ...?
WHAT DO YOU MEAN ...?
SHUT UP. I'M JUST GETTING TO THE IMPORTANT PART.
TON
!

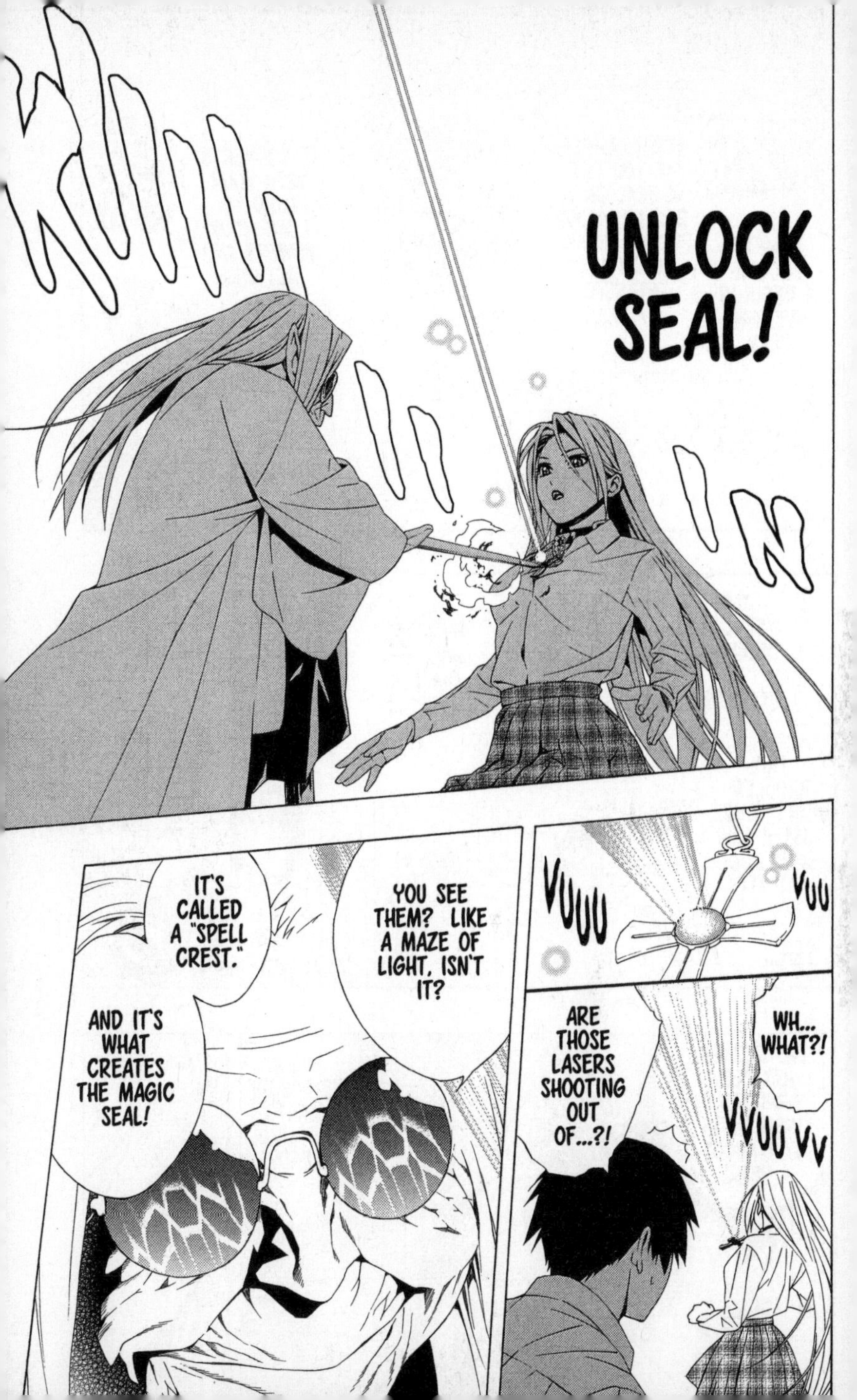
UNLOCK SEAL!
VUUU
VUU
WH... WHAT?!
ARE THOSE LASERS SHOOTING OUT OF...?!
VVUUU VV
YOU SEE THEM? LIKE A MAZE OF LIGHT, ISN'T IT?
IT'S CALLED A "SPELL CREST."
AND IT'S WHAT CREATES THE MAGIC SEAL!

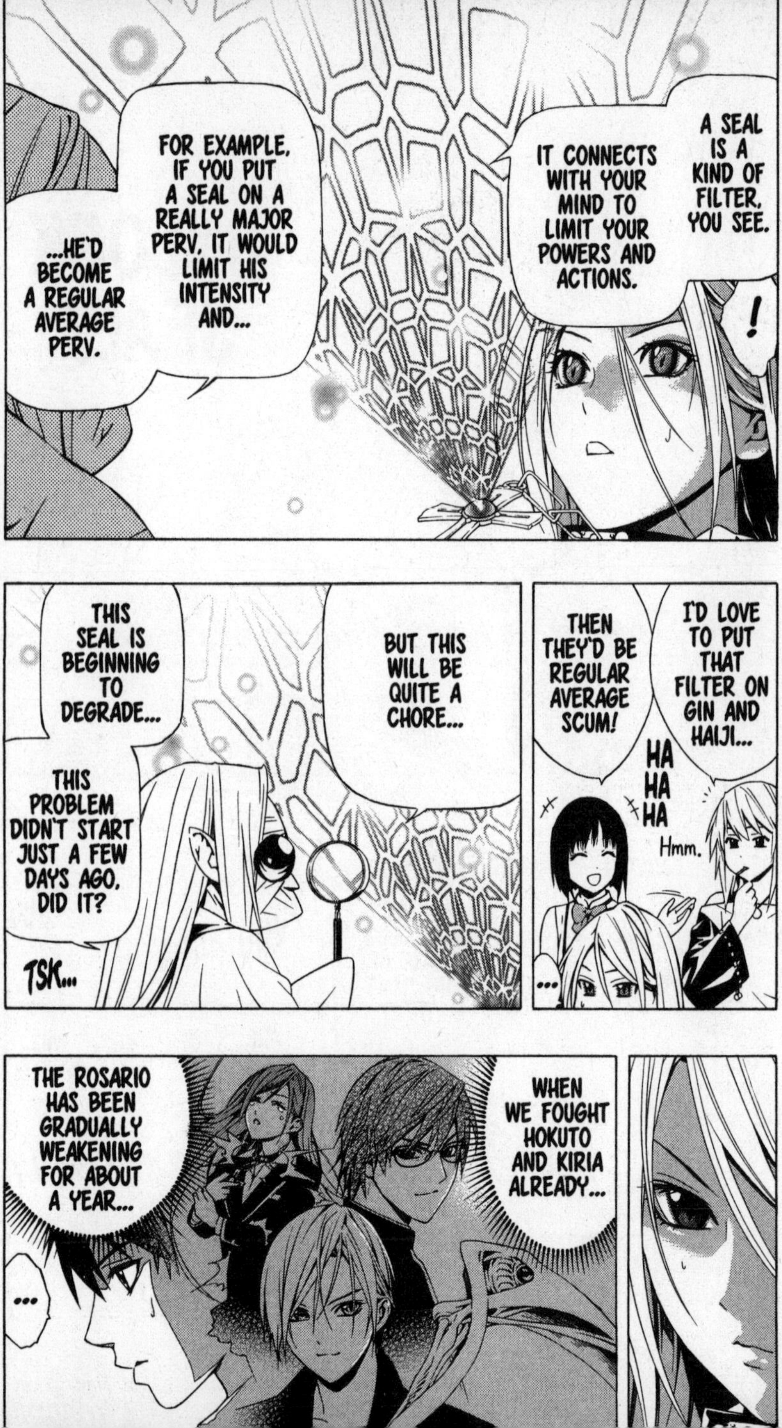
A SEAL IS A KIND OF FILTER, YOU SEE.
IT CONNECTS WITH YOUR MIND TO LIMIT YOUR POWERS AND ACTIONS.
!
FOR EXAMPLE, IF YOU PUT A SEAL ON A REALLY MAJOR PERV, IT WOULD LIMIT HIS INTENSITY AND...
...HE'D BECOME A REGULAR AVERAGE PERV.
I'D LOVE TO PUT THAT FILTER ON GIN AND HAIJI...
THEN THEY'D BE REGULAR AVERAGE SCUM!
HA HA HA
Hmm.
...
BUT THIS WILL BE QUITE A CHORE...
THIS SEAL IS BEGINNING TO DEGRADE...
THIS PROBLEM DIDN'T START JUST A FEW DAYS AGO, DID IT?
TSK...
WHEN WE FOUGHT HOKUTO AND KIRIA ALREADY...
THE ROSARIO HAS BEEN GRADUALLY WEAKENING FOR ABOUT A YEAR...
...

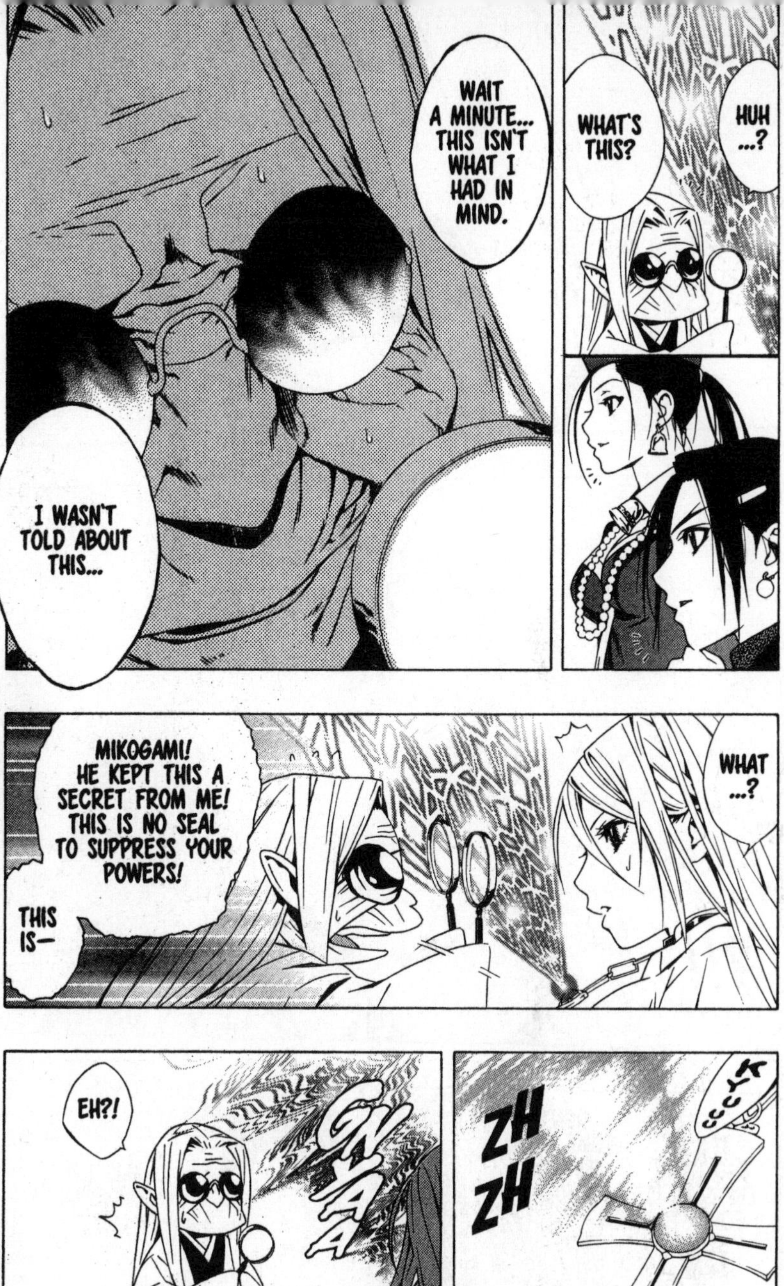
HUH ...?
WHAT'S THIS?
WAIT A MINUTE... THIS ISN'T WHAT I HAD IN MIND.
I WASN'T TOLD ABOUT THIS...
WHAT ...?
MIKOGAMI! HE KEPT THIS A SECRET FROM ME! THIS IS NO SEAL TO SUPPRESS YOUR POWERS!
THIS IS—
KYUCCC
ZH ZH
GNYAA
EH?!

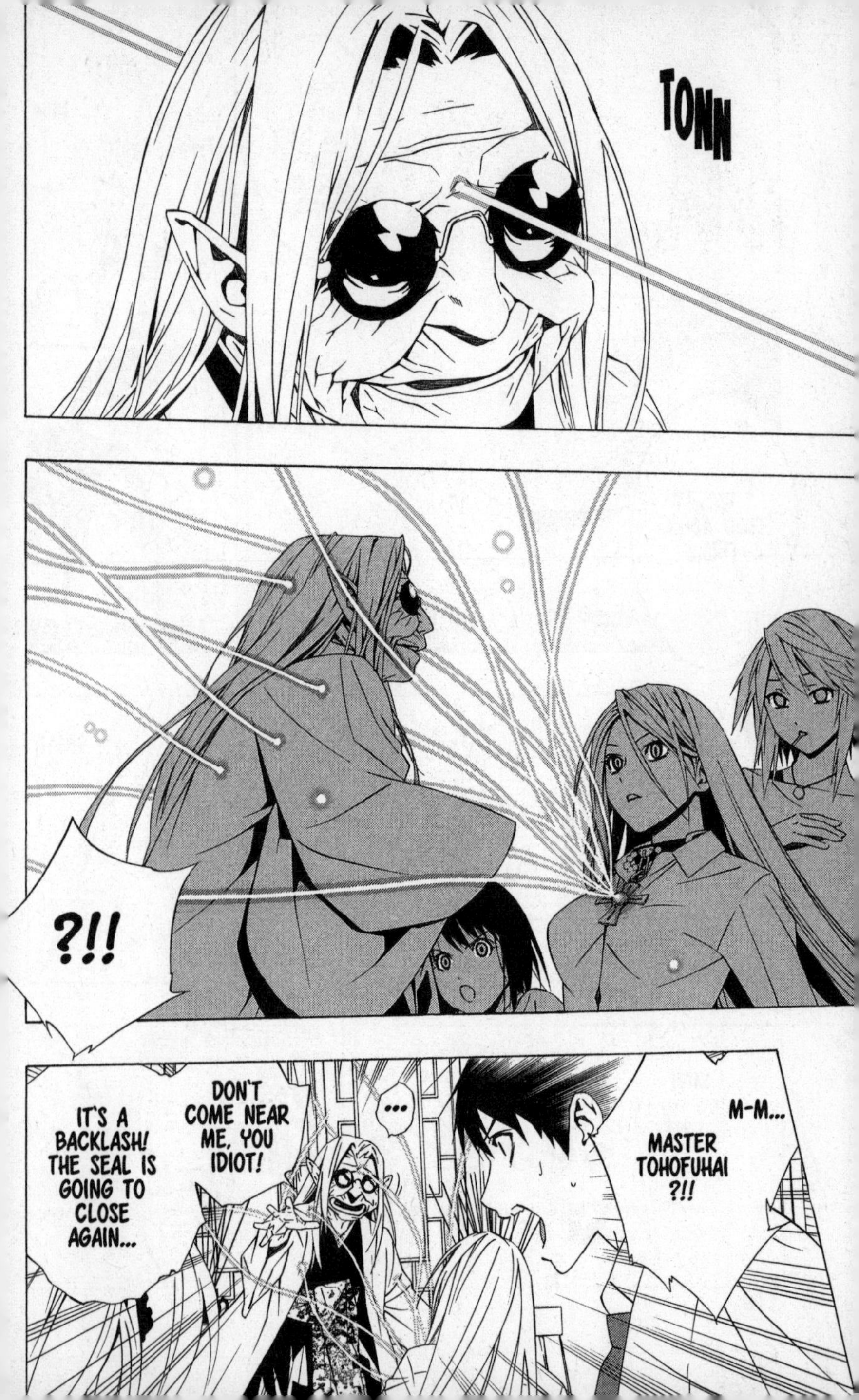
TONN
?!!
M-M...
MASTER TOHOFUHAI ?!!
...
DON'T COME NEAR ME, YOU IDIOT!
IT'S A BACKLASH! THE SEAL IS GOING TO CLOSE AGAIN...

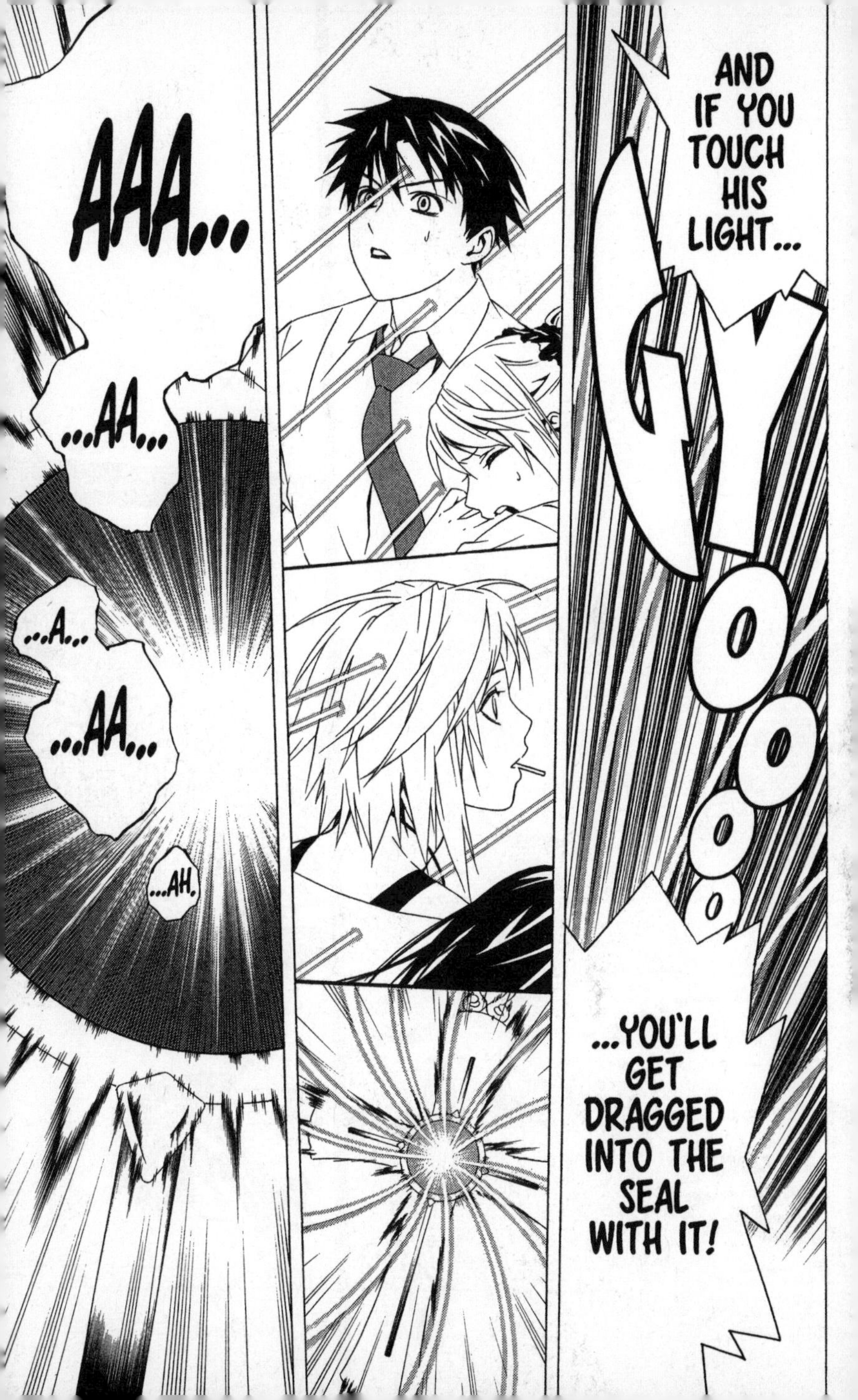

AND IF YOU TOUCH HIS LIGHT...
GYOOOO
...YOU'LL GET DRAGGED INTO THE SEAL WITH IT!
AAA...
...AA...
...A...
...AA...
...AH.

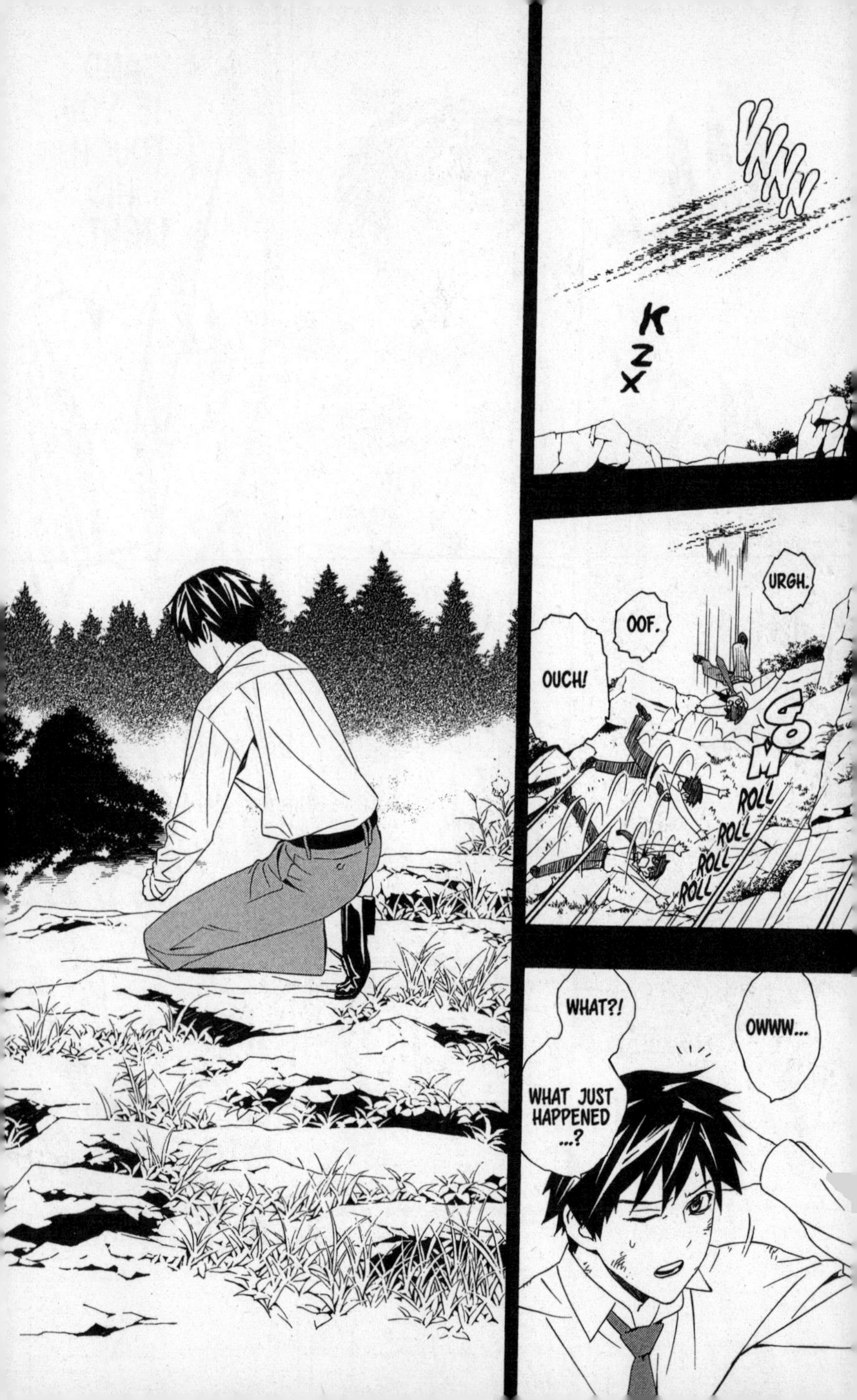
VNNNN
KZX
URGH.
OOF.
OUCH!
GOM
ROLL
ROLL
ROLL
ROLL
OWWW...
WHAT?!
WHAT JUST HAPPENED ...?

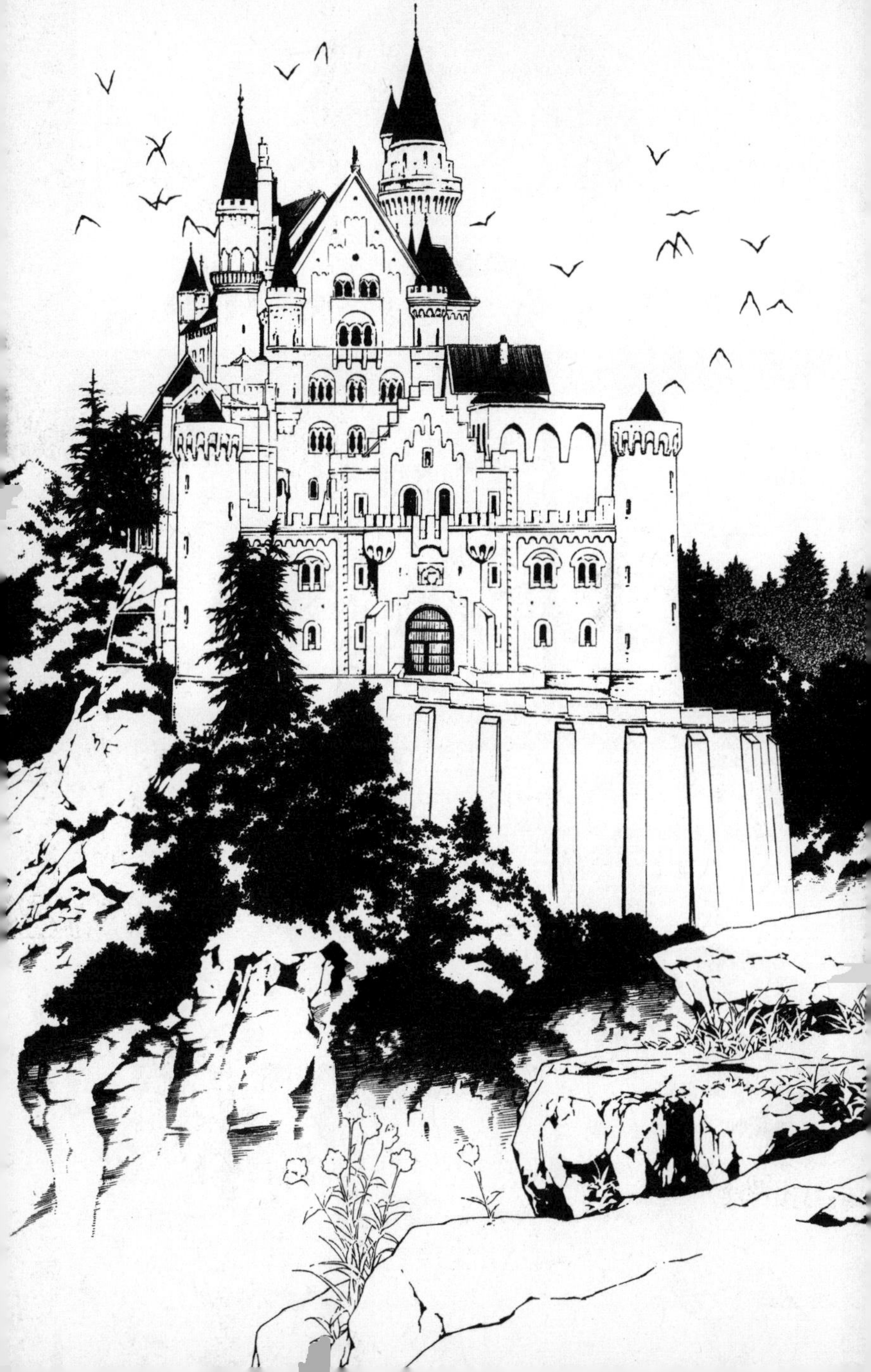

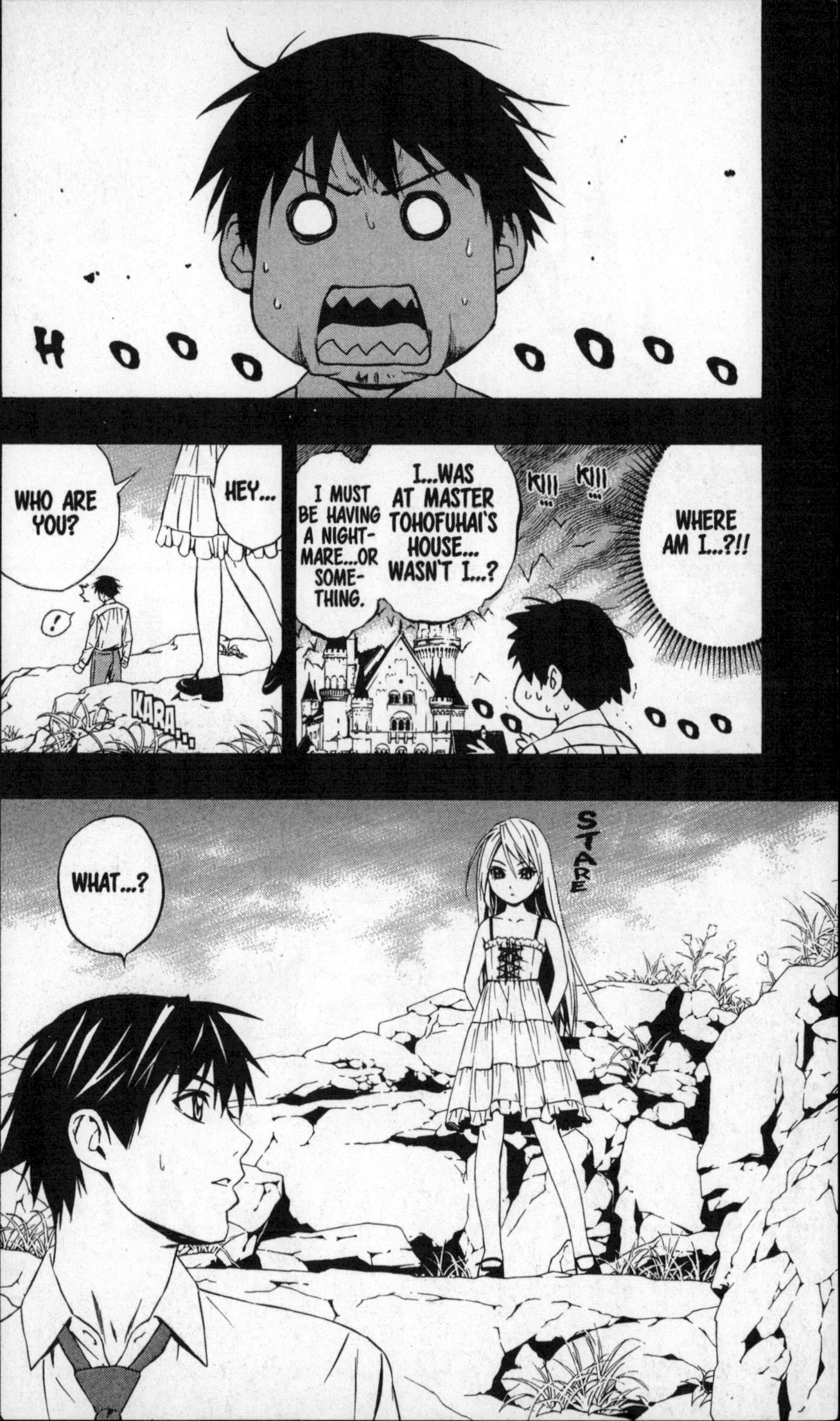
HOOOOOOOOO
KIII KIII
WHERE AM I...?!!
I...WAS AT MASTER TOHOFUHAI'S HOUSE... WASN'T I...?
I MUST BE HAVING A NIGHTMARE...OR SOMETHING.
HEY...
WHO ARE YOU?
!
KARA...
STARE
WHAT...?

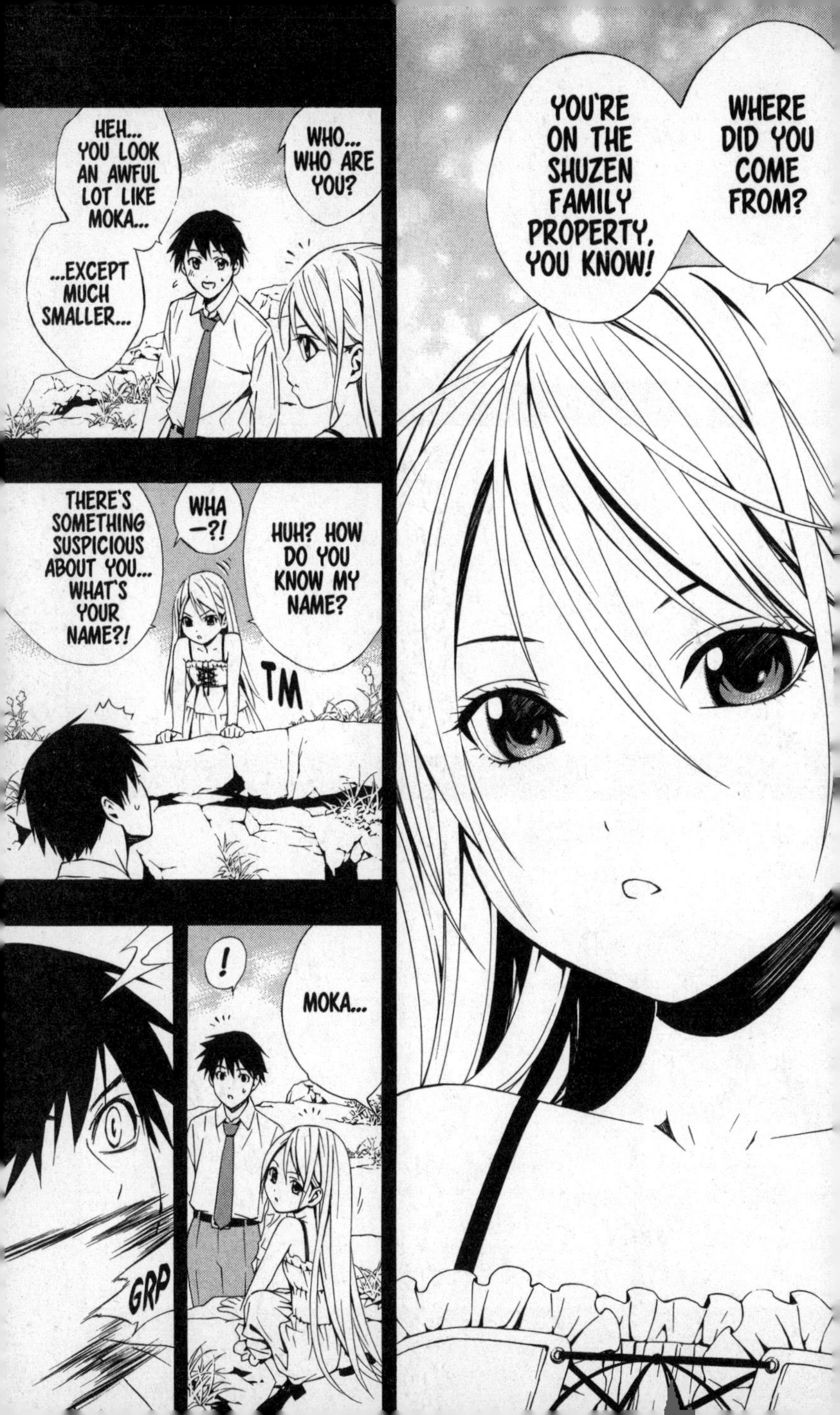
WHERE DID YOU COME FROM?
YOU'RE ON THE SHUZEN FAMILY PROPERTY, YOU KNOW!
WHO... WHO ARE YOU?
HEH... YOU LOOK AN AWFUL LOT LIKE MOKA...
...EXCEPT MUCH SMALLER...
HUH? HOW DO YOU KNOW MY NAME?
WHA—?!
THERE'S SOMETHING SUSPICIOUS ABOUT YOU... WHAT'S YOUR NAME?!
TM
MOKA...
!
GRP

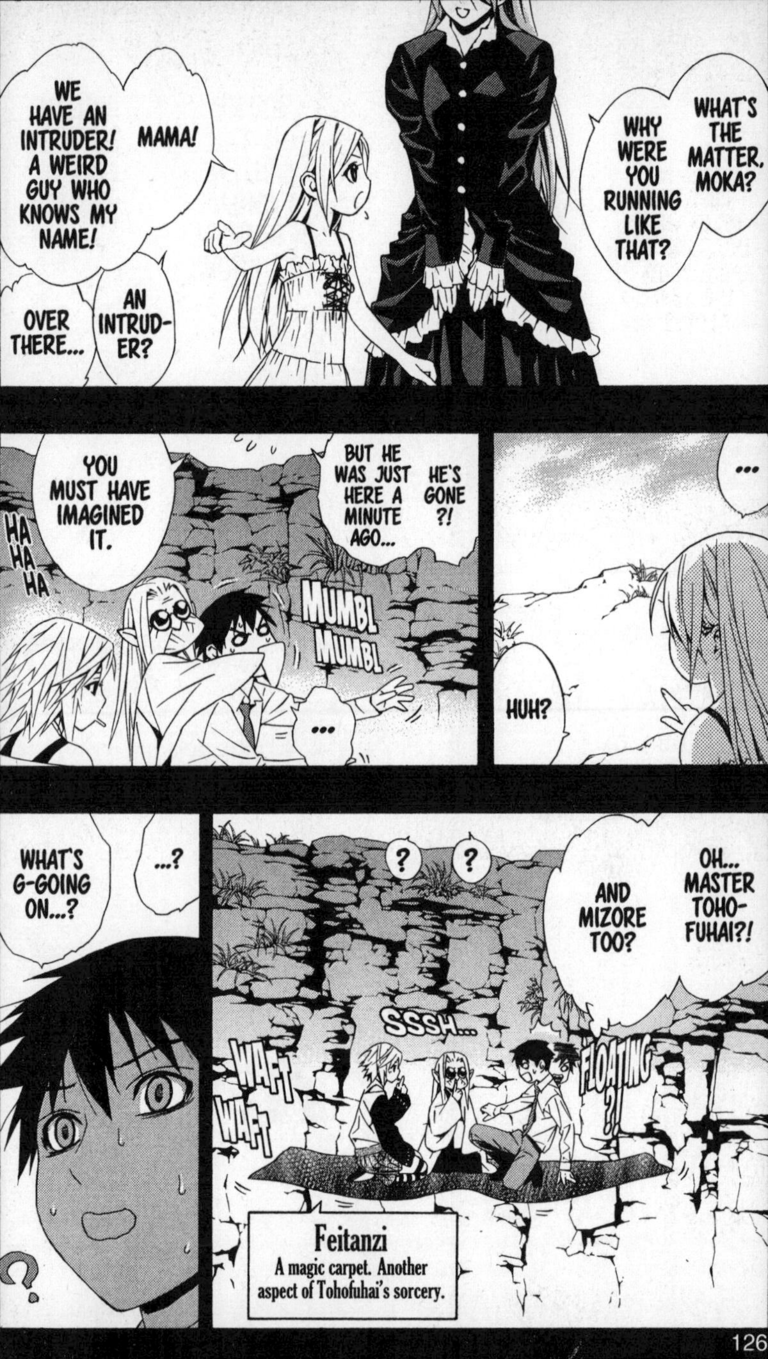
WHAT'S THE MATTER, MOKA?
WHY WERE YOU RUNNING LIKE THAT?
MAMA!
WE HAVE AN INTRUDER! A WEIRD GUY WHO KNOWS MY NAME!
AN INTRUDER?
OVER THERE...
...
HUH?
HE'S GONE?!
BUT HE WAS JUST HERE A MINUTE AGO...
YOU MUST HAVE IMAGINED IT.
HA HA HA
MUMBL MUMBL
...
OH... MASTER TOHOFUHAI?!
AND MIZORE TOO?
?
?
SSSH...
FLOATING?!
WAFT WAFT
Feitanzi
A magic carpet. Another aspect of Tohofuhai's sorcery.
...?
WHAT'S G-GOING ON...?

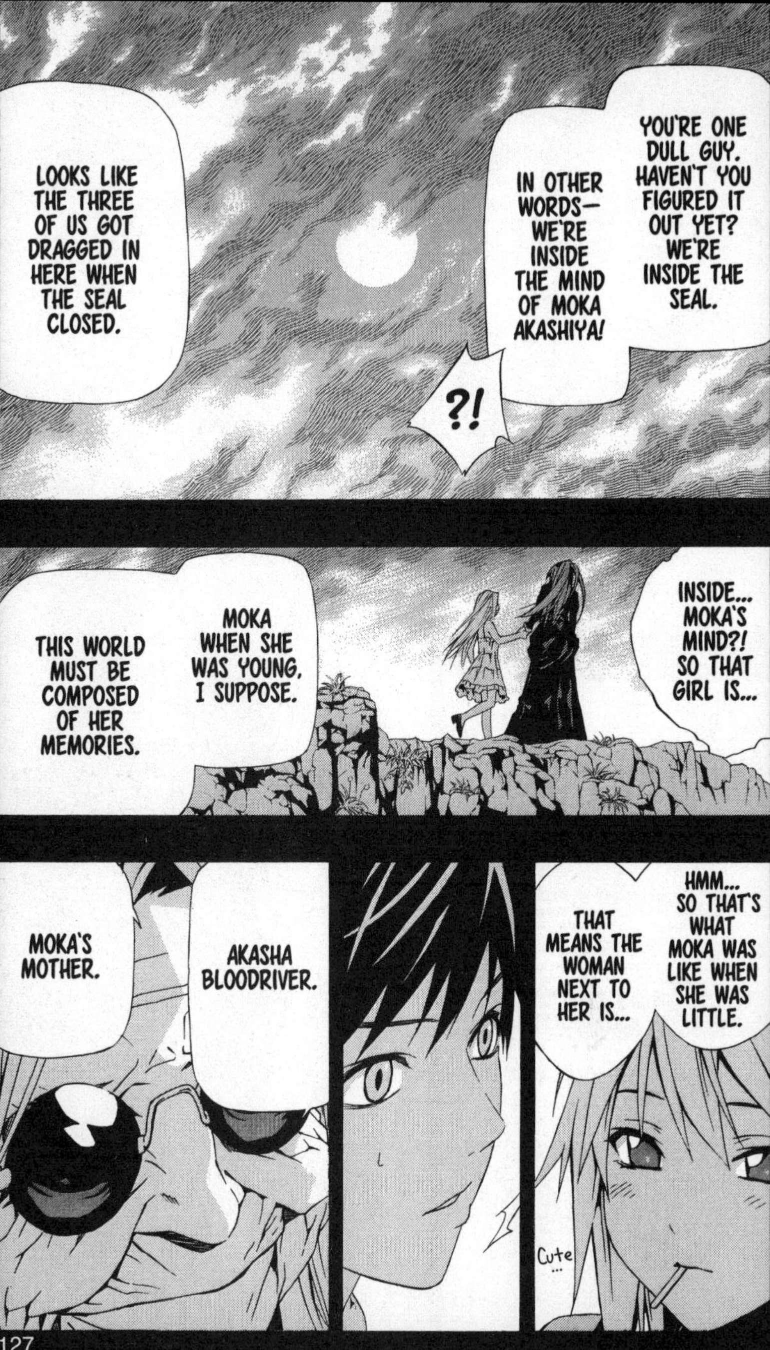
YOU'RE ONE DULL GUY. HAVEN'T YOU FIGURED IT OUT YET? WE'RE INSIDE THE SEAL.
IN OTHER WORDS— WE'RE INSIDE THE MIND OF MOKA AKASHIYA!
LOOKS LIKE THE THREE OF US GOT DRAGGED IN HERE WHEN THE SEAL CLOSED.
?!
INSIDE... MOKA'S MIND?! SO THAT GIRL IS...
MOKA WHEN SHE WAS YOUNG, I SUPPOSE.
THIS WORLD MUST BE COMPOSED OF HER MEMORIES.
HMM... SO THAT'S WHAT MOKA WAS LIKE WHEN SHE WAS LITTLE.
THAT MEANS THE WOMAN NEXT TO HER IS...
Cute...
AKASHA BLOODRIVER.
MOKA'S MOTHER.

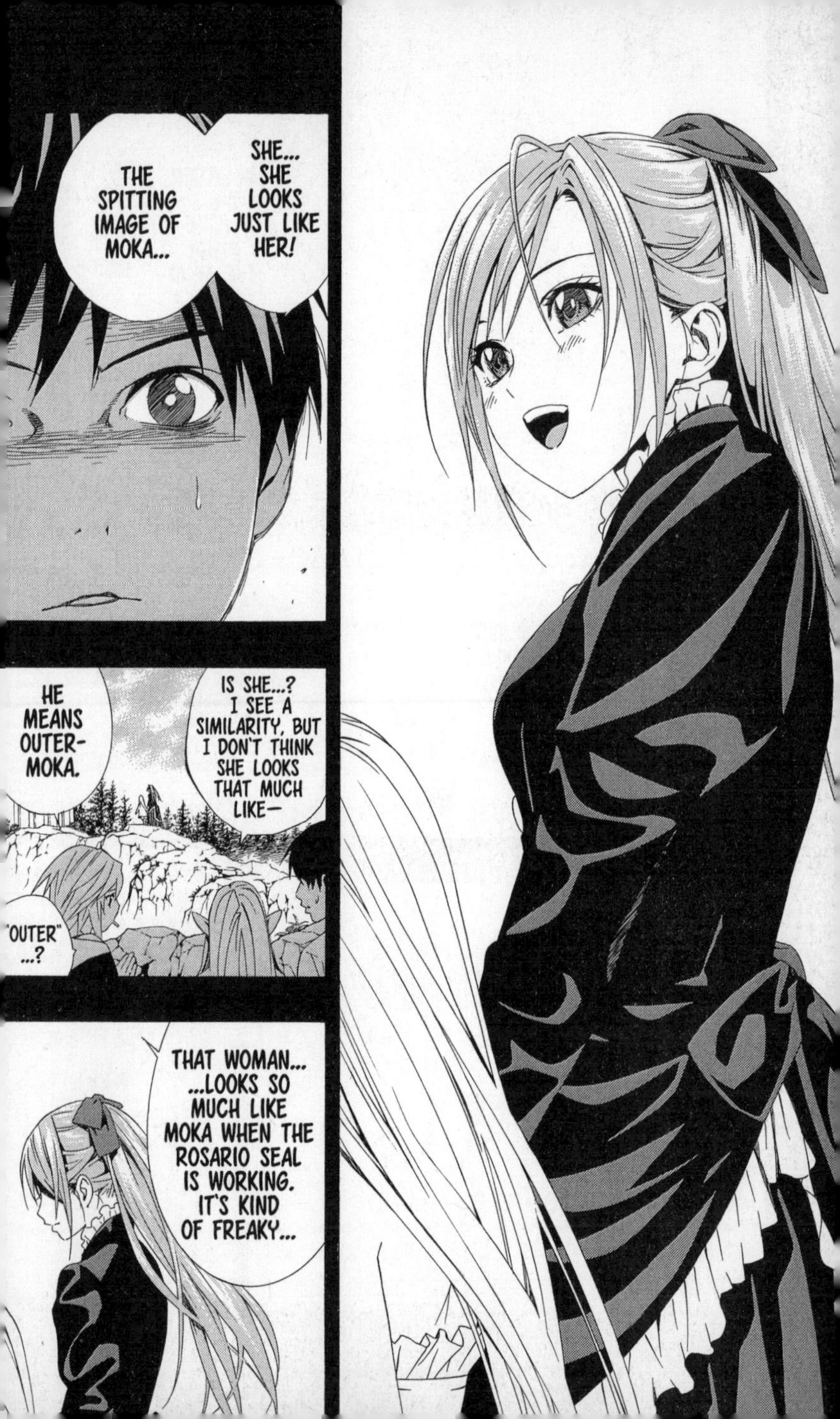
SHE... SHE LOOKS JUST LIKE HER!
THE SPITTING IMAGE OF MOKA...
IS SHE...? I SEE A SIMILARITY, BUT I DON'T THINK SHE LOOKS THAT MUCH LIKE—
HE MEANS OUTER-MOKA.
"OUTER" ...?
THAT WOMAN... ...LOOKS SO MUCH LIKE MOKA WHEN THE ROSARIO SEAL IS WORKING. IT'S KIND OF FREAKY...

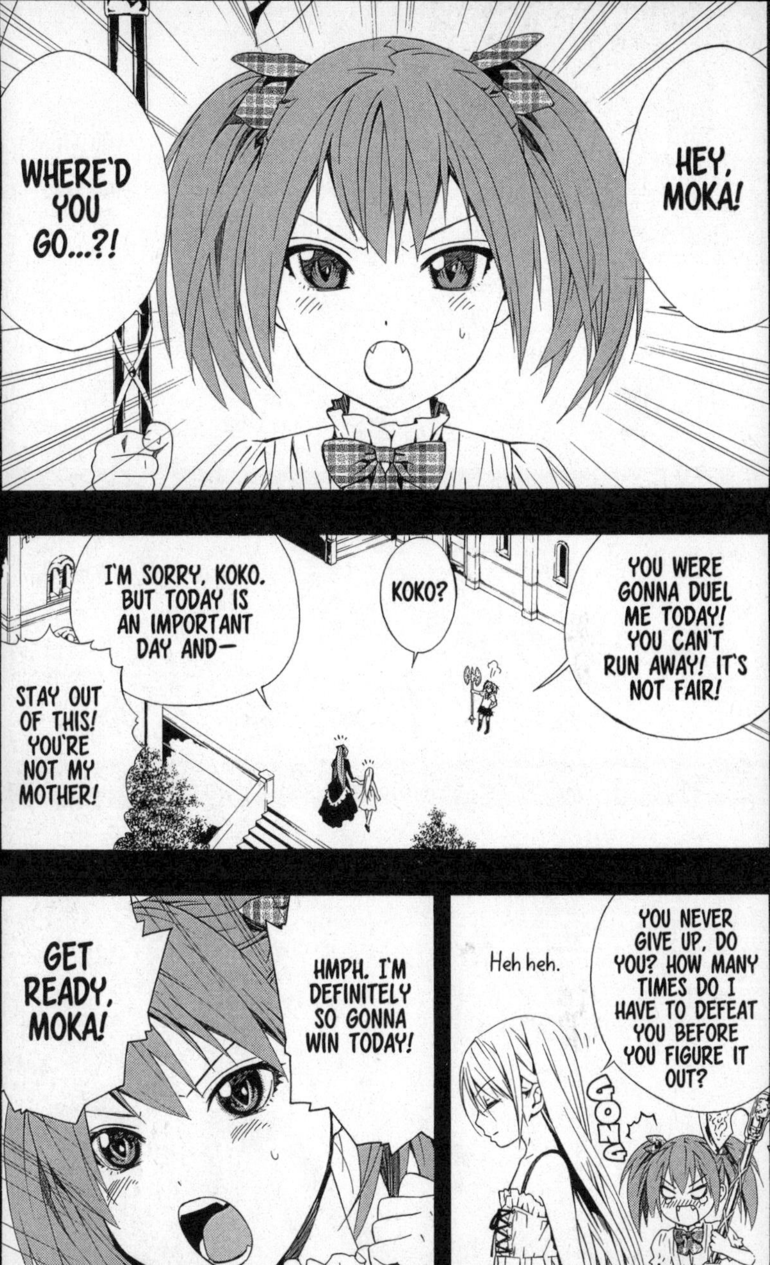
HEY, MOKA!
WHERE'D YOU GO...?!
YOU WERE GONNA DUEL ME TODAY! YOU CAN'T RUN AWAY! IT'S NOT FAIR!
KOKO?
I'M SORRY, KOKO. BUT TODAY IS AN IMPORTANT DAY AND—
STAY OUT OF THIS! YOU'RE NOT MY MOTHER!
YOU NEVER GIVE UP, DO YOU? HOW MANY TIMES DO I HAVE TO DEFEAT YOU BEFORE YOU FIGURE IT OUT?
Heh heh.
GONG
HMPH. I'M DEFINITELY SO GONNA WIN TODAY!
GET READY, MOKA!

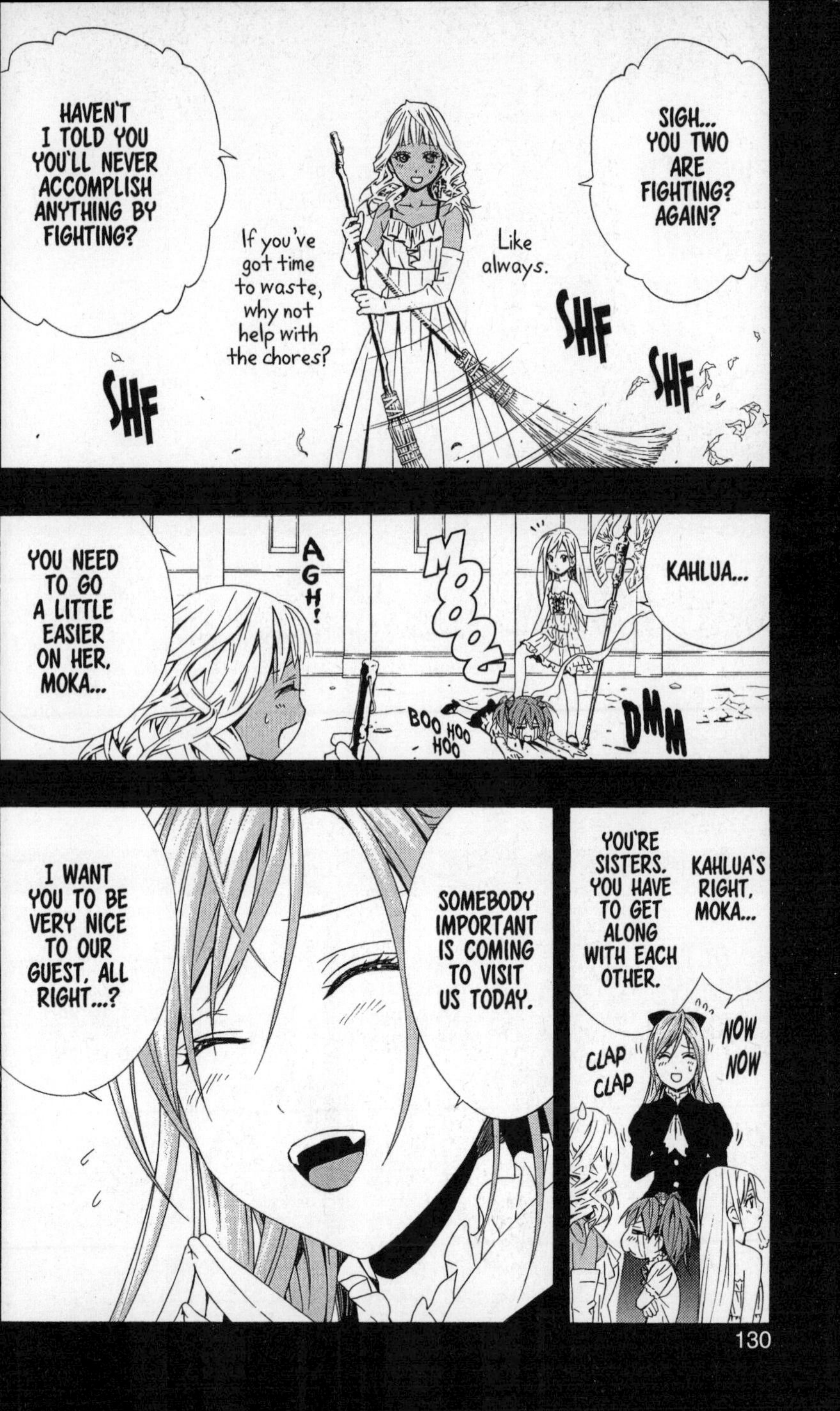
SIGH... YOU TWO ARE FIGHTING? AGAIN?
Like always.
If you've got time to waste, why not help with the chores?
HAVEN'T I TOLD YOU YOU'LL NEVER ACCOMPLISH ANYTHING BY FIGHTING?
SHF
SHF
SHF
KAHLUA...
DMM
MOOOG
AGH!
BOO HOO HOO
YOU NEED TO GO A LITTLE EASIER ON HER, MOKA...
KAHLUA'S RIGHT, MOKA...
YOU'RE SISTERS. YOU HAVE TO GET ALONG WITH EACH OTHER.
NOW NOW
CLAP CLAP
SOMEBODY IMPORTANT IS COMING TO VISIT US TODAY.
I WANT YOU TO BE VERY NICE TO OUR GUEST, ALL RIGHT...?

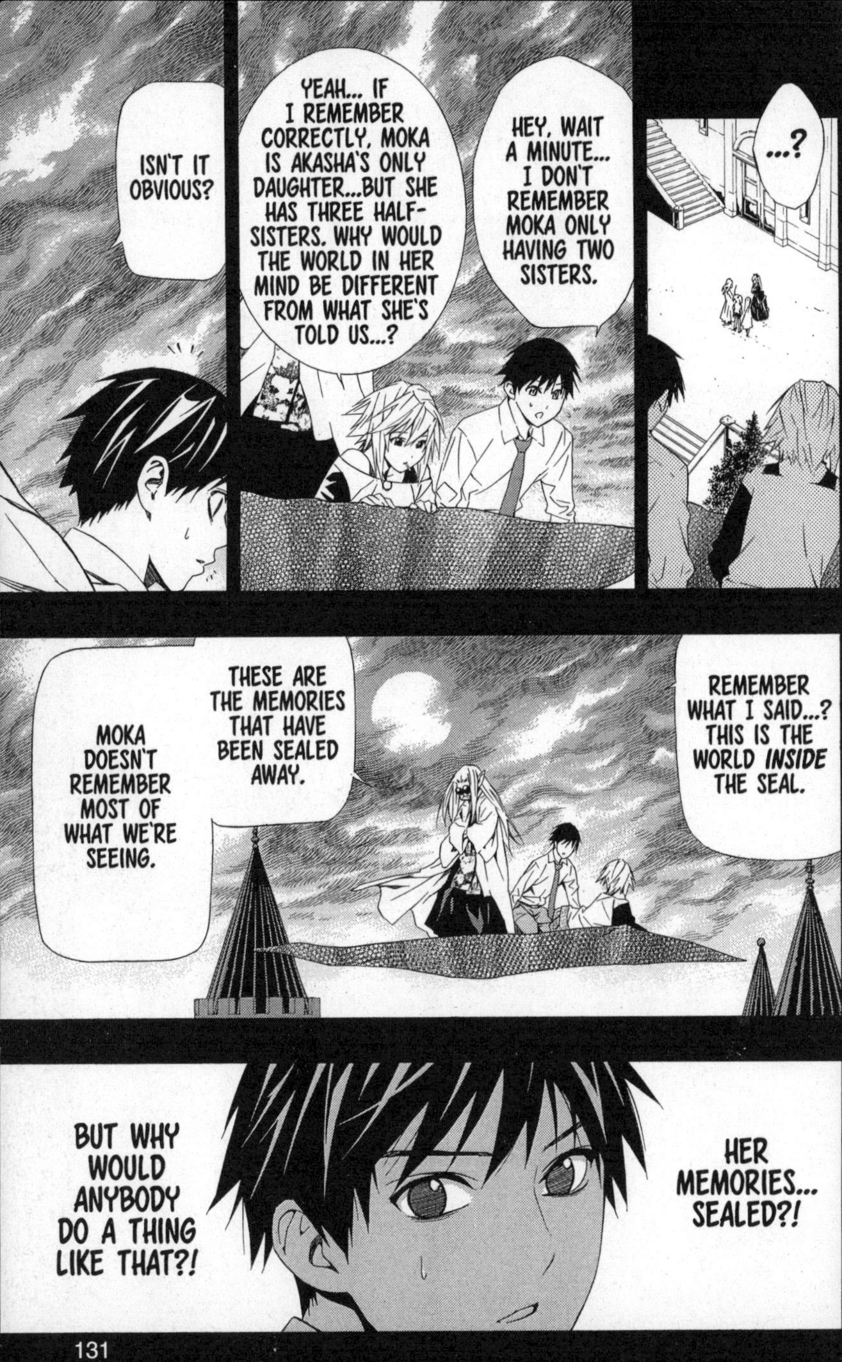
...?
HEY, WAIT A MINUTE... I DON'T REMEMBER MOKA ONLY HAVING TWO SISTERS.
YEAH... IF I REMEMBER CORRECTLY, MOKA IS AKASHA'S ONLY DAUGHTER...BUT SHE HAS THREE HALF-SISTERS. WHY WOULD THE WORLD IN HER MIND BE DIFFERENT FROM WHAT SHE'S TOLD US...?
ISN'T IT OBVIOUS?
REMEMBER WHAT I SAID...? THIS IS THE WORLD *INSIDE* THE SEAL.
THESE ARE THE MEMORIES THAT HAVE BEEN SEALED AWAY.
MOKA DOESN'T REMEMBER MOST OF WHAT WE'RE SEEING.
HER MEMORIES... SEALED?!
BUT WHY WOULD ANYBODY DO A THING LIKE THAT?!

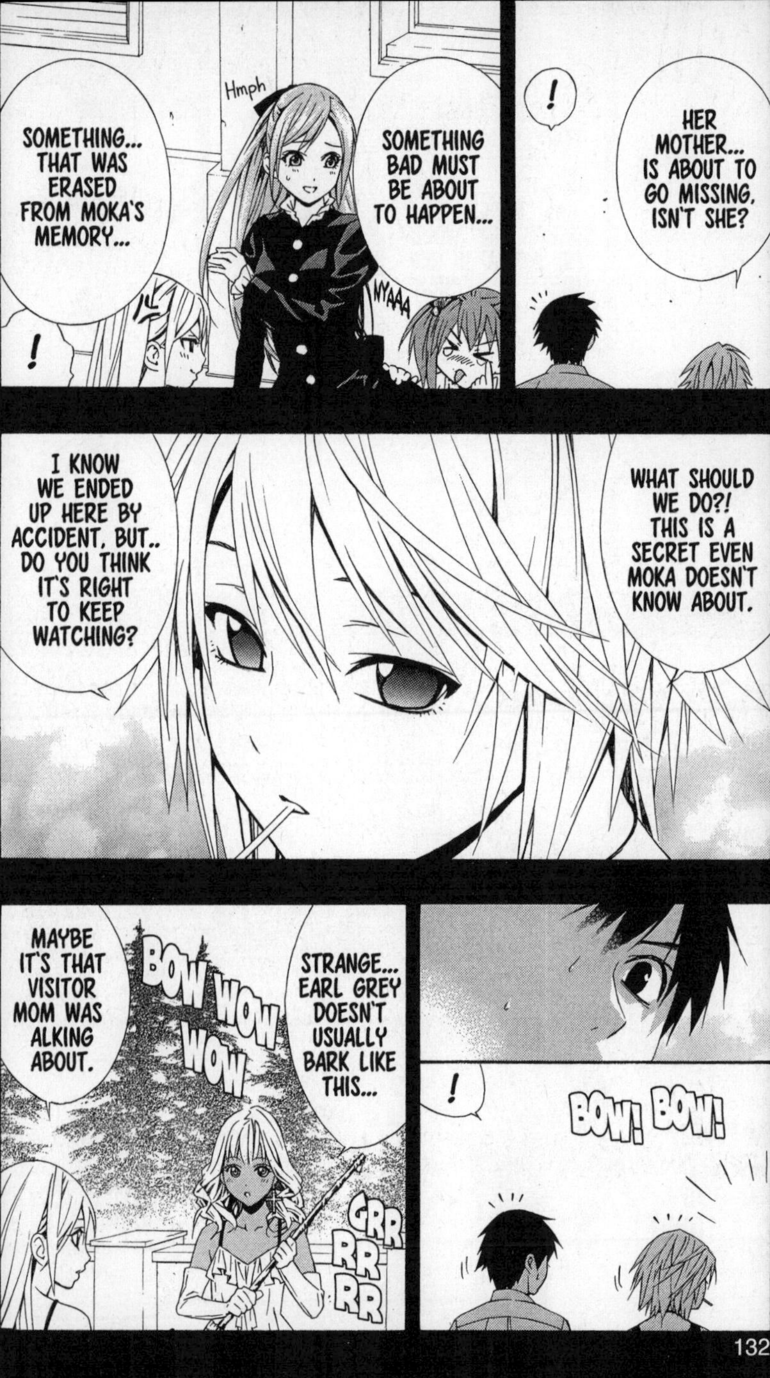
!
HER MOTHER... IS ABOUT TO GO MISSING, ISN'T SHE?
SOMETHING BAD MUST BE ABOUT TO HAPPEN...
Hmph
SOMETHING... THAT WAS ERASED FROM MOKA'S MEMORY...
NYAAA
!
WHAT SHOULD WE DO?! THIS IS A SECRET EVEN MOKA DOESN'T KNOW ABOUT.
I KNOW WE ENDED UP HERE BY ACCIDENT, BUT.. DO YOU THINK IT'S RIGHT TO KEEP WATCHING?
!
BOW! BOW!
STRANGE... EARL GREY DOESN'T USUALLY BARK LIKE THIS...
BOW WOW WOW
MAYBE IT'S THAT VISITOR MOM WAS ALKING ABOUT.
GRRRRRRR

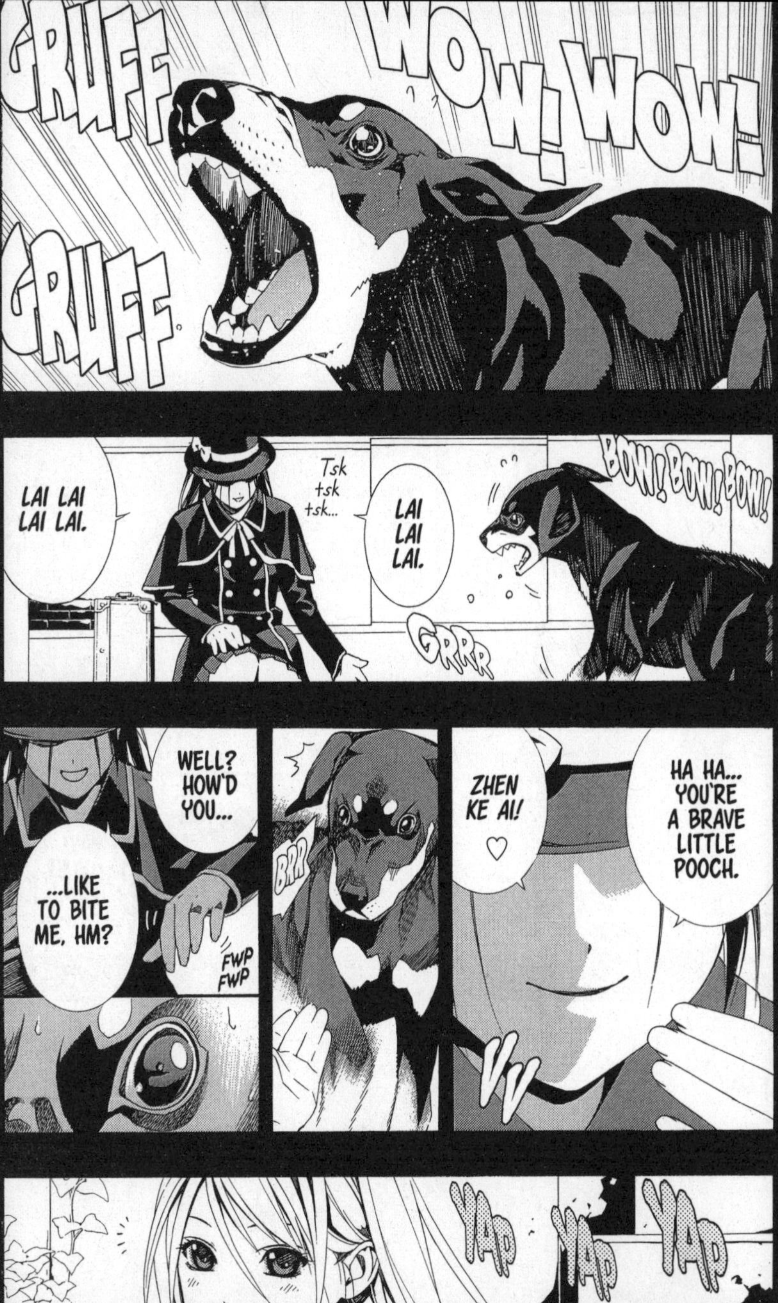
WOW! WOW!
GRUFF
GRUFF
BOW! BOW! BOW!
GRRR
LAI LAI LAI.
Tsk tsk tsk...
LAI LAI LAI LAI.
HA HA... YOU'RE A BRAVE LITTLE POOCH.
ZHEN KE AI! ♡
BRR
WELL? HOW'D YOU...
...LIKE TO BITE ME, HM?
FWP FWP
YAP
YAP
YAP

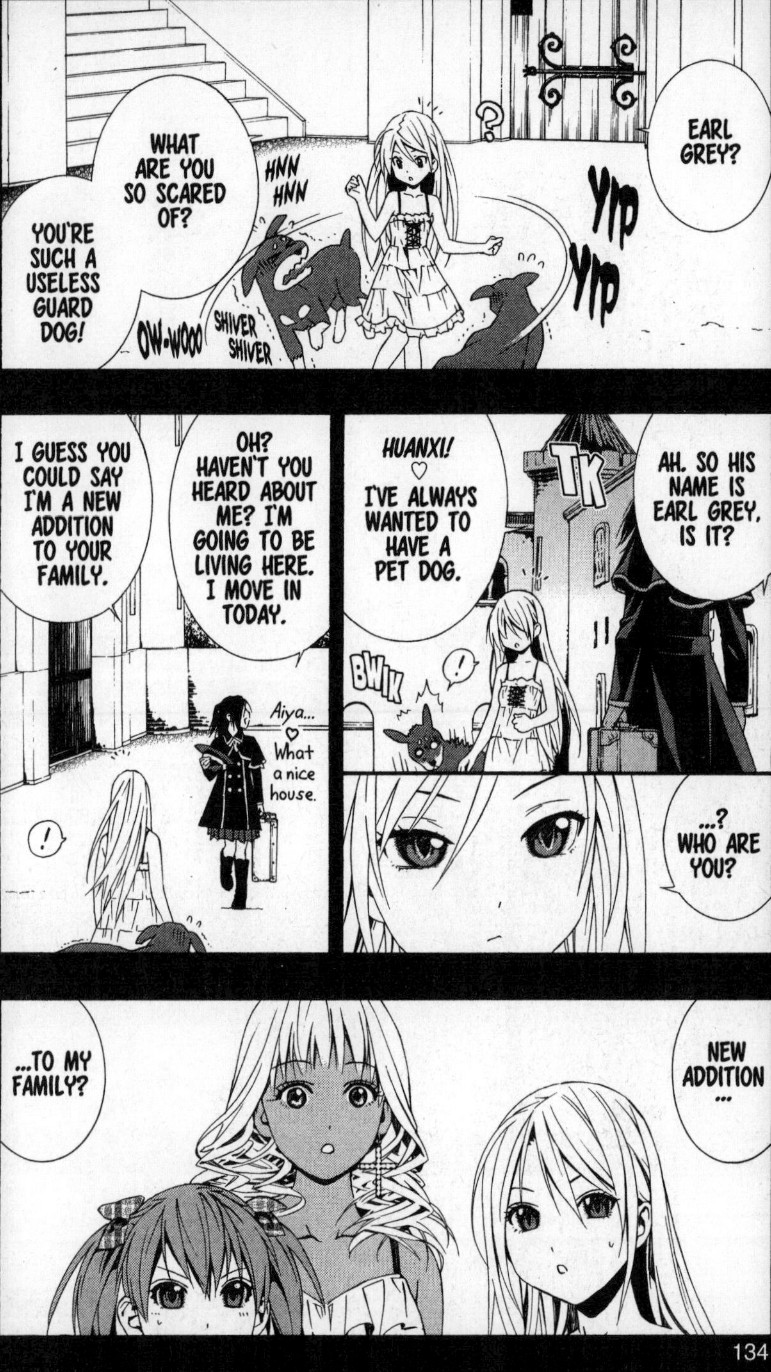
EARL GREY?
YIP YIP
WHAT ARE YOU SO SCARED OF?
HNN HNN
YOU'RE SUCH A USELESS GUARD DOG!
OW-WOOO
SHIVER SHIVER
AH. SO HIS NAME IS EARL GREY, IS IT?
TK
HUANXI! ♡ I'VE ALWAYS WANTED TO HAVE A PET DOG.
BWIK
!
...? WHO ARE YOU?
OH? HAVEN'T YOU HEARD ABOUT ME? I'M GOING TO BE LIVING HERE. I MOVE IN TODAY.
I GUESS YOU COULD SAY I'M A NEW ADDITION TO YOUR FAMILY.
Aiya... ♡ What a nice house.
!
NEW ADDITION...
...TO MY FAMILY?

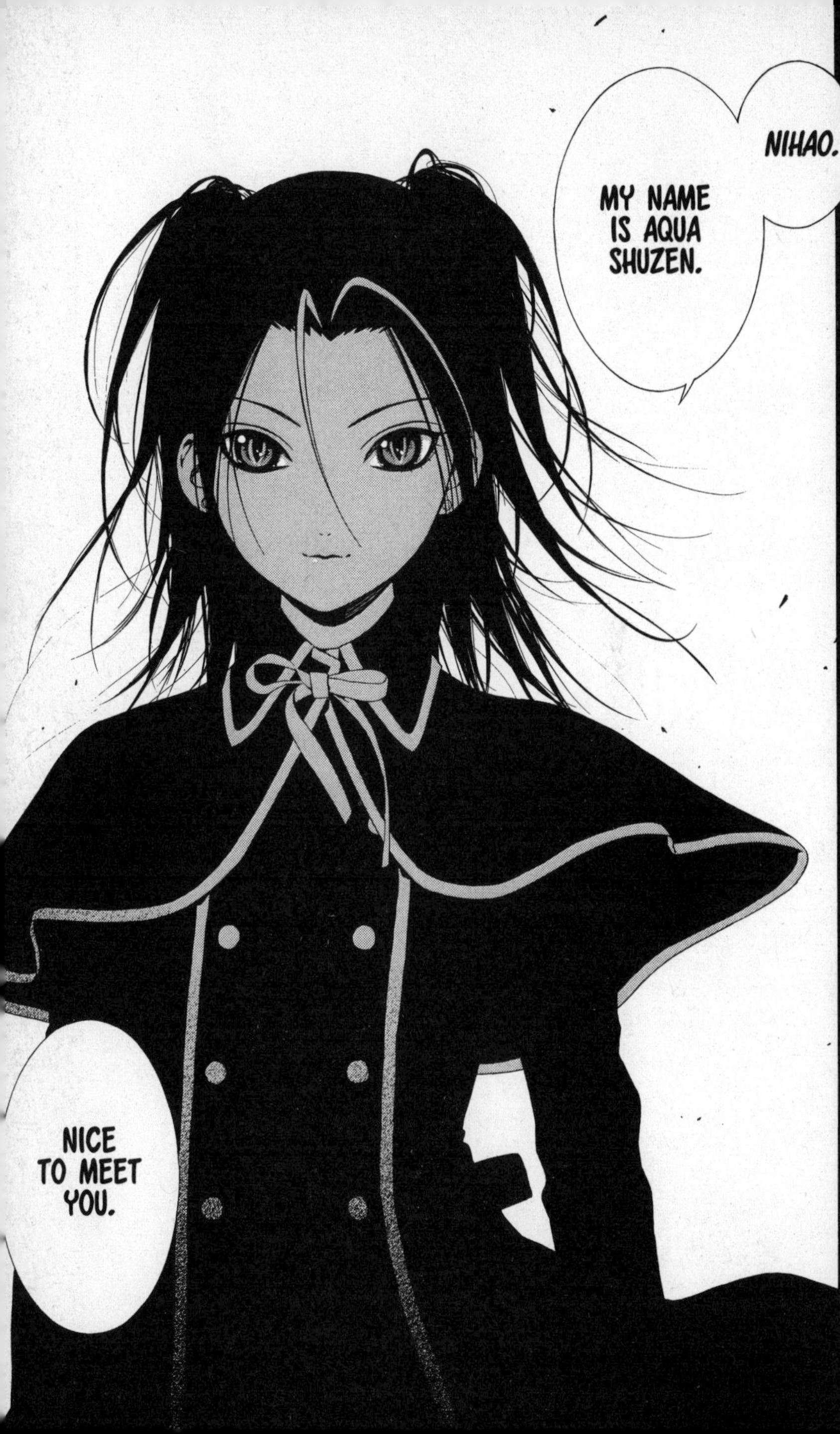
NIHAO.
MY NAME IS AQUA SHUZEN.
NICE TO MEET YOU.

# 30: Eldest Daughter

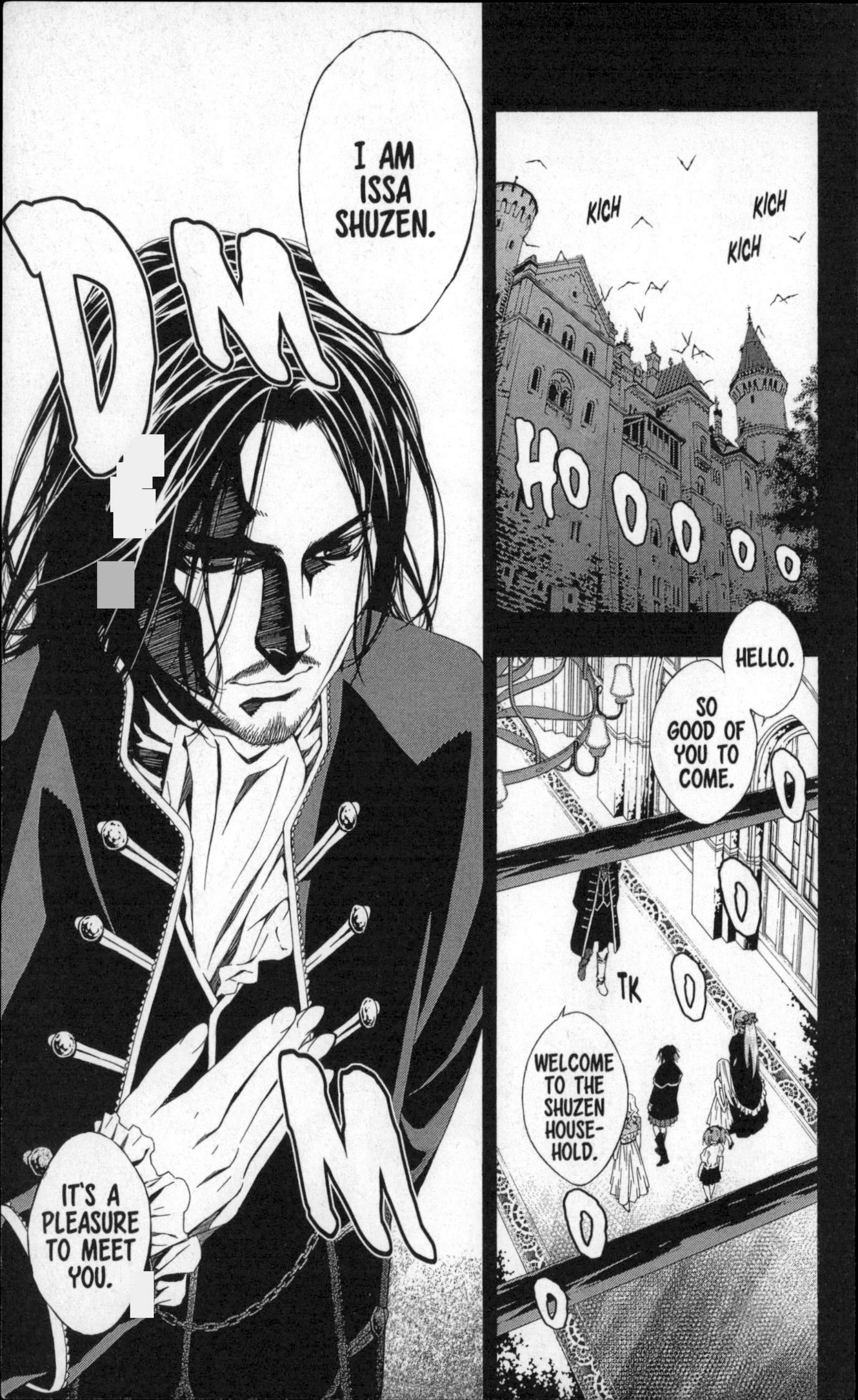
KICH
KICH
KICH
HOOOOO
HELLO.
SO GOOD OF YOU TO COME.
OOOO
TK
WELCOME TO THE SHUZEN HOUSE-HOLD.
OO
I AM ISSA SHUZEN.
DMM
IT'S A PLEASURE TO MEET YOU.

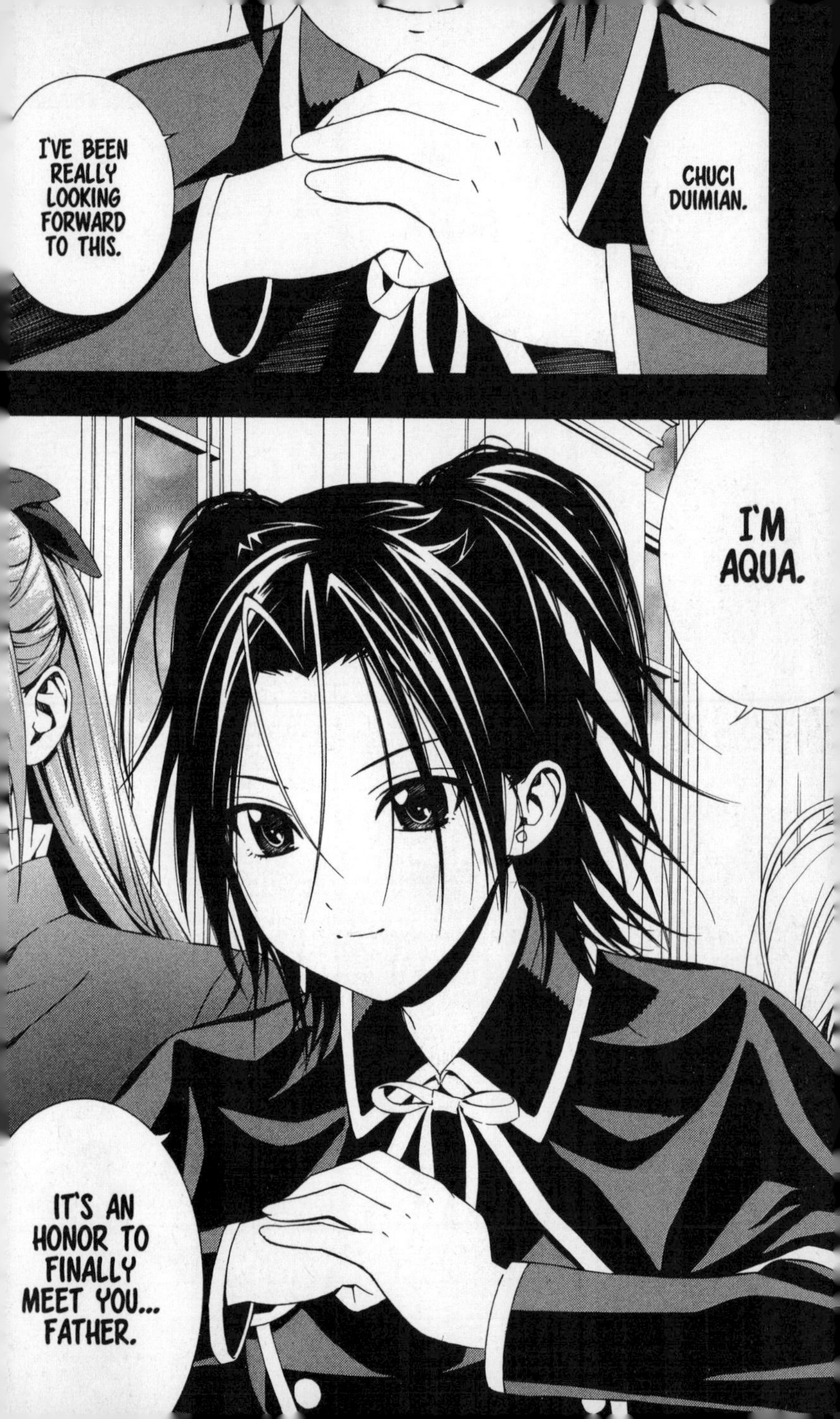
CHUCI DUIMIAN.
I'VE BEEN REALLY LOOKING FORWARD TO THIS.
I'M AQUA.
IT'S AN HONOR TO FINALLY MEET YOU... FATHER.

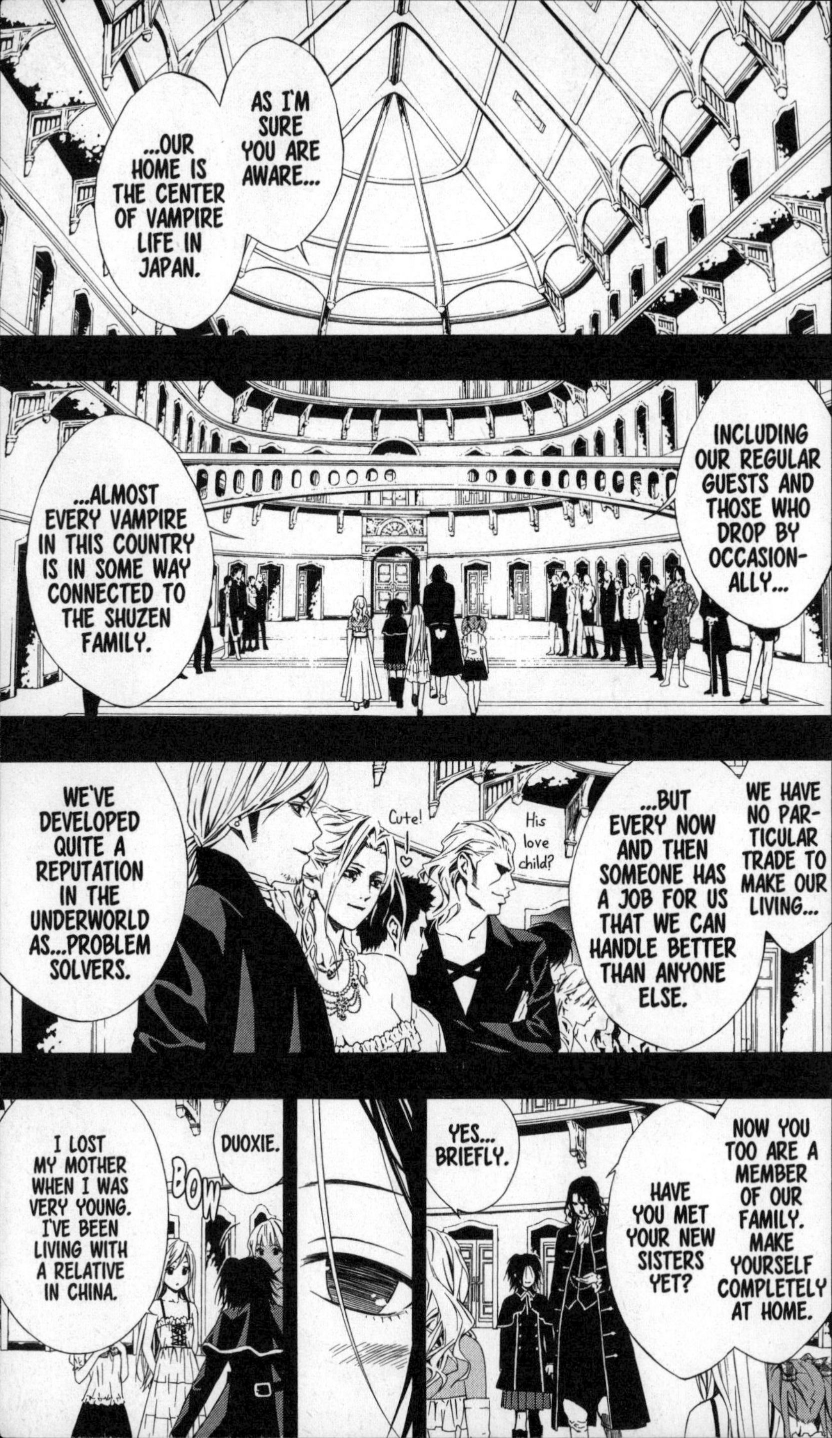
AS I'M SURE YOU ARE AWARE...
...OUR HOME IS THE CENTER OF VAMPIRE LIFE IN JAPAN.
INCLUDING OUR REGULAR GUESTS AND THOSE WHO DROP BY OCCASION-ALLY...
...ALMOST EVERY VAMPIRE IN THIS COUNTRY IS IN SOME WAY CONNECTED TO THE SHUZEN FAMILY.
WE HAVE NO PAR-TICULAR TRADE TO MAKE OUR LIVING...
...BUT EVERY NOW AND THEN SOMEONE HAS A JOB FOR US THAT WE CAN HANDLE BETTER THAN ANYONE ELSE.
His love child?
Cute!
WE'VE DEVELOPED QUITE A REPUTATION IN THE UNDERWORLD AS...PROBLEM SOLVERS.
NOW YOU TOO ARE A MEMBER OF OUR FAMILY. MAKE YOURSELF COMPLETELY AT HOME.
HAVE YOU MET YOUR NEW SISTERS YET?
YES... BRIEFLY.
DUOXIE.
BOW
I LOST MY MOTHER WHEN I WAS VERY YOUNG. I'VE BEEN LIVING WITH A RELATIVE IN CHINA.

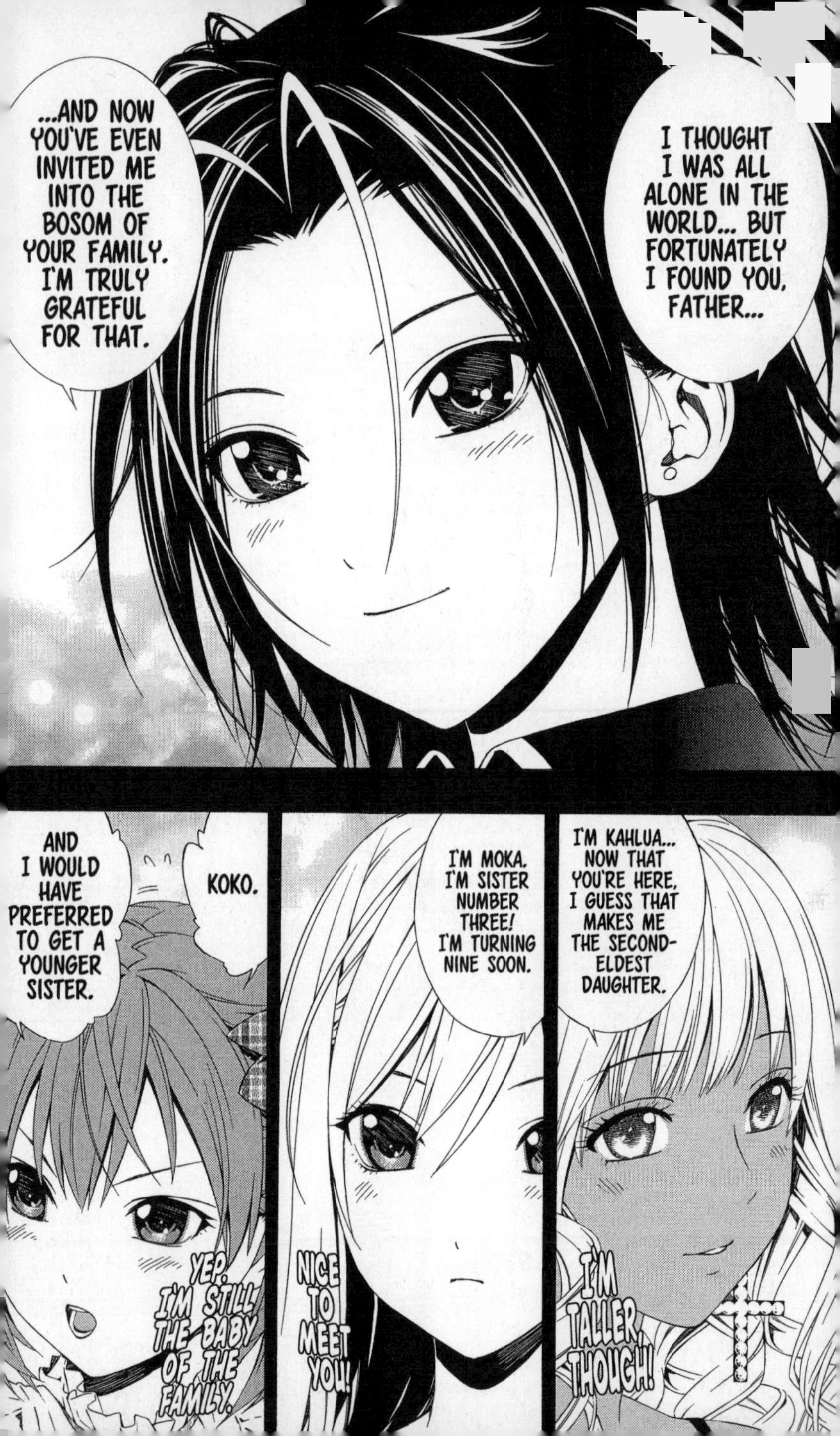
I THOUGHT I WAS ALL ALONE IN THE WORLD... BUT FORTUNATELY I FOUND YOU, FATHER...
...AND NOW YOU'VE EVEN INVITED ME INTO THE BOSOM OF YOUR FAMILY. I'M TRULY GRATEFUL FOR THAT.
I'M KAHLUA... NOW THAT YOU'RE HERE, I GUESS THAT MAKES ME THE SECOND-ELDEST DAUGHTER.
I'M TALLER, THOUGH!
I'M MOKA. I'M SISTER NUMBER THREE! I'M TURNING NINE SOON.
NICE TO MEET YOU!
KOKO.
AND I WOULD HAVE PREFERRED TO GET A YOUNGER SISTER.
YEP. I'M STILL THE BABY OF THE FAMILY.

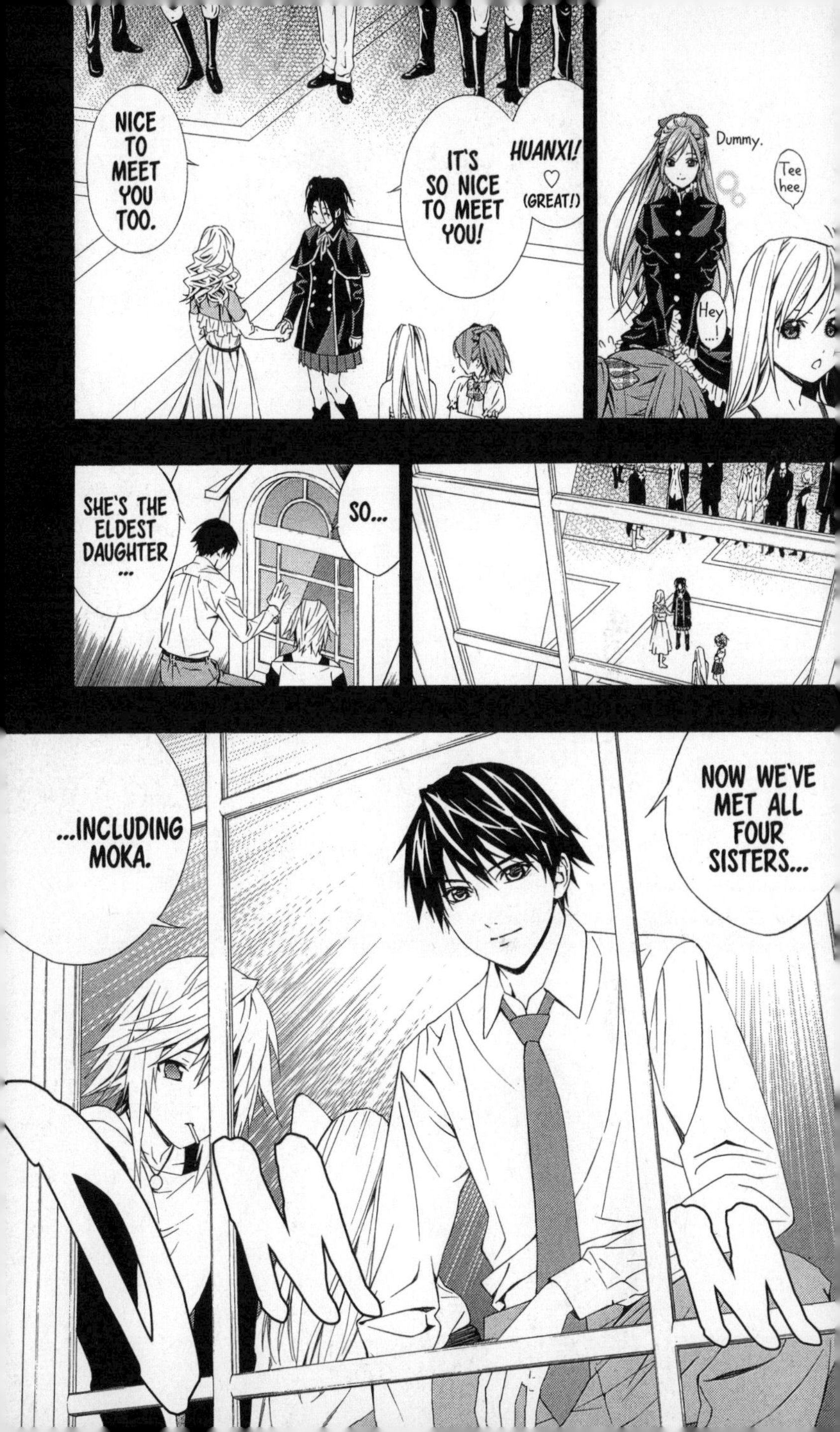
Tee hee.
Dummy.
Hey...!
HUANXI! ♡ (GREAT!)
IT'S SO NICE TO MEET YOU!
NICE TO MEET YOU TOO.
SO...
SHE'S THE ELDEST DAUGHTER...
NOW WE'VE MET ALL FOUR SISTERS...
...INCLUDING MOKA.

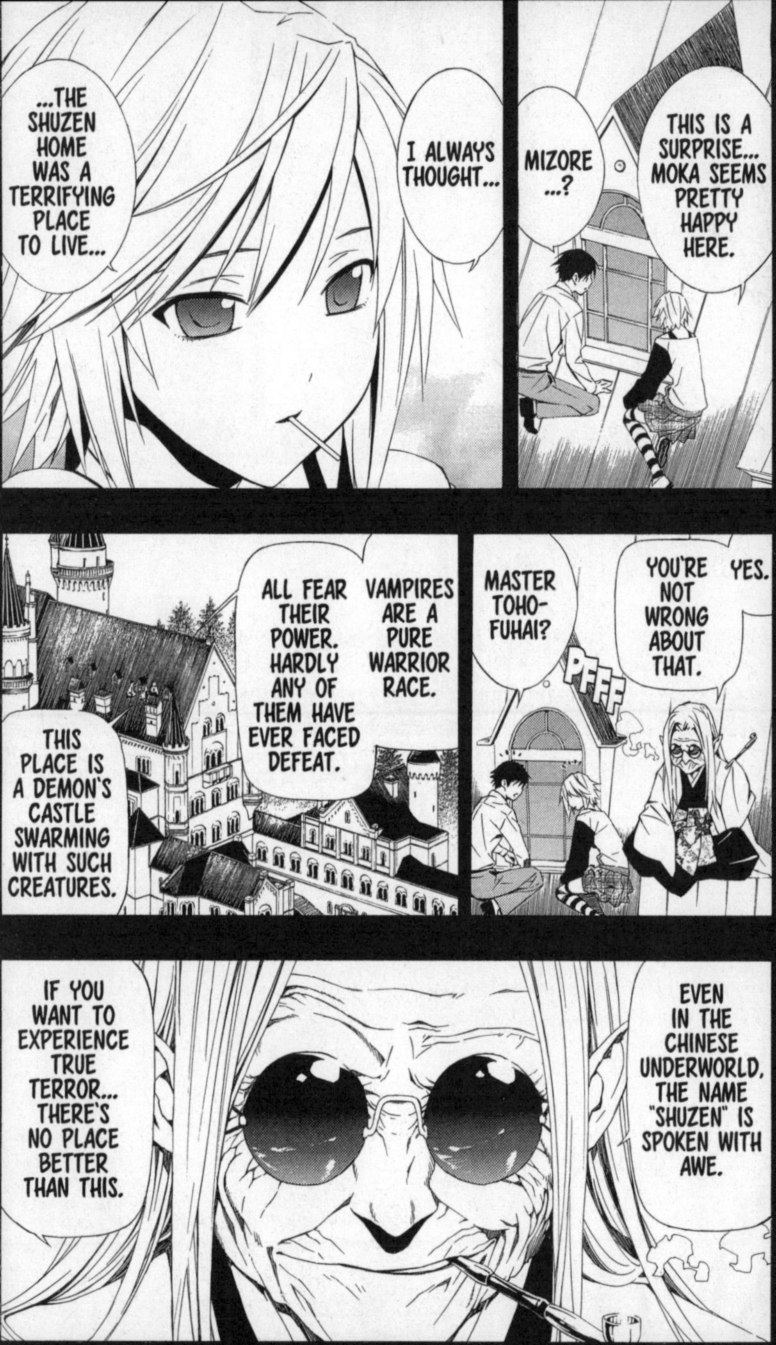
THIS IS A SURPRISE... MOKA SEEMS PRETTY HAPPY HERE.
MIZORE ...?
I ALWAYS THOUGHT...
...THE SHUZEN HOME WAS A TERRIFYING PLACE TO LIVE...
YES.
YOU'RE NOT WRONG ABOUT THAT.
MASTER TOHO-FUHAI?
PFFF
VAMPIRES ARE A PURE WARRIOR RACE.
ALL FEAR THEIR POWER. HARDLY ANY OF THEM HAVE EVER FACED DEFEAT.
THIS PLACE IS A DEMON'S CASTLE SWARMING WITH SUCH CREATURES.
EVEN IN THE CHINESE UNDERWORLD, THE NAME "SHUZEN" IS SPOKEN WITH AWE.
IF YOU WANT TO EXPERIENCE TRUE TERROR... THERE'S NO PLACE BETTER THAN THIS.

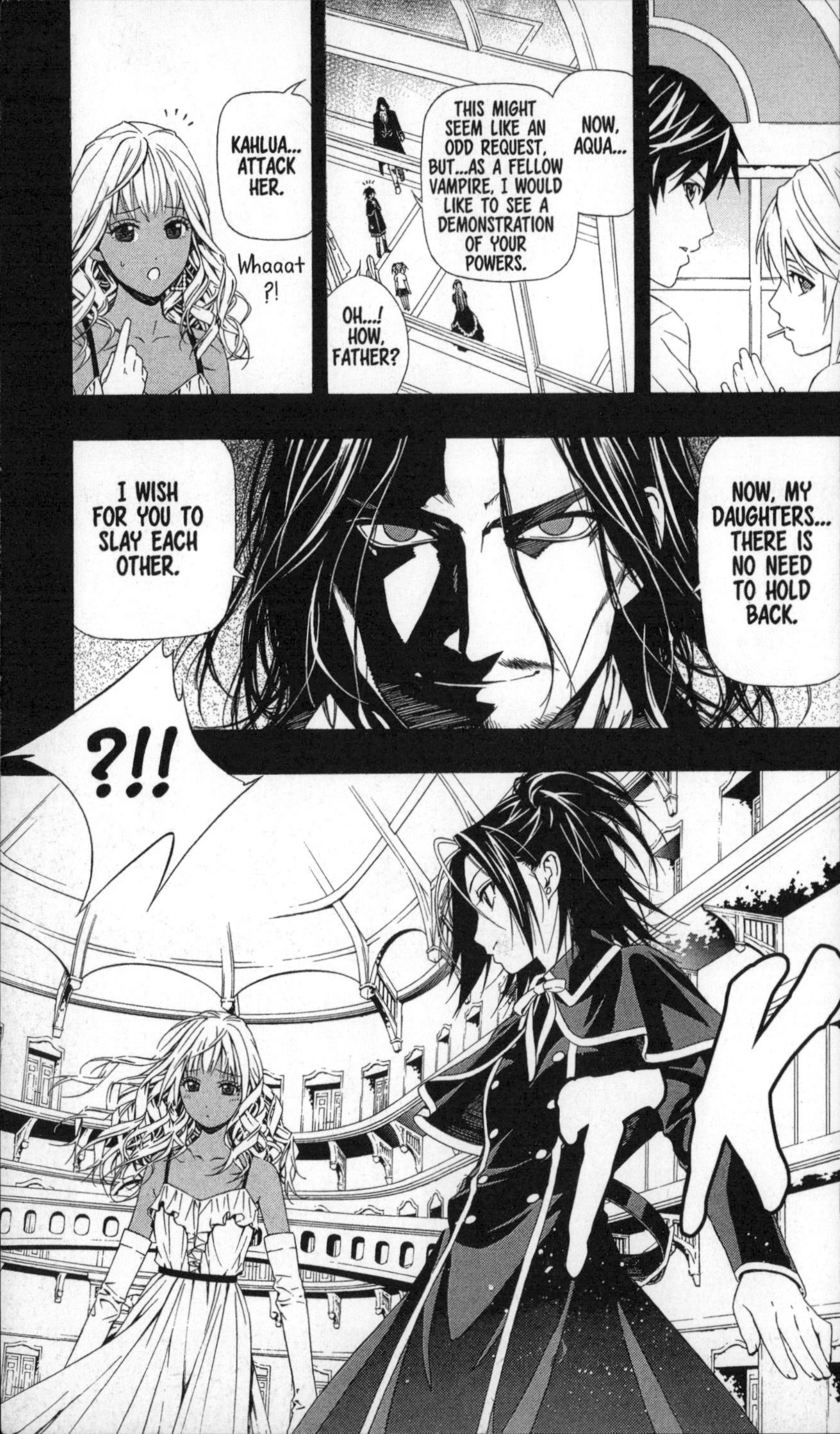
NOW, AQUA...
THIS MIGHT SEEM LIKE AN ODD REQUEST, BUT...AS A FELLOW VAMPIRE, I WOULD LIKE TO SEE A DEMONSTRATION OF YOUR POWERS.
OH...! HOW, FATHER?
KAHLUA... ATTACK HER.
Whaaat ?!
NOW, MY DAUGHTERS... THERE IS NO NEED TO HOLD BACK.
I WISH FOR YOU TO SLAY EACH OTHER.
?!!

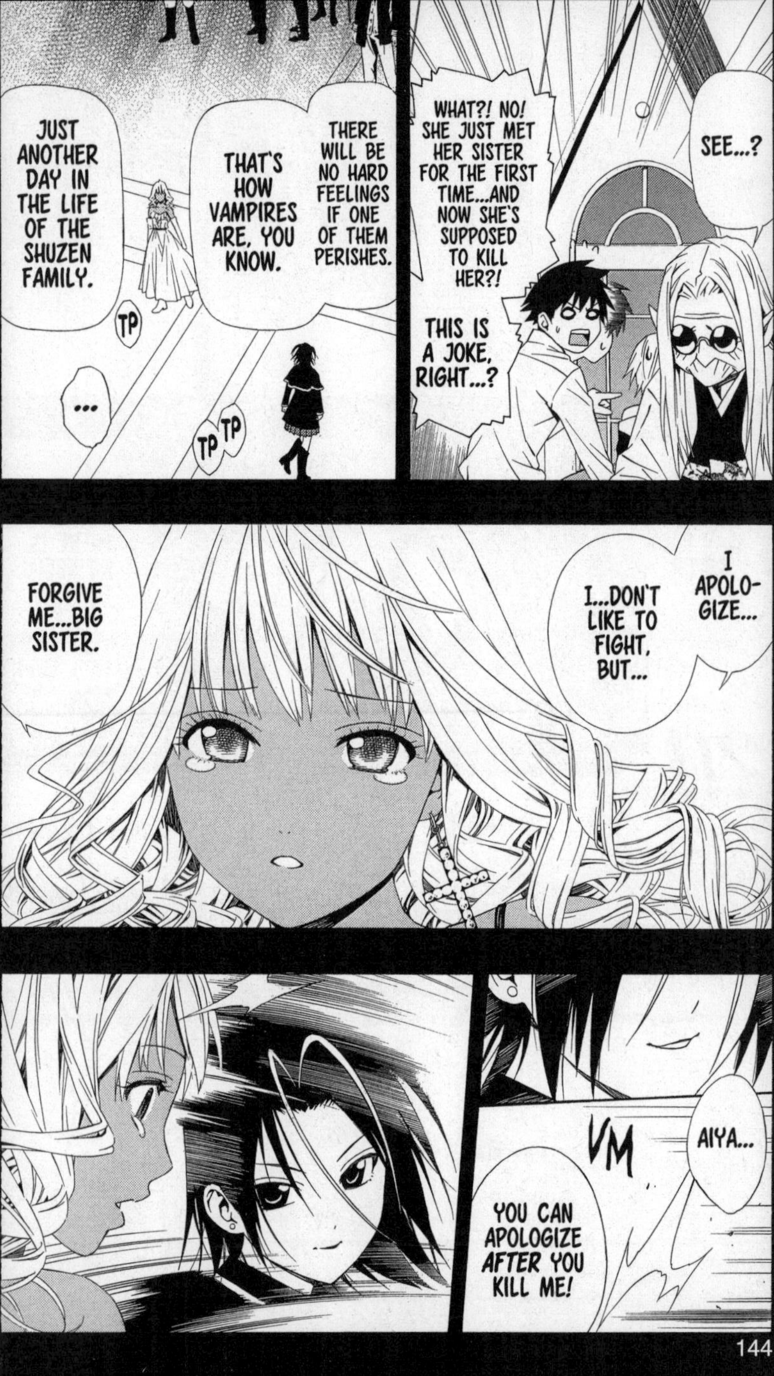
SEE...?
WHAT?! NO! SHE JUST MET HER SISTER FOR THE FIRST TIME...AND NOW SHE'S SUPPOSED TO KILL HER?!
THIS IS A JOKE, RIGHT...?
THERE WILL BE NO HARD FEELINGS IF ONE OF THEM PERISHES.
THAT'S HOW VAMPIRES ARE, YOU KNOW.
JUST ANOTHER DAY IN THE LIFE OF THE SHUZEN FAMILY.
TP
...
TP TP
I APOLOGIZE...
I...DON'T LIKE TO FIGHT, BUT...
FORGIVE ME...BIG SISTER.
AIYA...
VM
YOU CAN APOLOGIZE AFTER YOU KILL ME!

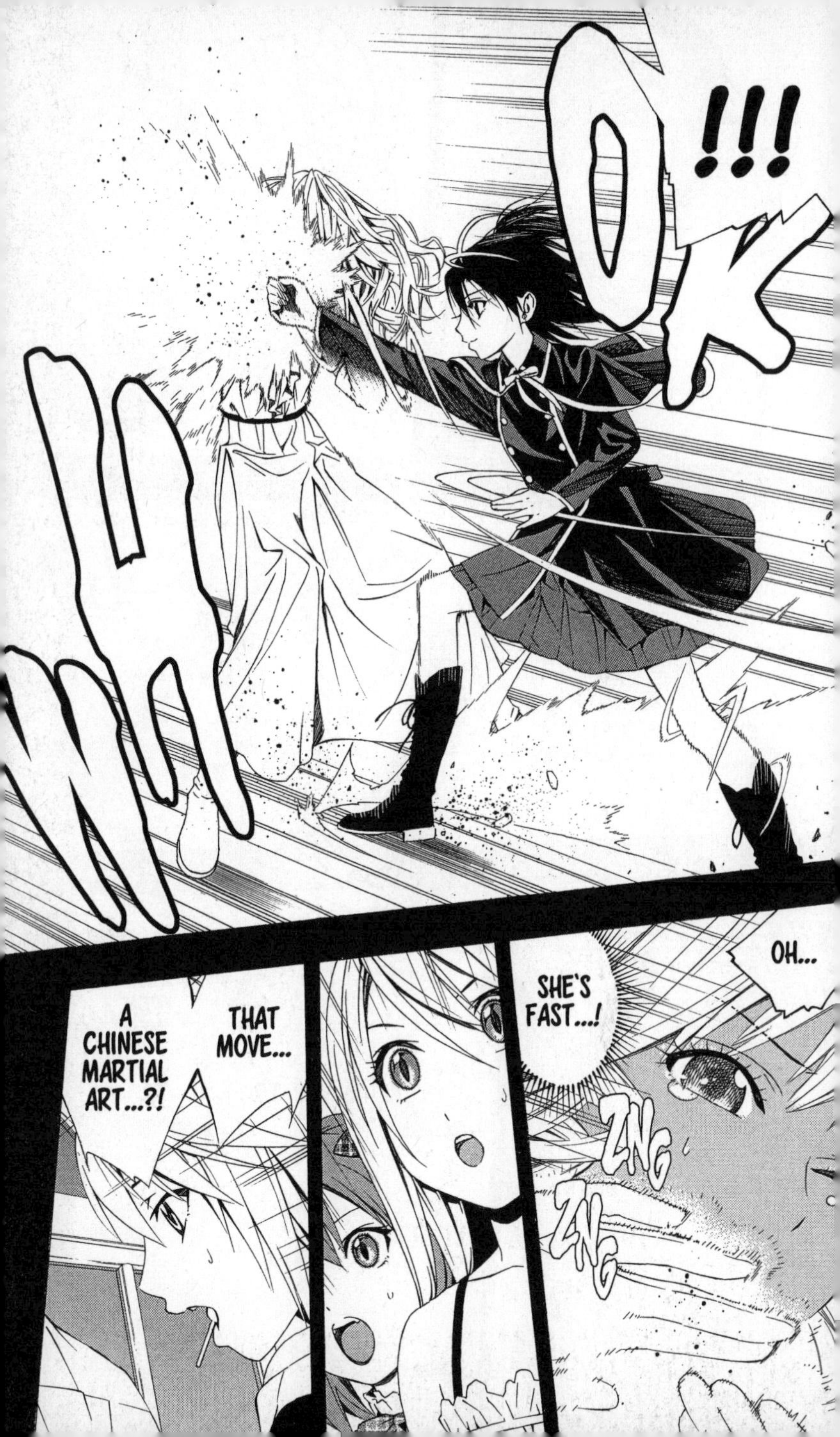
OH...
SHE'S FAST...!
ZNG
ZNG
THAT MOVE...
A CHINESE MARTIAL ART...?!

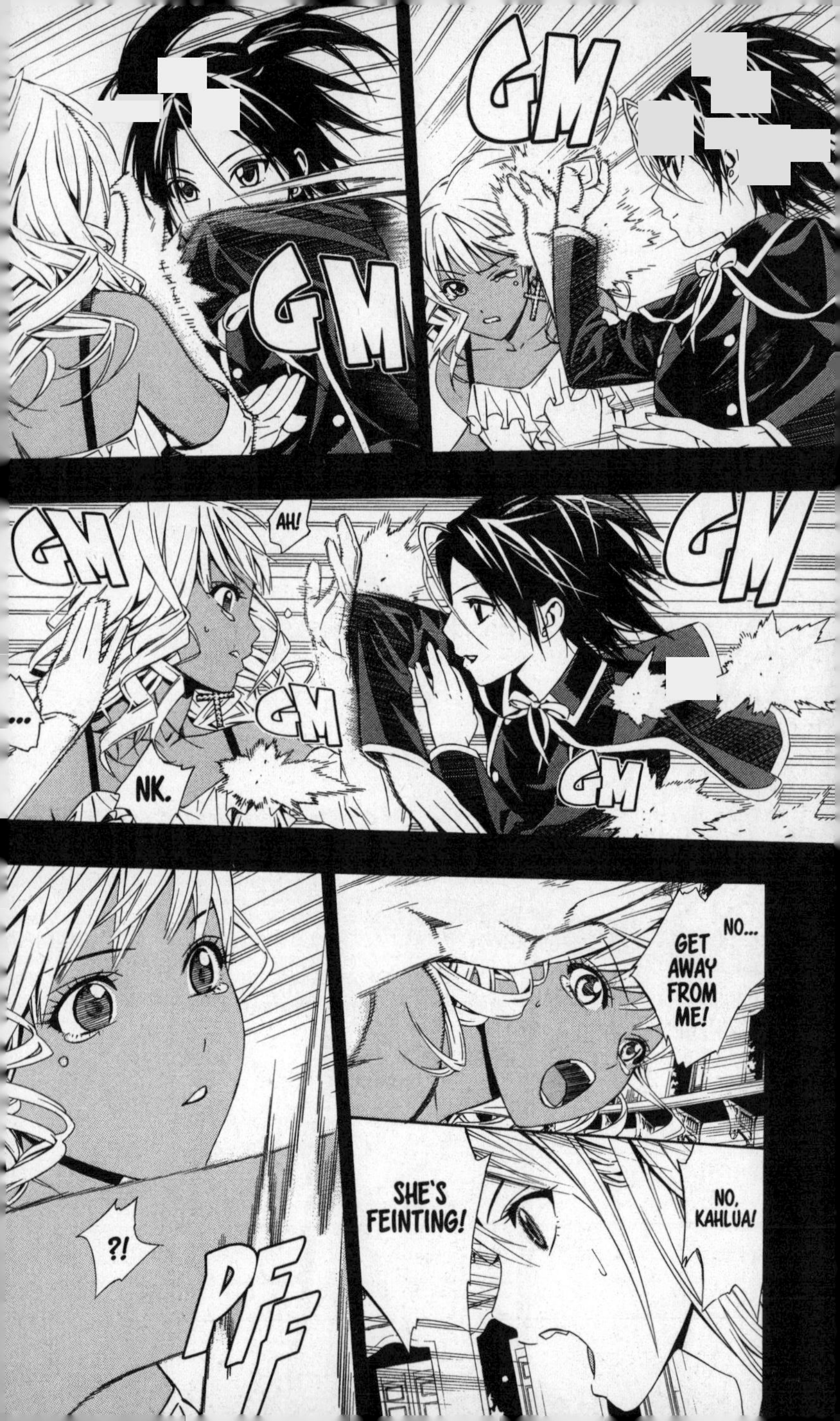
GM
GM
GM
AH!
GM
GM
GM
...
NK.
NO...
GET AWAY FROM ME!
NO, KAHLUA!
SHE'S FEINTING!
?!
PF

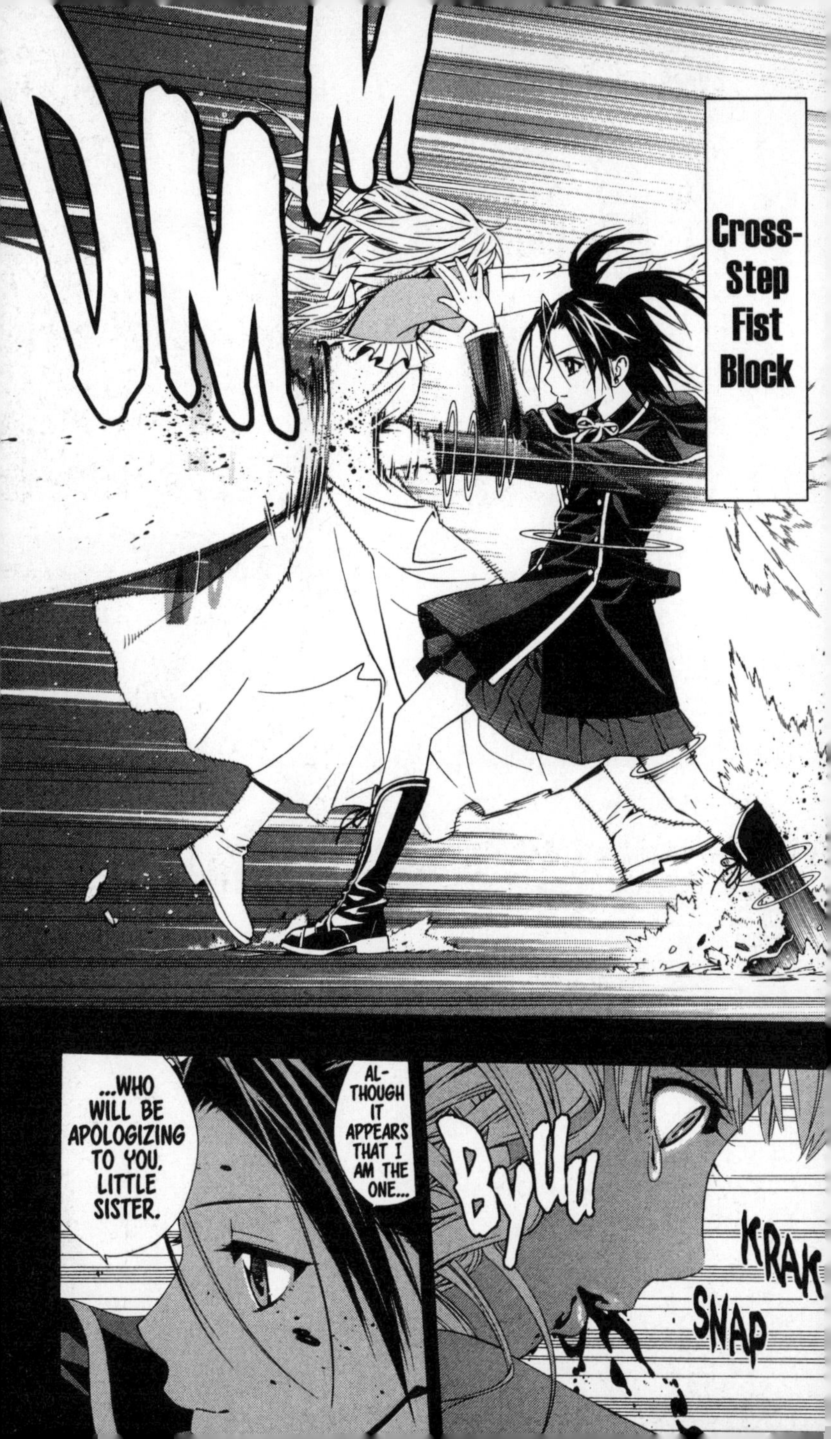

Cross-Step Fist Block
KRAK
SNAP
ByUu
ALTHOUGH IT APPEARS THAT I AM THE ONE...
...WHO WILL BE APOLOGIZING TO YOU, LITTLE SISTER.

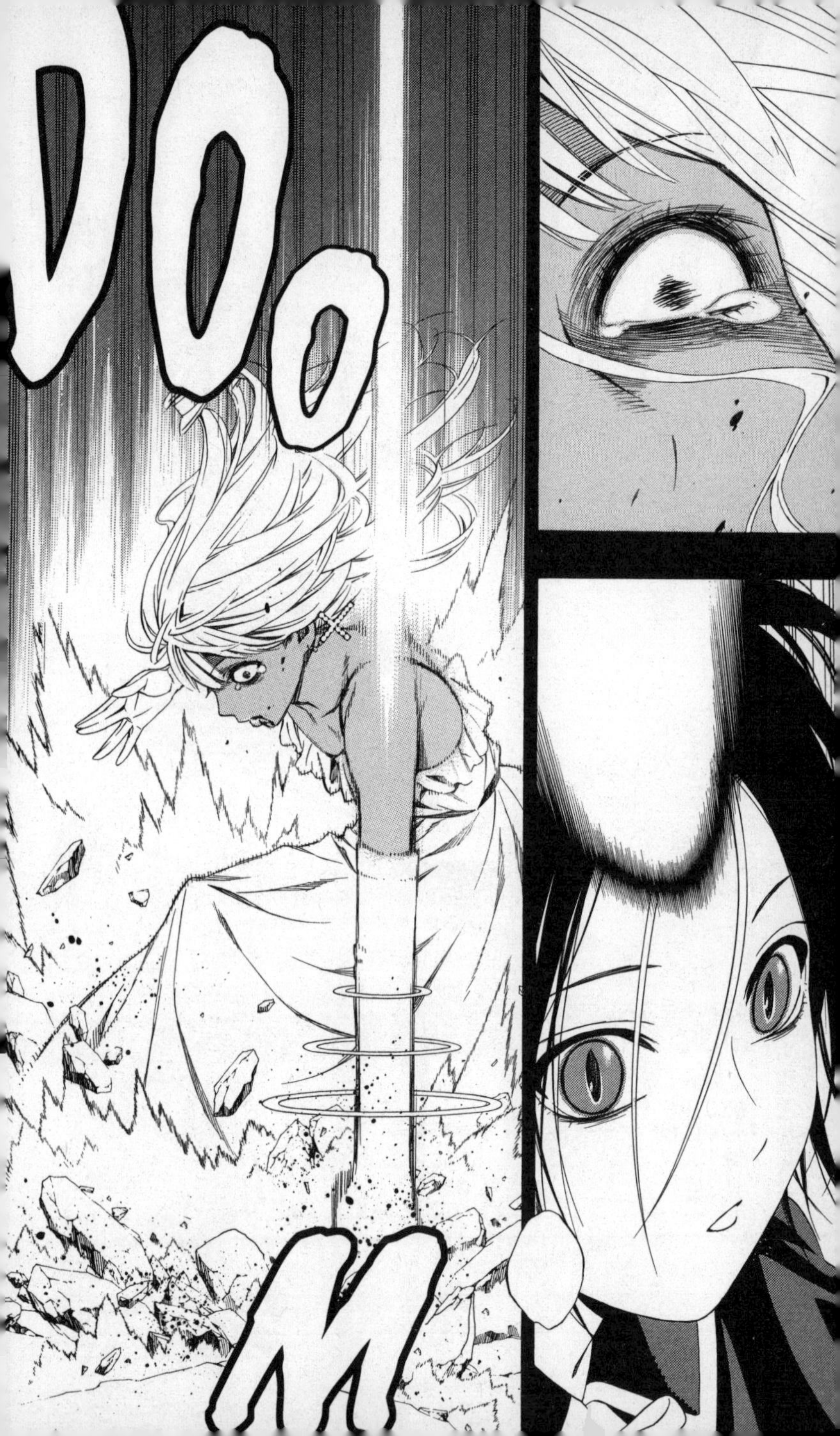
DOOOM

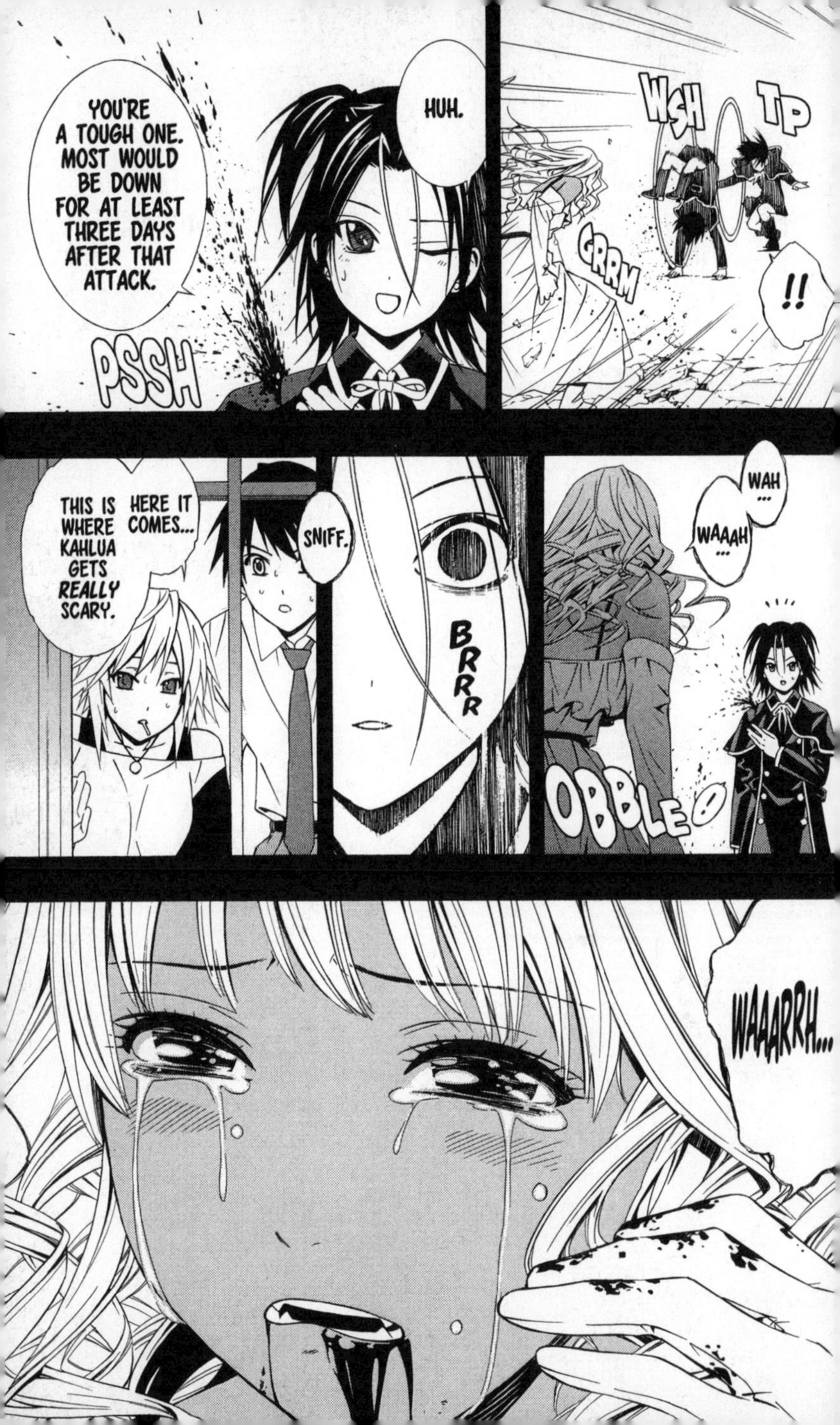
TP
WSH
!!
GRRM
HUH.
YOU'RE A TOUGH ONE. MOST WOULD BE DOWN FOR AT LEAST THREE DAYS AFTER THAT ATTACK.
PSSH
WAH...
WAAAH...
OBBLE
BRRR
SNIFF.
HERE IT COMES...
THIS IS WHERE KAHLUA GETS *REALLY* SCARY.
WAAARRH...

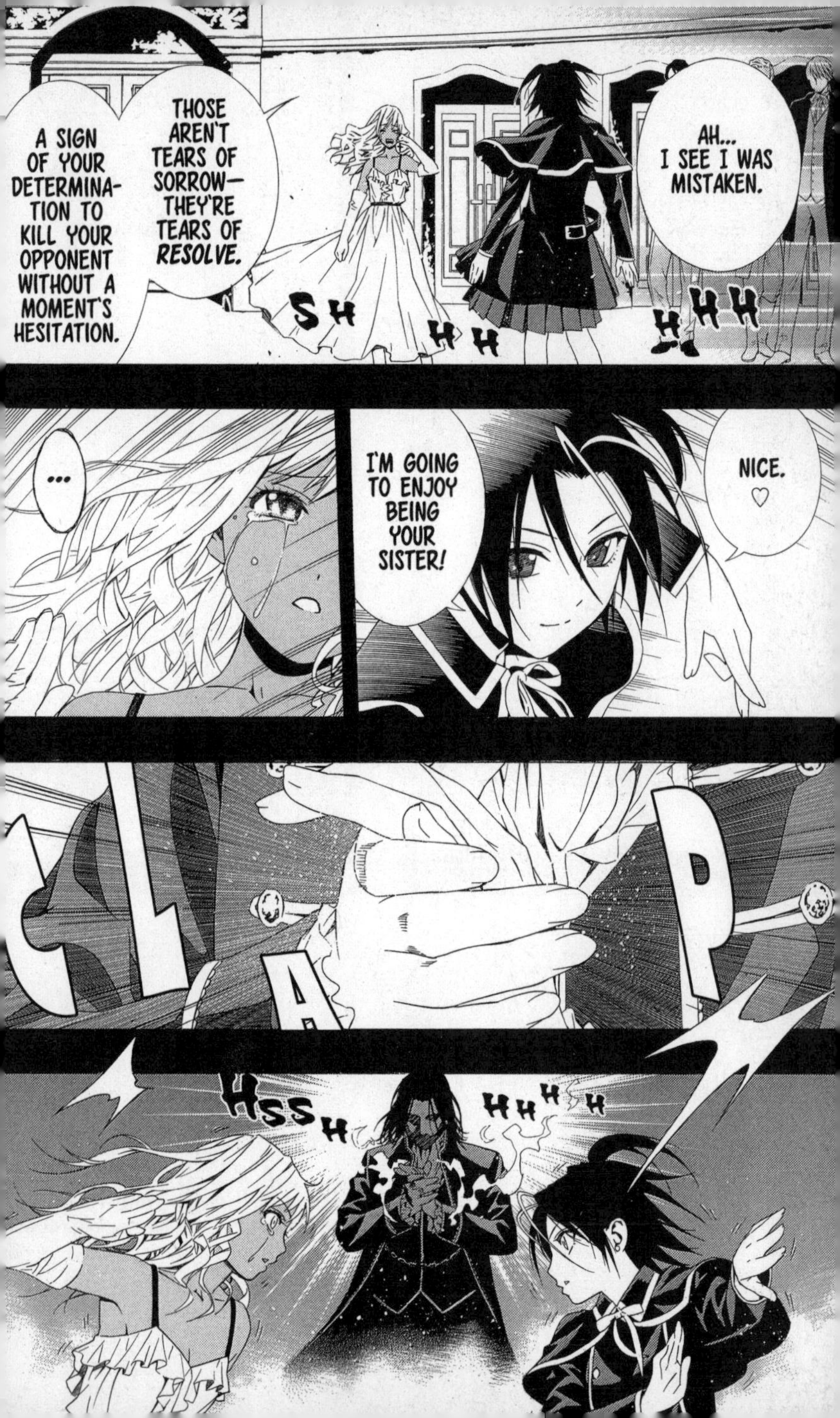

AH... I SEE I WAS MISTAKEN.
THOSE AREN'T TEARS OF SORROW—THEY'RE TEARS OF *RESOLVE.*
A SIGN OF YOUR DETERMINATION TO KILL YOUR OPPONENT WITHOUT A MOMENT'S HESITATION.
HHHH
SHHH
NICE. ♡
I'M GOING TO ENJOY BEING YOUR SISTER!
...
CLAP
HHHHH
HSSH

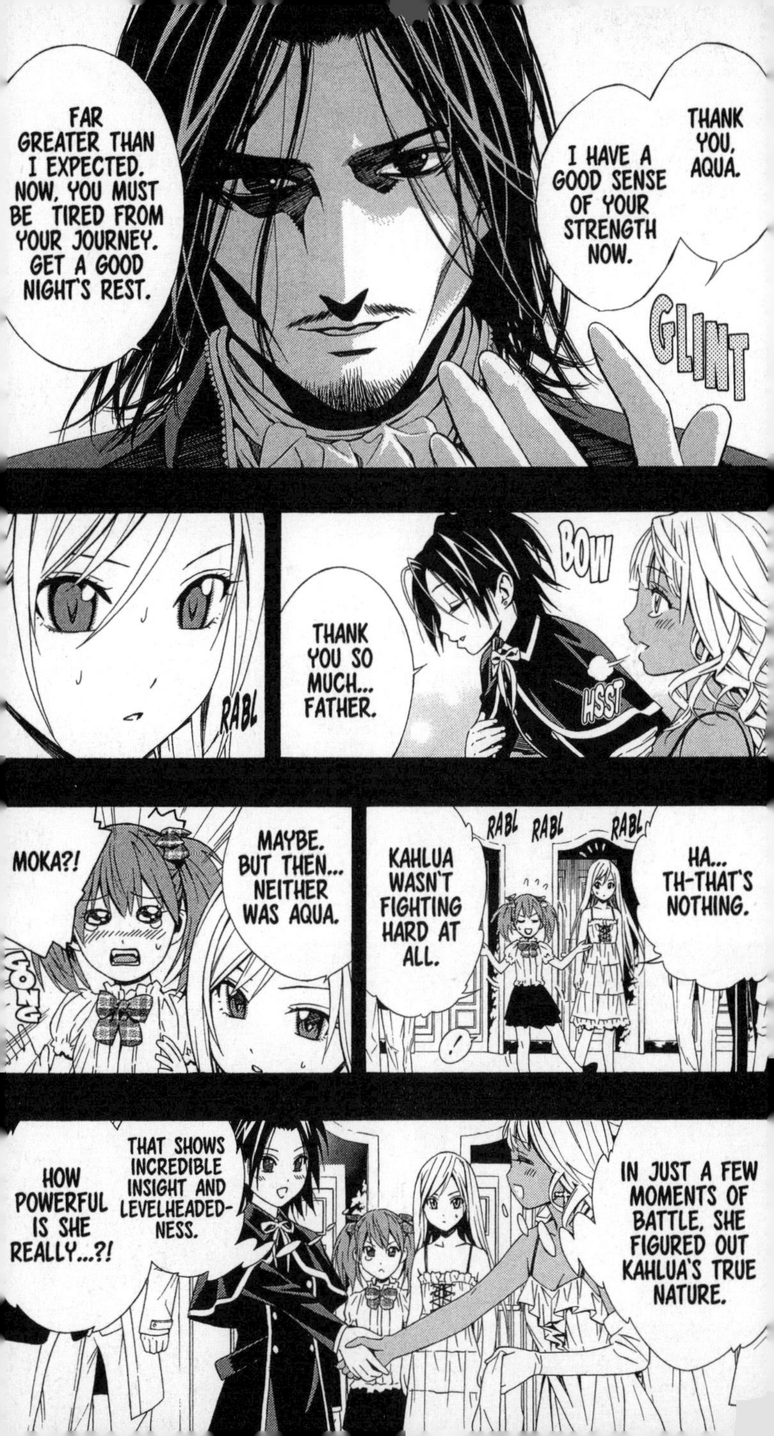
THANK YOU, AQUA.
I HAVE A GOOD SENSE OF YOUR STRENGTH NOW.
GLINT
FAR GREATER THAN I EXPECTED. NOW, YOU MUST BE TIRED FROM YOUR JOURNEY. GET A GOOD NIGHT'S REST.
BOW
HSST
THANK YOU SO MUCH... FATHER.
RABL
HA... TH-THAT'S NOTHING.
RABL RABL RABL
KAHLUA WASN'T FIGHTING HARD AT ALL.
!
MAYBE. BUT THEN... NEITHER WAS AQUA.
MOKA?!
GONG
IN JUST A FEW MOMENTS OF BATTLE, SHE FIGURED OUT KAHLUA'S TRUE NATURE.
THAT SHOWS INCREDIBLE INSIGHT AND LEVELHEADED-NESS.
HOW POWERFUL IS SHE REALLY...?!

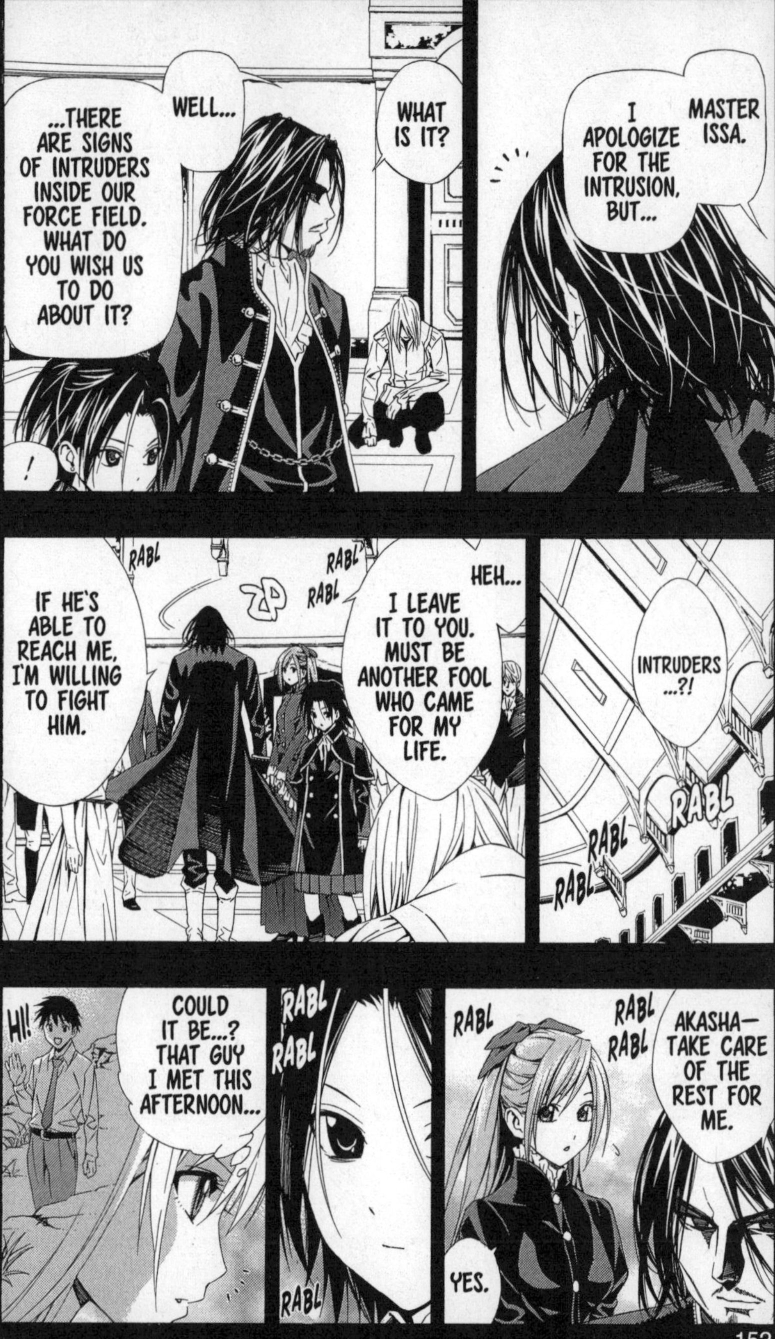
MASTER ISSA.
I APOLOGIZE FOR THE INTRUSION, BUT...
WHAT IS IT?
WELL...
...THERE ARE SIGNS OF INTRUDERS INSIDE OUR FORCE FIELD. WHAT DO YOU WISH US TO DO ABOUT IT?
!
INTRUDERS ...?!
RABL
RABL
RABL
HEH...
I LEAVE IT TO YOU. MUST BE ANOTHER FOOL WHO CAME FOR MY LIFE.
RABL
RABL
RABL
IF HE'S ABLE TO REACH ME, I'M WILLING TO FIGHT HIM.
RABL
RABL RABL
AKASHA—TAKE CARE OF THE REST FOR ME.
YES.
RABL
RABL
RABL
COULD IT BE...? THAT GUY I MET THIS AFTERNOON...
HI!

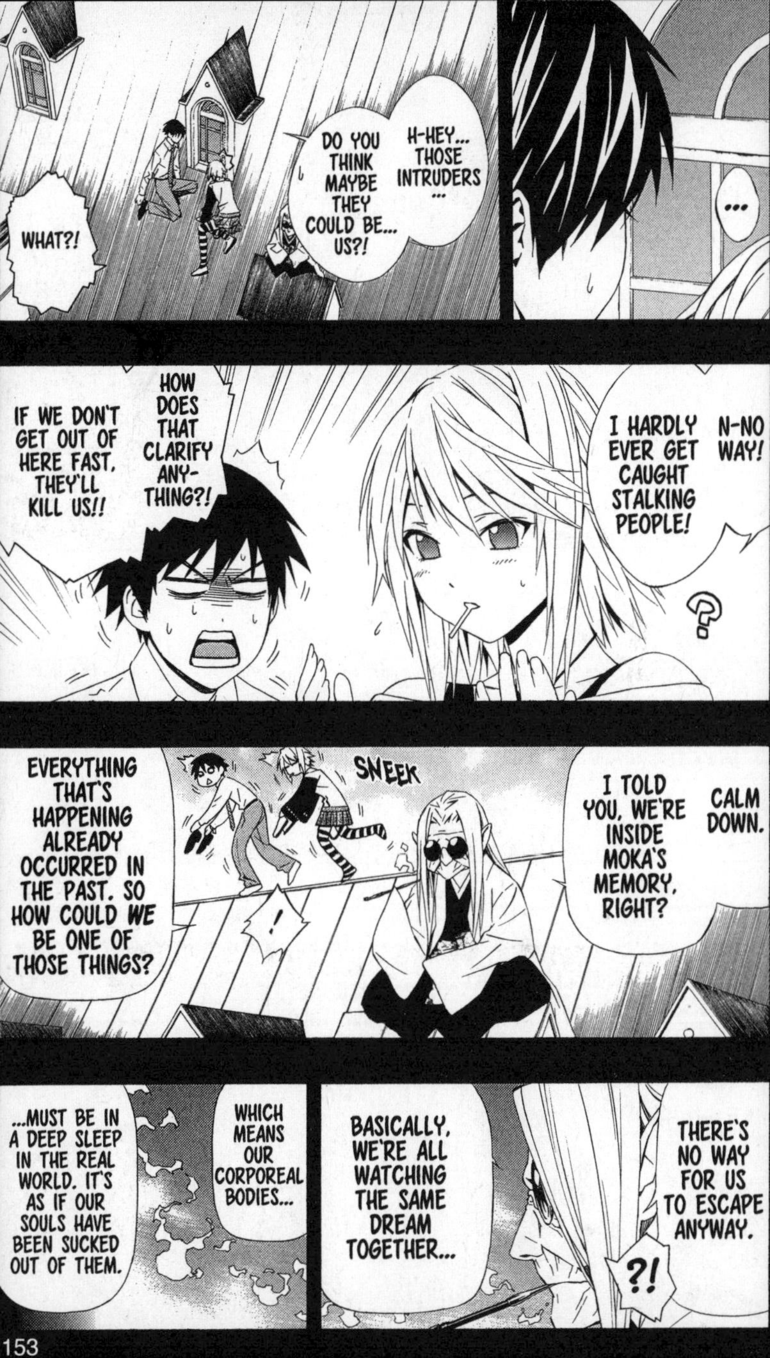
...
H-HEY... THOSE INTRUDERS...
DO YOU THINK MAYBE THEY COULD BE... US?!
WHAT?!
N-NO WAY!
I HARDLY EVER GET CAUGHT STALKING PEOPLE!
?
HOW DOES THAT CLARIFY ANY-THING?!
IF WE DON'T GET OUT OF HERE FAST, THEY'LL KILL US!!
CALM DOWN.
I TOLD YOU, WE'RE INSIDE MOKA'S MEMORY, RIGHT?
SNEEK
!
EVERYTHING THAT'S HAPPENING ALREADY OCCURRED IN THE PAST. SO HOW COULD WE BE ONE OF THOSE THINGS?
THERE'S NO WAY FOR US TO ESCAPE ANYWAY.
?!
BASICALLY, WE'RE ALL WATCHING THE SAME DREAM TOGETHER...
WHICH MEANS OUR CORPOREAL BODIES...
...MUST BE IN A DEEP SLEEP IN THE REAL WORLD. IT'S AS IF OUR SOULS HAVE BEEN SUCKED OUT OF THEM.

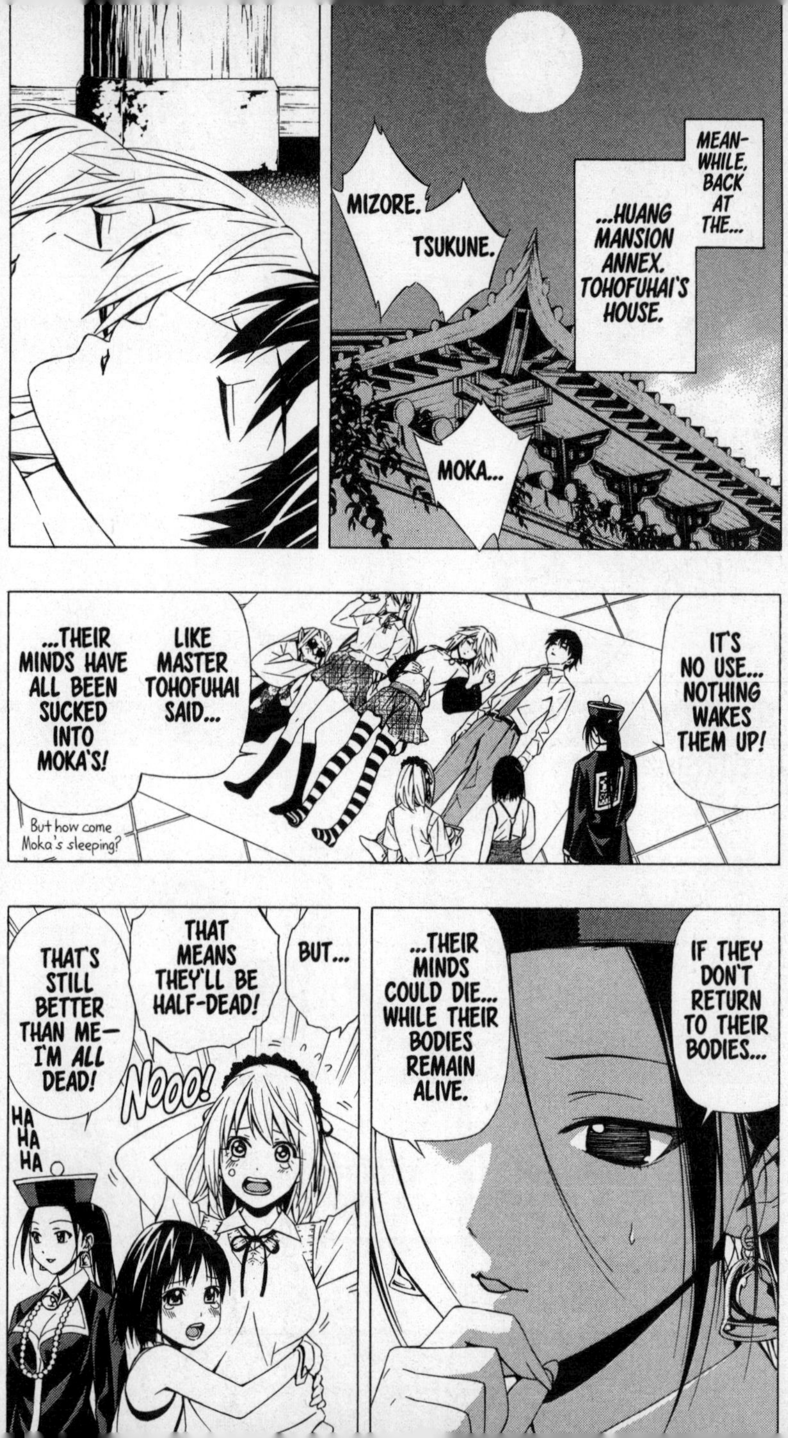
MEAN-WHILE, BACK AT THE...
...HUANG MANSION ANNEX. TOHOFUHAI'S HOUSE.
MIZORE.
TSUKUNE.
MOKA...
IT'S NO USE... NOTHING WAKES THEM UP!
LIKE MASTER TOHOFUHAI SAID...
...THEIR MINDS HAVE ALL BEEN SUCKED INTO MOKA'S!
But how come Moka's sleeping?
IF THEY DON'T RETURN TO THEIR BODIES...
...THEIR MINDS COULD DIE... WHILE THEIR BODIES REMAIN ALIVE.
BUT...
THAT MEANS THEY'LL BE HALF-DEAD!
NOOO!
THAT'S STILL BETTER THAN ME— I'M ALL DEAD!
HA HA HA

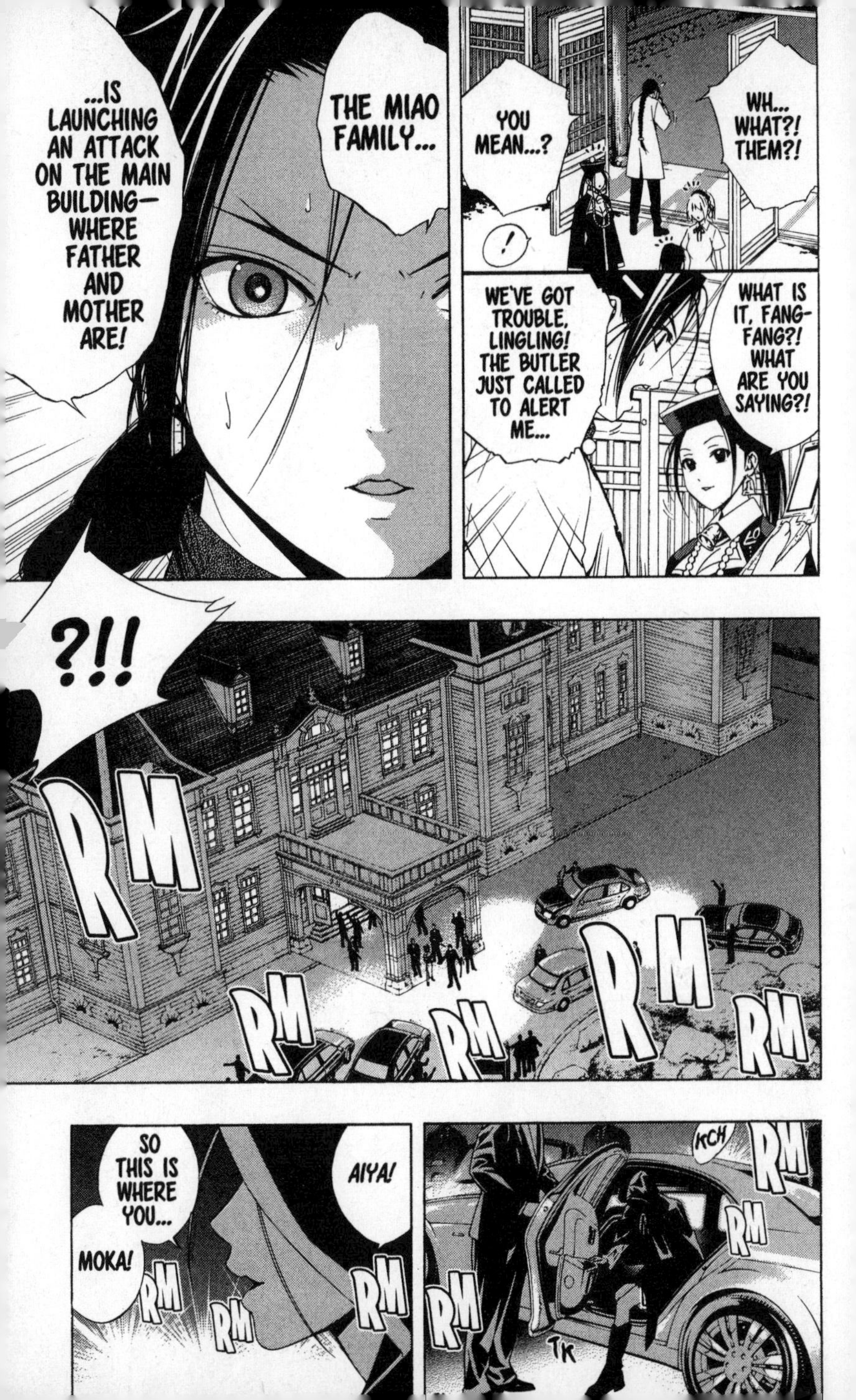
WH... WHAT?! THEM?!
YOU MEAN...?
!
WHAT IS IT, FANG-FANG?! WHAT ARE YOU SAYING?!
WE'VE GOT TROUBLE, LINGLING! THE BUTLER JUST CALLED TO ALERT ME...
THE MIAO FAMILY...
...IS LAUNCHING AN ATTACK ON THE MAIN BUILDING—WHERE FATHER AND MOTHER ARE!
?!!
RM
RM
RM
RM
RM
RM
KCH
RM
RM
RM
TK
AIYA!
SO THIS IS WHERE YOU...
MOKA!
RM
RM
RM

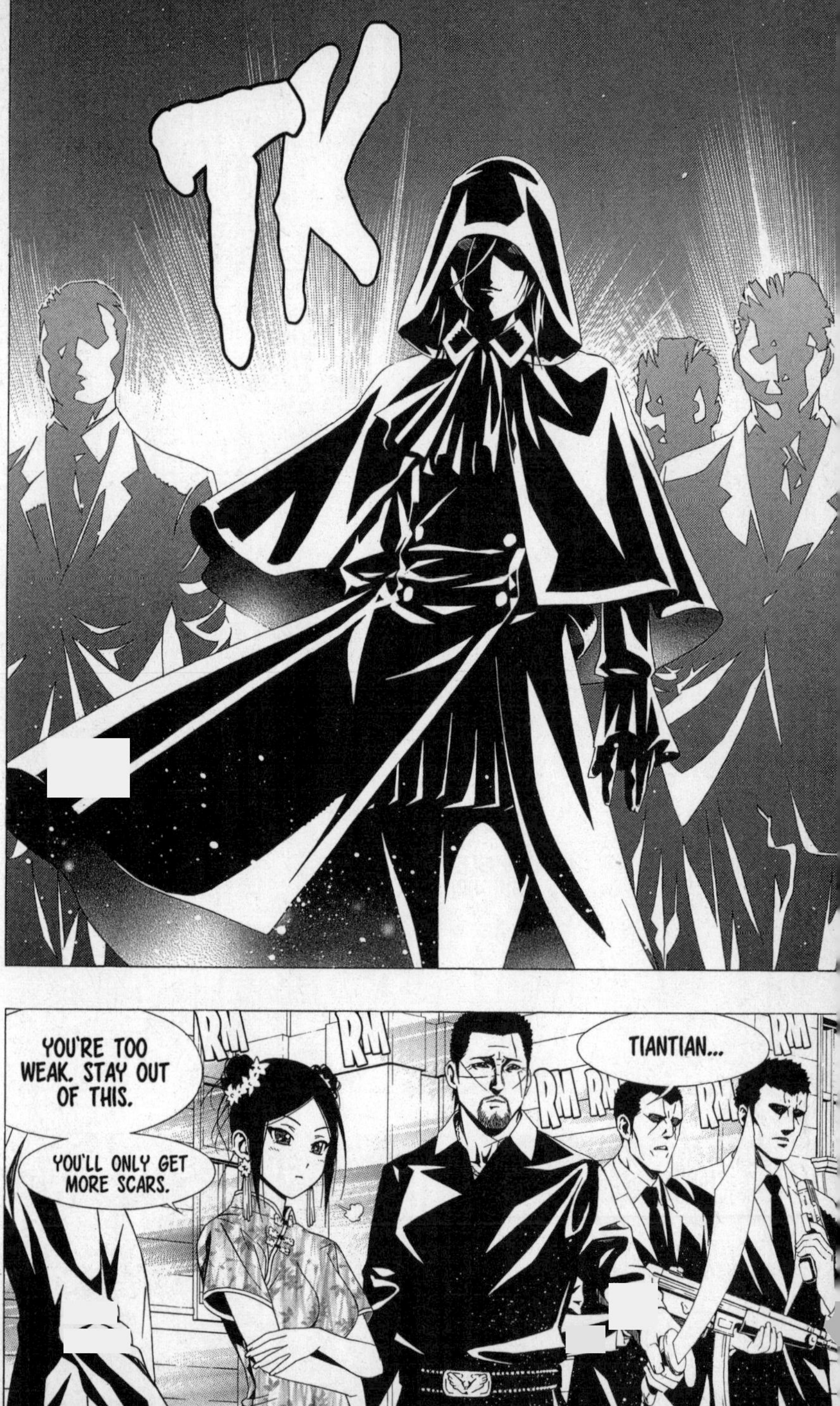
TK
RM RM RM RM RM RM
TIANTIAN...
YOU'RE TOO WEAK. STAY OUT OF THIS.
YOU'LL ONLY GET MORE SCARS.

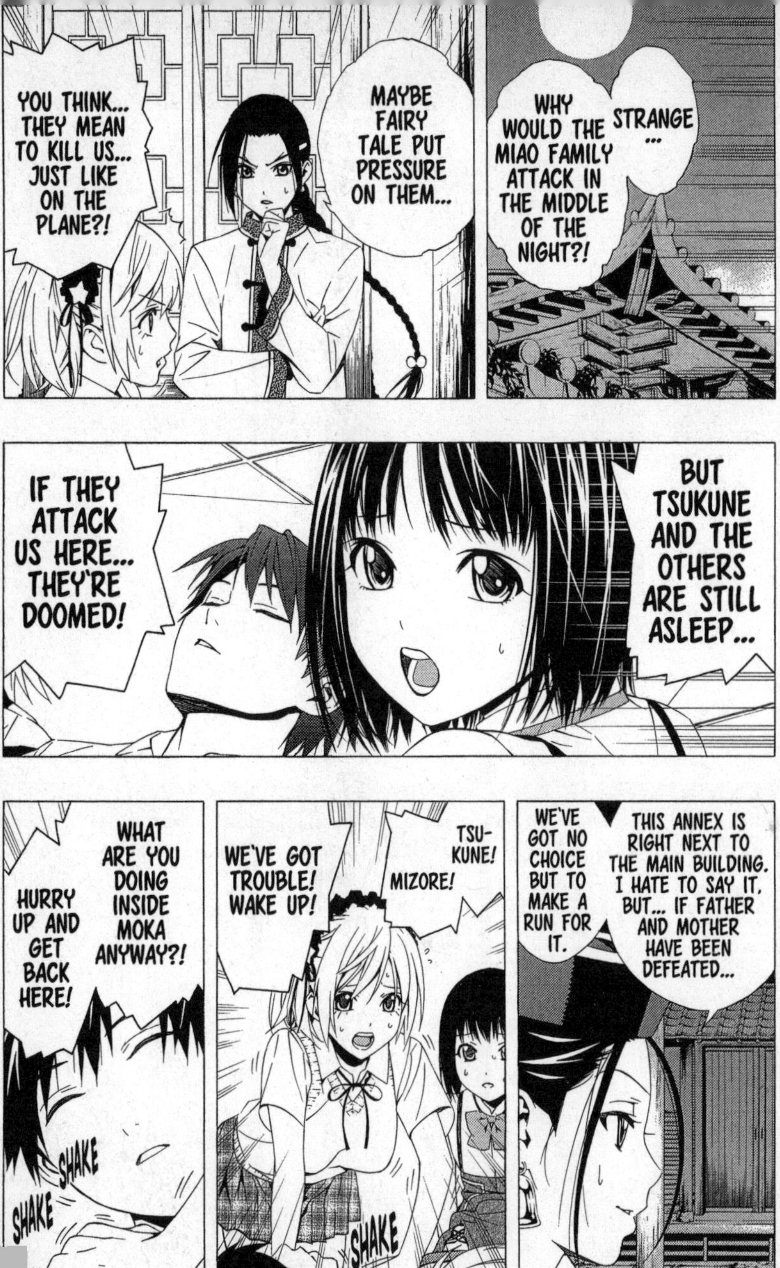
STRANGE...
WHY WOULD THE MIAO FAMILY ATTACK IN THE MIDDLE OF THE NIGHT?!
MAYBE FAIRY TALE PUT PRESSURE ON THEM...
YOU THINK... THEY MEAN TO KILL US... JUST LIKE ON THE PLANE?!
BUT TSUKUNE AND THE OTHERS ARE STILL ASLEEP...
IF THEY ATTACK US HERE... THEY'RE DOOMED!
THIS ANNEX IS RIGHT NEXT TO THE MAIN BUILDING. I HATE TO SAY IT, BUT... IF FATHER AND MOTHER HAVE BEEN DEFEATED...
WE'VE GOT NO CHOICE BUT TO MAKE A RUN FOR IT.
TSU-KUNE!
MIZORE!
WE'VE GOT TROUBLE! WAKE UP!
SHAKE
WHAT ARE YOU DOING INSIDE MOKA ANYWAY?!
HURRY UP AND GET BACK HERE!
SHAKE
SHAKE

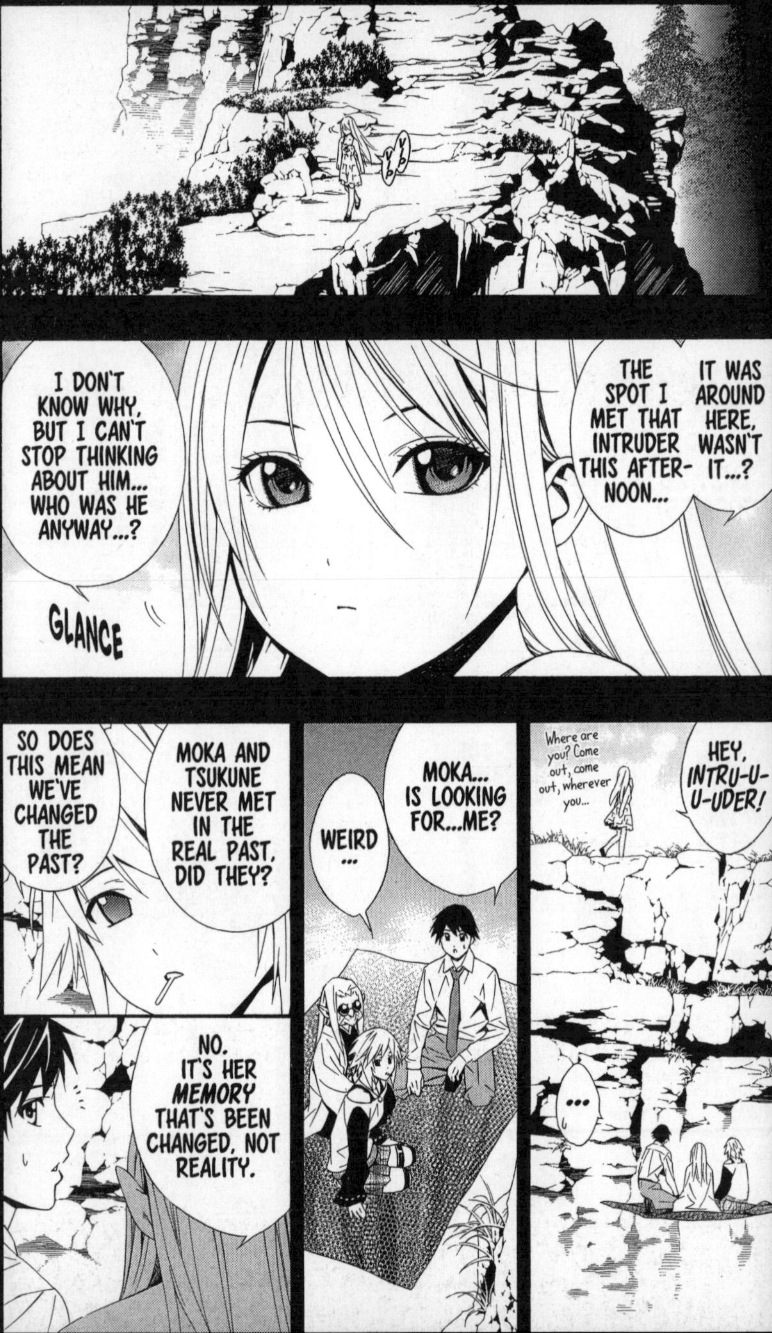
VIP VIP
IT WAS AROUND HERE, WASN'T IT...?
THE SPOT I MET THAT INTRUDER THIS AFTERNOON...
I DON'T KNOW WHY, BUT I CAN'T STOP THINKING ABOUT HIM... WHO WAS HE ANYWAY...?
GLANCE
HEY, INTRU-U-U-UDER!
Where are you? Come out, come out, wherever you...
...
MOKA... IS LOOKING FOR...ME?
WEIRD...
MOKA AND TSUKUNE NEVER MET IN THE REAL PAST, DID THEY?
SO DOES THIS MEAN WE'VE CHANGED THE PAST?
NO. IT'S HER MEMORY THAT'S BEEN CHANGED, NOT REALITY.

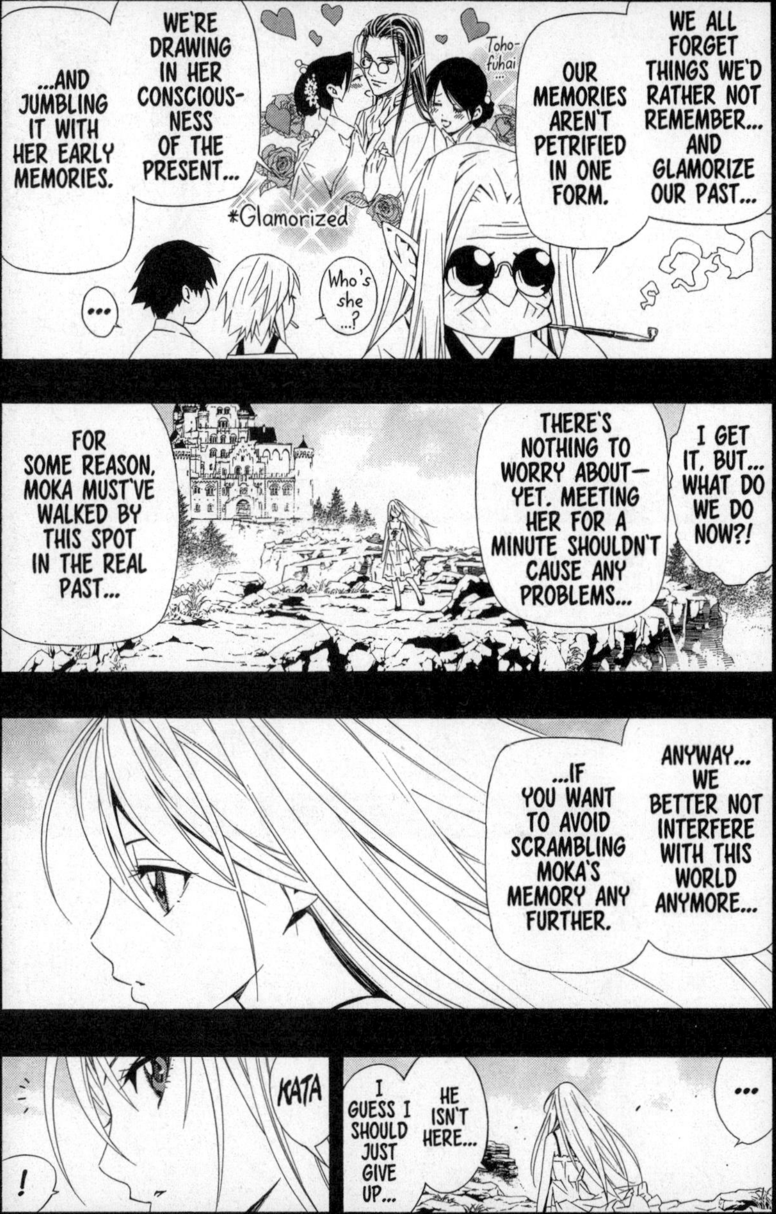

WE ALL FORGET THINGS WE'D RATHER NOT REMEMBER... AND GLAMORIZE OUR PAST...
OUR MEMORIES AREN'T PETRIFIED IN ONE FORM.
Toho-fuhai...
WE'RE DRAWING IN HER CONSCIOUSNESS OF THE PRESENT...
...AND JUMBLING IT WITH HER EARLY MEMORIES.
*Glamorized
Who's she...?
...
I GET IT, BUT... WHAT DO WE DO NOW?!
THERE'S NOTHING TO WORRY ABOUT—YET. MEETING HER FOR A MINUTE SHOULDN'T CAUSE ANY PROBLEMS...
FOR SOME REASON, MOKA MUST'VE WALKED BY THIS SPOT IN THE REAL PAST...
ANYWAY... WE BETTER NOT INTERFERE WITH THIS WORLD ANYMORE...
...IF YOU WANT TO AVOID SCRAMBLING MOKA'S MEMORY ANY FURTHER.
...
HE ISN'T HERE...
I GUESS I SHOULD JUST GIVE UP...
KATA
!

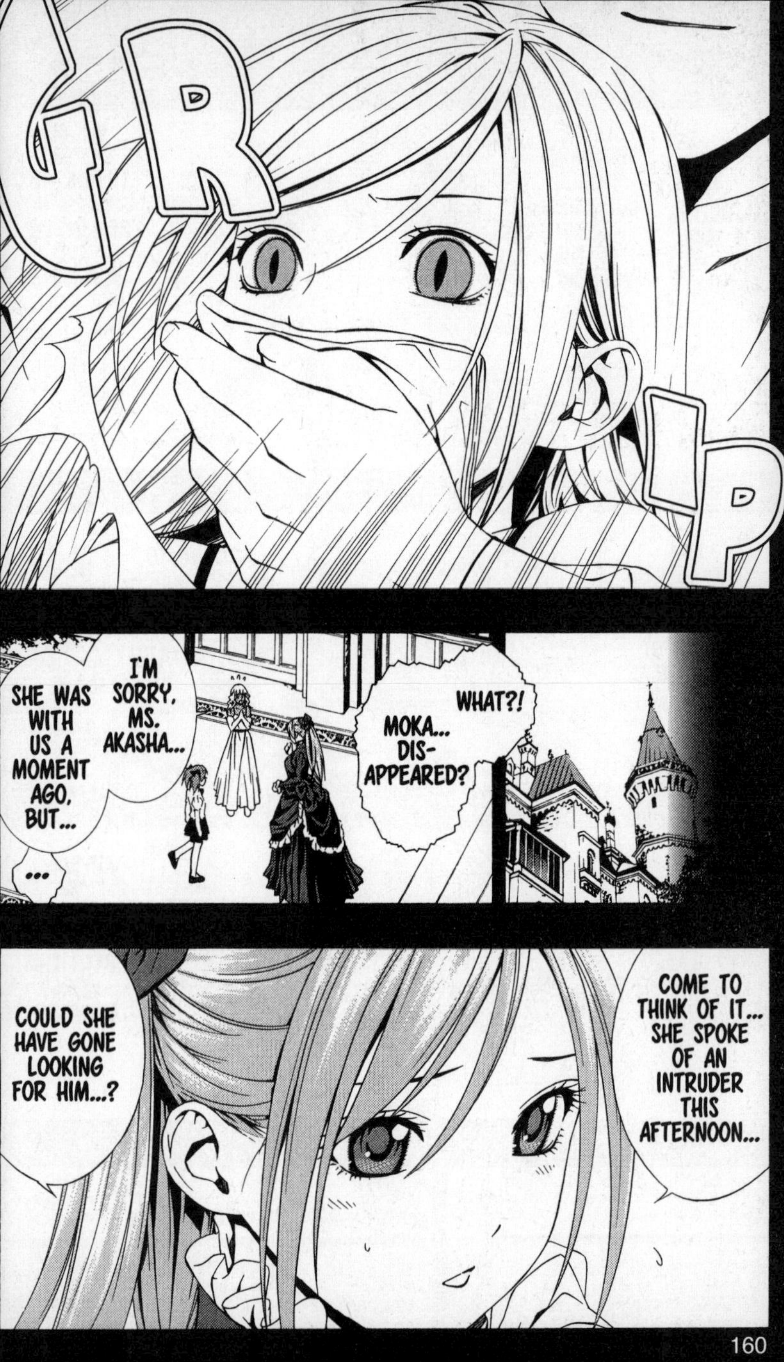
GRIP
WHAT?!
MOKA... DIS-APPEARED?
I'M SORRY, MS. AKASHA...
SHE WAS WITH US A MOMENT AGO, BUT...
...
COME TO THINK OF IT... SHE SPOKE OF AN INTRUDER THIS AFTERNOON...
COULD SHE HAVE GONE LOOKING FOR HIM...?

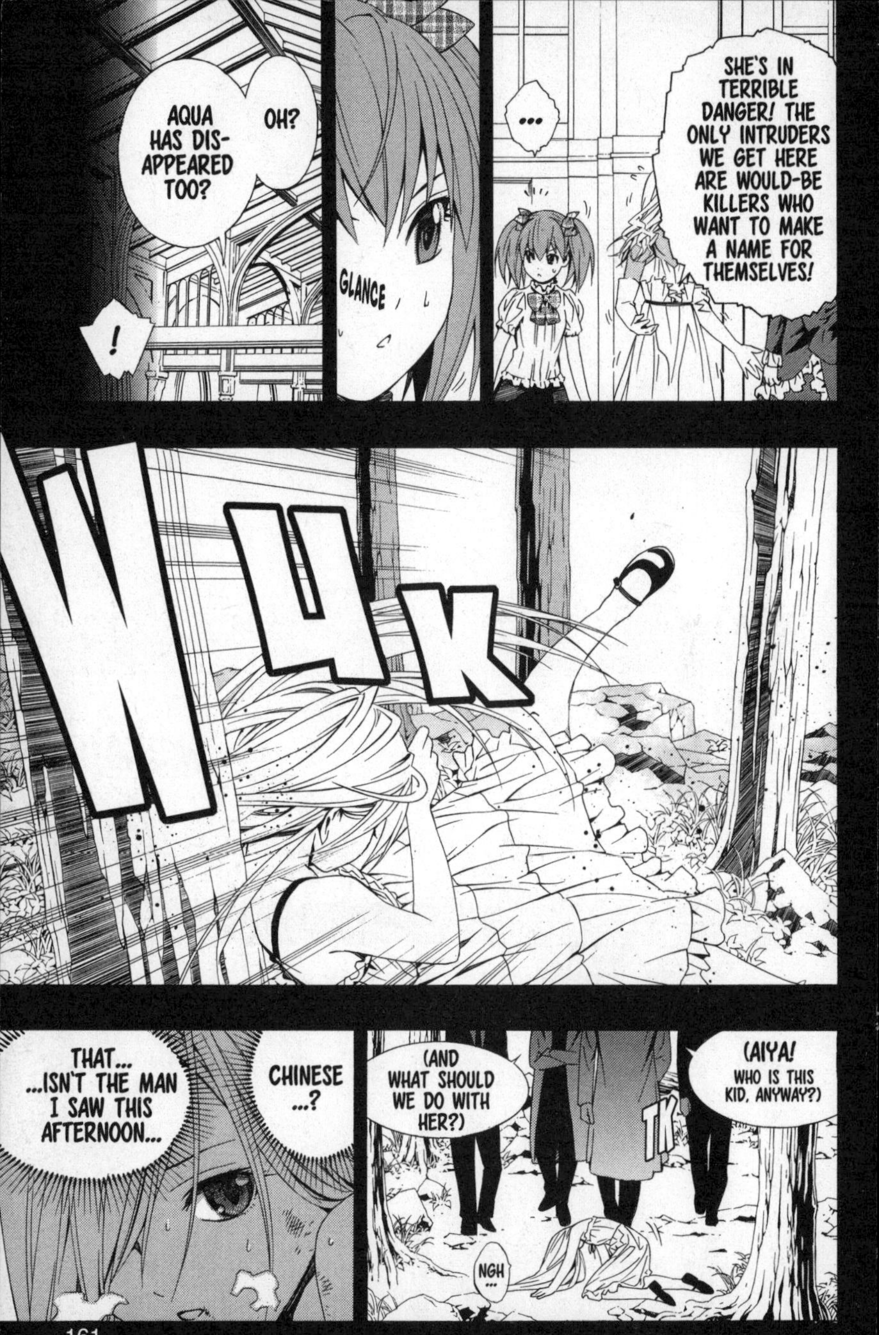
SHE'S IN TERRIBLE DANGER! THE ONLY INTRUDERS WE GET HERE ARE WOULD-BE KILLERS WHO WANT TO MAKE A NAME FOR THEMSELVES!
...
GLANCE
OH?
AQUA HAS DIS-APPEARED TOO?
!
WHAK
(AIYA! WHO IS THIS KID, ANYWAY?)
TK
(AND WHAT SHOULD WE DO WITH HER?)
NGH...
CHINESE ...?
THAT... ...ISN'T THE MAN I SAW THIS AFTERNOON...

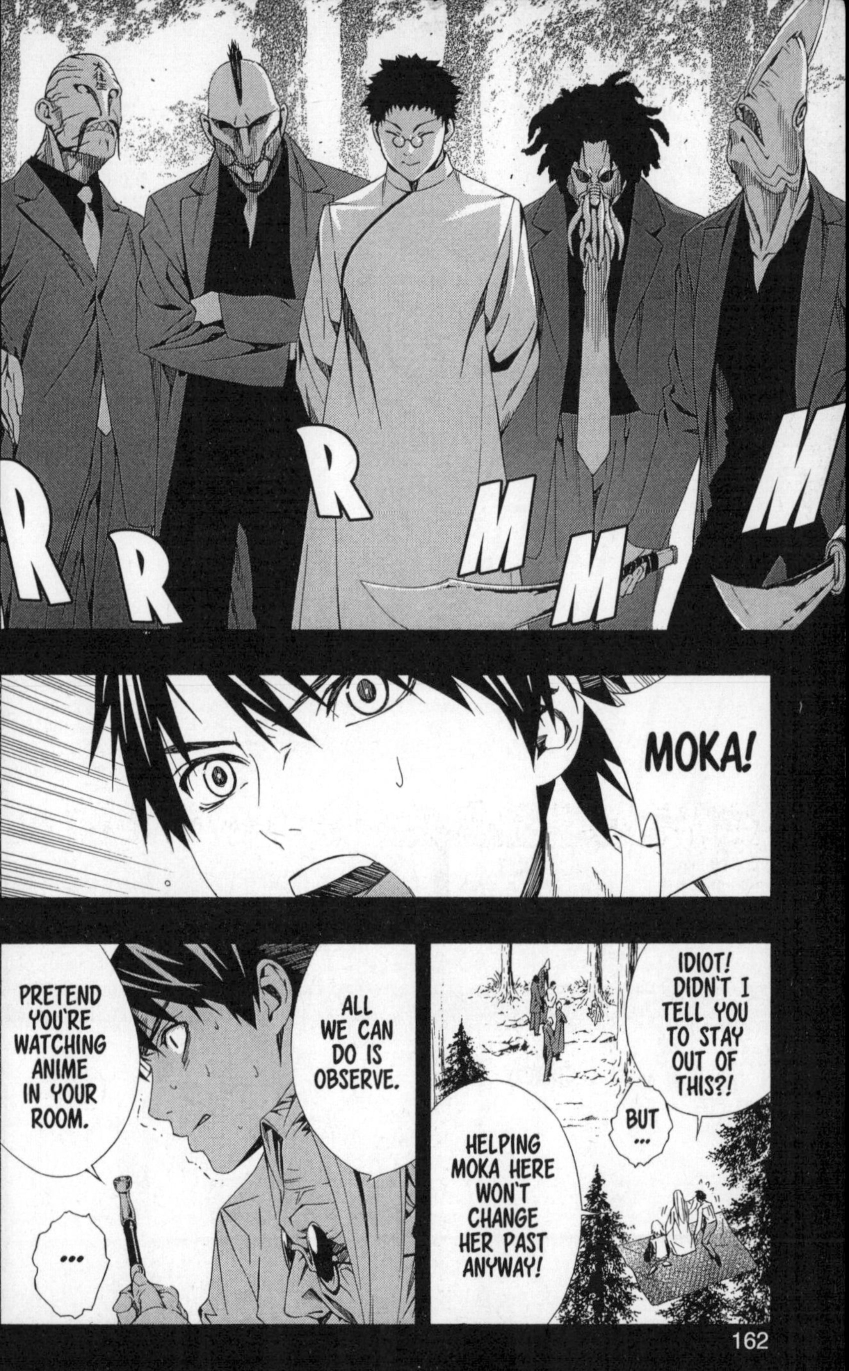
RRRMMM
MOKA!
IDIOT! DIDN'T I TELL YOU TO STAY OUT OF THIS?!
BUT...
HELPING MOKA HERE WON'T CHANGE HER PAST ANYWAY!
ALL WE CAN DO IS OBSERVE.
PRETEND YOU'RE WATCHING ANIME IN YOUR ROOM.
...

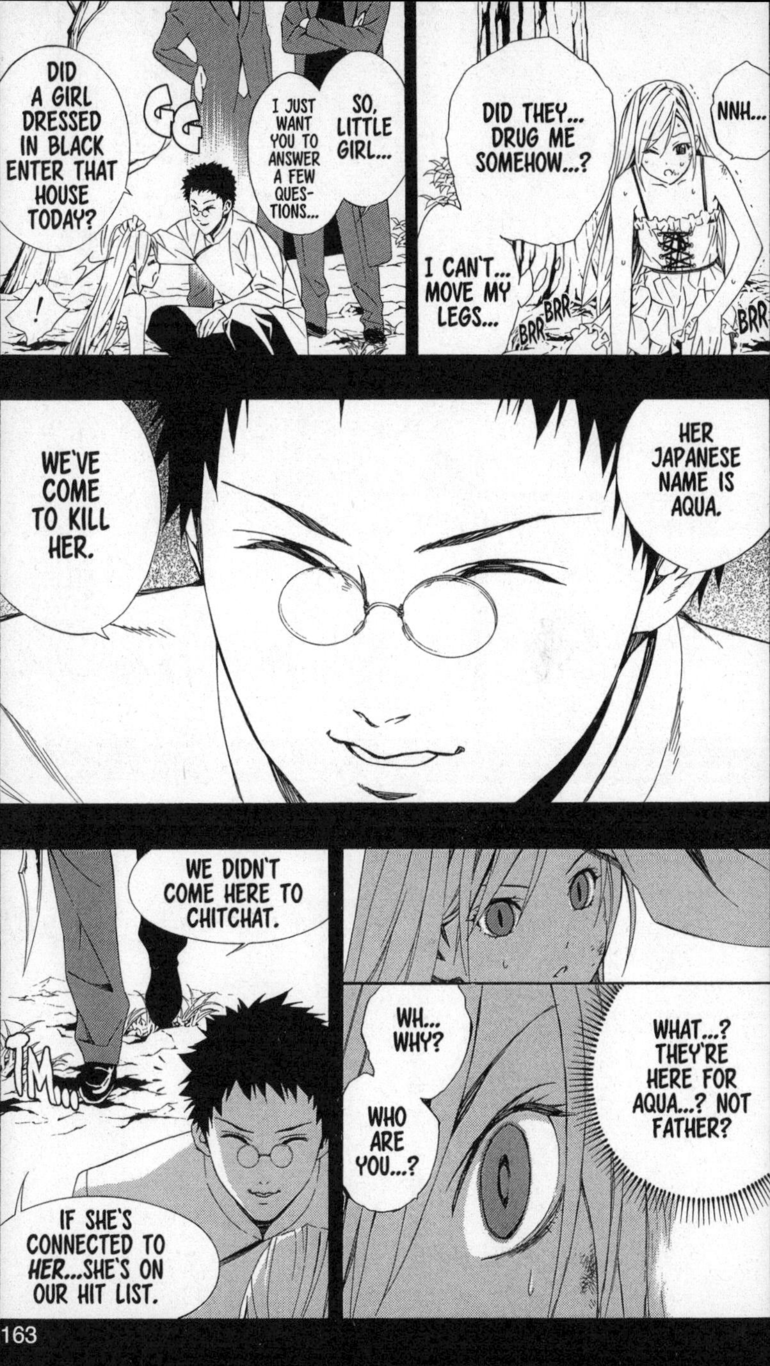
NNH...
DID THEY... DRUG ME SOMEHOW...?
I CAN'T... MOVE MY LEGS...
BRR BRR
BRR
SO, LITTLE GIRL...
I JUST WANT YOU TO ANSWER A FEW QUES- TIONS...
DID A GIRL DRESSED IN BLACK ENTER THAT HOUSE TODAY?
GG
!
HER JAPANESE NAME IS AQUA.
WE'VE COME TO KILL HER.
WHAT...? THEY'RE HERE FOR AQUA...? NOT FATHER?
WH... WHY?
WHO ARE YOU...?
WE DIDN'T COME HERE TO CHITCHAT.
IF SHE'S CONNECTED TO *HER*...SHE'S ON OUR HIT LIST.

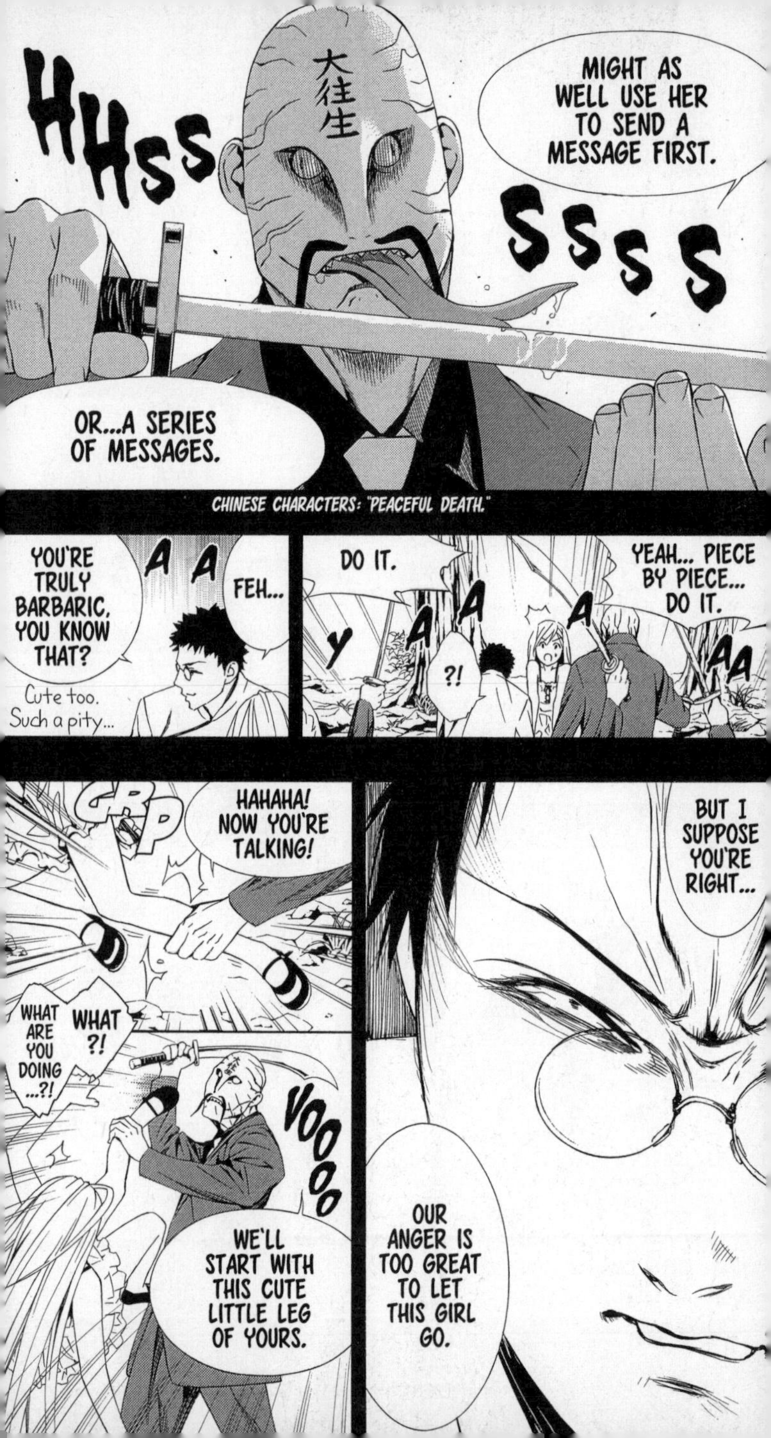
大往生
MIGHT AS WELL USE HER TO SEND A MESSAGE FIRST.
SSSS
HHSS
OR...A SERIES OF MESSAGES.
CHINESE CHARACTERS: "PEACEFUL DEATH."
YEAH... PIECE BY PIECE... DO IT.
AA
A
DO IT.
A
A
?!
Y
FEH...
A A
YOU'RE TRULY BARBARIC, YOU KNOW THAT?
Cute too. Such a pity...
BUT I SUPPOSE YOU'RE RIGHT...
OUR ANGER IS TOO GREAT TO LET THIS GIRL GO.
HAHAHA! NOW YOU'RE TALKING!
GRP
WHAT?!
WHAT ARE YOU DOING...?!
VOOOO
WE'LL START WITH THIS CUTE LITTLE LEG OF YOURS.

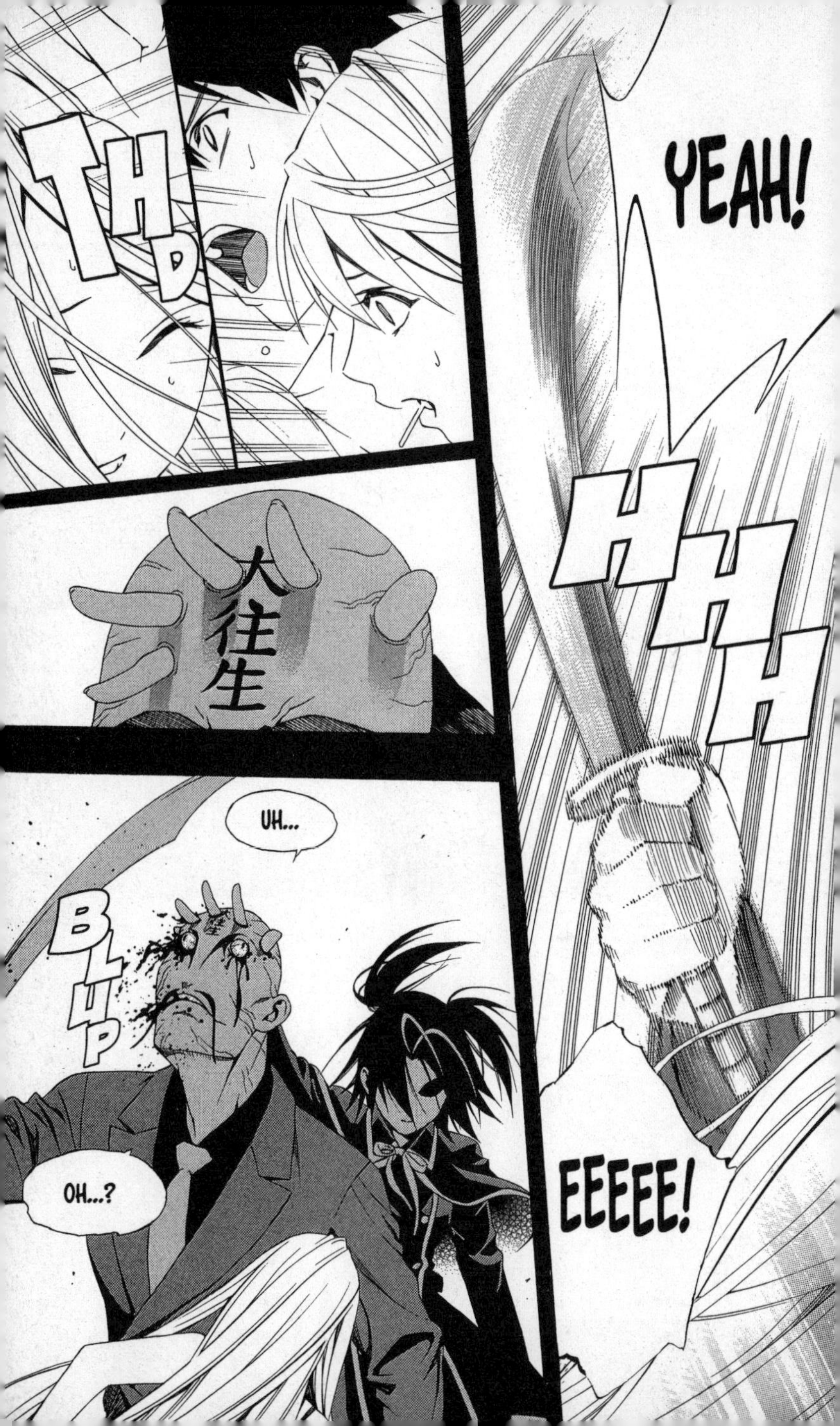
YEAH!
HHHH
EEEEE!
THD
大往生
UH...
BLUP
OH...?

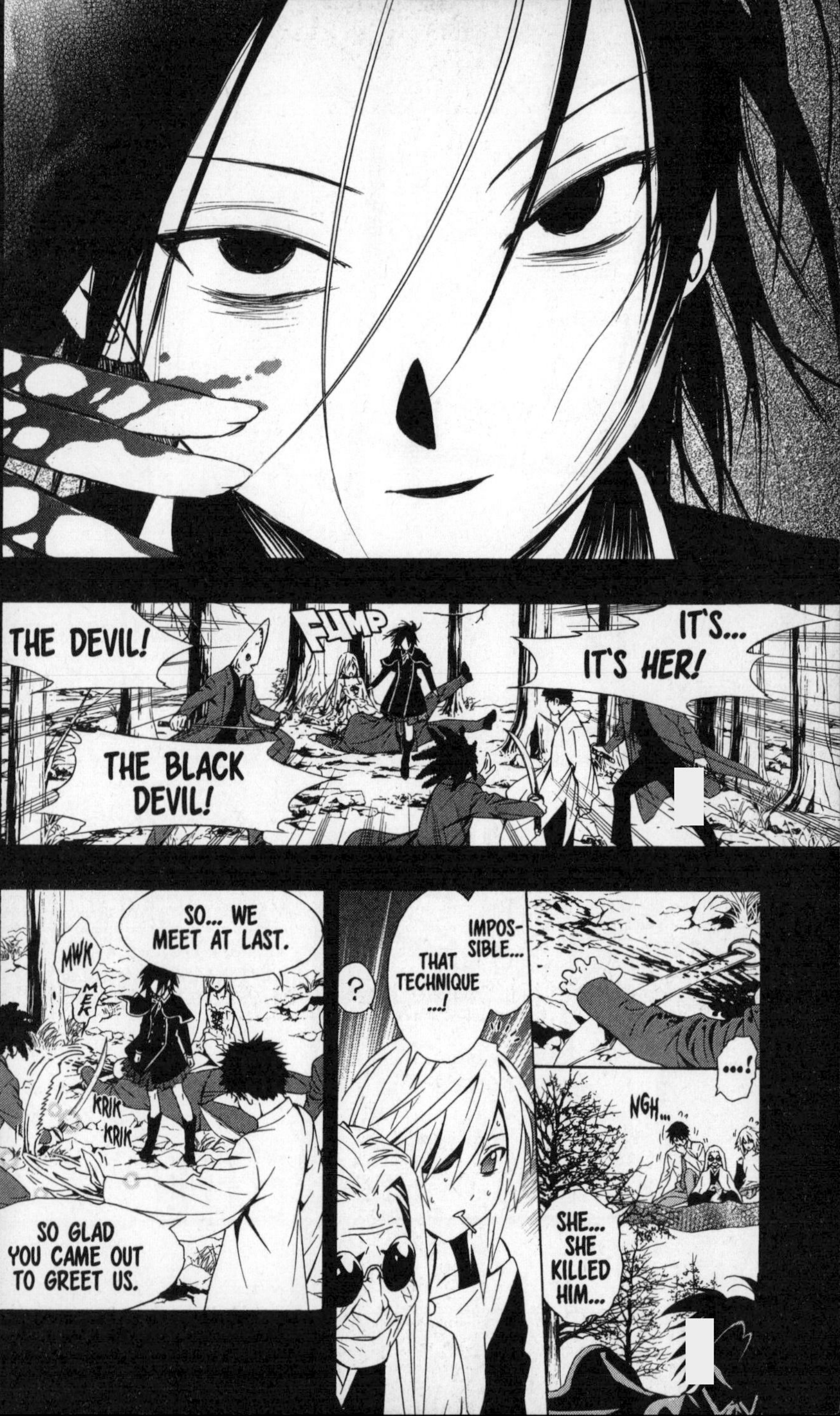
IT'S... IT'S HER!
FUMP
THE DEVIL!
THE BLACK DEVIL!
...!
NGH...
SHE... SHE KILLED HIM...
IMPOSSIBLE... THAT TECHNIQUE ...!
?
SO... WE MEET AT LAST.
MWK
MEK
KRIK KRIK
SO GLAD YOU CAME OUT TO GREET US.

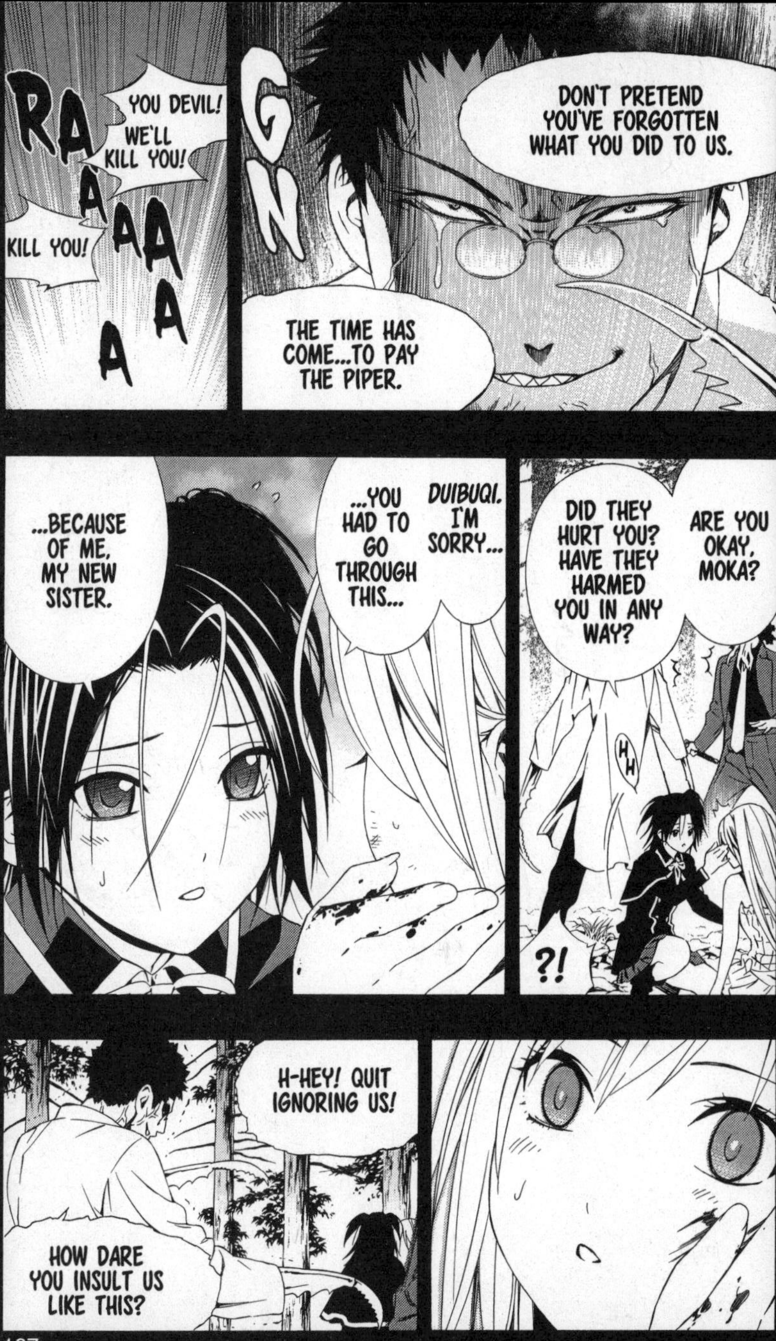
DON'T PRETEND YOU'VE FORGOTTEN WHAT YOU DID TO US.
GN
THE TIME HAS COME...TO PAY THE PIPER.
YOU DEVIL!
WE'LL KILL YOU!
RAAAAAAA
KILL YOU!
ARE YOU OKAY, MOKA?
DID THEY HURT YOU? HAVE THEY HARMED YOU IN ANY WAY?
HH
?!
DUIBUQI. I'M SORRY...
...YOU HAD TO GO THROUGH THIS...
...BECAUSE OF ME, MY NEW SISTER.
H-HEY! QUIT IGNORING US!
HOW DARE YOU INSULT US LIKE THIS?

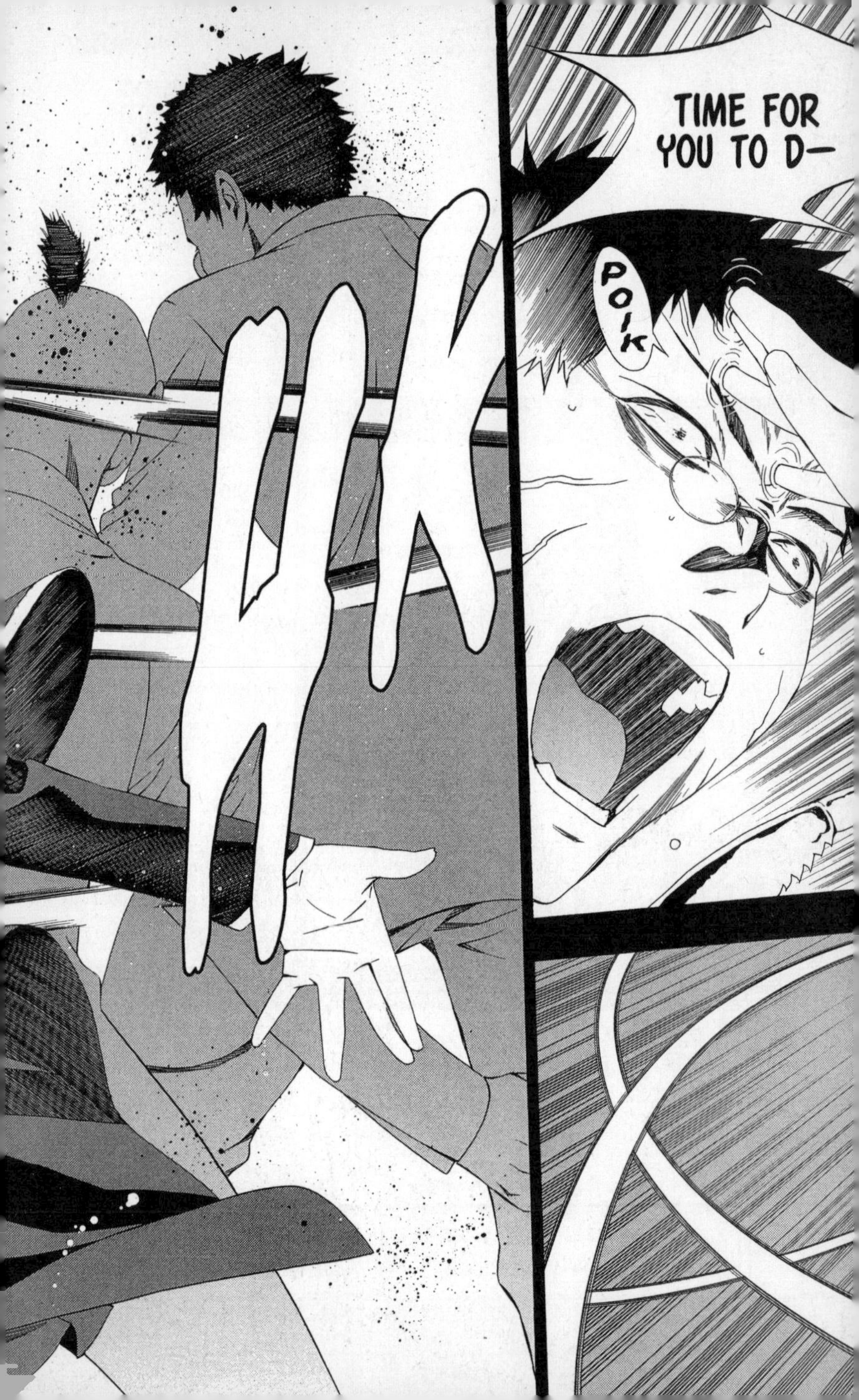
TIME FOR YOU TO D—
POIK
HIK

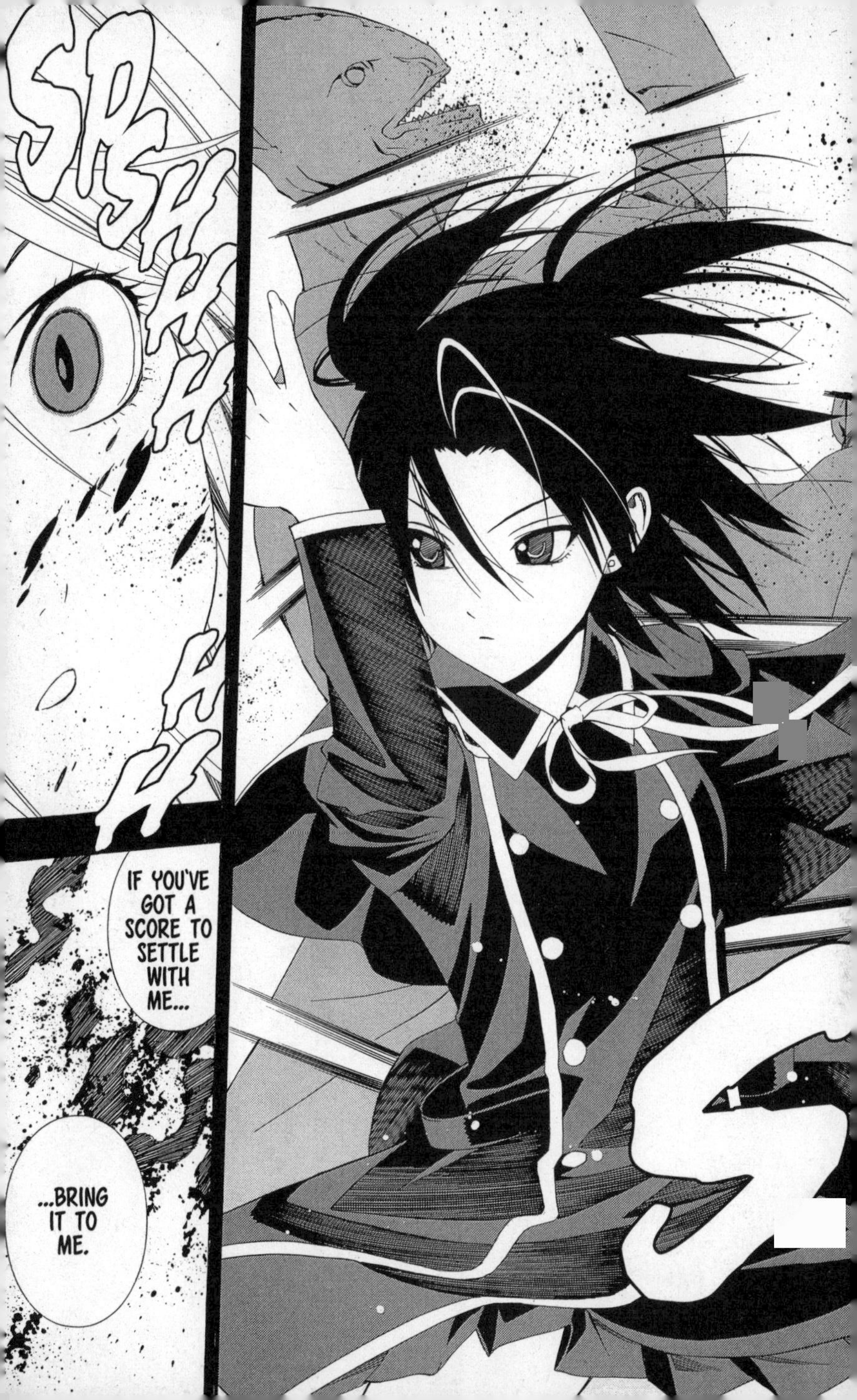
S
SPSHHHHH
IF YOU'VE GOT A SCORE TO SETTLE WITH ME...
...BRING IT TO ME.

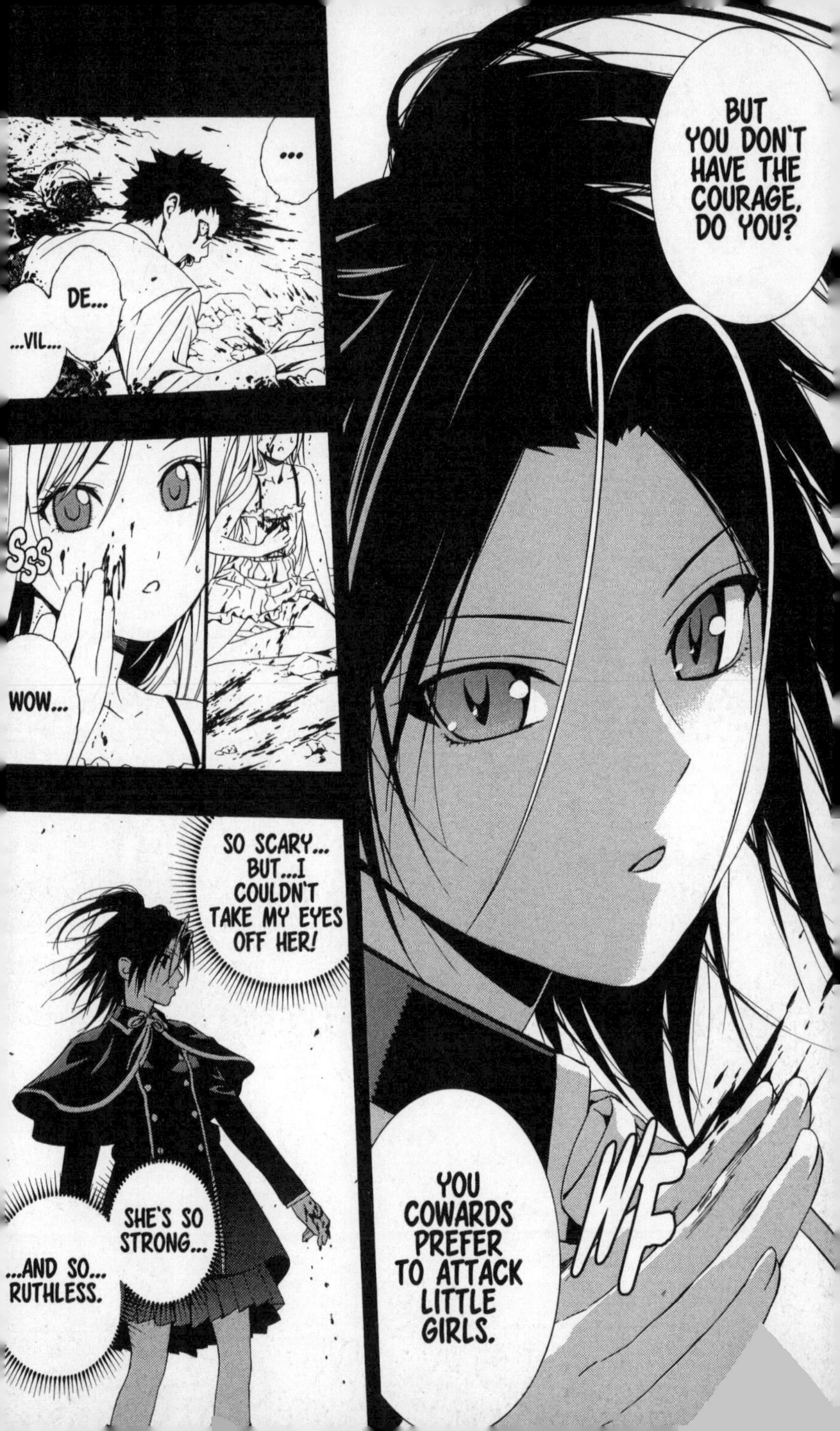
BUT YOU DON'T HAVE THE COURAGE, DO YOU?
YOU COWARDS PREFER TO ATTACK LITTLE GIRLS.
...
DE...
...VIL...
SSS
WOW...
SO SCARY... BUT...I COULDN'T TAKE MY EYES OFF HER!
SHE'S SO STRONG...
...AND SO... RUTHLESS.

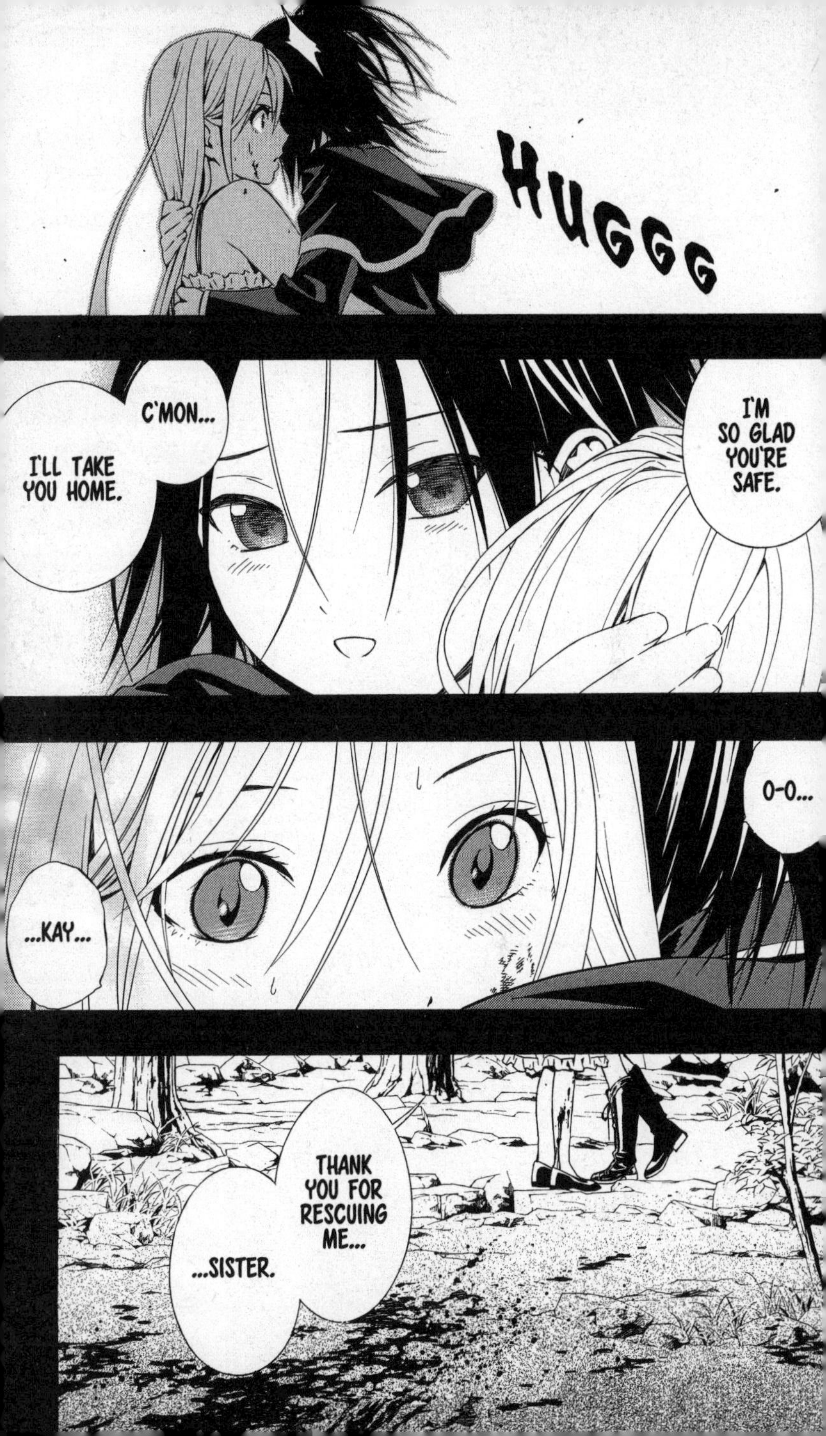
HUGGG
I'M SO GLAD YOU'RE SAFE.
C'MON...
I'LL TAKE YOU HOME.
O-O...
...KAY...
THANK YOU FOR RESCUING ME...
...SISTER.

ROSARIO+VAMPIRE

Season II

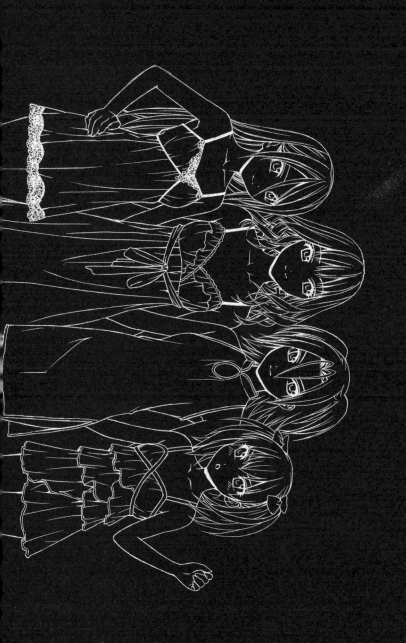

# ROSARIO + VAMPIRE

## Season II

This end-of-volume theater takes place right after Tsukune and the others reach Hong Kong (between Chapter 27 and Chapter 28).

**Meaningless
End-of-Volume
Theater**

## VII

## • Welcome to Hong Kong •

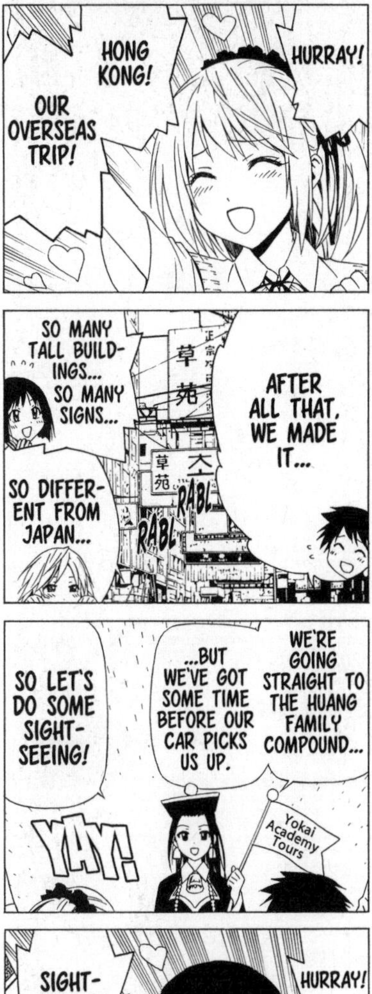
HURRAY!
HONG KONG!
OUR OVERSEAS TRIP!
AFTER ALL THAT, WE MADE IT...
SO MANY TALL BUILDINGS... SO MANY SIGNS...
RABL
RABL
SO DIFFERENT FROM JAPAN...
WE'RE GOING STRAIGHT TO THE HUANG FAMILY COMPOUND...
...BUT WE'VE GOT SOME TIME BEFORE OUR CAR PICKS US UP.
SO LET'S DO SOME SIGHT-SEEING!
Yokai Academy Tours
YAY!
HURRAY!
SIGHT-SEEING!
FREE TIME!

## • The Right Person •

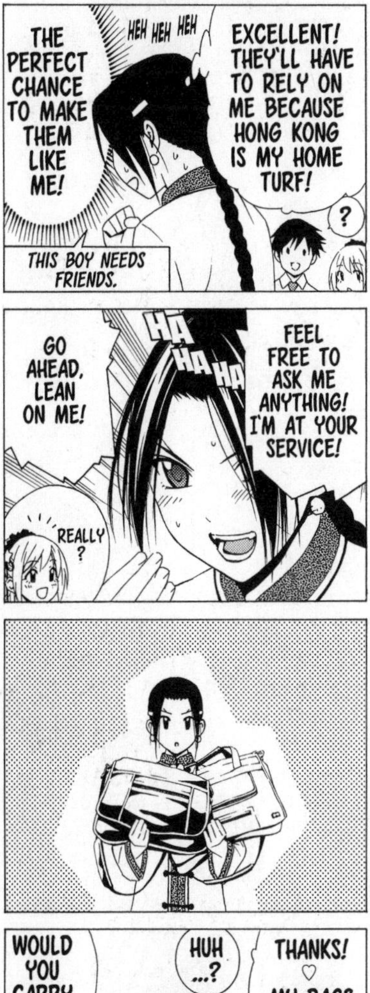
EXCELLENT! THEY'LL HAVE TO RELY ON ME BECAUSE HONG KONG IS MY HOME TURF!
HEH HEH HEH
THE PERFECT CHANCE TO MAKE THEM LIKE ME!
?
THIS BOY NEEDS FRIENDS.
FEEL FREE TO ASK ME ANYTHING! I'M AT YOUR SERVICE!
HA HA HA
GO AHEAD, LEAN ON ME!
REALLY ?
THANKS! ♡ MY BAGS WERE SO HEAVY.
HUH ...?
Not on purpose.
WOULD YOU CARRY OURS TOO?

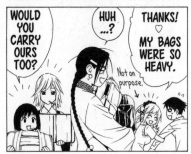

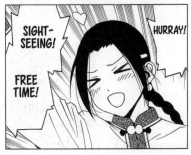

## • 2D OVERSEAS •

W-WAIT... I MEANT I'D BE YOUR TOUR GUIDE... NOT YOUR BELLHOP!
GARA GARA
HUF... HUF...
AND YOUR INTERPRETER. YOU NEED AN INTERPRETER, RIGHT?
NAH. WE'RE FINE.
See?
EXCUSE ME. COULD YOU GIVE ME DIRECTIONS?
STRAIGHT AHEAD, THEN VEER RIGHT AT THE Y.
THANK YOU!
HUH? KURUMU! YOU SPEAK CHINESE?
'COURSE NOT.
THEN HOW COULD YOU TALK TO THAT LADY?!
HA!
JUST DON'T...
...THINK ABOUT IT TOO MUCH.

## • DEEP •

PEEP
WHY ARE YOU HIDING, MIZORE?
WHAT'S IT LOOK LIKE? I'M STALKING THEM.
EVEN IN HONG KONG?!
HONG KONG IS NICE...
BUT WATCHING TSUKUNE SIGHTSEEING IS MY KIND OF SIGHTSEEING.
THAT'S... DEEP.
WOW...
YOU'RE IN MY WAY!

Please send questions and fan letters to ➡ Rosario+Vampire Fan Mail, VIZ Media, P.O. Box 77010, San Francisco, CA 94107

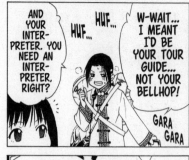

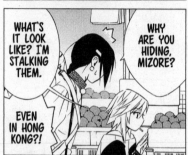

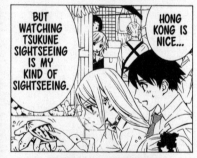

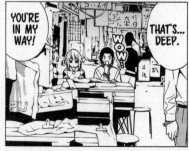

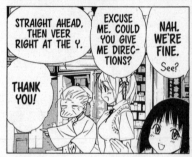

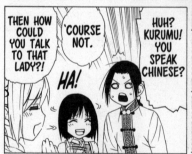

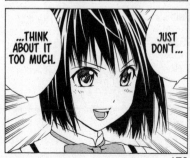

# Rosario+Vampire

## Akihisa Ikeda

**• Staff •**

Makoto Saito
Nobuyuki Hayashi
Rika Shirota

**• Assistants •**

Kenji Tashiro
Tomoharu Shimomura
Yuichi Ozaki
Soshi Kurotani

**• 3DCG •**

Takaharu Yoshizawa

**• Editor •**

Takanori Asada

**• Comic •**

Kenju Noro

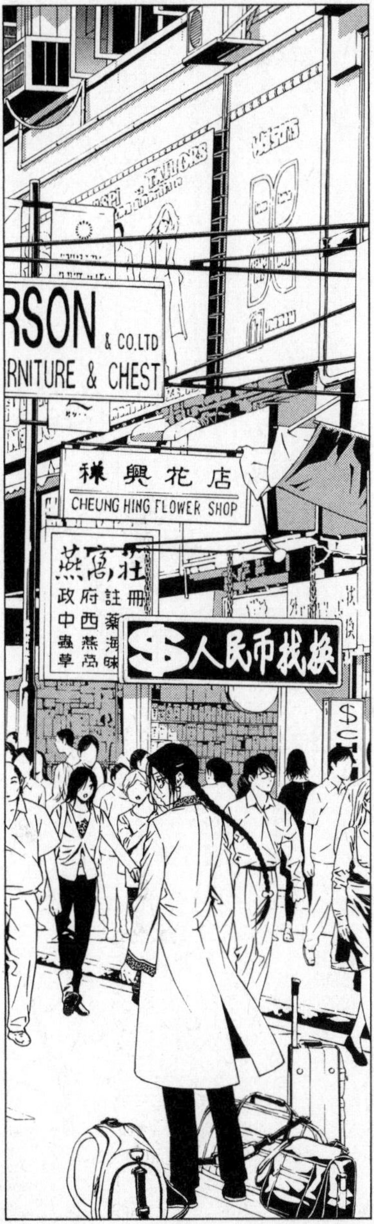
RSON & CO.LTD
RNITURE & CHEST
CHEUNG HING FLOWER SHOP
$人民币找换

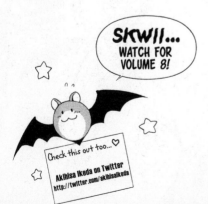

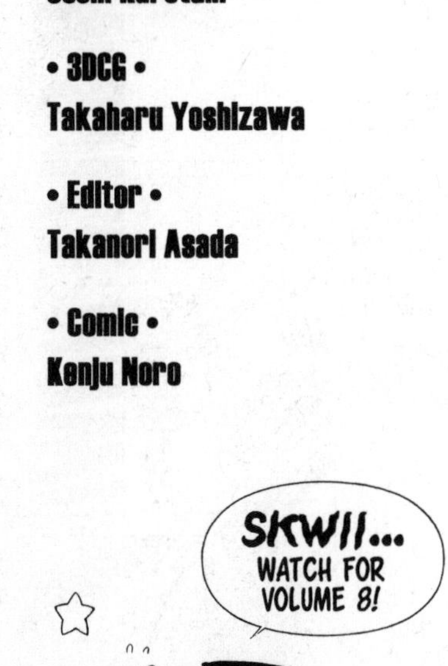
SKWII... WATCH FOR VOLUME 8!
Check this out too...♡
Akihisa Ikeda on Twitter
http://twitter.com/akihisaikeda

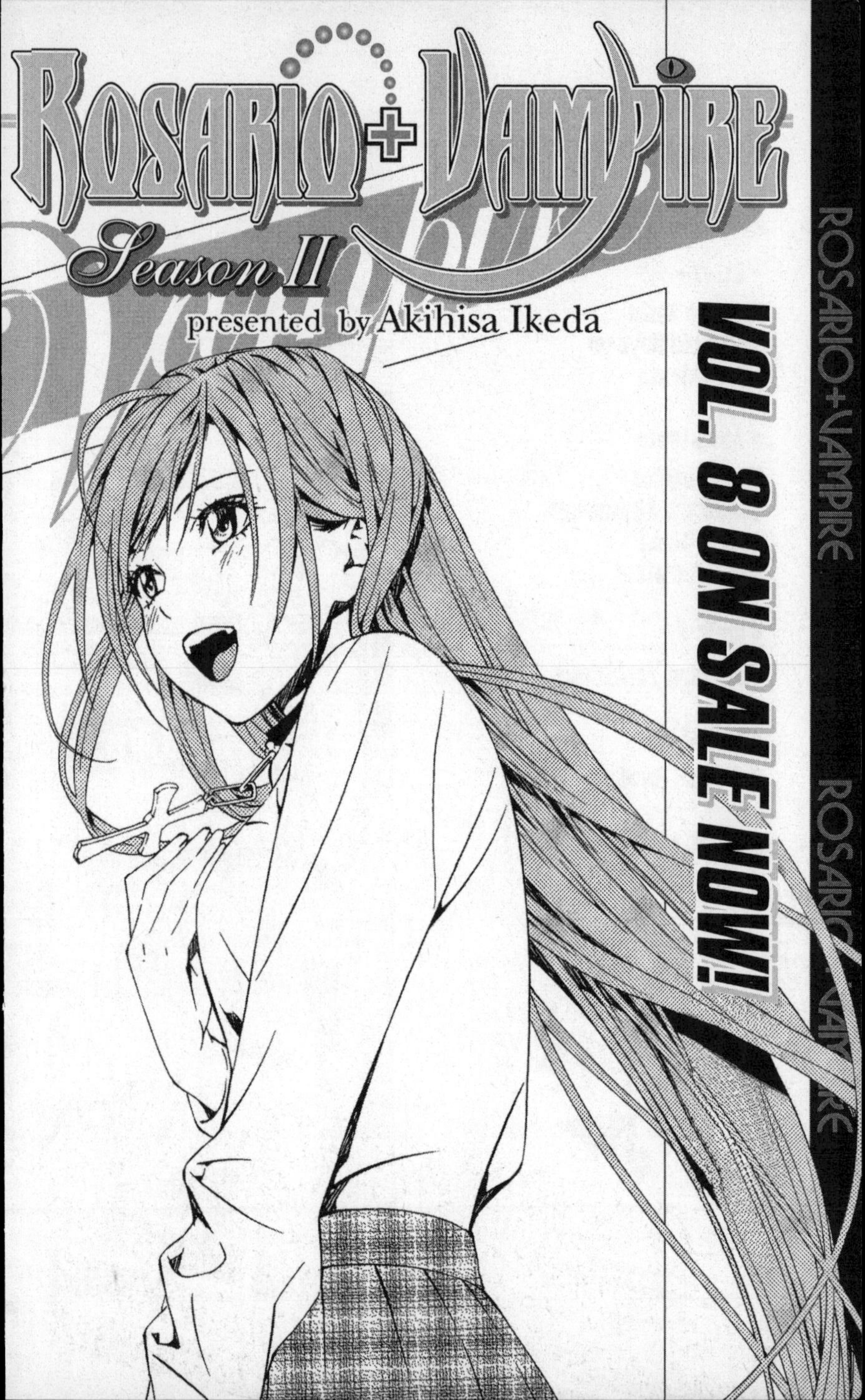
ROSARIO+VAMPIRE
Season II
presented by Akihisa Ikeda
VOL. 8 ON SALE NOW!
ROSARIO+VAMPIRE
ROSARIO+VAMPIRE

NEXT VOLUME...
WHEN THE HIDDEN PAST IS REVEALED, THE DOOR TO THE TRUTH WILL OPEN...

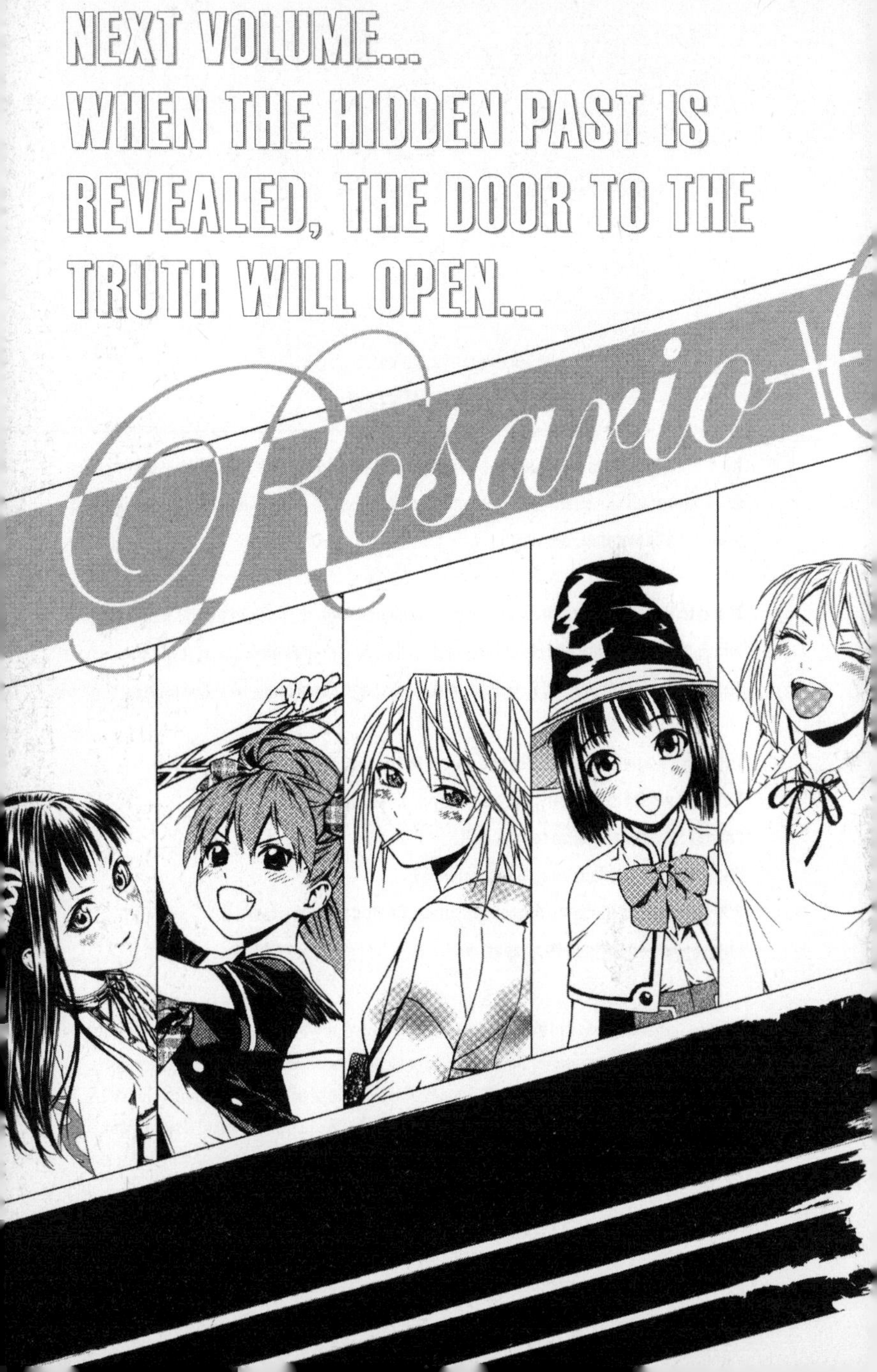
Rosario+

## *AKIHISA IKEDA*

How time flies! This is already the seventh volume of Season II. I've been working hard to establish all the characters, but the story is about to take a sharp turn right around... now! (That's my plan, anyway.)

If you were to compare the story to the game of shogi, this would be the middle part, where the pieces start to clash into each other. And if you think about it in terms of plot structure—Introduction, Development, Twist, and Conclusion— this would be the twist.

I did say I was about a third of the way into the entire story arc in volume 4...
But that would mean only twelve volumes in all, wouldn't it?
I'm not sure it's all going to fit... (LOL)
What fate awaits Tsukune and his friends?
Will I be able to continue drawing without fleeing from my task...?
I hope you all continue to support me!

Akihisa Ikeda was born in 1976 in Miyazaki. He debuted as a mangaka with the four-volume magical warrior fantasy series *Kiruto* in 2002, which was serialized in *Monthly Shonen Jump*. *Rosario+Vampire* debuted in *Monthly Shonen Jump* in March of 2004 and is continuing in the magazine *Jump Square (Jump SQ)* as *Rosario+Vampire: Season II*. In Japan, *Rosario+Vampire* is also available as a drama CD. In 2008, the story was released as an anime. Season II is also available as an anime now. And in Japan, there is a Nintendo DS game based on the series.

Ikeda has been a huge fan of vampires and monsters since he was a little kid. He says one of the perks of being a manga artist is being able to go for walks during the day when everybody else is stuck in the office.

# ROSARIO+VAMPIRE: Season II
# 7

SHONEN JUMP ADVANCED Manga Edition

## STORY & ART BY **AKIHISA IKEDA**

Translation/Tetsuichiro Miyaki
English Adaptation/Gerard Jones
Touch-up Art & Lettering/Stephen Dutro
Cover & Interior Design/Ronnie Casson
Editor/Annette Roman

ROSARIO + VAMPIRE SEASON II © 2007 by Akihisa Ikeda
All rights reserved. First published in Japan in 2007 by SHUEISHA Inc.,
Tokyo. English translation rights arranged by SHUEISHA Inc.

Printed in the U.S.A.

Published by VIZ Media, LLC
P.O. Box 77010
San Francisco, CA 94107

10 9 8 7 6 5 4 3 2
First printing, January 2012
Second printing, September 2014

www.viz.com

www.shonenjump.com

**CRYPT SHEET FOR**

# ROSARIO+VAMPIRE: SEASON II, VOL. 8

## *THE SECRET OF THE ROSARIO*

**TEST 8**

**TO SUPPRESS A VAMPIRE WHO LONGS TO DESTROY THE WORLD...**

a. suppress yourself

b. express yourself

c. second-guess yourself

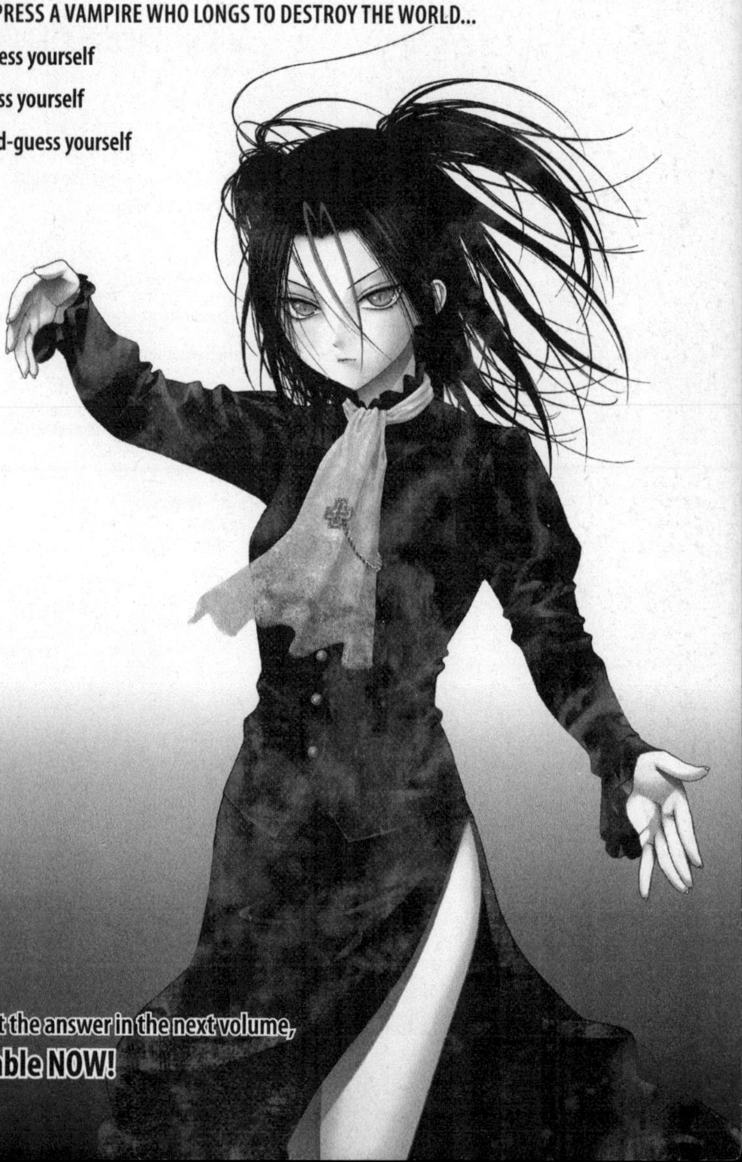

**Find out the answer in the next volume, available NOW!**

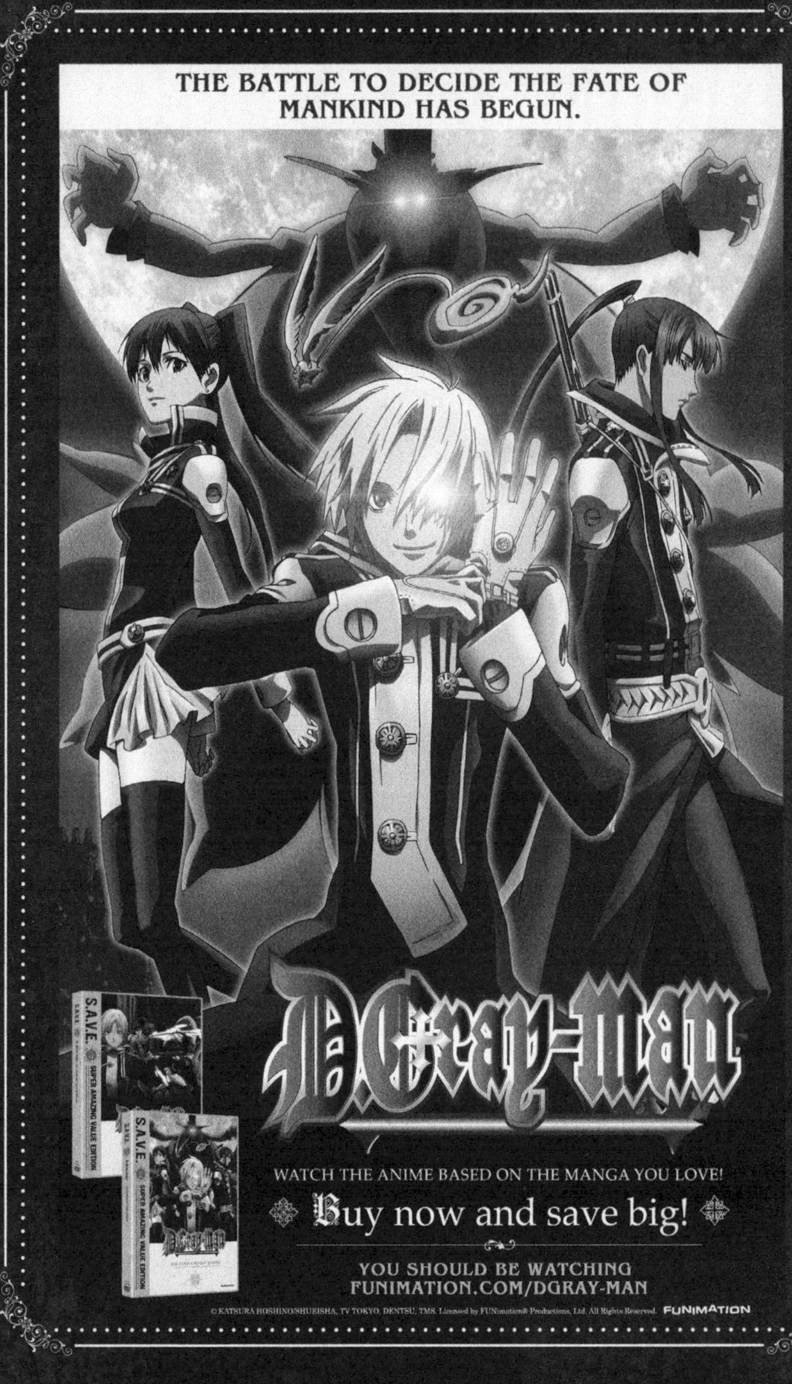
THE BATTLE TO DECIDE THE FATE OF
MANKIND HAS BEGUN.
D.Gray-man
S.A.V.E.
SUPER AMAZING VALUE EDITION
WATCH THE ANIME BASED ON THE MANGA YOU LOVE!
Buy now and save big!
YOU SHOULD BE WATCHING
FUNIMATION.COM/DGRAY-MAN
© KATSURA HOSHINO/SHUEISHA, TV TOKYO, DENTSU, TMS. Licensed by FUNimation® Productions, Ltd. All Rights Reserved.
FUNIMATION

# You're Reading in the Wrong Direction!!

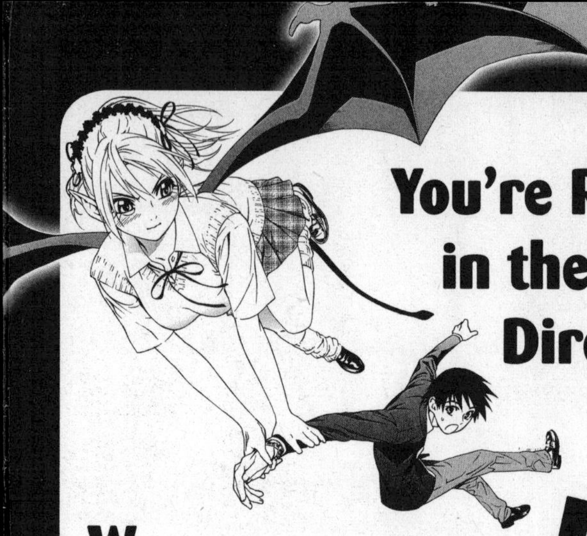

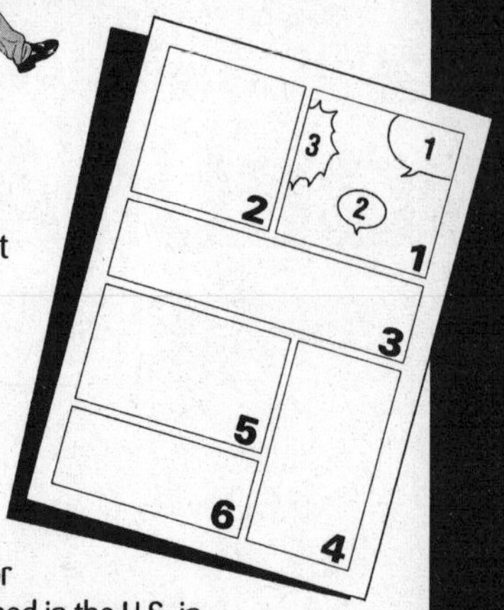
1
2
3
1
2
3
4
5
6

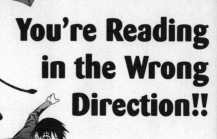

**W**hoops! Guess what? You're starting at the wrong end of the comic!

...It's true! In keeping with the original Japanese format, **Rosario+Vampire** is meant to be read from right to left, starting in the upper-right corner.

Unlike English, which is read from left to right, Japanese is read from right to left, meaning action, sound effects and word-balloon order are completely reversed... something which can make readers unfamiliar with Japanese feel pretty backwards themselves. For this reason, manga or Japanese comics published in the U.S. in English have sometimes been published "flopped"—that is, printed in exact reverse order, as though seen from the other side of a mirror.

By flopping pages, U.S. publishers can avoid confusing readers, but the compromise is not without its downside. For one thing, a character in a flopped manga series who once wore in the original Japanese version a T-shirt emblazoned with "M A Y" (as in "the merry month of") now wears one which reads "Y A M"! Additionally, many manga creators in Japan are themselves unhappy with the process, as some feel the mirror-imaging of their art skews their original intentions.

We are proud to bring you Akihisa Ikeda's **Rosario+Vampire** in the original unflopped format. For now, though, turn to the other side of the book and let the haunting begin...!

—Editor